Children of Ham

Freed Slaves and Fugitive Slaves on the Kenya Coast, 1873 to 1907

African Modernization and Development Series

Paul Lovejoy, Series Editor

Tom Smith, Bombay African, freed slave resident of Frere Town, near Mombasa, and Chief Engineer of the "Dove," the Church Missionary Society's steamer, ca. 1875

Children of Ham

Freed Slaves and Fugitive Slaves on the Kenya Coast, 1873 to 1907

Fred Morton

Westview Press
BOULDER • SAN FRANCISCO • OXFORD

African Modernization and Development Series

This Westview softcover edition is printed on acid-free paper and bound in library-quality, coated covers that carry the highest rating of the National Association of State Textbook Administrators, in consultation with the Association of American Publishers and the Book Manufacturers' Institute.

Copyright © 1990 by Westview Press, Inc.

Published in 1990 in the United States of America by Westview Press, Inc., 5500 Central Avenue, Boulder, Colorado 80301, and in the United Kingdom by Westview Press, 36 Lonsdale Road, Summertown, Oxford OX2 7EW

Library of Congress Cataloging-in-Publication Data
Morton, Fred, 1939–
  Children of Ham : freed slaves and fugitive slaves on the Kenya
coast, 1873 to 1907 / by Fred Morton.
    p. cm. — (African modernization and development series)
  Includes bibliographical references and index.
  ISBN 0-8133-8002-2
  1. Kenya—History—To 1895. 2. Freedmen—Kenya. 3. Fugitive
slaves—Kenya. 4. Slavery—Kenya—History. I. Title. II. Series.
DT433.57.M67 1990
967.62'01—dc20   90–46433
                                                     CIP

Printed and bound in the United States of America

The paper used in this publication meets the requirements of the American National Standard for Permanence of Paper for Printed Library Materials Z39.48-1984.

10   9   8   7   6   5   4   3   2   1

To

Rob Gregory, Rod Macdonald, and Alan Smith

Contents

Maps

Plates

Acknowledgments

Thanks are due to a great many who provided assistance to my family and me on the long road to this book's completion, but only a few individuals can be recognized here. Those named below hold special importance and deserve to share in any credit that may be earned by this volume. They are likewise exempt from blame for any fault or error, which shall be the responsibility of the author.

Children of Ham has emerged from comments on my Ph.D. dissertation and related articles on Kenya coastal history, as well as on the initial drafts of this manuscript, including its graphics. For their scholarly advice, technical help, and encouragement, I wish to thank Jim Allen, Lynn Arts, Cynthia Brantley, Judy Butterman, Christine Carson, Dick Cashmore, the late Neville Chittick, the late Michael Crowder, Fred Cooper, Barbara Ellington, Nathan Fedha, Rob Gregory, Rene Haller, Tom Herlehy, Rose and James Juma, the late James Kirkman, Willie Lamouse-Smith, Rod Macdonald, Esmond Martin, Suzanne Miers, the late David Miller, David Milton-Thompson, Barry Morton, Jim and Jenny Musen, James O'Brien, David Parkin, Terence Ranger, Richard Roberts, Edward Rodwell, Achmed Salim, Hamo Sassoon, Alan Shellhause, Gill Shepherd, Nancy Shepherd, George Shepperson, Alan Smith, Tom Spear, Bob Strayer, Don Suddick, Romilly Turton, and the history departments at the University of Botswana and the University of Nairobi.

Cooperation of the staffs of many repositories and libraries made it possible for me to assemble the scattered record of late nineteenth-century coastal Kenya. I am especially grateful to the personnel of the Bird Memorial Library, Syracuse University; the Bodleian and Rhodes House libraries, Oxford University; the British Museum, London; the Center for Africana Microform Project, Chicago; the Church Missionary Society, London; East African Railways, Nairobi; East African Standard, Nairobi; the Fort Jesus Museum, Mombasa; the India Office, London; the Kenya National Archives, Nairobi; the Land Office, Nairobi; the Methodist Mission, Ribe; the Methodist Missionary Society, London; the Public Record Office, London; the Royal Geographical Society Library, London; the School of Oriental and African Studies Library, London; the United Society for the Propagation of the Gospel Archives, London; the University of Botswana Library, Gaborone; and the Wahlert Memorial Library, Loras College.

Children of Ham would not have been possible without the financial assistance received toward doctoral studies, which provided the groundwork. Major support came from Syracuse University and its Program of Eastern African Studies, for preliminary research in Kenya in 1969-70, and from the Fulbright-Hays Dissertation Research Abroad Program, for archival and field-work in 1972-73 in England and Kenya. Their sponsorship is sincerely appreciated. Gratitude is also extended to Syracuse University, for research assistance in Syracuse during the proposal stage, to Tina Higginson and the Bamburi Chalets, for enabling work to continue in Kenya until 1975, to the

Xerox Corporation, Dayton, Ohio, for photocopying, and to Loras College, for photocopying, laser printing, and postal expenses.

I am personally indebted to Paul Lovejoy for encouraging me to write this volume and for his many valuable comments thereon.

Kindness and tolerance are the most cherished forms of support, especially in times of difficulty. Especially deep appreciation is felt toward the following:

> Pat and Rob Gregory, Glenna and Byron Morton, Irmgaard and Gerhardt Schauderna, Kathleen and Bob Shellhause, Nancy and Eva Shepherd, Gill Shepherd and Peter Loizos, and Blanche and Clyde Williams, for opening their homes and making provisions for my family and me during the years of research and writing;
>
> Befukwe wa Kagumba, the late Nzaka wa Kunya, and their wives and children, who accepted me into their compounds, fed, sheltered, and taught me, and in so many other ways aided my efforts to conduct fieldwork;
>
> The residents of Rabai, for their patience and help in learning about the first and second generations of ex-slaves on the coast;
>
> Rob Gregory, for his example as a scholar, teacher, gentleman, spouse, and parent; and
>
> Sue, for her sacrifices and honesty.

The manuscript was processed on an Apple Macintosh™ SE computer. Final copy was prepared with Microsoft Word 4.0 and Aldus PageMaker 3.2. Maps were created with Superpaint 2.0 and are the work of the author. Camera-ready copy was produced on an Apple LSW printer.

Fred Morton

Introduction

On the Kenya coast, slavery was a brand transmitted as a birthmark. It was, as the Miji Kenda of the coastal hinterland would say, *k'autsuka hiraka*, not quickly cleansed. To the Muslim Swahili and Arab, the slave was *hayawana* (a brute) and *'adua 'Ilahi u Rasul* (an enemy of God and the Prophet), who was owned and ruled in accordance with God's will. Slaves and their descendants were *watoto wa Hami* (the children of Ham), cursed by God to be the slaves of the children of Shem and Japhet.

The notion that slaves were ordained inferiors was also popular among European Christians. One Protestant bishop's comment about freed slave children in Mombasa is typical of European attitudes toward coastal slaves and ex-slaves in general: "From their earliest," he asserted, "[they] have been taught and grown up in all possible wickedness."[1] Christian and Muslim alike thought of slaves and ex-slaves as God's children but as those children who stood furthest from His Grace. All Christians or Muslims, apart from a rare individual or two, presumed the children of Ham to be incapable of salvation, felt no responsibility for their suffering, and opposed steps toward their unconditional freedom. Slaves and ex-slaves were expected to receive their blessings insofar as they served their superiors.

Slaves were the means by which coastal Kenya was attached to the commercial empire of the Busaidi of Zanzibar, whereas slaves and freed slaves were used by British officials and missionaries in establishing themselves in the same territory. Under the Busaidi, slaves raised grain on the Kenya coast to feed Busaidi-controlled Zanzibar and Pemba. British officials and missionaries then campaigned against the slave trade to gain leverage over the Busaidi. Slavery itself was a side issue. Crown officials and missionaries needed slaves and freed slaves to build their stations, swell lists of converts, man caravans, and staff junior positions. Slaves and ex-slaves possessed value insofar as they advanced powerful interests, just as quests for power overrode saving lives and protecting individuals. Political contenders on the coast--whether Busaidi sultans and governors, British officials and missionaries, or coastal leaders and communities-- regarded slaves and ex-slaves as laborers or followers to be used. Protection was offered on terms equivalent to servitude. On the Kenya coast, the powerful coerced the weak and treated them as rank inferiors.

Before slavery was abolished in 1907, slaves and "freed" slaves had to seize their own freedom. They had to capture and control their own land and establish their own communities. Opportunities arose because of the political and military

---

1 Hannington to Stock, 8 May 1885, G3A5/02, Church Missionary Society Archives, London (CMS).

conflicts raging in the late nineteenth century. Fugitive slaves (*watoro*) established settlements beyond territories controlled by coastal slave owners or imperial officials and in the crevices separating hinterland groups. Freed slaves also took control of mission stations neglected by European missionaries and admitted *watoro*. Freed slaves and *watoro* formed organized, self-governing communities that expanded through agriculture, trade, and fresh intakes of *watoro*.

Their success, though limited, was sufficient to make them pariahs. Independent communities such as these upset calculations of the powerful, who counted obedient slaves or freed slaves as assets and discounted runaway slaves or assertive freed slaves as liabilities. As a rule, European missionaries distanced themselves from maroons,[2] while British and Muslim officials reviled them as the "worst characters on the coast" and sent combined forces against them. Protecting and sustaining these enclaves was a constant challenge. Maroons and freed slaves met it by communicating with one another, forging alliances with neighbors, making treaties with enemies, acquiring arms, and going to war.

Children of Ham: Freed Slaves and Fugitives Slaves on the Kenya Coast, 1873 to 1907 is a chronological account of the repeated bids for freedom made by slaves and ex-slaves on the Kenya coast and of the obstacles placed in their way by the British, the Busaidi Arabs, and the peoples of the coast. Efforts to escape slavery are as old as slavery itself on the Kenya coast, but the principal story begins in 1873, when Britain pressured the sultan of Zanzibar to abolish the ocean-going slave trade. Thereafter, political and military conflict intensified on the coast, while opportunities for slaves to escape increased accordingly. This period, ending roughly with the abolition of the legal status of slavery in 1907, corresponds to the imperial scramble from its earliest stages to the effective establishment of European rule.

Chapter One argues that coastal slavery was harsh and the desire to escape it strong, with opportunities for flight determined by changing external circumstances. It challenges the standard accounts, based on Frederick Cooper's arguments, which portray nineteenth-century coastal slavery as fundamentally benign and the Kenya coast during this period as static. Other, methodological, differences with regard to emphasis, sources, and chronology are highlighted.

Chapter Two relates the stories of three communities of *watoro* that flourished during the violent era of the slave trade. The oldest and largest *watoro* group was that of the Gosha, who settled on the banks of the Juba river in Somaliland. The other two were the *watoro* attached to Ahmed b. Fumo Luti ("Simba") of Witu and to Mbaruk b. Rashid of Gasi. The combined population of these three groups totalled in the thousands. In the decades they survived, *watoro* suffered great hardship and inflicted great harm on others. At constant risk of being recaptured, *watoro* often became marauders themselves; they attacked

---

[2] Maroon, meaning a fugitive slave, especially one belonging to a settlement of other fugite slaves, is a term borrowed from the Americas. It was not used as a designation by observers in East Africa at the time.

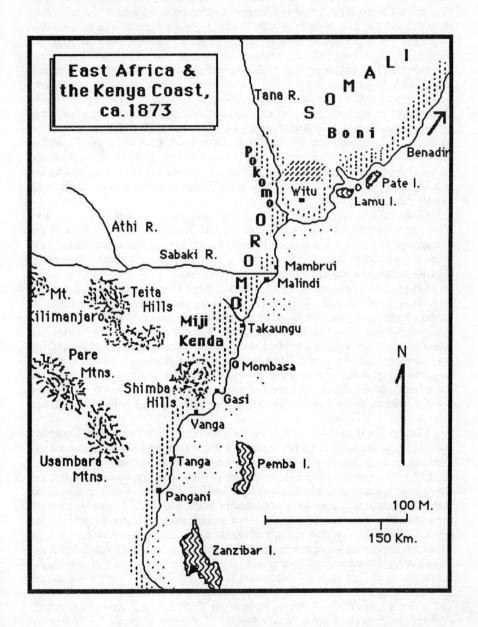

East Africa &
the Kenya Coast,
ca.1873

coastal plantations, killed and raided for slaves, defied coastal authorities, flirted with imperialists, and ultimately confronted the British. Their stories demonstrate the extremes to which runaways were prepared to go to avoid slavery. Their experiences, nevertheless, underscore themes common to all ex-slaves.

Chapter Three is an account of how freed slaves became disenchanted with the Church Missionary Society (CMS) at Frere Town, East Africa's most ambitious experiment for the settlement of recaptives of the British Naval Patrol in the Indian Ocean. Missionary racism and authoritarianism, and the missionary alliance with Busaidi and British officials, were underlying factors, as was the missionaries' persecution of the freed slave elite known as the "Bombay Africans." Frere Town declined within years of its founding in 1874, abandoned its support of adult freed slaves, and, after an abortive uprising in 1880, lost the confidence of coastal slaves, who had thought European missionaries had come to help fight their battles.

Chapter Four recounts the relationship between missionaries and fugitive slaves in the Mombasa, Takaungu, and Malindi hinterlands, climaxing with the emergence of Fuladoyo, a *watoro* Christian community. *Watoro* expected help from missionaries, but ultimately they alone faced their former owners and Busaidi troops in a sequence of battles in the 1880s.

Chapter Five tells the story of one of Kenya's most remarkable personalities, the ex-slave deacon William Henry Jones, and his efforts in the 1880s to create a freed slave community at Rabai that incorporated *watoro* and indigenous Africans of the hinterland. Rabai's rapid growth under Jones's leadership illustrates how the children of Ham attempted to gain acceptance on something approaching their own terms. Rabai's success was temporary, not from want of imagination or effort, but because Jones's community challenged the might of the coastal slave owners, undermined white control of the Church Missionary Society, and threatened the legitimacy of the new Imperial British East Africa Company.

Chapter Six reassesses the role of the Imperial British East Africa Company (IBEACO) in its relations with *watoro*, freed slaves, and slaves. From its establishment in November 1888 to its withdrawal from the coast in July 1895, the IBEACO reinforced the military power of slave owners, stimulated demand for slave labor, and ignored slave trading. The IBEACO participated in attacks on maroon villages, fomented the destruction of Witu, and tracked down *watoro* for their owners. Though the IBEACO expected slave owners to ameliorate conditions of slavery and though they enforced laws to that effect through Busaidi officials, the Company discouraged manumission and opposed abolition.

Chapter Seven measures the cost to ex-slaves and slaves of the establishment of the East Africa Protectorate in July 1895. Under Arthur Hardinge, the Protectorate followed the IBEACO's policies on slavery and runaway slaves and actively undermined attempts to have the legal status of slavery abolished. Perhaps the greatest tragedy in the history of slavery of the Kenya coast was occasioned by the manner in which the Protectorate established its authority. Hardinge's first step--putting down armed Mazrui resistance in Takaungu and Gasi districts--led straight to the Anglo-Mazrui War of 1895-96. Thousands of innocent slaves suffered as war victims. British and Mazrui combatants regarded slaves as potential allies or enemies and their crops as having potential value to the other side. Slaves were therefore coerced, dispersed, attacked, or killed and their crops and trees destroyed. The war, together with the pro-slave owner policy of the Protectorate, led to a mass exodus of slaves from coastal plantations.

Chapter Eight challenges Frederick Cooper's argument that with abolition slaves became squatters on old plantations. Evidence shows that in the 1890s only a few ex-slaves remained in plantation districts, whereas the vast majority fled. The post-abolition experience is too diverse to be served by the squatter paradigm. The chapter examines ex-slave groups and the lives of individual ex-slaves--farmers, town dwellers, mission adherents, chiefs, and administrators--to demonstrate their creative efforts to divest themselves of the mark of slavery, reduce their vulnerability, and, in some cases, continue fighting their old enemies. Distilling their stories into a single conclusion risks overlooking countless variables of time, personality, and place, but one thing can be said: following abolition, some children of Ham gained opportunities to improve their material lives, but the abolition of the legal status of slavery enabled few to alter their status as social and political inferiors.

1

Slavery and Escape

William Jones, 1861:
> Cruelly did the other fellow creatures suffer who came
> with me from my country; but I was free....[1]

1. *Slavery on the Kenya Coast*

Modern plantation slavery was introduced on the Kenya coast no earlier than the 1820s, but within decades slaves made up nearly 25 per cent of the population. Of an estimated 168,000 people living between Tanga and the Lamu archipelago in 1887, slightly more than 40,000 were slaves.[2] Since the early nineteenth century, when the slave markets in Kilwa and Zanzibar expanded, coastal Kenya had become a slave-importing region in which all coastal groups--Arab, Swahili, Miji Kenda, Oromo, Pokomo, Somali, and Wata--used slave labor. Slaves of the Kenya coast performed a variety of tasks and roles, such as artisans, soldiers, and domestics, but the large majority worked as field hands near the coastline and became the mainstay of a lucrative grain-export trade. Furthermore the majority of slaves lived in areas suitable for farms and plantations. Three such areas of importance had emerged by 1873. The first was the *barani* (mainland), opposite the Lamu archipelago. The *barani* was developed as a millet-, rice-, and sesame-producing region in the 1820s by the Bajuni, and other island dwellers, after Sultan Seyyid Said of Zanzibar established Busaidi rule in the archipelago and improved Lamu's port.[3] The second slave area was established at Takaungu by the Zaheri Mazrui following their eviction from Mombasa in 1837 by the forces of Sultan Said.[4] The third was the Malindi hinterland, developed in the

---

[1] From the autobiography of William Jones, CI3/067, Church Missionary Society Archives, London (CMS).

[2] Figures from R.F. Morton, "Slaves, Fugitives, and Freedmen on the Kenya Coast, 1873 to 1907"(Syracuse: Syracuse University Ph.D. dissertation, 1976), 46, 398-402.

[3] Lamu also became the seat of Said's governor. M. Ylvisaker, *Lamu in the Nineteenth Century: Land, Trade, and Politics* (Boston: Boston University African Studies Center, 1979), 109-110.

[4] Morton, "Slaves, Fugitives, and Freedmen," 57-60; P. L. Koffsky, "History of Takaungu, East Africa, 1830-1896" (Madison: University of Wisconsin Ph.D. Thesis, 1977), 31-95. See ch. 2.

1860s by Said's successors as Zanzibar's breadbasket. In addition to Lamu, Takaungu, and Malindi, small numbers of agricultural slaves were located in the rural suburbs of Mombasa and other southern ports, and in the southern coastal hinterland.[5]

Slavery preexisted the plantations, but in mild form. In the early nineteenth century slaves were owned by leading townsmen. The Mazrui governors of Mombasa were the largest slave owners, prior to their ouster by the Busaidi, and turned out large groups of slaves for public works and military service. Male slaves were especially important to the Mazrui and to the rival political groups in Mombasa as personal retainers who could be called upon for military support. Such slaves, along with the children of slave concubines, were grafted onto existing lineages.[6] In later years, slavery underwent considerable change as a result of the expansion of grain production in Lamu, Takaungu, and Malindi. Large-scale slave importation resulted in more pernicious forms of slavery based on coercion and on exclusion from coastal society.

By the 1840s, the burgeoning slave community constituted a large and differentiated underclass on the coast. Collectively they were known as *watumwa* or *waja*. Those recently arrived, called *mateka* or *waja na ngoma*, occupied the bottom rung. New slaves were regarded as *wajinga* ("fools," "ignoramuses"), whose unfamiliarity with the Swahili language and culture suited them only to the simple, unskilled tasks. They worked primarily in the fields, but some fished, worked as boatmen, or provided general labor in the towns. Slaves who had lived for a while on the coast and their offspring (*vivyalia* in Mombasa, *wazalia* in Lamu) performed domestic chores or became skilled artisans in the towns. Male Slaves (*watwana*), or young lads (*vitwana*) ranked from the domestics (*watumwa wa nyumba*), working as pages, personal attendants, and messengers, up to the *mafundi*, who were the artisan builders, tailors, carpenters, and metalworkers. Women slaves (*wajakazi*, girls *vijakazi*) not employed in the fields worked mainly in their owners' domiciles. Slave concubines (*masuria*, sing. *suria*), ranked above other female slaves in the home and, alone among slaves, were liable to have their children regarded by the father as free. The daughter of a *suria*, however, could be made a *suria* herself.[7] Slaves distinguished among themselves according to dress and their owners' social status. They used the term *mjoli* ("fellow slave") to refer to their rank peers rather than to any *mtumwa*.[8] Regardless, the freeborn regarded slaves collectively as an inferior, nonassimilable group.

---

[5] Morton, "Slaves, Fugitives, and Freedmen," 61-9; F. Cooper, *Plantation Slavery on the East Coast of Africa* (New Haven: Yale University Press, 1977), 81-102.

[6] T. Boteler, *Narrative of a Voyage of Discovery to Africa and Arabia*. 2 vols. (London: Richard Bentley, 1835), II, 208; J. Gray, *The British in Mombasa, 1824-1826* (London: Macmillan, 1957), 124.

[7] See the case of Kaizuia in Mohamed b. Sudi b. Mbaruk to Craufurd, 14 Dec. 1898, CP 67/ 14, Kenya National Archives, Nairobi (KNA).

[8] Slave terminology is derived from L. Krapf, *A Dictionary of the Suahili Language* 2nd ed. (Ridgewood: Gregg Press, 1964); A.H.J. Prins, *The Swahili-Speaking Peo-*

Legally slaves had mere chattel status. Islamic law, of which the Sunni school was used along the coast, enjoined owners to treat slaves well, provide for their upkeep, respect their rights of property and family, and manumit them as a pious act. But the law was not consistently enforced until 1890; no higher authority was prepared to censure owners except in cases of extreme cruelty.[9] To the freeborn, slaves were kinless persons. A common term for slaves, *waja*, underlines their plight: newcomers, those without local roots or families.[10] The exercise of full privileges within coastal Muslim society depended on freeborn legitimacy and the relative position of one's family within the freeborn community. Freed slaves (*wahuru*) thus lacked the family ties necessary for leaving the slave class. *Uhuru* was an unprotected, though legal, status that carried no importance in the social sphere, and manumitted slaves were commonly re-enslaved. Slavery was itself an inherited, though kinless, status for which association with the owner's family determined one's home. The children of slaves (*wazalia*, lit. "those born here") became the dependents, if not slaves, of their parents' owner and his or her family.

As a class, slaves were identified exclusively with manual labor and dark skin color. "Work is the badge of the slave," noted Charles New who lived in the Mombasa area in the 1860s. In the estimate of freeborn Swahili, work was "disgraceful."[11] Debasement of manual labor among freeborn Muslims is a trend noted by other contemporary observers.[12] Among freeborn women, seclusion (*utawa*) represented a parallel development. Spending time outdoors was for slaves, an attitude observed as well by New during his visit in 1865 to Takaungu, where he chatted with two young married Arab women and an old female slave attendant. When New criticized the practice of seclusion, which, he claimed had "blanched [the women's skin] to a sickly whiteness," it was not the Arab women who rebutted him, but the slave:

---

ples of Zanzibar and the East African Coast (Arabs, Shirazi and Swahili) (London: International African Institute, 1952), 69; F. Johnson, ed., *A Standard English-Swahili Dictionary* (Oxford: Oxford University Press, 1939); H.K. Binns, *A Swahili-English Dictionary* (London: Society for the Promotion of Christian Knowledge, 1925).

[9] Cooper, *Plantation Slavery*, 25; Hardinge to Kimberley, 26 Feb. 1895, C.7707, 27-31; M. Beech, "Swahili Life" (Fort Jesus Library typescript, n.d.); M.K. Mazrui, *Historia ya Utumwa katika Uislamu na Dini Nyingine* (Nairobi: n.p., 1970).

[10] New Arab settlers, usually Hadrami, who arrived steadily in small numbers, were *waja na maji*, 'newcomers from over the water'. Though freeborn persons with Arab clan connections, they were normally barred from marrying into older coastal Muslim families.

[11] C. New, *Life, Wanderings, and Labours in Eastern Africa*, 3rd ed., (London: Frank Cass, 1971), 64. See also Krapf to Venn, 7 Jun. 1845, CA5/M1, 613, and Krapf's "Memoir on the East African Slave Trade," CA5/016, CMS.

[12] H. Greffulhe, "Voyage de Lamoo a Zanzibar," *Bulletin de la Société de Géographie et d'Etudes Coloniale de Marseille*, 12(1878), 212; Wilson to de Winton, 10 Aug. 1890, FO 403/138, 161; Gissing to Kirk, 14 Sep. 1884, FO 541, 243.

"Ah," she said, "that may be, but it is not so here. The Waungwana [free-born persons] must remain indoors, while the slave woman only go out into the sun, and on this account," said she, "look at me. I am black, while these children are almost white."[13]

Cooper has argued that, because many freeborn persons were black, color lines did not correspond with class division, but this was not so.[14] What appears to have been the case was that slaves, being as they were black Africans, imbued their skin color with inferior social rank and encouraged dark-skinned, freeborn Swahili to pose as non-Africans.

Race consciousness among coastal freeborn is revealed in their notions of group descent. During the nineteenth century on the Kenya coast, the historical traditions of many established clans began to affirm southern Arabian or Omani origins. Many accounts of "Shirazi" or other, usually Africanized, origins were submerged or eliminated. The ascendancy of the Arab ancestral myth followed the period of the post-Portuguese influx into East Africa of Shafi Arabs from the Hadramaut, which according to J.S. Trimingham, "was responsible for remolding Swahili culture and imprinting it with the dominant stamp it bears today." Trimingham claims that the "Arab racial myth, together with the strong Arabism of Hadrami influence, caused the Arab element to dominate, whereas the earlier exotic traditions had succumbed to both Arabism and Bantuization."[15] Evidence that the Arab myth was accepted on the Kenya coast exists in the *Kitab al-Zanuj* ("Book of the Blacks"), a late nineteenth century account which relates the story of the founding of towns on the Kenya coast by Yemini Arabs of the "Tubba' himyarite."[16] The *Kitab al-Zanuj* places emphasis on several important clans of Mombasa, such as Changamwe, Kilifi,

---

[13] S.B. Barton, "Extracts from the Journals and Letters of the late Rev. Charles New," UMFC *Magazine* (1878), 27-8. See also Tritton to commissioner, 30 Jan. 1903, CP 85/111, KNA.

[14] Cooper, *Plantation Slavery*, 12, 27, 199, 267 (Cooper's work is discussed in this chapter's section, "The Historiography of Coastal Slavery," below). For the ideology of Arab "whiteness" and Arab racism, see J.P. Glassman, "Social Rebellion and Swahili Culture: the Response to German Conquest of the Northern Mrima" (Madison: University of Wisconsin Ph.D. dissertation, 1988), 107-8, 176-7.

[15] *Islam in East Africa* (Oxford: Clarendon, 1964), 22. "Among freemen there was a distinction between those free in origin (*asili*), having a genealogy (*nisba*), and the 'freedmen' (freed by a document, *kartasi*), and his descendants whose status was that of client to the former master's family." Ibid, 146. See also A.H. El-Zein, *The Sacred Meadows: a Structural Analysis of Religious Symbolism in an East African Town* (Evanston: Northwestern University Press, 1974), 51f.

[16] The *Kitab al-Zanuj* originated most likely in the last quarter of the nineteenth century. In the early twentieth century versions were located in Mogadishu, Kismayu, Witu, and Malindi. A full text of the *Kitab*, combining the first three above mentioned versions, is printed in Arabic together with an Italian translation in E. Cerulli, *Somali: Scritti vari Editi Ed Inediti*, 2 vols. (Rome: Instituto poligrafico, dello stato P.V., 1957), I, 233-92.

Mtwapa, and Mombasa, the names of which are alleged to represent certain places in southern Arabia. In light of earlier Mombasa clan traditions, which attest to "Shirazi" origins, the *Kitab al-Zanuj* version appears to be spurious, likely written to promote locally the notion of Arab descent.[17] Of greater importance here, the *Kitab al-Zanuj* encouraged members of established clans not only to claim Arab origins, but to distinguish themselves racially, as well as in terms of descent--i.e., historically--from Africans. According to the *Kitab al-Zanuj*, the origin of the Africans is accounted for in the legend of Ham, the accursed son of Noah:

> Ham was very handsome in appearance and gracious of feature, but God changed his color and [that] of his progeny because of the curse of Noah, who cursed Ham with the blackening of the features and blackening the faces of his progeny. And that his children were the slaves of the children of Sham and Japhet.

> And he made them numerous and he multiplied them. When the Prophet of God (Noah) divided the land among his sons, Africa was dealt to Ham. The latter begat sons who are the blacks, whose hair does not go beyond their ears as we now see them.[18]

It was perhaps a natural outcome in a Muslim society in which ancestry played a vital role that the growing presence of a black slave class would lead to the acceptance of the Hamitic myth in popular ideas of race. In 1845 Ludwig Krapf heard it circulating in Mombasa:

> I did not know before, that the name of Ham is known to the Suahelees. [To them] Ham signified a black man and a slave. If for instance a slave would take too much liberty in the presence of his master, the latter would say to him: get thee hence, thou son of Hami, thou art a slave and no Unguana [*mngwana*], which means a free man, or a Lord. All the white people, the Wasungo, Arabs, and Indians are called Unguana, in opposition to the blacks and slaves, or watoto wa Hami [children of Ham].[19]

Rendered inferior by color, birth, and occupation, slaves were reduced to objects of abuse. European observers, mostly resident missionaries, witnessed many incidents of severe punishment and cruelty inflicted on slaves, especially in the towns. In Mombasa the means of demanding obedience were harsh. "The instruments by which household discipline is maintained," remarked Charles

---

[17] For an elaboration of these points in the context of Miji Kenda historiography, R.F. Morton, "New Evidence regarding the Shungwaya Myth of Miji Kenda Origins," *IJAHS*, 10, 4(1977), 628-43.

[18] Cerulli, *Somali*, I, 254 (from the Italian translation).

[19] Journal from 13 to 27 Mar. 1845, CA5/M1, 577, CMS. *Wasungo* (*wazungu*) = European. Krapf used the Swahili term for freeborn status, *ungwana*, instead of for free born persons (*mwungwana*, pl., *waungwana*). For the myth of Ham as part of Lamu's free born oral tradition, see Zein, *Sacred Meadows*, 199-213.

New, "are the stick, fetters, manacles, chains, and kongo [long forked stick] and
the stocks, and they are not infrequently used."[20] Other observers of New's time
bear him out. W.S. Price, a CMS missionary who arrived in Mombasa in 1875
to establish the Frere Town settlement, felt that "[although] some are kind in
their treatment of their slaves, others are simply brutal."[21]

> "Even here in one day," from my own window I have seen 1. a poor woman with
> heavy chains on her legs, so that she could only jerk herself along a few inches
> at a time, and carrying a load on her head; 2. a little girl of about 8 or 9 with an
> iron chain on her neck several feet in length, which was coiled up in a basket
> on her head, and at the same time carrying a burden in her hands, 3. a little boy
> of the same tender age, in similar condition, 4. a poor man emaciated and cover-
> ed with sores, who in consequence of his heavy chains and extreme weakness,
> could only move along in a sitting posture on his hands!

Price wrote of a slave carpenter who, when trying to visit his wife in another
part of town, was set upon by a mob of persons "who thrashed him with sticks
within an inch of his life. He was truly in a pitiable state." Price appealed to the
Governor, who took action against the offenders, but, as Price noted, "there are
some scores of similar cases every week in Mombasa, in which poor wretches
have no appeal."[22] Price's experiences were not isolated. Until the late 1880s
missionaries at Frere Town and other outlying stations recorded many cases of
slaves who had fled to the missions in chains, manacles, or bearing physical evidence of severe beatings.[23] Europeans outside the mission also commisserated
with the slaves' suffering. "That many of the Mombasa slave owners are cruel
masters," wrote the British consul in Zanzibar, "needs no proof."[24]

Punishment for slaves who tried to run away could be particularly harsh,
even for children. New once encountered two youths heavily fettered and forced
to carry heavy loads because they had tried to escape. In Lamu, in the 1880s
slave children were "dragging about the streets a great pole fastened by a ring to
their necks as a punishment," presumably for running away.[25] Adults were dealt
with more severely. In 1882 one particularly gruesome incident occurred in

---

[20] New, *Life*, 503. For similar forms of punishment in the 1840s, Krapf, "Memoir
on the East African Slave Trade," CA5/016, CMS, and idem, *Dictionary of the Suahili
Language*, cv *mkatale* ("stocks").

[21] Price to Wright, 29 May 1875, CA5/M4, 92, CMS.

[22] Price journal, 25 Mar. 1876, CA5/023, CMS.

[23] Handford quarterly report, 25 Mar. 1876, CA5/011, CMS; Price journal, 22 Apr.
1876, CA5/023, CMS; Ramshaw to Bushell, 2 Feb. 1881, UMFC *Magazine*, Jul.
1881, 149; Howe to Editor, 19 Jun. 1896, *Missionary Echo*, 3(1896)--regarding an
Mgindo slave who ran away in the 1880s. See also the extracts of letters from
Menzies and Felkin in Hutchinson to Granville, 14 Jan. 1881, FO 541/49, 200-01.

[24] Kirk to Granville, 4 Apr. 1881, FO 541/49, 246.

[25] F. Jackson, *Early Days in East Africa*, 2nd ed. (London: Dawsons of Pall Mall,
1969), 21.

Mombasa, where a slave had injured his master in a scuffle and ran away to hide in the outlying farms.

> Then [the master] called some men, and told them to have a regular hunt for this slave, and whoever saw him to shoot him. They did so, and in the afternoon of the same day they found him, and one of the pursuers shot him in the leg. They then tied a rope round him, and dragged him right into Mombasa, a distance of about two miles. There is a pole standing in the bazaar, and here his master ordered Serengi [the runaway slave] to be suspended, still alive, head downwards. An Arab then came forward, and before crowds of spectators....*beheaded him, and drank his life's blood.*[original emphasis] [26]

This story, written for young church school readers in England and probably embellished for effect, is nevertheless believable in its basic particulars.[27] Other instances of the execution of runaways have been recorded, and coastal owners dealt ruthlessly with runaways settled in the coastal hinterland.

For the cruel treatment of slaves, no other coastal town matched the notoriety of Malindi in the mid-1860s. New and Thomas Wakefield, who spent three weeks there in 1866, came away appalled. Wakefield wrote that it was common for slaves to receive lashings in the public market place and to be left tied to the post for beatings from passers-by.[28] According to New, "the treatment of slaves was to the last degree heartless and cruel; it was indeed a reign of terror."

> We saw them beaten over the head with large sticks in the most wanton manner. The "mkatali" [stocks] where the victims were retained day and night were always full. Men were slung by their wrists to the flagstaff, and thrashed upon their bare backs within an inch of their lives. Others trailed through the town, and along the beach, long beams of wood, attached to heavy iron collars about their necks. Others shuffled about with immense "pingu" [irons] upon their ancles. Others had heavy collars upon their necks, to which was attached a length of chain filling a large basket, which they had to carry about them wherever they might go.[29]

---

[26] R.C. Ramshaw, "Stories about East Africa," in *Welcome Words*, 16(1882), 158-59.

[27] Ramshaw, missionary at Ribe, identified his informant for this story as an Islamized Ribe man who knew personally the master in question.

[28] E.S. Wakefield, *Thomas Wakefield : Missionary and Geographical Pioneer in East Equatorial AFrica* (London: Religious Tract Society, 1904), 83.

[29] New, *Life*, 166-67. New and Wakefield interceded in Malindi on behalf of a man who suffered a beating in the market place, only to discover twelve years later that the victim had not been a slave after all, but a thief who had been caught for the third time. Wakefield, "Fourth Journey to the Southern Galla Country in 1877," *PRGS*, 4(1882), 371. This shows that the missionaries could misconstrue events and that the Malindi crowds did not single out slaves for abuse. Mob justice was to be expected in Malindi, which was then only a rough, pioneer town. It is safe to assume, however, that these experienced missionaries could normally recognize slaves apart from free men and that they did not misrepresent conditions in Malindi. Their accounts were

2. The Historiography of Coastal Slavery

Attention to slavery, and in particular to slaves' hardships, has been slow to surface in the published literature. The curse of Ham, as it were, seemingly extends to the telling of Kenya coastal history. On the coast, as in so many other parts of East Africa, hegemonists have received the attention, much of it flattering. Among colonialist historians such as Coupland, Hemphill, Lloyd, Lyne, and Oliver, Britain's fight against the East African slave trade is a major theme, British officials and missionaries the principal actors, but slavery and imperialism's effects on slaves are usually ignored.[30] The colonialists' predilection, of seeing upright heroes where a forest of villains stood, persisted among the next generation of revisionist historians, whose aim was "decolonizing" coastal history. In revisionist works, which began to appear in the 1960s, the spotlight turned on resistors to foreign domination. Revisionists play down the fact that leading opponents of Busaidi and British imperialism were slave owners.[31] Spear denies that non-Muslim coastal Kenyans used slave labor, and Sheriff ignores the existence of coastal slavery altogether.[32] Revisionists, moreover, building on the work of Fred Berg, portray slave-owning Muslim and non-Muslim coastal societies as harmoniously intertwined until the

---

not based on hearsay but on first-hand observations, and they were corroborated by the experiences of their porters.

[30] R. Coupland, *East Africa and its Invaders* (Oxford: Clarendon, 1938); idem, *The Exploitation of East Africa*, 2nd ed. (London: Faber & Faber, 1968); M. deK. Hemphill, "The British Sphere, 1884-94," in R. Oliver and G. Mathew, ed., *History of East Africa, Vol. I* (Oxford: Clarendon, 1963), 391-432; C. Lloyd, *The Navy and the Slave Trade* (London: Frank Cass, 1968); R.N. Lyne, *An Apostle of Empire: Being the Life of Sir Lloyd William Mathews, K.C.M.G.* (London: George Allen and Unwin); R. Oliver, *Sir Harry Johnstone and the Scramble for Africa* (London: Faber, 1957); idem, *The Missionary Factor in East Africa* (London: Longmans & Green, 1952). .

[31] T. Cashmore, "Sheikh Mbaruk bin Rashid bin Salim el Mazrui," in N. Bennett, ed., *Leadership in Eastern Africa* (Boston: Boston University Press, 1968); T. Ranger, *Dance and Society in Eastern Africa* (London: Heinemann, 1975); A. Salim, *The Swahili-speaking Peoples of Kenya's Coast 1895-1965* (Nairobi: East African Publishing House, 1973); R. Strayer, *The Making of Mission Communities in East Africa* (London: Heinemann, 1978); Ylvisaker, *Lamu*. A notable exception to the revisionist tendency is C.S. Nicholls, *The Swahili Coast; Politics, Diplomacy and Trade on the East African Littoral, 1798-1856* (London: George Allen & Unwin, 1971), which however deals with the period before coastal slavery reached its peak.

[32] T. T. Spear, *The Kaya Complex: a History of the Mijikenda Peoples of the Kenya Coast to 1900* (Nairobi: Kenya Literature Bureau, 1978), 98-9, passim; A. Sheriff, *Slaves, Spices & Ivory in Zanzibar: Integration of an East African Commercial Empire into the World Economy, 1770-1873* (London: James Curry, 1987). Sheriff's work, which constitutes the only neo-Marxist analysis of East African slavery and the slave trade, is based on research in the 1960s and early 1970s and makes but token use of studies that have appeared since.

imperial impact.[33] Insofar as they acknowledge slavery, revisionists represent slaves as victims largely of British rule. They also ignore anthropologist A. H. M. el-Zein, who argues that freeborn Muslims in nineteenth-century Lamu despised and mistreated slaves as a matter of course.[34] Zein's path of inquiry halted with his death in 1979, and his methodology has since been assailed.[35]

It has been the revisionist road, instead, that has been extended and widened, notably by Frederick Cooper's study of nineteenth-century plantation slavery. Cooper's work is the first to portray slaves as active members of coastal societies and vital participants in the economy, and he does so in a manner that is both imaginative and brilliant.[36] His analytical framework, flexible enough to absorb the revisionists intact, has accommodated all subsequent studies of the coast.[37] Cooper's East Africa is the one commonly represented in discussions of comparative slavery in Africa, Arabia, and the western hemisphere. In Kenya coastal historiography, his work has been integrative and transitional. Cooper has merged the colonialist historians, who used East Africa as their canvas, with the revisionists, who produced local and ethnic studies, and he has laid the foundation for the present generation of thematists, who isolate elements on the Kenya coast for comparative use in Africa and elsewhere.

Colonialists, revisionists, and thematists share with Cooper important common ground. Their perspective is that of the hegemonist. Even the colonialists, who trumpeted the call against the slave trade, were inclined to sympathize with slave owners and exculpate their institutions. In all such studies, the powerful nurture and protect the weak. Coastal slavery is a benign system in which paternalism prevails. Slaves occupy a subordinate but protected position in a society built on reciprocal obligations between freeborn and slave as rein-

---

[33] F.J. Berg, "Mombasa under the Busaidi Sultanate. The City and its Hinterlands in the Nineteenth Century" (Madison: University of Wisconsin Ph.D. thesis, 1971).

[34] Zein *Sacred Meadows*. For a summary of Zein's view of slavery, see ch. 8.

[35] P. Romero Curtin, "The Sacred Meadows: a Case Study of 'Anthropologyland' vs. 'Historyland'," *History in Africa*, 9(1982), 337-46; also P.W. Romero, "'Where Have All the Slaves Gone?' Emancipation and Post-Emancipation in Lamu, Kenya," *JAH*, 27(1986), 508.

[36] Cooper, *Plantation Slavery*.

[37] F. Cooper, *From Slaves to Squatters: Plantation Labor and Agri-culture in Zanzibar and Coastal Kenya, 1890-1925* (New Haven: Yale University Press, 1980); idem, "Islam and Cultural Hegemony: the Ideology of Slaveowners on the East African Coast," in P.E. Lovejoy, ed., *The Ideology of Slavery in Africa* (Beverly Hills: Sage Publications, 1981), 271-307; C. Brantley, *The Giriama and Colonial Resistance in Kenya, 1800-1920* (Berkeley: University of California Press, 1981); P. Romero Curtin, "Laboratory for the Oral History of Slavery: the Island of Lamu on the Kenya Coast," *American Historical Review*, 88, 4 (Oct. 1983), 858-82; M. Strobel, *Muslim Women in Mombasa* (New Haven: Yale University Press, 1979); idem, "Slavery and Reproductive Labor in Mombasa," in C.C. Robertson and M.A. Klein, ed., *Women and Slavery in Africa* (Madison: University of Wisconsin Press, 1983), 111-29; R. Pouwels, *Horn and Crescent: Cultural Change and Traditional Islam on the East African Coast, 800-1900* (Cambridge: Cambridge University Press, 1987).

forced by Islamic values. An exception would appear to exist in the work of Glassman, who rejects the "big man" approach in history and explores initiative and resistance below, including from runaway slaves. Yet, with regard to slaves and slavery, Glassman defers to Cooper's interpretation.[38]

Formidable as the Cooper position may seem, evidence in its support derives largely from written sources for the period after 1890, when slavery was in decline. Cooper and those who have followed his lead make little or no distinction between the post-1890 period, when conditions of slavery were ameliorated, and roughly the three decades prior to 1890, when slavery was at its peak. Though it has become *de rigueur* for researchers to collect oral data in the field, informants interviewed in the late twentieth century have yet to demonstrate that they can distinguish between slavery as practiced at different times in the nineteenth century. Neither Cooper nor any one else has tried systematically to make such distinctions themselves. In their versions, as in those of their informants, slavery and the society of which it was part exist in a stable, if not entirely static, form, and function in a synchronic past. Cooper's versions of change and process in the nineteenth century, and revisions arising therefrom, are for the most part arbitrary models, having been constructed without reference to an independently verifiable chronology.[39] Such versions are difficult to reconcile, for example, with the rapid, often violent, tumble of events that occurred on the coast in the half century before slavery became illegal. For most of this period, social and political stability in any of the slave-owning coastal communities was rare.

It may be that benign forms of slavery were practiced on the coast, but it would appear that such was possible only after 1890, when Islamic laws governing slavery were enforced by Busaidi governors with the backing of the British.[40] Before then, with the exception of Mombasa after 1884, slavery operated without governmental regulation. It was subject instead to the wishes of individual owners and freeborn residents. The pre-1890 record of slavery is thin, but it reveals, when separated from the later evidence, a much harsher form of exploitation than has been suggested by Cooper. The case that at least the earlier forms of slavery were based on coercion is further strengthened when combined with the record of resistance to slavery mounted by freed slaves and fugitive slaves.

In comparative terms, the experience of slaves on the Kenya coast may have been generally less dehumanizing and their physical suffering less than was

---

[38] J.P. Glassman, "The Runway Slave in Coastal Resistance to Zanzibar: the Case of the Witu Sultanate" (Madison: University of Wisconsin M.A. Thesis, 1983). Glassman's dissertation on the northern Mrima, insofar as it deals with slavery, is largely derived from coastal Kenya evidence and Cooper's conclusions thereof. "Social Rebellion and Swahili Culture," 141-239. For Glassman on Witu, see ch. 2, notes 52 and 65.

[39] An exception is Ylvisaker's *Lamu,* which adopts a chronological approach. Yet, Ylvisaker slices her study into separate topics covering parallel time periods, overlooks connections, and omits reconstructing the whole.

[40] See ch. 6.

the case in such places as St. Domingue, Surinam, Fernando Po, or even Alabama. Kenya's slaves, however, were provided with no opportunity of comparing themselves with slaves elsewhere, and it is unlikely that any of their owners were aware of the differences. Slaves measured their lives by the treatment they received, by their opportunities to blend with or rise among freeborn people, and by similar yardsticks applied to the generation they created. As the record shows, thousands of slaves on the Kenya coast tried to escape. Before 1890, no more than a small fraction, however, perhaps as few as one-tenth, succeeded in removing themselves from slavery. Most slaves eschewed flight, not because slavery was benign, but because the risks while running away were great, the penalties for capture harsh, and the security of maroon communities marginal in the best of times.

3. *Early Marronage: Koromio and Mwazangombe*

Marronage was common on the Somalia coast and Juba river in the early nineteenth century, but on the Kenya coast and in its hinterland escape from slavery was almost impossible until the 1870s.[41] Along the Kenya coast, even manumitted slaves were unprotected. Some slave owners decreed manumission, and Sunni law accorded free status to those manumitted. Protection of manumitted slaves, of even those with written documents, however, depended on voluntary observance of the law, which was lax. At one time, Mombasa attracted manumitted slaves from other Kenya port cities because of its reputation for tolerance, but reenslavement occurred even there.[42]

Few slaves who fled their masters avoided recapture. All coastal communities owned slaves and, as a rule, cooperated in the seizure and return of fugitives. The Digo of the Shimba hills raided one another as well as their neighbors, journeyed inland to trade for slaves, and supplied the ports of Wasin and Tanga, sources of slaves for Pemba.[43] The Giriama and other Miji Kenda in the hills west of Mombasa purchased slaves from coastal Muslims, journeyed to Pare to procure slaves for trade on the coast, and raided one another for the same purpose.[44] Localized slave raiding occurred most often in times of famine when conditions forced the Miji Kenda into acts of desperation. There were enough

---

[41] For southern Somalia, see "Gosha" in ch. 2.

[42] Krapf, "Memoir of the East African Slave Trade," CA5/016, CMS; also David to Wright, 10 Oct. 1878, CA5/M5, 247, CMS.

[43] R.F. Burton, *Zanzibar: City, Island and Coast* 2 vols. (London: Tinsley Bros., 1872), II, 111-2; J. Christie, *Cholera Epidemics in East Africa* (London: Macmillan, 1876), 229-31; Erhardt journal, 10 Aug. 1853, CA5/09, CMS; Erhardt to Venn, 27 Oct. 1854, CA5/M2, 624, CMS.

[44] Rebmann journal, 7/8 Jun. 1848, CA5/024, CMS; Krapf journal, 16 Mar. 1851, in CMS *Intelligencer*, 2(1851), 212; Sparshott to Wright, 21 Nov. 1868 and 24 Jul. 1869, CA5/026, CMS; Wakefield journal, 3 Jan. 1872, in R. Brewin, *Memoirs of Mrs. Rebecca Wakefield,* 2nd ed. (London: Hamilton & Adams, 1879), 202; Binns diaries, cv. 22 Nov. 1879; Mugomba to Wakefield, n.d., *Welcome Words*, 14(1880),

instances of local kidnapping and similar occurrences in famine-free years, however, to indicate that easy profits as well as hard times drove the Miji Kenda to prey on each other. The Kamba, who lived near the Miji Kenda, sold slaves at their Jimba market, fifteen miles west of Mombasa, and until the 1880s raided their neighbors for slaves.[45] Both they and the Miji Kenda received bounties for returning runaways to coastal Muslims.

The hinterland north of Mombasa, west of the towns of Takaungu and Malindi, was controlled by the pastoral Oromo and their dependent hunting relatives, the Wata and Liangulo.[46] The Oromo prohibited strangers from settling among them and confined the Swahili to the coastal strip south of Kilifi and the Miji Kenda to the hills west of Mombasa. The Oromo owned slaves whom they used as agricultural laborers, domestics, and concubines.[47] Young men purchased male slaves in order to sever and dry their penises, which as *gutu* ("war trophies"), adorned the Oromo coiffure and elevated the possessor to the ranks of the brave and marriageable.[48] Oromo attacked the new plantations areas around Takaungu in the 1840s, killing slaves and taking others, a pattern which continued following the development of grain plantations in the Malindi area in the 1860s. In both areas they commanded tribute for abstaining from slave raids and allowing Swahili traders to pass through their territory.[49]

Initially the Oromo and Wata permitted maroon settlements in their territory. In the 1840s slave runaways from the coast founded the settlement of Koromio in the hilly reaches of the left bank of the Rare river at its mouth. There they welcomed other runaways, organized a community, and allied with the Oromo and Wata. Koromio's proximity to Takaungu nevertheless exposed it

---

4; Handford to Lang, 4 May 1884, G3A5/01(1884), CMS; Smith to Kirk, 18 May 1885, C. 4776, 644.

[45] Binns to Hutchinson, 6 Apr. 1881, G3A5/01(1880-81); Handford to Lang, 21 Jan. 1885, G3A5/02, CMS; Taylor to Lang, 17 Mar. 1885, CMS.

[46] For an account of these people, see R.F. Morton, "A Reappraisal of the History of the Wata Hunters of the Kenya Coast in the Pre-Colonial Era," *Kenya Historical Review* (1978/79).

[47] Krapf, "Memoir of the East African Slave Trade," CA5/016, CMS; W. Yates, *Dado: or, Stories of Native Life in East Africa* (London: A. Crombie, 1886), 17-22, 102; Binns Jilore report, Feb. 1877, CA5/03, CMS; David Godoma report, [1878?], CA5/06, CMS; W.W.A. Fitzgerald, *Travels in the Coastlands of British East Africa and the Islands of Zanzibar and Pemba* (London: Chapman and Hall, 1898), 131; Wata(Sanye) also purchased slaves on the coast. W.E.H. Barrett, "Notes on the Customs and Beliefs of the Wa-Giriama, etc., British East Africa," *JRAI*, 41(1911), 33.

[48] Krapf, "Memoir on the East African Slave Trade," CA5/016, CMS. For a picture of an Oromo and his *gutu*, see Wakefield, *Thomas Wakefield*, 45 opp.

[49] Krapf journal, CA5/M1, 634, 737, CMS; Wakefield to UMFC, 25 Nov. 1865, UMFC *Magazine*, Jun. 1866, 430; New to Wakefield, 17 May 1870, UMFC *Magazine*, Nov. 1870, 752; Kirk to Granville, 6 Nov. 1873, C.1064, 102; Holmwood Report in Prideaux to Derby, 8 Feb. 1875, C.1588, 404; Gissing to Kirk, 14 Sep. 1884, FO 541/26, 243.

to danger, and in late December 1848 it was attacked by a combined force from Takaungu and Mombasa. According to the missionary, Ludwig Krapf, the raiders "burned down the houses, and captured many women and children. Some men were killed. The remainder fled to the Dahalo (Wata) country, or hid themselves in forests and caves."[50]

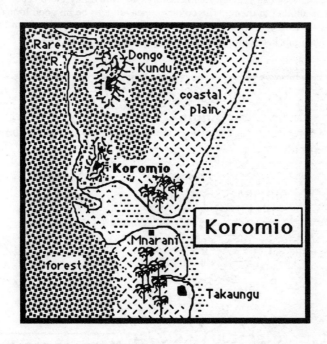

About the same time, discord in the interior southwest of Mombasa led to the founding of another maroon village. The settlement was established in the Shimba hills by a Miji Kenda known as Mwazangombe, who after quarreling with his brother broke away away and began to build up his power locally by attracting runaway slaves from the Mombasa area.[51] In 1843 Mwazangombe's village was reported to contain between three and four thousand maroons.[52]

---

[50] Krapf journal, 29 Dec. 1848, and "Memoirs of the East African Slave Trade," CA5/016, CMS; Morton, "Slaves, Fugitives, and Freedmen," 125-6, 128-9.

[51] Krapf journal, 15 Jul.. 1848, CA5/016, CMS; Burton, *Zanzibar*, II, 105-06. See also Thompson diary, 30 Jul. 1917, CP 19/82, KNA. It is possible that Mwazangombe's original group had earlier lived at Gasi, from which they were displaced by the Uthmani Mazrui in the late 1830s. Koffsky, "History of Takaungu," 14, quoting Sheikh [Fathili b.] Omar Al-Bauri's history of Takaungu.

[52] Krapf to Venn, 22 Oct. 1845, CA5/M1, 701, CMS. Krapf later revised this estimate to "400 families." Krapf to Venn, 9 Dec. 1847, CA5/M2, 120, CMS.

Krapf understood from reports received while he was in Mombasa that Mwazangombe, as the maroon settlement was already known, had grown through active
recruitment among slaves on the coast. The maroons, Krapf wrote,

> have always cottages ready for newcomers, who receive food from a common
> stock until they can provide for themselves by cultivating the piece of ground
> which is allotted to them....The colony endeavours to be on good terms with the
> pagans around, by whose instrumentality they get their supplies from the coast.
> They have muskets [and their] colony is strongly fortified.[53]

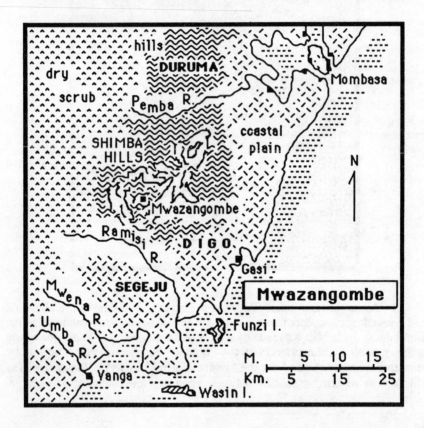

Mwazangombe appears nevertheless to have troubled the neighboring Digo and
caused havoc on the Usambara-Tanga caravan route, which had to be rerouted
away from their vicinity.[54]

---

[53] "Memoir on the East African Slave Trade," 1853, part 3, CA5/016, CMS.

[54] Krapf journal, 15/19 Jul. 1848, CA5/016, CMS; idem, "Memoir of the East African Slave Trade."

Mwazangombe survived only a short while as an open refuge for runaways. Plans were afoot in 1848 in Mombasa to launch an attack on the village. No record of an attack survives, but threats alone may have been enough to halt the flow of runaways, because Mwazangombe soon began delivering up runaway slaves to their masters for a fee. According to New, the original maroons had little room for expansion in what was a crowded area and so decided to limit their numbers.[55] Mwazangombe's residents also had to contend with their Digo neighbors, who were raiding for slaves in the region and selling them on the coast.[56] The maroons survived by allying with Muslim slave owners. The people of Mwazangombe developed ties with the Mazrui of Gasi, who after Mbaruk b. Rashid's accession to power in 1865 frequently rebelled against Busaidi rule on the southern coast. Mbaruk used slaves and runaways to do his fighting. By 1874 Mwazangombe was a mere dependency of Gasi.[57]

4. *Later Opportunities*

In the 1860s conditions on the Kenya coast under Busaidi control changed so substantially that freed slaves and runaways were able at least by the 1870s to sustain confrontations with slave owners. Change overall was the result of two parallel discontinuities: in the hinterland, collapse of the Oromo led to the redistribution of people, while along the coastline, strict enforcement of anti-slave trade proclamations led to the redistribution of power.

Events in the coastal hinterland constituted the more abrupt, and violent, change. In the early 1860s the Oromo, who had controlled the hinterland unchallenged for nearly two centuries, were faced by more numerous and determined pastoralists. On the southern coast, periodic states of alarm were brought about by the cattle raiding of Iloikop Maasai and related peoples from the interior, all referred to on the coast as "Kwavi." The Duruma, Ribe, and Giriama of the Mombasa hinterland were among those who lost their herds and withdrew into their fortified hilltop *kaya*, coming out only to cultivate nearby fields. As the Kwavi returned annually, their raiding extended farther north. By 1865 Kwavi had reached the Sabaki river and depleted the herds of the Oromo, who then withdrew from the Kilifi-Sabaki hinterland.[58] By then the Oromo were already under extreme pressure from Somali expanding southward from the Benadir hinterland. The Somali, who raided for cattle and slaves all the way to the Tana river, decimated the Oromo and took control of the grazing lands between the Tana and the Juba rivers.[59] Thereafter the Oromo ceased to be a significant

---

[55] New, *Life*, 49.

[56] Erhardt Journal, 10 Aug 1853, CA5/09, CMS; Erhardt to Venn, 27 Oct. 1854, CA5/M2, 624, CMS.

[57] Price journal, 29 Dec. 1874, CA5/023, CMS. See also Thompson diary, 30 Jul. 1917, CP 19/82, KNA.

[58] Morton, "Reappraisal of the History of the Wata."

[59] R. Brenner, "Reise in den Galla-Landern, 1867 bis 1868," *Petermann's Mittheilungen* (Gotha), 5(1868), 176-7; Ylvisaker, *Lamu*, 90. See ch. 2.

factor on the Kenya coast, except as refugees on Methodist mission stations and commodities in the slave trade.

By the 1870s colonization of the hinterland vacated by the Oromo was well underway. In the south, the pioneer settlers were Miji Kenda, who ventured out of their hilltop and forest strongholds and planted small agricultural colonies in the hills west of Takaungu. Predominant among them were families of Giriama, who by the 1880s were settled as far north as Mt. Mangea. In time the Giriama would become the principal occupants of the hinterlands of Mombasa, Takaungu, Malindi, as well as the arid district between the Sabaki and Tana rivers.[60] In the north the hinterland remained largely open, visited regularly as it was by Somali. In the forests, however, communities of agriculturists and hunter-gatherers took root. The forest dwellers, located mainly in the Lamu hinterland, were Pokomo, Oromo, and Wata refugees churned up by the raids, but there were coastal Bajuni and Nabahani, too.

The hinterland colonists also included runaway slaves from coastal plantations and port towns. In the 1860s plantation slaves from the Lamu *barani* started fleeing to the Utwani forest, where they joined maroon settlements and became part of the Nabahani sultanate of Witu. On the southern coast in the 1870s, fugitive slaves from the Mombasa-Malindi coast established Fuladoyo and Makongeni, west of Malindi and Takaungu, respectively. Gone with the Oromo were old arrangements with slave owners for the recapture and return of runaway slaves. New settlers in the hinterland were not opposed to slavery but did see themselves as rivals of plantation owners. By and large they were agriculturists who produced grain and other crops for export. Without the capital to emulate the plantation principle, they operated as families, with relatives, or as part of small, loosely-organized communities. After the 1860s the hinterland was developed as a grain-exporting region by small farmers--Miji Kenda, Pokomo, Bajuni, and maroons.

Meanwhile, along the coastline, Britain was beginning to restrict the slave trade at the very time when coastal Kenyans were expanding their role as consumers and conveyors of slaves. During the reign of Sultan Majid (1856-1870), Zanzibar's economy suffered from depressed clove prices and British restrictions on the slave trade. Enforcement of the 1845 Treaty, which outlawed slave exports north of Lamu, and the 1862 Treaty, which banned "northern Arabs" (principally from the Hadramaut) from operating in East Africa's slave markets, had the side effect of stimulating legal sales of slaves and slave labor enterprises within the sultanate.[61] The Kenya coast in particular attracted heavy investment in slaves for large-scale agriculture. In the 1860s thousands of newly-imported slaves converted vacant stretches between the Kilifi and Sabaki rivers into the Sultan's principal grain-exporting region and spurred Malindi's revival as a major

---

[60] Brantley, *The Giriama*, 8-32.

[61] Sheriff, *Slaves, Spices & Ivory*, 223, 228.

coastal port.[62] At the same time, Swahili traders in Mombasa and smaller southern ports were travelling to the interior to acquire slaves for the Kenya coastal market.[63] The northern Kenya coast also absorbed an important share of internal (and therefore still legal) slave traffic, because it was within walking distance of Benadir markets unaffected by the 1845 treaty. During the 1860s, when Lamu's hinterland was depopulated by Somali attacks on the Oromo, the Somali established an overland trade route from Lamu to the Benadir coast of southern Somalia. The Benadir ports, which the Sultan included in his dominions but did not control, soon became an important slave market for traders from the northern Indian Ocean who were prohibited from visiting Lamu and points south. Scattered and defenseless Oromo were also enslaved and exported via the overland route.[64]

With such alternatives available, Majid and his successor, Barghash (1870-1888), cooperated with the British in terminating the seaborn export trade, which at any rate was an economic resource monopolized by Arabs operating outside his dominions and a political weapon used by Britons meddling in his affairs. During the 1860s, therefore, the Sultan's governors, whose responsibilities heretofore had involved adjudicating local disputes and dealing with rebellious communities, began restricting the slave trade at water's edge while investing in land and slave-based agriculture. The governor (his proper title being *liwali*, pl. *maliwali*) was inclined to become, in other words, a self-promoter with outside backing. Two governors in particular, Sud b. Hamid of Lamu and Salim b. Khalfan of Malindi (and from 1884, of Mombasa) determined many of the policies of the Busaidi's Kenya coastal administration and strengthened their personal economic and political power with British support. Sud and Salim, enriched from slave-related ventures, were popular with the British for their active assistance in enforcing the treaties, which after all were directed against the slave trade rather than at slavery. *Maliwali* and other officials who proved uncooperative were gradually removed from office by the sultan, whose troops enforced the treaties. Although the new bureaucracy satisfied British requirements it operated without British supervision until the mid-1880s. And thus, for a time, *maliwali* were able to connive in the illegal slave trade being carried on in the Mombasa hinterland.

Local reactions to the proclamations varied. Old enemies of the sultan, such as the Mazrui and Nabahani, were prone to act defiantly, but to little avail. Rebellion merely exposed their weakness and afforded the sultan's *maliwali*, as well as the British, opportunities to demonstrate their strength. Rather than invoke the sultan's wrath, coastal folk resorted to *fitina* (complaints) as a means of saddling his administration. They increased pressure on the nearby *liwali* to

---

[62] E.B. Martin, *The History of Malindi: a Geographical Analysis of an East African Coastal Town from the Portuguese Period to the Present* (Nairobi: East African Literature Bureau, 1973), 56-61; Cooper, *Plantation Slavery*, 81-4.

[63] Sheriff, *Slaves, Spices and Ivory*, 170; Berg. "Mombasa under the Busaidi Sultanate," 238-42

[64] Ylvisaker, *Lamu*, 116-7. See also ch. 2

settle disputes, punish neighbors, discipline hinterland peoples, control missionaries, and capture runaway slaves. Most coastal folk played the *maliwali* like the *maliwali* played the British; in return for expressions of loyalty and service, they expected help in protecting special interests. Thus, while building his personal estate, each *liwali* was busy brokering a hundred local truces, each renegotiable the following day, and lending his power this way and that to maintain equilibrium. Such a balancing act, performed with anxiety until *maliwali* consolidated their hold, was eventually followed by a show of authoritarianism.

In the meantime, slaves were discovering opportunities created by corresponding dislocations of power along the coastline. Rates of escape rose with the intensity of disputes, while runaway slaves became the source of new conflicts. On missions built or expanded near Mombasa following the 1873 proclamation, runaway slaves drew missionaries and freed slaves into confrontations with slave owners, *maliwali*, and even the British. Rebellions against coastal authority were another attraction. Maroons assisted freeborn opponents of the sultan and his governors, and in Witu they promoted a conflict that began in the 1860s and lasted for three decades.

2

Watoro

Runaway slaves, known on the coast as *watoro* ("people who run away"), survived by shifting loyalties or locations, altering appearances, and acting new roles. Escape required initiative. And, for those hoping to stay alive in the seething hinterland, taking the initiative often meant committing a cold-blooded, preemptive act--in the form of stealing, kidnapping, raiding, or killing. Security meant living in harsh environments, instilling fear among neighbors, and deploying casual violence. As a rule, *watoro* were slave dealers. And they were present up and down the East African coast, as one observer noted, "from the Rovuma [river] to Cape Guardafui."[1]

Some *watoro* bore arms for freeborn Muslims. It would be a mistake to regard them as dependents of wealthy patrons or akin to the armed slaves who made up the personal retinue of many coastal leaders, such as Hamis b. Kombo, leading elder of the Mombasa Swahili and plantation lord at Mtwapa, and the Mazrui governors of Takaungu. They used armed slaves to patrol their districts, engage in the slave trade, and eventually fight the British.[2] *Watoro* however, such as those attached to the Nabahani of Witu and the Mazrui of Gasi, more closely resembled hired guns, who were capable of leaving town when it suited them or turning on their employer. They were active, not passive, elements, disinclined to wait or take orders.

Like runaways in all parts of the coast, *watoro* looked out for themselves. They made poor "loyal servants," having earned no rewards for being timid, submissive, or trusting.

1. *Gosha*

Thickest of skin were the Gosha of southern Somalia, who founded communities in the 1830s that survived into the twentieth century. Gosha's

---

[1] Miles to Granville, 17 Nov. 1881, C. 3160, 257. In addition to the *watoro* of the Kenya and Somali coast discussed in this book, see Glassman, "Social Rebellion and Swahili Culture," 218-31, for *watoro* activity on the coast opposite Zanzibar.

[2] See ch. 7. Shaw to Lang, 4 and 30 Jun. 1887, and Parker to Stock, 8 Jun. 1887, G3 A5/O4, CMS; Holmwood to Salisbury, 12 Apr. 1896, FO 403/226, 175. Kirk to Granville, 16 Feb. 1885, FO 84/1724; Gissing to Kirk, 14 Sep. 1884, FO 541/26, 239; de Winton to Euan Smith, 1 Aug. 1890, FO 403/138, 160; F. Lugard, *Diaries*, M. Perham, ed. 4 vols. (Evanston: Northwestern University Press, 1959-63), I, 239. For other examples of armed slave retainers, Cooper, *Plantation Slavery*, 91, 190-93.

early history, however, reads more like a suicidal tale than a success story. They built their refuge on the banks of the Juba river, infested with tsetse, mosquitoes, and crocodiles. Thick foliage along the Juba river valley provided natural defence for their villages, which attracted other settlers. Eventually these river *watoro* became known on the Benadir coast as "WaGosha" (people of the bush).[3] When the river also became an important link in the overland slave trade, the Gosha participated, and fed the trade with their own. Yet, while *watoro* preyed on one another, their corporate security increased. Shrewd leaders gained protective external allies, obtained guns, and repelled Somali slave owners wanting to destroy their settlements. Apart from the writings of Cassanelli, the history of the Gosha *watoro* is relatively obscure, because the Zanzibari and British paid no attention to the Somali coast until the mid-1870s, and little attention thereafter.

The Gosha were the past possessions of Somali in the Webe Shebelle and Trans-Juba areas. Slaves were imported into Somaliland before 1800, but traffic reached substantial levels in the 1840s, when traders from Kilwa and other southern ports began organizing supplies. Soon hundreds, probably thousands, of slaves were laboring in the Webe Shebelle flood plains cultivating cash crops. Slave-grown durra, sesame, and orchilla weed became major exports of the Benadir, and in the 1860s slave-raised cotton spurred a local textile export industry.[4] Slave import numbers are uncertain, but the Benadir coast was one of Zanzibar's largest markets. In 1875, two years after the sea traffic was prohibited, over-land traders were supplying the Somali plantations with an estimated 10,000 slaves annually.[5] Slaves were trekked from Kilwa and the newer

---

[3] Simons to IBEACO, 26 May 1890, FO 403/138, 31. Gosha is a Bantuized rendering of *gosh* (Somali for "dense bush"); Wa- is a prefix meaning ("people of...") in KiSwahili and many other Bantu languages.

[4] L.V. Cassanelli, *The Shaping of Somali Society: Reconstructing History of a Pastoral People, 1600-1900* (Philadelphia: University of Pennsylvania Press, 1982), 165-8; prior to the development of cash-crop agriculture, the Somali coast exported Galla slaves brought by caravan to the Benadir. They were exported to the Red Sea, Persia, and India. Christie, *Cholera Epidemics*, 137-8. The 1840s also mark the period when Sultan Seyyid of Zanzibar was trying to stave off British and French trading influence on the Benadir by offering good trading terms to the Geledi clan, and providing them with guns and powder. Nicholls, *Swahili Coast*, 298-300; Sheriff, *Slaves, Spices and Ivory*, 71-3, 165-6.

[5] Kirk to Derby, 29 Nov. 1875, C. 1829. Kirk's estimate, though based on what he was told at the Benadir port of Merka, might seem high considering that in 1874 Holmwood visited the Benadir and obtained no information. Holmwood to Prideaux, 17 Nov. 1874, C. 1588, esp. 7 and 10-11; also P.H. Colomb, *Slave-Catching in the Indian Ocean: a Record of Naval Experiences* (London: Dawsons of Pall Mall, reprint, 1968), 33-4, 47. The size of the slave population was nevertheless substantial. As Kirk had noted in 1873 after a visit to Mogadishu, Barawa, Merka, and Warsheikh, the bustling sesame and orchilla weed trade from Merka and Mogadishu "explains why Somali-land takes so many slaves, that are not exported to Arabia as is popularly imagined, but retained for work in the land itself." J. Kirk, "Visit to the Coast of Somali-land," *PRGS*, 17, 5(1872/73), 340-2. As late as 1945, former slaves and their descendants constituted a large, despised caste in Somalia, "an even lower

coastline depots of the Mrima. When the Ogaden and Herti Somali defeated the Oromo and expanded west of the Juba toward the Tana river, they also enslaved their enemy's women and children, many of whom were exported from the Somali coast.[6] Apart from working as field hands, slaves were used as domestic servants, concubines, and soldiers. They were present in large numbers in the Benadir towns. West of the Juba, Ogaden used slaves as herders.[7]

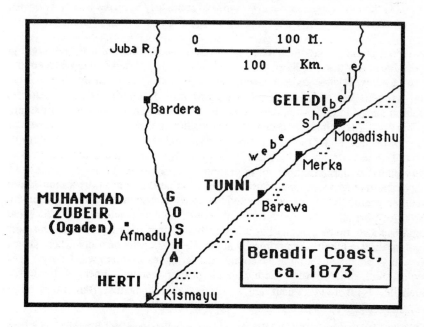

From the earliest period, slaves of the Somali escaped. They fled south of the Juba river and established maroon settlements on the islands opposite the

caste than the Bon of Southern Somalia and the Sab of the North." A census conducted by the British during the Second World War identified 34,900 people of slave descent in the Juba river and Webe Shebelle areas and in the towns of Barawa, Merka, Havai, and Mogadishu, "Somali Handbook," cv. Gosha (127), Kabole(143), Makanne(148), and Former Slaves (160-1), FJL: See also I.M. Lewis, *Peoples of the Horn of Africa: Somali, Afar and Saho* Ethnographic Survey of Africa; North Eastern Africa, part 1(London: International African Institute, 1955), 41-2.

[6] Sparshott to CMS, 21 Nov. 1868, CA5/026, CMS. Brenner, "Reise in den Galla Landern," 177; idem, "Forshungen in Ost-Afrika," *Petermann's Mittheilungen*, 10 (1868), 457-8. Christie, *Cholera Epidemics*, 137-8; K. Macdougall, "Notes on the Decline and Extermination of the Galla," 31 Mar. 1915, DC/MAL/2/3, KNA.

[7] Holmwood to Prideaux, 17 Nov. 1874, C. 1588, 11-3; Hardinge report, 20 Jul. 1897, C. 8683, 18; Lewis, *Peoples of the Horn*, 125-8; Cassanelli, *Shaping of Somali Society*, 170-2.

mainland controlled by the Oromo. Like their Somali ex-masters and in contrast to the Oromo, the maroons professed Islam. In 1824, the British naval reconnaissance operating from Mombasa encountered numbers of "Soalese [Swahilis] who...were originally runaway slaves" on the Juba islands, along the coast between Kiu and the Juba river.

> They adopt the Arab costume and Mohammedan faith; and, from what we observed in the little communication we had with them, they appeared to be very docile, tractable people. They trade in a slight degree with the Gallah [Oromo].... [8]

By then it is likely that other runaway slaves owned by Somali had found refuge in the Juba river town of Bardera. In 1819 a Mogadishu sheikh made Bardera the base of a new Islamic reformist religious community, later led by Sheikh Ibrahim Hassan Jeber.[9] The Bardera Muslims attempted to purify Islamic practices, prohibit social indulgences, and banish local cults of saint worship. In the late 1830s or 1840s, they attempted to spread their beliefs through *jihad*, which reached its peak under the leadership of Sherif Abdirahman and Sherif Ibrahim.[10] According to Cassanelli, Bardera's "militant phase" coincided with the arrival in the vicinity of "large numbers of migrating [Darood] nomads" from the north.[11] But at the time McQueen and Harris understood that Bardera "under Sultan Abder Rahman" had been "founded on a sudden spirit of discontent showing itself by the slave portion of the community of small tribes surrounding."[12] The issue requires more investigation, but it is significant that sherifs Abdirahman and Ibrahim directed their *jihad* primarily at the Webe Shebelle districts, where slaves were most abundant, and that the counterattack against Bardera was led by Yusuf Mohammad, sultan of the Geledi clan, the principal slave owners of the lower Shebelle.[13] In 1844, Yusuf led a force of 40,000 against Bardera, razed it,

---

[8] Boteler, *Narrative*, II, 220-1. For the islands, see Rebmann and Erhardt's 1856 map in E. Stock, *The History of the Church Missionary Society: its Environment, its Men and its Work*, 2 vols. (London: Church Missionary Society, 1899-1916), II, 136; and the islands named Burgal, Tula, Tovai, and Kwayama in C. W. Haywood, "The Bajun Islands and Birikau," *Geographical Journal*, 85(1933), 64 map. They later became known as the Bajun islands after the people who colonized them in the second half of the nineteenth century. For Bajuni traditions vaguely recalling the original inhabitants, J.T. Juxon Barton, "Report on the Bajun Islands,"*Journal of the East Africa and Uganda Natural History Society*, (Mar. 1922), 33-7.

[9] L. Krapf's account of the founding "twenty five years ago" of "Barder, on the River Jub," 19 Mar. 1844, CA5/M2, 267-9. Cassanelli, *Shaping of Somali Society*, 136-7, using oral evidence and also dating Bardera's founding in 1819, identifies Sheik Ibrahim as the founder, but Krapf specifies Ibrahim as successor.

[10] *Shaping of Somali Society*, 137-8.

[11] Ibid., 137, 140-1.

[12] W.C. Harris, *The Highlands of Aethiopia*, 3 vols. (London: Longman, Brown, Green, Longmans, 1844), notes on end map dated 1843 entitled "Abyssinia," by M. McQueen with additions by Harris.

[13] When Kirk visited the Benadir in 1873, slave-grown grain exports came from

slaughtered the males, and enslaved the females.[14]

After the sacking of Bardera, *watoro* settlements sprang up along the lower Juba river.[15] Unlike the lower Shebelle, the Juba river was not used for plantation agriculture and seldom resorted to for watering by Somali pastoralists; crocodiles infested the river, and dense bush, thick with tse-tse fly, paralleled much its course. The first runaways who entered the area ran away from the Barawa hinterland and were of coastal Tanzanian, or Zigua, origin. Under the leadership of Majandero and later a woman diviner named Wanakuka, they founded small villages along the Juba banks, fished, and cultivated small grain fields. They were assisted with seed by a small community of Lashunle Somali, and with river skills by Boni hunter-gatherers. Eventually the Zigua pioneers were able to defend themselves against Somali and Oromo pastoralists occupying the regions to the east and west, respectively. By 1865, six villages were established, with an estimated population of 4,000.[16]

Soon, many more runaways gained refuge along the river. Cassanelli speculates that the *watoro* population increased because of manumission in coastal towns, the liberation of slaves captured by the British naval patrol off the Benadir coast, and the escape of slaves from caravans trekking overland between 1874 and 1876.[17] More important, however, was the Somali-Oromo war, which began in 1866, spread west toward the Tana, and accelerated movement of Somali clans on both sides of the Juba river. According to a contemporary

---

"River Geledi" [Shebelle]. Kirk, "Visit to Somali-land," 342. "Cassanelli, *Shaping of Somali Society*, 138-46, presents the Geledi-Bardera clash as a religio-political conflict, without considering the possibility that Bardera directly threatened the slave-based economy of the lower Shebelle. Sheriff has also noted Bardera's interference in the long-distance trade in slaves and ivory. *Slaves, Spices and Ivory*, 165. Cassanelli's argument that the Geledi were, individually, not large slave owners may also need closer investigation. Yusuf's son and successor, Ahmad Yusuf, in 1874 had 2,000 soldiers under his command, "principally slaves." Holmwood to Prideaux, 17 Nov. 1874, C. 1588, 13.

[14] Krapf to CMS, 22 Dec. 1844, CA5/M1, 513, CMS. Cassanelli, relying on C. Guillain, *Documents sur l'histoire, la géographie et le commerce de l'Afrique Orientale*, 3 vols (Paris: Arthus Bertrand, 1856-58), III, 42-3, gives 1843 as the year of the battle, and omits mention of enslavement. *Shaping of Somali Society*, 138 and note.

[15] In 1892, "some thirty or forty years back." F.G. Dundas, "Expedition up the Jub River through Somali-land, East Africa," *Geographical Journal*, 1(Mar. 1893), 213; idem, "Explorations of the Rivers Tana and Juba," *The Scottish Geographical Journal*, 9 (1893), 113-26. For a survey of Gosha history, L.V. Cassanelli, "Social Construction on the Somali Frontier: Bantu Former Slave Communities in the Nineteenth Century," in I. Kopytoff, ed., *The African Frontier* (Bloomington: Indiana University Press, 1987), 216-38. Cassanelli's oral evidence suggests the Gosha maroons may have originated as early as the 1830s (219).

[16] Cassanelli, "Former Bantu Slave Communities," 221-2; Hardinge to Salisbury, 1 Oct. 1897, FO 403/244, 77; F. Elliott, "Jubaland and its Inhabitants," *Geographical Journal*, 41(June 1913), 559.

[17] "Former Bantu Slave Communities," 222.

account, the Somali clans east of the Juba, having "forgotten their enmity [toward one another]...crossed the Juba in masses and stood,...in January [1867], level with the coast village of Kiunga."[18] Once the Oromo were routed, however, Somali groups jostled with one another for territory. The Herti moved southwest along the coast and defended their position against the Tunni trying to expel them from the northeast.[19] Such conflicts took place in the Juba river vicinity and made it easier for Somali-owned slaves to escape. As with Witu, which absorbed many new runaways in the late 1860s when turmoil became common in the Lamu hinterland, the Somali conquest had as one of its many by-products the rapid growth of Gosha.[20] Whereas only six *watoro* villages existed in 1865, more than eighty stood twenty years later.

As new villages came into existence, they remained small and separated from one another. Cultivation was confined to *desheks* next to the river bank, and thick bush was allowed to grow on the three landed sides of each village.[21] The staple crop was maize, while millet, sesame, cotton, bananas, and cotton were also grown.[22] Villages were relocated often, on both banks, to improve fishing, cultivation, and no doubt to return the surrounding bush, used as a latrine and fuel source, to fallow. By scattering themselves in many small villages, rather than concentrating in large towns, the Gosha made it difficult for Somali to drive them out. Any attack on one village would be an alarm to the inhabitants of others, whose women and children could cross the river to safety, while the men came to their neighbors' defense.

Somali expansion ultimately embroiled the *watoro* in the slave trade. The Muhammad Zubeir (Ogaden) and Tunni, who traded slaves before the war, led the campaigns against the Oromo and benefitted from the sudden burst in the export of Oromo slaves and cattle along the northern coast. Somali conquest was at least in part, if not primarily, motivated by their desire to expand slave trading activities.[23] Murgan Yusuf, sheikh of the Muhammad Zubeir at Afmadu in the

---

[18] Brenner, "Reise in den Galla-Landern," 177. Kiunga is situated on the present Kenya-Somali border, 150 km. south of the mouth of Juba river. By late 1866, the slave market in Lamoo was "overstocked with [slaves], owing to war existing between two tribes on opposite sides of the Juba river...." G.L. Sulivan, *Dhow Chasing in Zanzibar Waters and on the Eastern Coast of Africa* (London: Sampson Low, Marston, Low, and Searle, 1873), 154.

[19] Ylvisaker, *Lamu*, 120, with reference to the conflict between the Mijertein [Herti] and Barawa Somali [Tunni].

[20] The nature, extent, and impact of the Somali-Oromo wars in the Tana-Juba region has yet to be explored in any detail. For Witu, see "Witu" below.

[21] Cassanelli, "Bantu Former Slave Communities," 222-3.

[22] Dundas, "Expedition up the Jub River," 214; Craufurd to AgAdmin, Mombasa; 31 Dec. 1893, CP 68/19, KNA; Jenner to Hardinge, 28 Jul. 1895, FO 403/ 210, 227.

[23] The Tunni Somali controlled the slave trading port of Barawa. In the 1860s the Ogaden area on the border of Ethiopia was the principal meeting place of Somali caravans channeling slaves down the Juba to the Benadir. Christie, *Cholera Epidemics*, 135-8. Ogaden expansion south ignited the Somali-Oromo wars, after the Oromo had

territory seized from the Oromo, later recounted a "series of successful fights" against the "Wardey" [Oromo] and the capture of 30,000 cattle and goats, and 8,000 women and children.[24] As the Oromo fled west, Herti Somali colonized the coast south of the Benadir to the port of Kismayu, which became a new slave outlet, while elements of the Tunni Somali, who controlled the Benadir port of Barawa, and the Muhammad Zubeir chased the Oromo all the way to the Tana river.[25] Traffic in Oromo slaves made this period, in Ylvisaker's words, "golden days for the traders."[26] In 1873 the land traffic between the Lamu hinterland and the Benadir began, and it was dominated by the Muhammad Zubeir, Herti, and Tunni, with their networks of intermediaries and dependents. At the Tana river the Somali met caravans arriving from the south and

> barter[ed] for the most miserable of the survivors who, if they recover, are sold in the extensive Bajuni country, ...or passed on to the Somali tribes up the Juba river, and to the Banadir ports.

The Somali also transferred to the Benadir slaves taken by the *watoro* of Witu from Lamu plantations.[27] Their trading network was served as well by Boni hunter-gatherers in the Bajuni hinterland, the followers of Avatula b. Bahero, and the Gosha of the Juba river.

The Gosha *watoro* acted as intermediaries between the Muhammad Zubeir and the Tunni of Barawa. Gosha traders rendezvoused with the Muhammad Zubeir under a large shade tree in an open field known as 'Regatta," located southeast of Afmadu, the Muhammad Zubeir's capital. Afmadu traders traveled to Regatta with cattle, goats, donkeys, and slaves; Gosha brought "friendless" women and children, recent runaways, grain, and tobacco. The Gosha then traded the slaves, and probably hides made from the stock obtained at Regatta, on the nearby coast controlled by the Tunni.[28] It is uncertain what the Gosha received

---

been weakened by small pox. Ylvisaker, *Lamu*, 90. Cassanelli, citing R. Turton ["Pastoral Tribes of Northern Kenya, 1800-1916," (London: University of London PhD thesis, 1970)], refers to Ogaden and Darod expansion into the Juba region as a pastoral response to agricultural and commercial growth on the Benadir, and as a significant "long-term consequence of the economic transformation of Somalia in the nineteenth century." *Shaping of Somali Society*, 180.

[24] Macdougall, "The Decline and Extermination of the Gallas," DC/MAL/2/3, KNA.

[25] Cassanelli, Shaping of Somali Society, 75, 180. Ylvisaker, *Lamu*, 120-1, re Mijertein [Herti] Somali. The Tunni appear on the maps of G.A. Fischer, *Petermann's Mittheilungen* (1886), map 19; IBEACO treaty map, FO 403/120, encl. in Alexander to Salisbury, 31 Oct. 1889; and D. Paulitschke, *Ethnographie Nordost-Afrikas* (Berlin: Geographische Verlagshandlung Dietrich Reimer, 1893).

[26] *Lamu*, 91, 117.

[27] Holmwood to Prideaux, 17 Nov. 1874, C. 1588, 7.

[28] Craufurd to Salisbury, 13 Jul. 1897, as well as the appended map, FO 403/227, 200. Gosha could not maintain stock in their tse-tse ridden areas. The bones scattered about Regatta when Craufurd passed through suggests that stock was immediately slaughtered (the Ogaden no doubt joining the feast), and the hides removed to the

in return, but before the 1880s it would have been confined to cloth and iron hoes. At any rate, proceeds from the middle trade did not offset the steep human price paid in Gosha. During the Regatta years, Gosha was plagued by murder, plunder, and civil strife.[29] Regatta coincided, too, with the rise of Gosha strong men.

The road from Gosha to Regatta led from the village of Nassib Bunda. Nassib was the runaway slave of Murgan Yusuf, sultan of Afmadu.[30] Of Yao origin, he joined the *watoro* on the Juba in the mid 1860s, where, allegedly, he ran afoul of the menfolk who accused him of luring away their women. By the early 1870s he had moved upstream with a band of followers and established the village which bore his name.[31] These were the years of Regatta, during which Nassib became the most powerful among several Gosha rivals, including Songollo Mafula and Makoma Maligo, whose villages were located downstream and further from Regatta. Nassib was known for his military prowess, courage, and knowledge of spiritual forces. According to one account, the Gosha believed he had the power to control the Juba's legion of crocodiles, which ate his enemies and carried their women to his village. He was "feared," a British official was later told, "as a wizard as well as a tyrant."[32] Though successful in building a powerful base inside Gosha, Nassib recognized that the Gosha altogether would have to become a force to reckon with. Thus, he nurtured contacts that strengthened the Gosha's position as well as his own. He learned, also, how conflict among slave owners could be turned to the *watoro*'s advantage.

Southern Somalia was ripe for intrigue. Divisions and conflict among the Somali had continued since the retreat of the Oromo. The Muhammad Zubeir and Herti competed for the cattle trade, while slave trade restrictions were beginning to tell on the Geledi and other cash-cropping clans of the Webe Shebelle, who regarded the Tunni, Bimal, and Herti clans along the coastline as their rivals. The sultanate of Zanzibar and the British were extremely unpopular among all Somali clans for restricting the slave trade and became even more so as the sultan tried to exercise direct authority over the Benadir ports. Coastal traders, who included Arabs and Asians, resented Zanzibar custom duties and competition from Zanzibar and British traders, whereas the Somali, many of whom were devout Sunni Muslims, resented the Ibadhi Muslim officials from Zanzibar and

---

coast for sale.

[29] Craufurd to Salisbury, 13 Jul. 1897, FO 403/227, 200.

[30] Hardinge to Salisbury, 1 Oct. 1897, FO 403/244, 78. Cassanelli's twentieth century sources provide several parallel accounts of Nassib's life before his arrival in Gosha, though none suggest that Nassib was owned by Murgan Yusuf or, for that matter, any other Ogaden. Hardinge wrote his account after interviewing Nassib privately. "Bantu Former Slave Communities," 226-7. "Bunda" was a Somaliized version of Pondo, which Hardinge and other British officials used in their correspondence.

[31] Cassanelli, "Former Bantu Slave Communities," 227. Cassanelli provides much valuable information about Nassib, based on Italian sources (ibid, 226-31).

[32] Hardinge to Salisbury, 1 Oct. 1897, FO 403/244, 78; Cassanelli, "Former Bantu Slave Communities," 228-9.

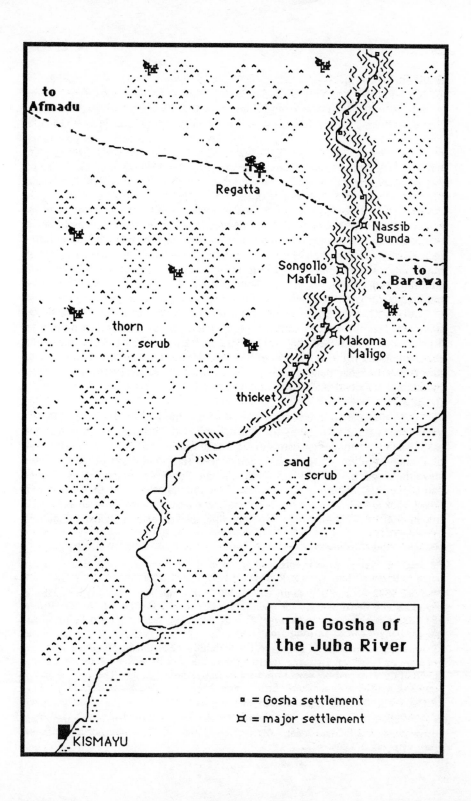

to
Afmadu

Regatta

Nassib
Bunda

Songollo
Mafula

to
Barawa

thorn
scrub

Makoma
Maligo

thicket

sand
scrub

The Gosha of
the Juba River

▫ = Gosha settlement
⌑ = major settlement

KISMAYU

despised British infidels, at whom they spat the word "kaffir."[33] Zanzibar and Britain had few natural allies on the Somali coast but wished, at the same time, to prevent outside powers from taking over the resources and harbors of the Benadir, which Zanzibar had for many years claimed as part of its dominions.[34]

Nassib's diplomacy reveals how Gosha moved to enhance its position a-midst these competing forces. He struck peace accords with small Somali clans who were capable enemies of large clans or who were dependent on Gosha's trading partners. He befriended, for example, the Bimal Somali of the Merka hinterland, who were old enemies of the Geledi, the largest slave-owning clan on the lower Shebelle and owners of many Gosha *watoro*. He accomplished the same with the pastoral Sheikal, dependents of the Tunni. The Bimal and Sheikal agreed to cease their raids on Gosha provided that Nassib guarantee the return of their runaway slaves.[35] Nassib neutralized his immediate neighbors by cooperating in the slave trade and helping to protect their investments in slaves while admitting runaway slaves only of Somali situated outside the Juba river valley trading network. By 1875, the principal partners in this network were the Tunni of Barawa, the Herti of Kismayu, the Muhammad Zubeir, and Nassib's Gosha followers. Nassib's membership was attested that year by the officers of the Khedive Ishmail who raised the Turkish flag in Barawa and Kismayu, and, after representations from the Tunni, recognized Nassib as Gosha's leader.[36] Juba traders expected that the Khedive's rule would increase the overland trade in slaves by ending Zanzibari and British interference in the export sea trade from the Benadir.[37]

The Juba network, however, was about to crumble. Within weeks after invading the coast, the Khedive's forces withdrew, and Zanzibar quickly returned to establish much stronger garrisons in the Benadir ports. The Herti were driven out of Kismayu. Sultan Bargash soon announced the prohibition of the overland slave trade and, by 1877, it had come to a halt. Southern Somalia at last formed part of the Busaidi empire administered from the major ports by the sultan's *maliwali*, backed by troops and junior officials, and accompanied by Arab and Hindu Indian traders. The hinterland Somali, their slaves, and the Gosha remained

---

[33] See, for example, the events leading up to the murder of Arthur Heale, British trader at Barawa, Holmwood to Prideaux, 17 Nov. 1874, C. 1588, 10-13.

[34] Since 1842. Nicholls, *Swahili Coast*, 296. For events inside southern Somalia in the 1870s and Zanzibar's bid for control, see Cassanelli, *Shaping of Somali Society*, 183-228; Coupland, *Exploitation of East Africa*, 229, 244-5; 271-99; Salim, *Swahili-speaking Peoples*, introduction.

[35] Cassanelli, "Former Bantu Slave Communities," 229; idem, *Shaping of Somali Society*, 223. Cassanelli respectively locates the Bimal between Barawa and the mouth of the Juba and between Jesiira and Mungiya further north. The Sheikal form a section of the Herab dependents of the Tunni. Lewis, *Peoples of the Horn*, 30, 149.

[36] Cassanelli, "Former Bantu Slave Communities," 227.

[37] Ylvisaker, *Lamu*, 96-9; E.R. Turton, "Kirk and the Egpytian Invasion of East Africa in 1875: a Reassessment," *JAH*, 11, 3(1970), 355-70; Coupland, *Exploitation of East Africa*, 271-99.

beyond Zanzibar's administration, yet each was affected by Zanzibar's control of the coast. Except for firearms and slaves, trade continued particularly in beef and hides, which benefitted cattle owners, including the Muhammad Zubeir. Sesame and cotton also enjoyed good markets. In the past the agricultural, slave-owning Somali profited from these and other cash crops, but after 1876 no longer could they replace the slave laborers who died, grew old, or ran away. Extracting labor from those who remained simply exacerbated the trend. The Somali of the Webe Shebelle grew even more resentful toward Zanzibar, for stopping the slave trade, and toward the Gosha, for giving refuge to their slaves.

Sometime in the early 1880s, Zanzibar recognized the Gosha *watoro* as loyal subjects and supplied them with firearms. Sultan Bargash's military commander, the Briton Lloyd Mathews, delivered hundreds of Enfield rifles to the Gosha, "as a protection against Somali raiders."[38] The Gosha also obtained muzzle-loaders, purportedly in the thousands, from Zanzibari traders. The lion's share appears to have gone to Nassib and his followers, who formed a small army of musketeers, archers, and spearmen.[39] The Gosha-Zanzibar alliance coincided, too, with Nassib's emergence as an Islamic mystic and sultan in the Arab style, complete with a personal secretary and correspondent.[40] Yet Nassib controlled only a handful of the many Gosha villages strung along the Juba, and other leaders contested his authority, because they, too, had firearms. The days of Regatta were probably not yet over, because the Muhammad Zubeir required herders for their expanding cattle holdings, and the Gosha needed hides to trade on the coast for guns. Ties with Zanzibar gained Gosha a measure of independence while perpetuating internal divisions. As with the defunct Juba network, so with Zanzibari-controlled coast: the Gosha *watoro* preyed on one other to avert re-enslavement by the Somali.[41]

2. *Witu*

Controlling the northern Kenya coast required the sultans of Zanzibar and their British backers to attack, rather than seek the support of, the local *watoro*. The difference is explained by the fact that the *watoro* were allied with Ahmed b. Fumo Luti (Simba), sultan of Witu in the Lamu hinterland, who resisted Zanzibari rule. Simba's *watoro* lived in semi-independent communities and gave military assistance to the sultan in return for legal adjudication and trade connections with which to obtain guns. On the northern coast the gun trade supported the slave trade, and *watoro* were deeply involved in both. Widespread insecurity on the mainland occasioned by slave raiding, potential attacks from the coast, and the Somali-Oromo conflict made guns essential. Simba seldom controlled the *watoro*, and his attempts at reconciliation with Zanzibar were often

---

[38] Hardinge to Salisbury, 1 Oct. 1897, FO 403/244, 79.

[39] Cassanelli, "Former Bantu Slave Communities," 228; Jenner to Hardinge, 28 Jul. 1895, FO 403/210, 227.

[40] Cassanelli, "Former Bantu Slave Communities," 228-9

[41] For the Gosha during the IBEACO period, see ch. 6.

disrupted by the desire of these maroons to remain independent. Simba's *watoro* refused to entrust their own protection to others, seeing that the overriding interests of the powerful would prove indifferent to their plight. The *watoro* hounded all who aspired to control the coast, while Lamu, Zanzibar, and Great Britain cooperated to eliminate Witu, this "nest," they called it, "of murderers, robbers, [and] fanatics."

Simba founded the sultanate of Witu in the 1860s, when members of the Nabahani family fled Pate island after their defeat at the hands of the sultan of Zanzibar, Seyyid Majid. Simba had supported his uncle, the sultan of Pate, rebelled with him against Majid, and followed him into exile at Kau. Simba succeeded his uncle, who by then had created the title, "Sultan of Witu." In 1860 Simba was invited by the leading elders of Pate and the sheikh of Siu to take up the sultanship of Pate in order to unify these two towns. He consented, and returned to Pate to receive popular support from all parts of the island. Sheikh Muhammad b. Bwana Mataka, the sultan of Siu, and other pro-Zanzibar groups such as the Bajuni townspeople of Faza under Mzee Seif, renounced loyalty to Majid and gave support to Simba. Majid responded quickly. From Zanzibar he dispatched his vizier, Seyyid Seleman b. Ahmad, who secreted troops into Pate town, secured local allies, and launched an attack on Simba's forces. Simba's support crumbled, and, in an opportunistic move that characterized his later actions, Mzee Seif of Faza switched his loyalty to Majid. Simba escaped to Siu and then, in order to avoid a crushing defeat, fled with his followers to Kau.[42]

In the next few years Simba's prospects of returning to Pate diminished as Majid eliminated his supporters in Siu and pressed Simba on the mainland. Majid imprisoned Bwana Mataka, along with his brother and all his sons, and installed his own governors in the island towns. From this time the towns of Pate and Siu declined, and numbers of Nabahani and other families left the island to settle in Lamu and Malindi, or to join Simba.[43] The Bajuni of Pate island remained on good terms with Zanzibar through the skillful maneuvering of Mzee

---

[42] Accounts of Pate history and Sultan Simba are based on two versions of the "Chronicle of Pate," as published in A. Werner, "A Swahili History of Pate," *Journal of the African Society*, 14, 54 (1915), 291-96, 393-413, and C.H. Stigand, *The Land of Zinj: Being an Account of British East Africa, its Ancient History and Present Inhabitants* (London: Frank Cass, 1966), 29-102, together with "Report on the Delimitation of the Sultan of Zanzibar's Territories on the Coast to the North of Lamou and in the Interior of Africa" in Kitchener to Rosebery, 30 Jun. 1885, FO 403/98, 44; Statement of Clemens Denhardt, 9 Apr. 1890, FO 403/137, 121; bw. Rehmet b. Ahmed Nabhani, "History of the Sultans of the Nabhani Tribes," ibid, 170; Mzee Seif, "History of the Nabahani Tribe," ibid, 171. See also G.A. Akinola, "Slavery and Slave Revolts in the Sultanate of Zanzibar in the Nineteenth Century," *Journal of the Historical Society of Nigeria*, 6, 2(Dec. 1972), 224-6; Ylvisaker, *Lamu*, 83-4; J.d.V. Allen, "Witu, Swahili History and the Historians," in A.I. Salim, ed. *State Formation in Eastern Africa* (New York: St. Martin's Press, 1985), 216-49.

[43] In 1874 Pate town contained only one hundred people. Holmwood agricultural and commercial report, in Prideaux to Derby, 8 Feb. 1875, C. 1588, 68; See also Fitzgerald, *Travels*, 387.

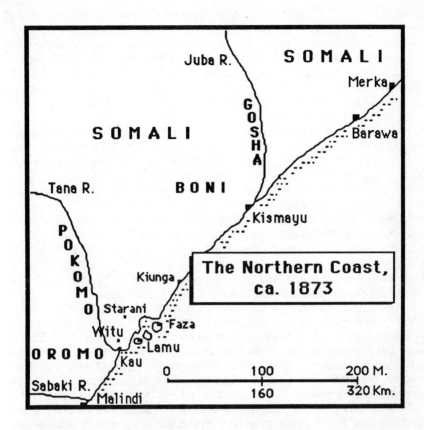

The Northern Coast, ca. 1873

Seif, and Faza became the dominant town of the island and the controlling center of the Pate coast up to Kiunga. Meanwhile, Simba, after staying one or two years at Kau, shifted with his followers to Witu in order to avoid clashes with Majid's troops, by 1865 under the command of his new governor of Lamu, Sud b. Hamed. In 1867 Sud attacked Witu but was repulsed.[44] The *liwali* 's failure was probably deliberate, his attack mounted only to convince Majid that the effort had been made. Simba's destruction was opposed by many Lamuans, who had kinship ties with the Nabahani; and Sud himself was connected to principal Lamu families by marriage and found it difficult to comply fully with the sultan's instructions when they ran counter to local sentiment.[45]

With the immediate threat of destruction gone, Simba added to Witu's security by keeping away from areas under Zanzibar's control and by making his

---

[44] New, *Life*, 257; Wakefield, *Thomas Wakefield*, 96; Werner, "Swahili History of Pate," 405; Ylvisaker, *Lamu*, 115.
[45] Haggard to Kirk, 26 Dec. 1884, FO 84/1679; Stigand, *Land of Zinj*, 98.

headquarters strong and defensible. In the decade or so after 1866 Simba avoided contact with Lamu and Kau. Majid and his successor, Bargash, kept the coastline firmly under their control and, as long as Simba did not renounce his allegiance or cause any trouble, were content to give him a small pension and leave him alone.[46] Apparently resigned to a life on the mainland, Simba and his followers concentrated their efforts on enlarging the town of Witu, farming, and securing the area. They located Witu in dense forest, surrounding it with timber walls, stockades, and thick doors.

As much as to fend off any possible attack from the coast, Simba needed strong defenses to maintain Witu's security among the peoples of the hinterland. From the late 1860s groups in the Tana-Lamu region were dislocated by incursions of Kwavi from the southwest and Somali from the northeast.[47] Most adversely affected were the Oromo, whose large herds acted like a magnet. Living as they were in small, scattered groups, the Oromo were helpless against well-armed and mobile Kwavi and Somali. The raiders killed many Oromo and stole their cattle.[48] Some Oromo fled south to settle near the Miji Kenda or lived among the Pokomo on the Tana river and turned to agriculture. Many who fled northeast from the Tana or southwest from the Juba region found safety at Witu. With Boni, Pokomo, and other refugees churned up by the Kwavi and Somali, the Oromo placed themselves under Simba's protection.

Simba further increased the population of Witu by harboring runaway slaves. He reportedly offered free status to all slaves crossing into his territory. As a result many slaves from the plantations of nearby Lamu, from Somali areas, and from distant parts of the coast fled to Witu where they received plots and took up agriculture. In the 1860s the runaways, together with numerous Pokomo, constituted the bulk of Witu's agriculturists, and it appears that the runaways intermarried freely with Pokomo and Boni residents. German traveller Richard Brenner gained the impression that Simba had banished slavery within his dominions, but it is clear from later reports that the people of Witu in time depended on slaves to develop its agricultural establishment. In the 1860s approximately one-third of the Witu population was made up of Swahili and Arab immigrants from Pate, Lamu, Takaungu, and Mombasa. They and Simba possessed many slaves, and the runaways, who settled in their own villages and accepted Simba's legal authority became slave owners themselves. Witu's estimated population as of 1870, by group, was Galla, Boni, Pokomo, and Doe, 15,000; Swahili and Arab, 13,000; and runaway slaves and other fugitives, 16,000. Though exaggerated, these figures reliably indicate Witu's heterogeneous makeup.[49]

---

[46] Miles to Granville, 17 Nov. 1882, C. 3160, 257. Bargash became sultan in 1870.

[47] Brenner, "Reise in den Galla-Landern," 176-7.

[48] Ibid; Yates, *Dado*, 82-8. Cf. ch. 1. Ylvisaker argues that the Oromo-Somali conflict was caused by Sud b. Hamed, governor of Lamu, but this seems farfetched. *Lamu*, 90-1.

[49] Brenner, "Reise in den Galla-Landern," 176-7; O. Kersten, *Baron Carl Claus von*

Witu grew rapidly into a loose federation of villages scattered throughout the surrounding forests. In the immediate neighborhood of Witu town were clustered the villages of Hamasi, Mohonda, Mawani, Chanja, Gongoni (Mogongoni), and Mominini. These villagers, known as the *watu wa Witu* ("people of Witu"), numbered, along with the townsmen of Witu, approximately six thousand in 1884.[50] To the east and north set deeply in the aboriginal Utwani forest were the heavily stockaded villages of Balana (or Balawa, itself a cluster of small villages), Balo, Katana (Katawa), Mtangamakundu, Panda Nguo, Pumwani, Ngavera, Ngomeni, and Mtoshani. Forest villagers were largely autonomous and, although they supported Simba and sought his mediation, often acted without his approval. The more single-minded and independent of the forest dwellers were the *watoro*. Known locally as the *wakengi* ("restless ones"), the maroons became as troublesome to Witu as they were vital to its interests.[51] Providing the bulk of Simba's forces, their settlements formed the vital line of defense against the Somali, and they controlled the key trading post of Katana. Important too among the forest dwellers were the Boni hunters, who with the runaways engaged in the ivory trade and gathered rubber for sale on the coast.[52] Above Simba the Boni recognized as their head, Avatula b. Bahero, of the Katwa clan of the Bajuni.[53] Avatula provided the forest dwellers with an important

---

der Decken's Reisen in Ost-Afrika in den Jahren 1859 bis 1865 (Leipzig: E. F. Winter'sche Berlagshandlung, 1869), II, 375, 377; E.F. Berlioux, *The Slave Trade in Africa in 1872* (London: Edward Marsh, 1872), 47-8. Berlioux's account of Witu appears to be based on Kersten and on Brenner's letters, some of which were not published. Glassman attributes Witu's source of *watoro* to be slaves of Lamu who had been forced to work harder by owners when their Asian creditors put the squeeze on slave owners to produce more crops to pay off debts after Zanzibar abolished the sale of slaves in the 1870s, which previously had been the readiest means of settling debts. This intriguing argument, which is unsupported by direct evidence, does not account for the sizeable presence of *watoro* in Witu in the 1860s. J. P. Glassman, "The Runaway Slave in Coastal Resistance to Zanzibar: the Case of the Witu Sultanate" (Madison: University of Wisconsin M.A. Thesis, 1983), 23, 54, 71-2. At any rate, the use of slaves as legal security against loans was not effectively eliminated until after the 1890 proclamation. See ch. 6.

[50] Haggard to Kirk, 25 Aug. 1884, FO 541/26, 232. Description of the towns of Witu is based on this and other of Haggard's reports together with the following: Rogers and Jackson report, 20 Jul. 1891, FO 403/159, 86; map in Euan Smith to Salisbury, 21 Aug. 1888, FO 403/106; map in Alexander to Salisbury, 31 Oct. 1889, FO 403/120; Capt. Rabenhorst, "Orientirungsplan," MPK/226(Public Record Office); Fitzgerald, *Travels*, 374; Greffulhe, "Voyage de Lamoo," 216.

[51] The mixed feelings with which the people of Witu regarded their maroon allies are revealed in names they gave to *wakengi* villages: e.g., Mtangamakundu ("throngs of vagabonds"), Katana ("cut one another"), and Balawa (from? *balaa* = "trouble," "calamity").

[52] Greffulhe, "Voyage de Lamoo," 216.

[53] Avatula was the brother of Amudu, Katwa headman of Bur Gavo, and gave as his full name, Avatula b. Bahero Somali. For a brief biographical sketch, Ylvisaker, *Lamu*, 88-9; also Fitzgerald, *Travels*, 465.

trading connection with the coast further north, where the *watoro* acquired guns and found a market for their slave trading.

During Simba's time Witu and the outlying districts grew prosperous from cash cropping and slave-based agriculture. After the 1860s it was common for observers in Witu to remark on the fertility of the area and the variety of crops under cultivation.[54] "The plantations," noted Lamu vice-consul J.G. Haggard after his visit to Witu in 1884, "are extensive and fruitful, the soil being very productive, a particularly large species of cocoanut is grown in them, of a superior kind to any I have seen in Zanzibar, Lamu, and elsewhere."[55] Others noted the excellent rice, which flourished in the surrounding marshes, and the large stands of maize, banana trees, and red peppers. In the Utwani forest clearings to the east and north, conditions were well suited to rice, millet, maize, and especially plantains, which flourished around Katana and the more lately constructed villages of Jongeni and Pumwani.[56] The forest also had an abundance of rubber vines, which were tapped seasonally by large numbers of Boni and *watoro* settlers.[57] Because of virulent tsetse fly in the Utwani forest, cattle were few, and Witu depended on the Somali for meat.[58] In order to maintain their large agricultural establishment, the people of Witu used many slaves to till the fields alongside the women.[59] Witu appears to have had the divisions of class and labor characteristic in other parts of the coast. In the 1860s most *watoro* engaged in agriculture, but by the 1880s they confined their labor to fighting and trading and stood socially on middle ground between slave and freeborn residents.[60]

---

[54] Kersten, *von der Decken*, II, 372, 377.

[55] Haggard to Kirk, 25 Aug. 1884, FO 541/26, 232.

[56] Rogers and Jackson report, 20 Jun. 1891, FO 403/159, 86; Rodd to Rosebery, 11 Aug. 1893, FO 403/183, 226; Mathews to Hardinge, 22 Jun. 1894, FO 403/195, 110; R. Rodd, *Social and Diplomatic Memories* (London: Edward Arnold, 1922), I, 322-9; Fitzgerald, *Travels*, 352f; C. Peters, *New Light on Dark Africa*, H. W. Dulcken, trans.(London: Ward & Lock, 1891), 66,68.

[57] Fitzgerald, *Travels*, 350; Rogers to Pigott, 21 May 1893, FO 403/183, 50; Mathews to Hardinge, 22 Jun. 1894, FO 403/195, 108; Hardinge report, 20 Jul. 1897, C. 8683, 16.

[58] Fitzgerald, *Travels*, 355-6. *Glossina morsitans*, the tse-tse specimen which Fitzgerald describes, is not found on the Kenya coast, but on the East African mainland well to the south. The Kenya coast has three kinds of tse-tse, *glossina pallidipes*, *glossina austeni*, and *glossina brevipalpis*, the latter two of which are relatively few and harmless. The *pallidipes*, which is medium in size, is aggressive and carries sleeping sickness. Today it is found in large numbers in the Witu area. Interview in Mombasa with J. van Etten, Tse-Tse Fly Research Officer, ICIPE Research Center (Nairobi), 1 Jul. 1974. Ylvisaker alleges that cattle-keeping was an important activity in Witu, but this could not have been the case. *Lamu*, 87.

[59] Haggard to Kirk, 25 Aug. 1884, FO 541/26, 232; Berkeley to Euan Smith, 23 Mar. 1891, FO 403/158, 41; Rodd to Rosebery, 5 Aug. 1893, FO 403/103, 222; Mathews to Hardinge, 22 Jun. 1894, FO 403/195, 111.

[60] Greffulhe, "Voyage de Lamoo," 215-6. Ylvisaker, *Lamu* (71 and footnote 59)

For some years after the seaborne slave trade, the slave owners of Witu depended for their supplies on the Lamu traders. The overland trade, which grew up after 1873, passed from the Ozi river through the neighborhood of Kau and Kipini to the mainland opposite Lamu.[61] This region was under the influence of the Lamu Swahili, and it appears that the people of Witu had easy access to the markets at Kimbo and Mkumbi, near Lamu. During the period of the overland route, which lasted until 1878/79, Witu made no attempt to control the access routes to Lamu that passed along the southern fringes of Witu territory.[62] Stability ensued.

As the overland trade stopped, Witu came into conflict with Lamu and the Sultan of Zanzibar. *Watoro* began raiding the Lamu mainland in 1880, stealing slaves and looting villages. The following year, the *watoro* of Katawa (Katana) raided the Lamu slave plantations in force. A retaliatory attack was routed by the maroons. In early 1882, Bargash and Simba agreed to restore law and order, but the *watoro* continued their depredations. Bargash held Simba responsible for the outrages and dispatched troops to Lamu. In 1882 Sud led them against Simba, only to suffer another defeat.[63]

Over the next few years the runaways raided at will for slaves in the Lamu area, crippling its agricultural production. By 1884 the rich grain areas west of Lamu, between Mkumbi and Mpekatoni, lay fallow. The vice-consul at Lamu, J.G. Haggard, toured this district in April and found Mkumbi abandoned with about one-half its people killed or carried away by *watoro* from Katana and other villages. Towns and farms from Mkumbi to Mpekatoni were affected similarly. "The Watoro," lamented Haggard, "at present are ruining this fine country." At Mpekatoni people were afraid to cultivate their farms, and land was reverting to bush. Not only slaves, but Swahili as well, were afraid of being carried off by the *watoro*. "I think more Swahili go away from this district to become slaves themselves," remarked Haggard, "than there are the people of other nations who arrived in this district to become slaves to the Swahili."[64]

Captives were either put to work in the Witu plantations or sold to the Somali. The Somali, who were old customers of the slave traders on the

---

implies that the *watoro* occupied a lowly position beneath the freeborn of Witu by virtue of the fact that the freeborn ate rice and the *watoro* cultivated only millet, but there is no evidence for such a statement and much evidence to the contrary.

[61] Holmwood to Prideaux, 17 Nov. 1874, C. 1588, 7. For a discussion of the slave trade prior to 1873, Ylvisaker, *Lamu*, 116-9.

[62] Such a theory explains why Holmwood makes no mention of Witu in his detailed 1874 report, which he based on extensive interviews and first-hand observation along the coast. C. 1588, 6-8. It contradicts Glassman's assertion that Witu exported its goods through Lamu in collaboration with Hadrami merchants and to the consternation of Lamu's *waungwana* (older established families). "Witu Sultanate," 71-2.

[63] Miles to Granville, 17 Nov. 1881, C. 3160, 663; Akinola, "Slavery and Slave Revolts," 226; Stigand, *Land of Zinj*, 97-98. Ylvisaker misdates these episodes to the "mid-1870s." *Lamu*, 92.

[64] Haggard to Kirk, 9 Apr. 1884, FO 541/26, 180-1.

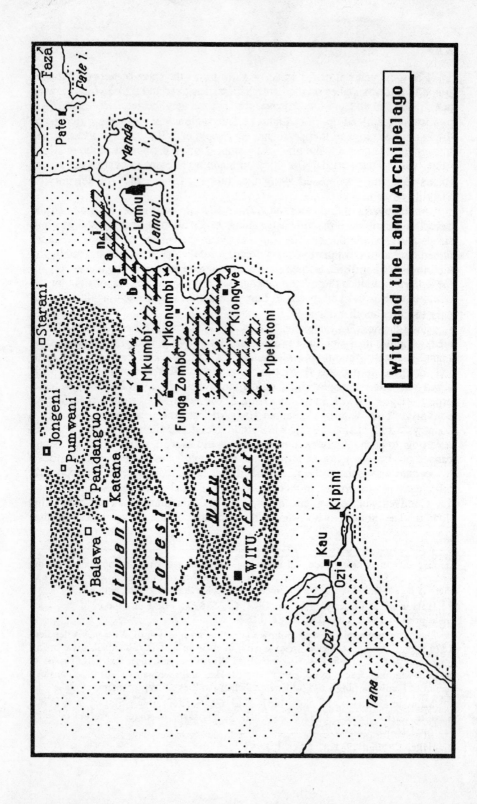

Witu and the Lamu Archipelago

northern coast and felt the pinch after the sea and overland trades closed down, obtained slaves with their new suppliers in Katana in exchange for cattle and gun-powder.[65] Repeating what was a normal cycle in so many other parts of East Africa where the slave trade had flourished, the *watoro* used the powder to raid for more slaves. To Witu's overall benefit, captured slaves revived its agricultural establishment, which had suffered from labor shortages since the late 1870s; the slave-for-powder trade also improved Witu's military position vis-a-vis the coast. Furthermore the troublesome Somali were neutralized.

Had he been able, Simba would nevertheless have prevented the *watoro* raids. In Zanzibar the sultan and the British held Simba responsible for the turmoil in Lamu, even though the raids and the slave trade were carried on from the Utwani forest settlements and beyond the limits of Simba's effective control. The raids also ran counter to Simba's coastal policy. From 1866 to 1880 Simba tried to avoid conflict with Lamu, where he had much popular support, by acquiescing to the authority of Zanzibar.[66] It is improbable that Simba would allow raids that weakened his support in Lamu and brought him into conflict with Zanzibar. The explanation given by the people of Lamu was that the *watoro* raided on their own and that Simba opposed them.[67]

As long as the raids continued, however, the likelihood of war increased, in which case Simba would need the support of the *watoro*. Unable to alienate the *watoro* element, the determining factor in Witu-coast relations, Simba stood by when militant Nabahani encouraged their raids and very likely supplied them with arms. Fumo Bakari, Simba's heir-apparent and regarded by observers as a "firebrand" and a "fanatic," was probably the foremost among the Nabahani supporters of the *watoro*.[68] It is evident from events following Simba's death in early 1889 that Fumo Bakari favored an assertive Nabahani sultanate, in contrast to his father-in-law's isolationist policies. His brief reign of two years was notable for his soldiers' raids on neighbors and open conflicts with Zanzibar and Britain. Mindful of the rising importance of the *watoro* in Witu affairs, Fumo Bakari most likely identified himself with the militant elements who were using

---

[65] Ibid, 180. The Somali obtained their powder overland from Ras Hafun, where it arrived by sea from Mukalla in the Yemen. Kirk to Granville, 23 Sep.1884, C. 4523, 66.

[66] Simba had paid allegiance to the sultan of Zanzibar from the time of his settlement on the mainland. Miles to Granville, 17 Nov. 1882, C. 3160, 257; sultan Ahmed to sultan of Zanzibar, n.d.[1885] in Kitchener to Rosebery, 30 Jun. 1886, FO 403/98, 53.

[67] Haggard to Kirk, 9 Apr. 1884, FO 541/226, 181. In 1881, when asked to disperse the runaways, Simba replied that "he was powerless to act." Miles to Granville, 17 Nov. 1882, C. 3160, 257.

[68] This also according to the opinion of the people of Lamu. Haggard to Kirk, 9 Apr. and 25 Aug. 1884, FO 541/226, 181, 231, resp. Haggard discounted "the common gossip" and decided that Simba was behind the raids after Simba's advisor treated Haggard rudely and pressured him to supply Witu with guns. Simba once had asked a British agent for guns, in order to put a stop to the excesses of the *watoro*. Miles to Granville, 17 Nov. 1881, C. 3160, 257.

the *watoro* to increase their influence. He would depend on their support to succeed to the sultanate.

Toward the end of 1884 a period of calm afforded Simba the chance to make a truce with the new *liwali* in Lamu, Said b. Hamed. In August it became apparent that the *watoro* were losing their supply of weapons and gunpowder. The powder trade with the Somali gradually ended after the British stopped the export of powder from Mukalla to the Somali coast. Witu's local source of guns at Makelli also disappeared.[69] With *watoro* activities diminished and the militant element losing support, Simba sought peace with Lamu. His chance came in October with the removal of Sud b. Hamed and the installation of Simba's tractable relative, Said b. Hamed. Simba quickly made a truce with Said and in the following months repledged his allegiance to Zanzibar.[70] Containing the militants in his camp remained a problem for the Witu sultan. His internal troubles were briefly resolved by a surge in slave trading in his district, which became an important transit point in the conveyance of slaves overland from the famine areas in the south to the Bajuni coast.[71] The famine trade, though brief, enabled the slave holders of Witu to compensate for their loss of supplies caused by the cessation of raiding and to enter into friendly relations with the Bajuni and their leader, Mzee Seif, the Nabahani's old enemy.[72] To Simba's added benefit, his people's involvement in the trade placed no strains on relations with Said. The *liwali* rigorously enforced anti-slave trade measures in the immediate vicinity of Lamu, where he was under scrutiny of the British vice consul, but he dispatched none of his forces to police Witu.[73] Said's actions reveal again the reluctance of the Lamu governors to take action against Witu without direct orders from Zanzibar. Said, like Sud before him, was restrained by his personal ties to prominent Lamu families and to the Nabahani of Witu, and wished to keep the peace by avoiding conflict with Simba and his followers.

On the other hand, events of the previous four years had convinced Bargash that Simba must be forced to submit openly to his authority. After the October

---

[69] Haggard to Kirk, 25 Aug. 1884, FO 541/226, 232; Kirk to Granville, 23 Sep. 1884, C. 4523, 66.

[70] Haggard to Kirk, 26 Dec. 1884, FO 84/1679; Simba to Bargash, n.d., and Simba to Said b. Hamid, n.d., in Kirk to Granville, 23 Jun. 1885, FO 403/94, 32E-F; Simba to Bargash, n.d.[1885] in Kitchener to Rosebery, 30 Jun. 1886, FO 403/98, 53.

[71] Haggard to Kirk, 26 Dec. 1884, FO 84/1679.

[72] Probably instrumental in the Witu-Bajuni connection was Avatula, then based in Starani in the Utwani forest. In 1889 it was revealed that for a number of years Mzee Seif had paid annual tribute to Avatula, a practice that likely originated in the slave trade days. Simons to Portal, 5 Oct. 1889, in Portal to Salisbury, 28 Oct. 1889, FO 403/120, 165. There can be no doubt that the 1884 traffic was sizeable. The extensive Bajuni plantations were cultivated almost entirely by slaves imported from the Mombasa hinterland, an area untapped by the slave trade until 1884. Fitzgerald, *Travels*, 586. The Bajuni passed along numbers of these slaves to the Somali of the Juba region.

[73] Haggard to Kirk, 8 Sep. 1884, in Kirk to Granville, C. 4523, 67-8; Haggard to Kirk, 26 Dec. 1884, FO 84/1679.

truce Bargash welcomed Simba's testimonies of allegiance and offered to recognize him as *liwali* of Witu, asking that Simba fly the Zanzibar flag and allow Bargash to station a token force there. Bargash did not press the last request, which Simba politely refused, but insisted that the flag be hoisted. Fearful of alienating his followers, Simba demurred. In January and February 1885 he implored Bargash to trust in his personal allegiance and asked for more time to comply.[74] Said b. Hamed, sensitive to Simba's predicament, urged Bargash's patience. Between March and May Bargash took no action. It proved to be a costly mistake. In late May it became known in Zanzibar that Simba had placed Witu under the protection of Germany. Bargash hastily dispatched heavy guns and seven hundred troops to Lamu, but the time to force Witu into submission had passed. Before the troops arrived in Lamu, Bismarck intervened by alerting German gunboats in East African waters and by informing the British foreign minister of Germany's readiness to defend Witu.[75] In the face of Germany's firm support of Simba, Bargash recalled his troops.

Prior to German intervention, Simba had been willing to place Witu under Zanzibari rule, but this old, disabled, and weary man was not about to control the turbulent elements in Witu. In 1885 Simba was nearing seventy, showing his years, and suffering from elephantiasis.[76] He had long ceased to be "the lion" in vigor and fighting spirit. Moreover Zanzibar's success in controlling the northern coast had discouraged Simba from reclaiming Pate for the Nabahani and from opposing the encroachments of Zanzibar rule in Witu itself. These factors irritated the militants, who included the Nabahani wanting to challenge Zanzibar on the northern coast, the people disobeying the sultan of Zanzibar's anti-slave trade measures, and the *watoro* and fugitives from justice fearing the loss of their freedom and an end to their military control of the mainland. It is clear, from his January and February letters to Said and Bargash, that Simba lacked Witu support on the question of allegiance to Zanzibar and that he delayed his submission in order to stifle internal conflicts and perhaps avert his own overthrow. At the same time Simba knew he could not put off Bargash indefinitely without risking a full-scale invasion, which likewise could have disastrous consequences. In late February 1885, therefore, when the brothers Clemens and Gustave Denhardt of the Tana Committee of the German Colonial Society appeared on the scene, Simba signed their treaty in exchange for German protection and gained what was probably the only means available to withstand the internal and external forces that threatened his position.[77]

---

[74] Simba to Said b. Hamed, 16 Jan. 1885, and Simba to Bargash, 29 Feb. 1885, in Kirk to Granville, 23 Jun. 1885, FO 403/94, 32E-F; Kitchener to Rosebery, 30 Jun. 1886, encls. 1,7, FO 403/98, 44,53.

[75] Bismarck to Munster, 2 Jun. 1885, as relayed in Munster to Granville, 6 Jun. 1885, FO 403/93, 65-6; Stigand, *Land of Zinj*, 98; Coupland, *Exploitation of East Africa*, 336.

[76] Haggard to Kirk, 25 Aug. 1884, FO 541/26, 229; Churchill to Euan Smith, 10 Aug. 1888, in Euan Smith to Salisbury, 21 Aug. 1888, FO 403/106, 146B.

[77] Ylvisaker claims that Simba's objectives to "attain economic and political inde-

The unwillingness of Simba to accept Zanzibari overrule stemmed not from a desire to preserve Witu's independence at all costs, but from a failure to curb the influence of the *watoro*. From the beginning Simba recognized the dangers of alienating the sultan of Zanzibar and tried to avoid troubles in the sultan's coastal dominions. Unfortunately the survival of Witu depended on defense against the Somali, whose intermittent raids were a danger throughout the period. The Somali threat was a strong inducement to allow maroon settlements to take root in the north of Witu territory, where they became a vital deterrent against Somali attacks. In the end, the decision to give asylum to runaway slaves was Witu's own undoing. *Watoro* raiding and destruction around Lamu embroiled Witu in repeated difficulties with the dominant powers, and, equally injurious, the *watoro* played an increasingly powerful and divisive role in the internal politics of Witu by supporting Nabahani who opposed any accommodation with Zanzibar and the British. This became apparent when the British displaced the Germans in 1888.[78]

3. *Gasi*

When the overland slave trade from the south gradually ended after 1876, slave trading in the Kenya coastal hinterland began. In the ensuing decade, coastal Muslims enslaved and exported thousands. Along the southern coast, the Mazrui of Gasi, under Mbaruk b. Rashid, were the most active in the trade. The stoppage of slave imports had challenged their long-standing position as slave suppliers to Pemba island and to mainland customers further north. Mbaruk also dreamed of restoring Mazrui rule to the coast. By stopping the southern trade, the Busaidi and British aroused Mbaruk's political ire as well as hurt his income. Mbaruk, impatient and aggressive, attempted to make up losses by raiding the nearby Shimba hills and challenged Busaidi authority by attacking loyalist settlements up and down the coast.

Slave raiding dispersed settled populations and ignited a scramble for security. Refugees from the Shimba hills and the surrounding areas fled Mbaruk's men and moved into the Mombasa hinterland. Not all were welcome. Nor was the Mombasa hinterland safe. At the time it suffered from intermittent Kwavi raids. Miji Kenda, taking refuge inside stockaded villages, neglected cultivation. Drought, disease, and a major famine followed. In 1884-5, Miji Kenda sold hundreds of children and dependents, whom they could not feed, to the Swahili around Mombasa and the Mazrui of Takaungu. They were put on dhows and marketed along the northern coast and beyond. Only some Giriama escaped hardship by moving into the fertile and watered hills parallel to the Takaungu and Malindi coast.

The Busaidi of the coast, strong and wealthy, were disinclined to waste time

---

pendence" were "enhanced" by the "intrusion of Europeans"(*Lamu*, 122). She also alleges that Simba accepted German protection because of a personal slight he received from the British vice-consul, Haggard, and an unspecified fear of an attack on Witu from Zanzibar (127).

[78] See ch. 6.

and resources destroying their opponents. The new rulers were developers, protective of their plantations and their slaves, kind to their local allies, and tolerant of other beliefs and persons of status. They were indifferent, however, to old Swahili families losing wealth and influence as well as to the desperate non-Muslims in the hinterland.

Groups disadvantaged by Busaidi rule, Muslim and non-Muslim alike, looked to Mbaruk of Gasi as their standard-bearer. Finding supporters from among the Miji Kenda and Swahili clan heads, Mbaruk had allies as far north as Lamu. Muslim town dwellers prevented a coast-wide revolt, however, by withholding their support. Town dwellers disliked the rebels' penchant for destruction. They preferred tolerant and peaceful Busaidi administration which, though it promoted the Sultan's economic interests, did not undermine their own. Mbaruk's followers were regarded as predators. Mbaruk acted without vision, apart from wanting to assert himself as a political leader, and his raids hurt legitimate trade, disrupted commerce between the coast and the hinterland, and threatened slave plantations.

Mbaruk employed runaway slaves, and his capital was defended by armed *watoro*. Many of Mbaruk's slave raiders had recently been slaves themselves. Armed *watoro* were anything but servile to their Muslim overlord, often acting as an independent, violent force. On their own initiative they raided for slaves, plundered wide areas, and traded slaves for guns and powder. After 1876 they played a role in every rebellion against Busaidi (and later British) rule. Their notoriety as the source of much suffering, economic disorder, and population movement, was widespread.

Mbaruk recruited among his own slaves, but most of his troops were comprised of runaway slaves who regularly sought asylum in his district. Long before Gasi became the headquarters of Mbaruk's rebellious activities, runaways received refuge and encouragement from the Mazrui living there. The colony of Mwazangombe in Digo country may have owed its origin to assistance received from Mbaruk's predecessor, Abdullah b. Hamis, and other Gasi Mazrui.[79] Mbaruk used runaways in his early fighting force, and during the years of his active rebellion they came to him directly from the coast or from runaway slave colonies near Mombasa and Takaungu.[80] Mbaruk also recruited runaways settled in Mwazangombe, and some of Mwazangombe's settlers accepted Mbaruk's authority when he used his interior retreat at Mwele. Others Mbaruk simply

[79] Krapf to Secy, 22 Oct. 1845, CA5/M1, 701, CMS; Guillain, *Documents*, III, 264; Burton, *Zanzibar*, II, 105-06; see also ch. 1.

[80] Price journal, 23 Oct. and 5 Nov. 1875, CA5/O23; Price to Miles, 7 Mar. 1882, G3A5/O1 (1882), CMS; Kirk to Allen, 26 Jan. 1883, MSS.Brit.Emp., s.18, G7, RH; Kirk to Granville, 9 Nov. 1883, C. 3849, 128; Handford to Lang, journal extracts, 25 Feb. 1884, G3A5/O1(1884), CMS; F.D. Lugard, *Rise of Our East African Empire: Early Efforts in Nyassaland and Uganda* 2 vols.(Edinburgh: William Blackwood, 1893), II, 223; Lyne, *Apostle of Empire*, 133; Binns to Hardinge, 7 Dec. 1898, C. 9502, 18; Cashmore, "Sheikh Mbaruk bin Rashid," 119.

coerced into joining his troops.[81] As escaped and hunted men, runaways had the qualities Mbaruk required. Without family or residential ties, they were suited for the risks of warfare and hardships of life on the move. Serving Mbaruk had its prospects. There was promise of adventure, means of upkeep, and the chance to become an *akida*, an officer with some wealth.

Seldom numbering more than one or two hundred, Mbaruk's soldiers were superior to any group armed with bows and arrows that dared to oppose them, and they moved at will in the countryside. Small parties commanded by Mbaruk's relatives or by an *akida* conducted raids. When attacking a town, Mbaruk used his soldiers as a core to lead more numerous irregular forces comprised of temporary allies and coerced Miji Kenda. Mbaruk supplied his soldiers with guns, ammunition, clothing, and, in good times, food and pay. For the most part, and especially during the long months of retreat and hiding from the sultan's forces, they lived off the land.

Europeans thought Mbaruk's men a hardened, boisterous, and undisciplined mob. The earliest description comes from Price, who traveled through the Shimba hills in 1882 in order to establish a mission site. Price, struck by the depopulating effects of Mbaruk's raids in the area, came face to face with one of the parties responsible. "They are well-built, hardy, desperate looking fellows," he wrote in his journal, "armed with good rifles and plenty of ammunition."[82] Eight years later, Price once again met Mbaruk's "dusky warriors," together with their leader, in Frere Town. Mbaruk's private rebellion was then in temporary abeyance. Mbaruk "was preceded by a hundred or more of his roughs--all armed with guns and swords--who came along shouting, blowing war horns, and firing, with all their might, as if they were going to attack us."[83] Mbaruk's "wild retainers" did no harm--several years had to pass before they had any grievance against the mission--but Price attributed their restraint to Mbaruk's presence. The Mazrui sheikh was known to shoot disobedient soldiers on the spot.[84]

Mbaruk was himself a calloused leader, who possessed great energy and ambition. As head of the Mazrui of Gasi from 1865 to 1896, he spent his entire reign in the vain attempt to subordinate the Mazrui of Takaungu and restore Mazrui hegemony on the southern Kenya coast.[85] Takaungu was the town of

---

[81] Price journal, 19 Dec. 1874, 7/8 Jan. 1875, CA5/023, CMS; see story of Mbega wa Mauya in Thompson tour diary, 30 Jul. 1917, CP 19/82, KNA.

[82] Price, notes, 1 May 1882, G3A5/01(1882), CMS.

[83] W.S. Price, *My Third Campaign in East Africa. A Story of Missionary Life in Troublous Times* (London: William Hunt, 1890), 230.

[84] Letter of Robson, 3 Dec. 1888, *Anti-Slavery Reporter*, 9, 1(Jan./Feb. 1889), 30-1. Mbaruk's men attacked Rabai in November 1895 during their war with the British (see ch. 7).

[85] Mbaruk was one of the younger sons of the last Mazrui governor of Mombasa, Rashid b. Salim, and spent most of his childhood in Gasi with members of the Uthmani (also rendered Athmani) branch of the Mazrui family who lived there after being driven out of Mombasa by Seyyid b. Sultan of Zanzibar in 1837. Mbaruk was then a lad of seven. For two brief biographies, Cashmore, "Sheikh Mbaruk bin Rashid bin

the Mazrui of the Zaheri (also rendered Zahoor) branch, who had gone into in exile as had the Uthmani after 1837. Hamis, as eldest son of Rashid b. Salim, led the Zaheri and was succeeded by Hamis's son, Rashid, in ca. 1850.[86]

The Zaheri-Uthmani feud, which began long before 1837, remained alive thereafter because the sultan of Zanzibar wished to keep the two branches apart. After Hamis b. Rashid died, it became clear that the Gasi branch was the stronger of the two when Mbaruk though himself not yet head of the Uthmani marched to Takaungu with his Uthmani relations, claimed the right to succession on the strength of his mother's Zaheri descent, and ousted Rashid. The sultan's troops in Mombasa then intervened, drove Mbaruk back to Gasi, and reinstated Rashid.[87] In 1865 Mbaruk succeeded Abdullah b. Khamis as head of the Uthmani and returned to Takaungu once more to assert his claim to rule the Zaheri. Mbaruk and his followers were repulsed, but in 1870 they returned in strength and defeated the Takaungu forces. Rashid sued for peace. Again the Busaidi intervened. Troops sent by Mombasa *liwali*, Ali b. Nasur, drove out Mbaruk's forces and imprisoned a number of his men.[88] The sultan was ready to protect Takaungu, an important grain-exporting center, but he feared alienating the Mazrui by treating Mbaruk harshly. The latter was left alone in Gasi and provided a regular subsidy.

In 1872 Mbaruk attacked Vanga on the southern coast and Likoni, on the southern mainland opposite Mombasa island. For the next sixteen years, he remained almost constantly at loggerheads with the sultan's governors and forces on the coast. After the attacks, Mbaruk was tracked down by the Sultan's forces at his forest stronghold at Mwele in the Shimba hills and forced to surrender. The sultan once more left him alone, before here assembled his followers and in 1873 attempted another rebellion.[89] In 1877 he raided around Mombasa, but the sultan's troops easily drove him out and forced him make a long retreat to the north.[90] Mbaruk once again recovered, and in 1882 his troops sacked Vanga for

---

Salim el Mazrui," 111-37; S. Chiraghdin, "Maisha ya Sheikh Mbaruk bin Rashid Al-Mazrui," *Journal of the East African Swahili Committee*, NS 1,2(Sep. 1960), 150-79. The final years of Mazrui rule in Mombasa are summarized in Coupland, *East Africa and its Invaders*, ch. 9, and Gray, *The British in Mombasa*, ch. 11, both entitled "The Fate of the Mazrui." Mbaruk's father, Rashid b. Salim, was put in chains and shipped to the dungeons of Bunder Abas, where he reportedly died of starvation.

[86] For genealogies and moiety chief lists, A. Hardinge memorandum, 26 Aug. 1895, C. 8274, 34-5.

[87] Cashmore, "Sheikh Mbaruk bin Rashid," 114; Hardinge memorandum, C. 8274, 31.

[88] Sparshott to Secy, 12 Jan. 1871, quoting from an undated letter of J. Rebmann, CA5/026, CMS; remarks of J. Rebmann to Pelly, in Frere to Granville, 5 Apr. 1872, C. 820, 86. To Mbaruk's great anger his men, who had been taken captive by the Zaheri before Nasur's troops arrived, were turned over to Nasur by Rashid b. Khamis.

[89] Cashmore, "Sheik Mbaruk bin Rashid," 115; M.A. Hinawy, *Al-Akida and Fort Jesus, Mombasa* (Nairobi: East African Literature Bureau, 1970), 29-35; Sparshott to Secy., 12 Dec. 1873, CA5/026, CMS.

[90] Greffulhe, "Voyage de Lamoo," 337-8.

the second time and raided once more around Mombasa and Malindi.[91] Sultan
Bargash then sent a large armed force to flush out Mbaruk and his followers an
to destroy Gasi and Mwele.[92] Mbaruk nearly lost his life at Mwele, and his
men were killed or scattered, but within three months his forces regrouped near
Rabai and went on a rampage in the mainland towns around Mombasa, where his
forces burned and looted farms and killed numbers of agricultural slaves.[93] In
July Mbaruk retreated when the sultan's troops took control of the area, and after
spending several months hiding in the bush he came to peaceful terms with
Bargash and was allowed once more to return to Gasi.[94] Ever restless, Mbaruk
then asked protection from the German government (a move made recently by
the Nabahani of Witu), before launching two more failed rebellions.[95]

Mbaruk's recalcitrance was fed by humiliation. Repeatedly the sultan had
rounded him up, administered light punishment, and set him free. Mbaruk aspired to unite the Mazrui, to avenge their ouster as governors of Mombasa, and
to raise the coast in revolt against the Busaidi. The sultan treated him instead as
a troublesome dependent. His repeated rebellions invited the sultan to imprison
or execute him, but the sultan sent him back to Gasi and kept him on an
allowance. Mbaruk's forays into the coastal towns and their environs dislodged
the sultan's authority for a mere day or two and gained Mbaruk the allegiance of
only a few.

Mbaruk was needed because he could supply slaves to Pemba, which became
an important clove producer after hurricanes decimated Zanzibar's plantations in
1872. The Mazrui of Gasi had old political ties with the Pemba aristocracy, and
the northern tip of the island lay only thirty miles from Gasi across the Pemba
channel. By 1874 caravans from the *mrima* coast opposite Zanzibar proceeding
north to Lamu shunted annually at Gasi an estimated three thousand slaves for
thousand slaves for export to Pemba.[96] As the southern route dried up, Mbaruk
and his *watoro* became the new suppliers of an "extensive Slave Trade with
Pemba," as Hardinge termed it, by raiding the Digo, Duruma, and
Kamba.[97] By 1878 they had depopulated the Shimba hills, and for another five
years Mbaruk's forces kept the southern coastal hinterland in turmoil.

---

[91] Miles to Granville, 10 Feb. 1882, FO 84/1620; Cracknall to Miles in Miles to
Granville, 6 Apr. 1882, C. 3547, 117; Binns to Miles, 6 Jul. 1882 in Miles to
Granville, 22 Jul. 1882, ibid., 134.

[92] Miles to Granville, 3 May 1882, FO 84/1621; Lyne, *Apostle of Empire*, 132.

[93] Miles to Granville, 4 Aug. and 28 Sep. 1882, FO 84/1622; Wakefield, *Thomas
Wakefield*, 172-80; Cashmore, "Sheikh Mbaruk bin Rashid," 117-8.

[94] Miles to Granville, 17 Nov. 1882, FO 84/1622; Kirk to Salisbury, 12 Feb. 1886,
FO 403/96, 114.

[95] Kirk to Salisbury, 12 Feb. 1886, ibid., 114; Handford to Lang, n.d., journal
extracts, 2 and 4 Mar. 1884; Handford to Lang, 17 May 1884, and Handford diary, 16
Sep. 1884, G3A5/01(1884), CMS; Taylor to Lang [Jul. 1886?], G3A5/03, CMS.

[96] Holmwood report in Holmwood to Prideaux, 17 Nov. 1874, C. 1588, 6-7; Lyne,
Apostle of Empire, 52-5; Sheriff, *Slaves, Spices and Ivory*, 54, 226.

[97] Hardinge to Salisbury, 12 Apr. 1896, FO 403/226, 174.

The country from Tanga to Mozungu, Virungani, Ada, Gora, Samburu,Mwa-njewa, are in a state of agitation....Civil war...[has] driven [the] inhabitants far and wide; while Mbaruku [Mbaruk] who represents the once powerful Mazurui [Mazrui] dynasty of Mombasa is also endeavouring by every mode in his power to give the finishing stroke by extracting large sums of money, cattle, goats, slaves, from the weak Wadigo, Waduruma, Wakamba and other tribes.[98]

Mbaruk did not molest the route from Chagga through the Shimba hills established by the Swahili.[99] Ada and Daluni were important links for slave caravans traveling to Vanga, and one of the main slave routes supplying Mombasa passed through the Shimba hills.[100]

In late 1878 peoples living on the fringes of the raiding zone began jostling for space. The Kamba were caught between the Duruma, who were being pushed north by Mbaruk's men, and the Rabai, who were entrenched in the hills west of Mombasa. The Kamba fought in turn against the Duruma, the Mazrui, the Jomvu, and the Rabai.[101] The Digo crowded into the Mombasa area, clashing with the Swahili of Mtongwe.[102] These struggles, at least between the Duruma and Kamba, produced captives for the slave trade.[103]

Upheavals in the hinterland also attracted the Sultan's troops. Ali b. Nasur,

---

[98] Jones, "Journey to Duruma," 7 Aug. 1878, CA5/014, CMS; See also Euan Smith to Salisbury, 26 Jul. 1888, FO 541/28, 300; Hardinge to Salisbury, 12 Apr. 1896, FO 403/226, 174.

[99] Smith to Kirk, 18 Jun. 1885, C.476, 646; Handford to Lang, 15 Apr. 1885, G3 A5/02, CMS; Gissing to Kirk, 26 Jun. 1884, FO 541/26, 216; E.C. Dawson, *James Hannington, First Bishop of Eastern Equatorial Africa: a History of His Life and Work, 1847-1885*, 2nd ed.(New York: Negro Universities Press, 1969), 334; Jackson, *Early Days in East Africa*, 147. By 1882 the Teita hills were a trading center in their own right. J.A. Wray, *Kenya, Our Newest Colony: Reminiscences* (London: Marshall Brothers, n.d.), 40; Binns to Wright, 29 Sep. 1879, CA5/03, CMS; Handford to Lang, 4 May 1884, G3A5/01(1884); Handford to Lang, 17 Dec. 1884, Hannington to CMS, 9 Mar. 1885, and Taylor to Lang, 17 Mar. 1885, G3A5/02, CMS; Morris to Lang, 11 Jan. 1888, FO 541/28.

[100] Price journal, 19 May 1882, G3A5/01(1882); Parker to Lang, 8 Jul. 1887, G3A5/04, CMS.

[101] The Rabai (properly ARavai) refers to the Miji Kenda group after whom the CMS named its mission station and who lived nearby. Wakefield to UMFC, 31 Jan. 1876, UMFC *Magazine*, (April 1876), 251; Jones "Journey to Duruma," 7 Aug. 1878, CA5/014, CMS; Binns diary, 9, 10, and 20 Dec. 1878, 11 Aug. 1879, 6 and 16 Oct. 1880, KNA; David to Wright, 28 Feb. 1879, CA5/06, CMS.

[102] Streeter to Wright, 14 Jun. 1879, CA5/027, CMS. Mtongwe is a district on the mainland southwest of Mombasa island. Fighting between the Digo and the Mtongwe Swahili followed fighting between the Digo and Mbaruk's forces in the South. Streeter to Wright, 30 Jan. 1879, CA5/M6, 23; David to Wright, 28 Feb. 1879, CA5/06, CMS.

[103] Mugomba to Wakefield, 10 Apr. [1879], *Welcome Words*, 14(1880), 4. Mugomba, Methodist evangelist at Mawsonville, in Duruma, alleged that 460 Duruma were sold into slavery by the Governor of Mombasa.

liwali in Mombasa (1875-1880) and Ali's successor, Muhammad b. Suleiman (1881-1884), wished to prevent Mbaruk from either creating alliances in the interior or establishing bases from which he could attack coastal towns. At one point, Suleiman was certain that CMS mission residents and Fuladoyans were in league with Mbaruk. The *liwali* thus obstructed a planned CMS mission in the Shimba hills and sent troops to punish the Digo for inviting the missionaries.[104] The governor was plotting an end to the CMS-Fuladoyo connection, but he also possibly feared that the presence of the CMS in the Shimba hills would result in the exposure of slave routes; missionaries had been aware of the traffic to the coast since late 1879.[105] He may also have wanted to prevent Mbaruk from obtaining mission firearms and Miji Kenda adherents. Whatever the reason, the struggle continued and at heavy cost to the weak and innocent.

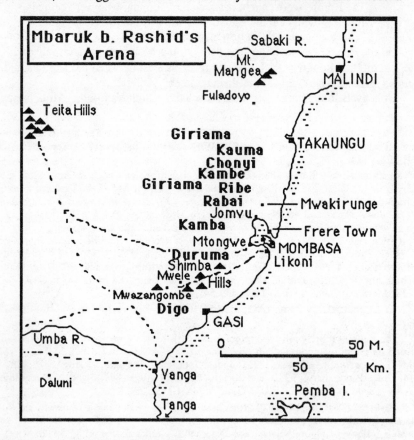

---

[104] Miles to FO, 31 May 1882 and Price to Miles, 20 May 1882, FO 84/1621; Price report, n.d. [June 1882], G3A5/01(1882), CMS.
[105] Price journal, 20 May 1882, G3A5/01(1882) and Binns to Wright, 29 Sep. 1879, CA5/03, CMS. See also section 3, "Fuladoyo," in ch. 4 .

In July 1882, Mbaruk's forces camped near the Rabai mission and coerced some Miji Kenda to support him, while entreating William Jones, then in charge of the station, to join him in attacking the coast. Jones prevaricated in order to keep mission settlers out of the plot, while Mbaruk raised about three hundred supporters from the nearby Rabai, nearby Ribe, Duruma, and Kambe. Prior to the raid, word had reached the *liwali* of Mombasa. He sent troops which quickly erected a stockade at Jomvu and built a makeshift fort near the Rabai mission, at present "Bomani." Mbaruk and his men thereupon deserted, leaving the Rabai to face the governor's troops alone. Jones appears to have then issued his Christian settlers with the mission's Snider rifles in support of the Rabai, who were nevertheless routed. The soldiers plundered the fields of the Rabai and their Ribe neighbors, destroying coconut palms and taking elders as prisoners to Mombasa. They captured many others, who were later sold into slavery. Meanwhile, Mbaruk's men skirted the *liwali's* troops and invaded plantations in the suburbs of Mombasa, burning crops and attacking the defenseless. At Mwakirunge they killed nearly all the agricultural slaves.[106] Two months later Mbaruk surrendered to Lloyd Mathews, the sultan's military advisor, and was allowed to return to Gasi without fine or punishment. The Rabai elders, who had been held in jail since August, were released in December and told if found associating with the mission, they would be returned to prison.[107]

During 1883 and 1884, the hinterland once again became a hunting ground. Takaungu's August 1883 attack on Fuladoyo sparked a war between maroons and coastal Muslims that pulled in the Giriama and engulfed the hinterland until the following May. Mbaruk used the occasion to mount yet another rebellion with the support of an estimated 250 Fuladoyans. In the face of an attack from the *liwali's* troops, he burned Gasi, established a camp at Mwaiba in the hills near Fuladoyo, and lured more maroons into his force. From there Mbaruk moved south to Tanga, where he beat off an attack from Mombasa (his first victory against the *liwali*). In retaliation, the rebels raided in the Mombasa hinterland and attacked a Swahili encampment near Rabai. Once more, the *liwali* locked up the Rabai elders as accomplices.[108] As soon as Mbaruk had emerged to threaten

---

[106] Binns to Lang, 7 Jul. and 10 Aug. 1882, Lane to Committee, 4 Jul. 1882, and Shaw to Lang, 28 Sep. 1882, G3A5/01(1882); Shaw to Lang, 23 Jan. 1883, G3A5/01(1883), CMS; Binns diaries, cv. 9 Jul. 1882, KNA; Cracknall to Miles, 4 Aug. 1882, Miles to Granville, 4 Aug. and 28 Sep. 1882, FO 84/1622; During to ?, 4 Aug. 1882, UMFC *Magazine* (January 1883), 55-6; Gissing to Kirk, 14 Sep. 1884, FO 541/26, 245; Mwangoma memoir, n.d., CP 67/15, KNA; Wakefield, *Thomas Wakefield*, 172-80; Cashmore, "Sheikh Mbaruk bin Rashid," 117-8; Salim, *Swahili-speaking Peoples*, 52.

[107] Miles to Granville, 17 Nov. 1882, FO 84/1623; Shaw to Lang, 23 Jan. 1883, G3A5/01 (1883), CMS; Kirk to Granville, 3 Jul. 1885, FO 403/94, 40.

[108] Kirk to Granville, 9 Nov. 1883, C. 3849, 128; Handford journal, 19 Jan., n.d.(quoting 10 Feb. 1884 letter from G. David), 25 Feb., 2 and 4 Mar. 1884, and Handford to Lang, 17 May and 12 Jul. 1884, G3A5./01(1884), CMS.

the governor's authority, he lost his followers. By September hunger caused mass desertions.[109]

In mid-1884 the hinterland was suffering from its worst famine of the century. Months of widespread insecurity had prevented cultivation, and Kwavi raids during 1883-84 removed large quantities of Giriama, Digo, and Duruma livestock. A severe drought hastened starvation. Famine affected a wide area from the Kenya coast to the Teita Hills and south to central Tanzania. For the Miji Kenda, the "Mwachisenge" famine, as they called it, caused great hardships and drove many to sell their children and relatives on the coast. "Hunger is depicted on every countenance," wrote John Handford from Frere Town. "I could write volumes of distress on every side. The Swahili are making a trade of it, for they are buying slaves for a few handfuls of corn."[110]

For six months following August 1884, Swahili up and down the coast traded actively in Miji Kenda slaves. Miji Kenda were purchased by the thousands, and many were exported.[111] Following the famine, the Mombasa area was the scene of a great increase in kidnapping in order to supply the export market. In 1885 and 1886 observers described this trade as "constant," "flourishing," and "increasing." The trade continued through 1887.[112] Kamba traders at Jimba in Miji Kenda territory leagued with Swahili to dispose of kidnapped Miji Kenda. They also were suspected of raiding parts of Miji Kenda.[113] Some Mazrui also took part in the famine trade and later turned to kidnapping. Salim b. Khamis of Takaungu put hundreds of destitute Miji Kenda to work as slaves in his plantations and exported others for resale on the Bajuni coast.[114] CMS missionary W.E. Taylor, who in 1887 made an extensive tour of Giriama country west of Takaungu, concluded that kidnapping, in addition to slaving during the 1884 famine, had contributed to severe depopulation. Many Giriama complained to Taylor about the loss of their relatives to Salim's men.[115]

Coastal rulers ignored the plight of those affected by the slave trade. Busaidi officials were there to suppress revolts, especially Mbaruk's, and punish

---

[109] Handford diary, cv. 16 and 18 Sep. 1884, G3A5/01(1884), CMS.

[110] Handford to Lang, 26 Nov. 1884, ibid. This file contains many other references to the famine.

[111] Among numerous references to the trade, see Haggard to Kirk, 8 Sep. 1884, and Kirk to Granville, 23 Sep. and 24 Oct. 1884, in C. 4523, 65, 67, 72, respectively; Kirk to Granville, 14 Mar. 1885, C. 4776, 110.

[112] Kirk to Granville, 14 Feb. 1885; Smith to Kirk, 18 May 1885, C. 4776, 628, 644, respectively; Taylor to Lang, 9 Jun. 1885, G3A5/02, England to Lang, 27 May 1886, G3A5/03, and Shaw to Lang, 4 Jun. 1887, G3A5/04, CMS.

[113] Handford to Lang, 21 Jan. 1885 and Handford to Hutchinson, 21 Jan. 1885, Taylor to Lang, 17 Mar. 1885, G3A5/02, CMS.

[114] In late 1884, the slaves on plantations around Mtondia near Takaungu were almost entirely from the coast. Gissing to Kirk, 14 Sep. 1884, FO 541/26, 240. For Takaungu's export of slaves, Haggard to Kirk, 8 Sep. 1884, C. 4523, 457.

[115] Taylor, "Diary of Itineration in Giryama," cv. 13, 17, and 19 Oct., 25 Nov. 1887, G3A5/05, CMS.

suspected co-conspirators. As for slavers, none were rounded up except in Mombasa, where anti-slave trade laws were enforced for the benefit of the British. Salim b. Khalfan, a well-known anglophile, was appointed *liwali* to implement the policy in 1884, when the British opened a vice consulate in Mombasa.[116] Soon he and the vice-consul identified slave dealers in the Mombasa area and prosecuted kidnappers, including high-born Swahili.[117] Salim became popular among local missionaries and other British for hard-line policies that led him, the vice-consul alleged, into "regrettable acts of positive tyranny towards the Arabs."[118] In Takaungu, however, the slave trade operated free of investigation.

In early 1885 Sultan Bargash summoned Salim of Takaungu to Zanzibar and imprisoned him, not for reasons connected with the slave trade then at its peak, but because he was then thought to be supporting his cousin, Mbaruk, in rebellion. British consul-general John Kirk then interceded. He feared Bargash's actions would endanger the "old friendship of the Mazrui for us" and drive Salim closer to Mbaruk, then in contact with the sultan of Witu and the Germans.[119] Kirk, who rated Salim as "the best and most energetic Governor I have seen on the coast," insisted that Bargash have Salim "released and returned with honour to his Governorship." The sultan complied.[120] In order for the sultan to please the British, he ferreted out and punished slave traders in Mombasa, whereas in Takaungu he set them free. Bargash, not unlike the British consul, was preserving power and influence for its own sake while, on the Kenya coast, slaving continued and insecurity prevailed.

4. *Watoro and the Slave Trade*

British officials were less forgiving of slave traders who happened to be *watoro*. As one British officer put it, *watoro* were "simply a horde of free-booters," and their communities, according to another, "nothing but inaccessible nest[s] of murderers, robbers, [and] fanatics...."[121] Their involvement in the

---

[116] As governor of Malindi from 1874 to 1884, he was popular with the British Admiralty, which presented him with a gold watch in appreciation of his assistance to the slave patrol. Gissing to Kirk, 14 Sep. 1884, FO 541/26, 242.

[117] Smith to Kirk, 31 May 1885, C. 4776, 122-3; Taylor to Lang, 9 Jun. 1885, G3 A5/02, CMS; Berg, 'Mombasa under the Busaidi," 294.

[118] Berkeley to Holmwood, 24 Jun. 1887, FO 403/102, 77-8. See also Shaw to Lang, 25 Jun. 1886, G3A5/03, CMS; Price, *Third Campaign*, 25.

[119] Witu had recently signed a treaty with the German Colonial Society that in turn was used by Germany to declare the Witu Protectorate on the Lamu mainland.

[120] Kirk to Granville, 16 Feb. 1885, FO 84/1724, and Kirk to Granville, 3 Jul. 1885, FO 403/94, 41.

[121] Miles to Granville, 17 Nov. 1881, C. 3160, 257; Euan Smith to Salisbury, 3 Oct. 1890, FO 403/139, 99. For similar remarks, Haggard to Kirk, 25 Aug. 1884, FO 541/26, 229; Jackson, *Early Days*, 26; A.H. Hardinge, *A Diplomatist in the East* (London: Jonathan Cape, 1928), 128-9.

slave trade was an irony often emphasized. Kirk regarded maroons in general as a menace to their fellows still in bondage. In his forwarding letter to vice-consul J.G. Haggard's first report on Witu, Kirk remarked that Haggard's account

> shows how hopeless it is to expect anything from such bands. Their history has always been the same on this coast. So far from helping the cause of freedom, they invariably become kidnappers and holders of slaves themselves.[122]

Kirk's remarks are echoed in many other reports of slave dealing carried on by the slave and ex-slave retainers of Mbaruk, Hamis b. Kombo, the Mazrui of Takaungu, and the maroons of the Mombasa-Malindi hinterland. They as well as the *watoro* of Witu and Gosha were liable to Kirk's charge.

Reprehensible behavior in itself, however, is insufficient proof that maroons rejected notions of law and order. To their credit, they established villages that lasted, elected leaders, raised crops, traded, and, at least in the case of Witu, attached themselves to the Nabahani in order to submit their internal disputes for judgment. *Watoro*, no matter how violent, desired social order and recognized the value of established political authority.

Though some surely vented aggression, most *watoro* deployed violence for one rational purpose or another. Nassib Bunda ran a slave trade operation as sinister as any on the East African coast, but his followers and those of his rivals increased, as did the population of Gosha. His methods were vile, but so were the times. He earned Cassanelli's sobriquet as an "African Spartacus," and deserved his salute as an "ardent foe of Somali domination."[123]

The *watoro* of Witu opposed submission to Zanzibar as a matter of life or death. Their Nabahani patrons, on the other hand, had little to lose other than political autonomy, an item of often modest value among coastal states of the nineteenth century. On several occasions, Simba and a number of his Nabahani followers were prepared to barter political independence away for peace. The *watoro* could not let this happen, because once Witu ceased to be a barrier, Zanzibari soldiers and the slave owners of the northern coast would find it easier to destroy their settlements, kill them, or return them to former owners. Before their raids became common, the ability of maroons to survive in their forest settlements already had made them a despised and feared element among the slave-holding subjects of the sultan.[124]

Maroon settlements threatened any society dependent on slaves. No matter how peacefully their settlements were established and administered, maroons were drawn into some form of war with the communities of their ex-masters. Within this context *watoro* raids for slaves along the Juba river, or on the Lamu mainland, or in the Mombasa hinterland, were part the war for survival. Raiding

---

[122] Kirk to Granville, 8 May 1884, FO 541/26, 179.

[123] Cassanelli, *Shaping of Somali Society*, 199; idem, "Former Bantu Slave Communities," 229.

[124] Greffulhe, "Voyage de Lamoo," 216

weakened their opponents while strengthening themselves. Slave owners lost their property, and *watoro* sold captured slaves for arms.

By involving themselves in slave dealing, some runaways were struggling to reduce their already numerous risks and hardships. As W.S. Price of the CMS observed, when reporting on three runaways who, after living off the slave trade in the Malindi area, applied to him for protection at Rabai:

> There are some hundreds of men of this class scattered over the country, who for the sake of protection are almost driven to connect themselves with Mbaruk or some other lawless chieftain who employs them upon plundering expeditions, but who nevertheless wd. be glad, if they had the chance, of maintaining themselves in a more honorable way.[125]

Motives for engaging in the trade and the advantages derived were not uniform throughout the coast, and the involvement of maroons can be viewed in light of the high priority they placed on survival. For the freeborn Muslims of the coast, slaves were a means to wealth, social elevation, influence, and leisure. For runaways, slaves were a means of getting arms and powder, of increasing the size of their fledgling settlements, and of placing more land under cultivation. Muslim coastal owners counted on slaves to improve their social prospects and their general standard of living, but maroons in the bush needed them to increase their security and food supply.

---

[125] Price diary, 23 Oct. 1875, CA5/023, CMS.

3

The Freed Slaves of Frere Town

In 1874, the Church Missionary Society (CMS) committed itself to the care of freed slaves in support of the British campaign against the East African slave trade. Their plan involved building a new mission station in East Africa and populating it with slaves captured by the British naval patrol and freed by the British consul at Zanzibar. Ground was broken the same year near Mombasa at a site named Frere Town. The new station was built in honor of Sir Bartle Frere, who represented Britain in negotiating the 1873 Treaty with Sultan Bargash abolishing the water-born slave trade. Frere Town was to stand as a plot of freedom in a land of slavery, give rise to a Christianized African community where Islam and African religions had dominated, and rejuvenate older mission stations among the Miji Kenda. Missionaries did not launch the Frere Town experiment alone. From the beginning they relied on the help of freed slaves who had been brought up and educated by the CMS in India. Nor was Frere Town popular among Mombasa residents. On many occasions, Frere Town needed the protection of the *liwali* of Mombasa, who along with other of the sultan's officials was responsible under provisions of the 1873 treaty for safeguarding the lives of liberated slaves.[1] Frere Town's history, which was particularly stormy in its early years, is akin to a running feud, between missionaries, coastal Muslims, and the freed slaves whom missionaries called "Nassickees," or "Bombay Africans."

1. The Bombay Africans

In May 1873, a few weeks before Frere and Bargash signed the 1873 treaty, a young freed slave carved on a tree in northwestern Zambia the initials of David Livingstone, who had died the previous day. The freed slave was Jacob Wainwright, product of the CMS African Asylum in India and who served as one of Livingstone's porters.[2] Just as Livingstone's firsthand reports of the East African slave trade had helped to create the pressure that led to the 1873 treaty, his

---

[1] Treaty between Her Majesty and the Sultan of Zanzibar for the Suppression of the Slave Trade, 5 June 1873, Article II, C. 820, 91.

[2] Wainwright was originally part of Lieut. L.S. Dawson's "Livingstone Search Expedition, which reached Livingstone at Unyanyembe in August 1872. Wainwright and four other freed slaves then joined Livingstone on his final journey, and they helped to carry Livingstone's remains to the coast. H.B. Thomas, "The Death of Dr. Livingstone: Carus Farrar's Narrative," *Uganda Journal*, 14, 2 (Sep. 1950), 115-28.

death in Wainwright's presence generated support for slaves freed through the treaty's enforcement. In the Spring of 1874, the freed slave issue was dramatized at Livingstone's funeral in Westminster Abbey by Jacob Wainwright himself, who attended as the "representative of Africa" and afterwards toured England addressing Anglican congregations as the guest of the CMS.[3] Nine months later Wainwright was in Mombasa to help the CMS establish Frere Town. Sir Bartles Frere, who promoted freed slave settlement after the death of Livingstone, his long-time friend, was an old admirer of William Salter Price, the CMS missionary who ran the freed slave mission establishment in India, known as the African Asylum. With Frere's encouragement, the CMS appointed Price in charge of the planned settlement near Mombasa.[4] Wainwright and other graduates of the African Asylum soon joined him. Together they established the station with the funds that poured in following Livingstone's death.[5] Because of their Indian connections, Price's former students were dubbed by East African missionaries as "Bombay Africans" or simply, "Bombays."

Most adult Bombay Africans who settled in Frere Town had left Africa as children. Liberated during the 1850s in the Indian Ocean and in port cities of southern Arabia and the Persian Gulf by the members of the British naval patrol, they were turned over to the British municipality in Bombay. European families cared for them until 1860, when they were collected into the African Asylum at the CMS Industrial Mission in Sharanpur, near the city of Nasik.[6] India put its mark on these children. Although missionaries encouraged the use of African languages, the children developed their own *patois* of Marathi, English, Hindustani, and Swahili.[7] Their close contact with missionaries also affected their self-images and appearances. As a rule they adopted biblical first names and the surnames of the missionaries charged with their care.[8] The Bombays who

---

[3] A.E. Fraser, *Livingstone and Newstead* (London: John Murray, 1913). Wainwright's figure appears in the engraving of Livingstone's funeral procession printed in the *London Illustrated News*, 25 Apr. 1874.

[4] Morton, "Slaves, Fugitives, and Freedmen," 297-8.

[5] Dawson, *James Hannington*,308; Stock, *History of the CMS*, III, 79.

[6] In 1853 George Candy, the Corresponding Secretary of the CMS in Bombay, and a German merchant and his wife, Mr. and Mrs. Theodore Zorn, established the first African Asylum in Bombay for freed slave boys and girls. In 1860, the CMS missionary C.W. Isenberg transferred the African Asylum from Bombay to its Industrial Mission at Sharanpur, to which the government began to place other children who over the previous years had not found homes. The Industrial Mission had been established in 1855 by W.S. Price for the care and training of Indian converts and indigents. Freed slaves in the Bombay area represented numerous groups in Eastern Africa. The majority, however, were either Galla from Abyssinia or Yao from Nyasaland. Isenberg to Venn, 11 May 1859, 12 Jan. 1861, and Jan. 1862; Isenberg's report to Howard, Jul. 1861, CI3/048, CMS; CMS *Proceedings*, 1857-58, 82; Stock, *History of the CMS*, II, 431.

[7] Deimler to Venn, 20 Dec. 1865; Deimler to Fenn, 15 Jan. 1873, CI3/035, CMS.

[8] Of the 114 known Bombay Africans (see Appendix I), forty derived their names

arrived in Frere Town had acquired strong preferences for British styles of dress. The women wore ankle-length, shirt-waisted dress, leggings, long sleeves, and collars. They combed their hair straight and bound it tightly behind the head. Men dressed in trousers and coats, some on occasion displaying elaborate combinations of wool suits with vest, cravat, high collar, boots, and felt hat. Like the women, Bombay men wore their hair straight and parted and combed it to the side.[9]

Education at the African Asylum also contributed to the Bombay's unique qualities. As youngsters they received instruction in English, Hindi, and Marathi, together with reading, writing, arithmetic, European geography, English history, and Bible studies. In their teens they were apprenticed in various trades,

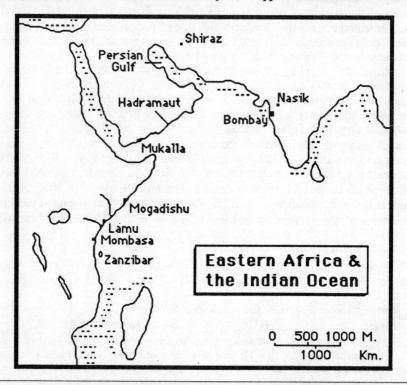

Eastern Africa & the Indian Ocean

0   500 1000 M.
      1000   Km.

from CMS missionaries in western India. Among the most common were Candy, Connop, Dickson, Farrar, Isenberg, Jerrom, and Matchett. The Bombays also took the names of prominent Englishmen (e.g., Russell, Wellington, Nelson), or made up English-sounding names of their own. Some were possibly given their surnames by missionaries, but they appear rather to have dropped willfully the use of their African names, which the missionaries used at the time of baptism. Compare Appendix I, which lists the names as they were used in East Africa, with those of Isenberg's pupils baptized in 1863. Isenberg to Venn, 31 Jan. 1863, CI3/048, CMS.

[9] Many poses in Bombay dress may be seen in photographs, dating from the 1870s, in the H.K. Binns albums, KNA.

the boys as smiths, weavers, carpenters, sailors, shoemakers, painters, and mechanics, the girls as cooks, seamstresses, and domestics. In addition to education and training, Christian habits were encouraged through daily worship services, and democratic principles of community life were reinforced through assembly meetings, where Asylum business was open to discussion and voting.[10]

From the establishment of the Asylum at Sharanpur, its founders, W.S. Price and C.W. Isenberg, looked forward to the day when their pupils might return to East Africa and spread Christianity, either as missionaries or exemplary lay members.[11] They encouraged the children to use African languages, taught them the history of Africa and the slave trade, and singled out those with an aptitude for religious work to receive training as evangelists and teachers.[12] J.G. Deimler, another CMS missionary who knew the youths, observed, however, that even among the more promising students education in India stood to hamper rather than help their return to East Africa. "I am afraid," he remarked, "that a prolonged stay and preparation [in India] may rather contribute to puff them up and estrange them in their feelings from their countrymen."[13]

In 1864 Isenberg and Price sent seven of the most promising Bombay Africans to assist Rev. Johann Rebmann, stationed seventeen kilometers west of Mombasa at Rabai, the oldest CMS station in East Africa. The Rabai station had been founded in 1844, and though Rebmann had been there since 1846, his efforts among the surrounding Miji Kenda were unfruitful. When the Bombays arrived, Rebmann had but two converts. His meager results for two decades' work stemmed from distaste for evangelistic work and a reluctance to remain for anything but short periods in Rabai itself. Rebmann and his wife spent most of their time in Mombasa or Zanzibar.[14] Rather than evangelize during these many years, Rebmann awaited instead some divine intervention. Perhaps for this reason the Bombay Africans made a strong impression on the old missionary. Reportedly, Rebmann wept when he first overheard them singing hymns in their private service.[15] The seven included three young men--Wiliam Jones, George David, and Ishmael Semler--who had excelled in their studies in India and were

---

[10] Isenberg to Venn, 12 Jan. 1861; Isenberg to Howard, Jul. 1861, CI3/048, CMS; New to UMFC, 9 Feb. 1863, UMFC *Magazine*, 1863, 334-5; H. Gundert, *Biography of the Rev. Charles Isenberg, Missionary of the Church Missionary Society to Abyssinia and Western India from 1832 to 1864* (London: CMS, 1885), 73; J. E. Harris, *The African Presence in Asia: Consequences of the East African Slave Trade* (Evanston: Northwestern University Press, 1971), 74-5.

[11] Isenberg to Venn, 12 Jan. 1861 and Jan. 1862, CI3/048, CMS.

[12] Isenberg to Venn, Jan. 1862, CI3/048, CMS; Gundert, *Isenberg*, 73-4; *Church Missionary Gleaner*, 1(1874), 127; W.F. Rampley, *Matthew Wellington: Sole Surviving Link with Dr. Livingstone* (London: Society for Promoting Christian Knowledge, n.d.[1930?]), 25-6.

[13] Deimler to Venn, 23 May 1862, CI3/035, CMS.

[14] Morton, "Slaves, Freedmen, and Fugitives," 230-33.

[15] Taylor to CMS, 20 Feb. 1865, CMS *Proceedings*, (1864-65), 180; Stock, *History of the CMS*, II, 432.

sent out as catechists. Jones and Semler were accompanied by their wives, both Galla freed slaves. In addition two sisters, Priscilla and Polly Christian, who had grown up at Sharanpur, were sent as prospective wives for Rebmann's converts.[16]

Rebmann soon lost his enthusiasm. Mutual ill-feelings grew between him and the men, who in turn became increasingly despondent. By 1870 two men had left, and two women had died. Only David, his wife, and Polly (nee Christian) Nyondo remained, and David was not happy with his work.[17] Rebmann believed the freed slaves lacked essential qualifications to be useful mission workers.[18] He regarded David and Semler, in spite of their training, as deficient in industrial skills, and he abandoned plans for them to replace Muslim workmen (probably slaves) on the station. Rebmann also obstructed the Bombay Africans from teaching and spreading the gospel. The missionary singled out Jones's teaching for praise, but Rebmann felt that he, like the others, was seriously hampered by an ignorance of Miji Kenda languages. Rebmann also felt that the Miji Kenda looked down on the Bombays as relatives of the slaves on the coast, who had been brought from Kilwa via Zanzibar.[19] Rebmann also faulted their religious commitment. "Their Christian character," he remarked, "has not had the benefit of the previous trial of those who, whether in heathen or Christian lands, are converted in the midst of their relatives and friends. Their Christianity is therefore one put on--rather than rooted and grown from within and through the comparison." Rebmann preferred his Miji Kenda converts.[20] He informed the

---

[16] Jones, David, and Semler had attended the Indo-British and Robert Money schools in Bombay and had trained for a time in the industrial section at Sharanpur. Priscilla Christian eventually married George David, whose wife died in India just prior to his departure for East Africa. Polly Christian became the wife of Isaac Nyondo, Rebmann's youngest and most devoted Rabai convert. Deimler to Venn, 31 Jan. 1865, and Deimler to Fenn, 27 Aug. 1874, CI3/035, CMS.

[17] Grace Semler died in 1866, whereupon Semler returned to India. In 1868 Jones and his wife, whose name does not appear in the CMS correspondence, left Rebmann and went to Zanzibar, where Jones worked under Bishop Steer of the UMCA. In 1870 Jones returned to Rabai, but when his wife died soon thereafter, Jones sailed for Bombay. Rebmann to Venn, 16 Nov. 1866, CA5/024, CMS; Sparshott to Venn, 24 Apr. 1868, CA5/026, CMS; Jones to Hutchinson, 16 Apr. 1870, CA5/01, CMS; David to Sparshott and Chancellor, 8 Jun. 1874, David to Hutchinson, 29 Nov. 1876, CA5/06, CMS.

[18] Rebmann to Venn, 27 Feb. 1866, CA5/024, CMS.

[19] "Unfortunately [in spite of] their civilized appearance they continually betray themselves by their speech (two of the girls also by their perforated lips) to belong to the tribes from which most of the slaves at Mombasa and among the Wanika are brought and which physically as a race, are evidently inferior to our people [sic], so that, knowledge of books being of no account with the heathen before he is converted, they have nothing to be proud of but their dress." Ibid.

[20] "Prominent among these in decision and worth of character, as well as in mental and moral power, stands Isaac [Nyondo]." Ibid.

CMS in London that he wished to have no additional freed slaves, from India or elsewhere.

Rebmann let the Bombay Africans know clearly, too, that he had no place for them. He lowered their status and injured in other ways their self-esteem.[21] While disallowing them salaries or a standard of living higher than the Africans around them, he issued them only small amounts of food and clothing and required the women to grind their own maize and fetch water. He withdrew small privileges such as shoes and tea, and he lessened the usefulness and prestige of their schooling by prohibiting the teaching of English and arithmetic.[22] Rebmann told them that they were a burden and reminded them often that they had once been slaves. Even George David, who stayed on after the departure of Semler and Jones, was subjected by Rebmann to repeated humiliations in front of others.[23] Rebmann's may have been an attempt to remove the things that separated the Bombays from other Africans, but the Bombays felt instead that they had been singled out for abuse. Whatever he expected from these, the first and best products of the African Asylum, they were unable or unwilling to provide.[24] T.H. Sparshott, who joined the Rabai mission in 1868, was initially sympathetic to the plight suffered by the Bombays in Rebmann's care, but his letters soon echoed the old missionary's attitudes. Even a visit to Sharanpur in 1872 failed to change his mind. "I cannot think that any help will be gained," Sparshott wrote to London, "from Africans trained in Bombay or any other foreign country. They are isolated in their affections and have no idea of becoming fellow country-men with Africans." It would be better for the mission, he thought, to depend on local African converts.[25]

---

[21] Sparshott to Venn, CA5/026, CMS. When Sparshott joined the CMS East Africa Mission in early 1868 the Bombays took their grievances to him, and it is on Sparshott's report that most of the above comments are based.

[22] According to Jones, Rebmann provided no instruction of any kind to his converts, or for that matter, to the Bombay Africans. Jones to Hutchinson, 16 Apr. 1870, CA5/01, CMS.

[23] David to Sparshott and Chancellor, 8 Jun. 1874, CA5/026, CMS.

[24] In this respect, Rebmann's experiences with freed slaves was similar to that of David Livingstone. In September 1865, soon after George David's party left for East Africa to join Rebmann, Livingstone visited Sharanpur and recruited nine young men from the Asylum for his final expedition in East Africa. Of Livingstone's "Nassick boys" as he called them, one died and another returned to India before the party left Zanzibar for the mainland. Of the remaining, three and possibly four deserted him, and a fifth was killed. The last two, Edward Gardiner and Nathaniel Gumba, stayed with Livingstone up to his death and helped to carry his body to the coast. Early in their travels with the missionary, however, Gardiner and Gumba (alias Mabruki) became Muslims and remained in East Africa to work as porters. Thomas, "Death of Dr. Livingstone," 120, 124-7; Livingstone to Waller, 27 Sep. 1865, MSS.Afr. s.16/1, RH.

[25] Sparshott to Hutchinson, 8 May 1872, CA5/026, CMS.

Asylum graduates were nevertheless ready to replace those whom Rebmann and Sparshott had driven out. And their enthusiasm to join the East African Mission persuaded the CMS to send them. In 1873, after his return to Mombasa and Rabai, Sparshott found himself receiving twenty Bombay Africans; another one hundred wished to come, failing which there would be "much breaking of heart." Sparshott dashed off a reply:

> May I beg the Committee to tell our Bombay friends to let them break their hearts, but not to send them here. I cd. send a thousand niggers from Mombas to Bombay if the society wd. pay their debts and passages and hold out the prospect of better pay with less work wh. I fear is the thought wh. influences nearly every one of these whose hearts are breaking.[26]

2. Price and the Frere Town Experiment

Sparshott's letter arrived in London after the CMS had decided to enlarge its East Africa mission in response to the news of Livingstone's death. Though plans were in the drafting stage, they necessarily included freed slaves, a direction in which the CMS had been moving since George David's party arrived to assist Rebmann. In 1867 the CMS had started an Educational Mission for liberated slaves in Port Victory, Mahe, in the Seychelles, but it failed for lack of British interest.[27] In 1871, when the official mood changed, the Society was encouraged by the Select Parliamentary Committee on the East African slave trade to try again on the coastal mainland, an idea also stressed in 1872-73 by the Frere Mission to East Africa. Such stations would absorb slaves captured by the British patrol. During Wainwright's visit to England the idea spread in CMS circles of setting up these stations with the assistance of freed slaves from the African Asylum; and the CMS, which had used freed slaves in Sierra Leone to spread Christianity in West Africa, became suddenly impatient that history repeat itself on the eastern side of the continent. The Society acted quickly on Frere's recommendation and appointed the head of the African Asylum, William Price, as the builder of a new freed slave mission in Mombasa.

London's decision arrived in India at an opportune time. Since 1870 many graduates of the Asylum had left Sharanpur to work in and around Bombay where they had trouble making ends meet despite their training. A few found work on the railway as smiths and carpenters, but others had to be content with unskilled jobs. During these lean times, the CMS maintained contact with the workers and their families through William Jones's itineration. Many had already expressed a desire to return to East Africa before the call came in 1873 and readily accepted the CMS offer of free passage to Mombasa in exchange for assisting

---

[26] Ibid, 12 Dec. 1873.

[27] E. Hutchinson, *The Slave Trade of East Africa* (London: Sampson Low, Marston, Low and Searle, 1874), 34f; CMS, *The Slave Trade of East Africa: Is it to Continue or Be Suppressed?* (London: CMS, 1868), 28-30.

Price.[28] They began leaving in late 1874. Jones was also able to recruit other freed slaves unconnected with the mission and living on the Government Model Farm in Bhargam. With the inducement of repatriation they also converted to Christianity and travelled with Jones to Mombasa in 1876.[29]

Price reached Mombasa in November 1874 and was later joined by William Harris, E.W. Forster, J. G. Pearson, and J.T. Last, all posted from England. While passing through Zanzibar, Price had also recruited Thomas Smith, an Asylum graduate then in the employ of the British consul. Price appointed Smith chief engineer and master of the CMS steam vessel, the "Dove."[30] The CMS instructed Price to enlarge the old mission station at Rabai and create a "Christian village" with the freed slaves.[31] Rebmann was completing his twenty-eighth year in Rabai when Price arrived, and the newcomer soon concluded the old man was "a positive hindrance to the progress of the Mission."[32] The mission station and the Mombasa hinterland were also unprotected from the rebel Mbaruk b. Rashid, whose runaway slave mercenaries visited Rabai within a month of Price's arrival.[33] Price therefore began to look for land near Mombasa, where the proposed settlement would be in direct contact with sultan's officials and within a day's journey of the British consulate in Zanzibar. Price arrived on the coast at the very moment when Britain was crushing Muhammad b. Abdullah's rebellion against the sultan. Muhammad was the sultan's *jemadar* (commander) in Fort Jesus whose troops seized control of the Fort in defiance of the Sultan's authority after he had been relieved of additional duties as *liwali* of Mombasa. Muhammad and his soldiers also made several attacks on Mombasa town. The revolt ended in January 1875 when several hundred of the sultan's troops arrived and pinned the rebels inside the fort, whereupon two British men-of-war bombarded the fort for three hours until the rebels surrendered.[34] This show of force underscored for coastal residents the might of the Busaidi-British

---

[28] Price to Fenn, 30 Jan. 1871, CI3/067; Deimler to Fenn, 15 Jan. 1873, 11 Mar. 1874, CI3/035, CMS.

[29] Deimler to Fenn, 11 Jan. 1876, CI3/035, CMS.

[30] Price to "friend," 19 Nov. 1874, CA5/023, CMS.

[31] Ludwig Krapf suggested to Price that the Shimba hills be explored as an alternative. Price to Hutchinson, 29 Oct. 1874. The CMS also wanted Price to plant a station near Mt. Kilimanjaro. Stock, *History of the CMS*, III, 83.

[32] Price to "friend," 27 Nov. 1874, CA5/023, CMS. Rebmann and the other CMS missionary, T.H. Sparshott, opposed Price's plans to set up a freed slave settlement and to use Bombay Africans in the mission project.

[33] Price's journal, 29 Dec. 1874, 7/8 Jan. 1875, CA5/023, CMS. The leader of the armed men was Abdullah, who asserted he and his eight men had come to break from Mbaruk and "join themselves to Mzungu, meaning myself, and that they wd gladly come and settle down under my protection and work honestly for a living." Price declined the request, because he believed Mbaruk's men were in conflict with the sultan's government. Abdullah and his group originated from Jilore and joined Mbaruk sometime in 1872-73. See "Early contacts" in ch. 4.

[34] Hinawy, *Al Akida and Fort Jesus*; Berg, "Mombasa under the Busaidi," 121-6.

alliance and made it possible for Price to receive tens of Bombay Africans arriving in early January and house them temporarily in Mombasa town.[35]

Price and the Bombay Africans were soon unpopular with the townspeople. "There is an uneasy feeling among some in the Town," Price recorded in his diary, "arising from a suspicion that my object is to set free all the slaves."[36] According to Sparshott, the Mombasans "view the movements of Mr. Price with great suspicion" and were particularly annoyed with the Bombay Africans who, he alleged, "intimidate the people by telling them 'the English are soon coming to take the place."[37] In late February 1875 feelings ran high after a public worship service on the island, and the acting *liwali*, Seif b. Suleiman, then tried to pressure Price's landlord to evict him.[38] In late March Suleiman's successor, Ali b. Nasur, obstructed Price's attempts to purchase land for the future freed slave settlement. Price had made the acquaintance of two Arabs willing to sell the CMS their adjoining plots in Kisauni, which was within easy reach of Mombasa town and had direct access to the sea. The owners, however, hesitated to sell because of the *liwali*'s harassment.[39]

Price then used his Zanzibar connections to quick effect. He wrote to the new consul in Zanzibar, John Kirk, friend of the late Livingstone and who had been appointed, as had Price, on the recommendation of Frere. Kirk interceded through Sultan Bargash, and the land transaction promptly went through.[40] The *liwali* was upset about this affair, but not because the mission had used Zanzibar to protect its interests. Nasur, though reputedly a "thorough Anglophobist," was in fact the sultan's loyal servant awaiting instructions. Nasur's concern was that the mission was creating opportunities for the sultan's enemies in Mombasa and along the coast. The two men who sold their land to Price were members of the Mazrui and Mandhry clans, which had been involved in resistance of one sort or another since the Busaidi takeover in 1837.[41] Nasur had

---

[35] Price journal, 4 Jan., 9 and 17 Feb., and 6 Mar. 1875, CA5/023, CMS; Price to Hutchinson, 4 Jan. 1875, CA5/M4, 9; CMS *Proceedings* (1874-75), 38, 50-1.

[36] Price journal, 1 Mar. 1875, CA5/M4, 54, CMS.

[37] Sparshott to Hutchinson, 15 Jul. 1875, CA5/M5, CMS, 113-4. Sparshott had an abiding dislike of the Africans from Sharanpur, whom he regarded as an "impudent and idle lot." Sparshott dubbed them the "Bombays," a contemptuous term that stuck. Price memorandum, 2 Feb. 1875, CA5/023, CMS.

[38] Price journal, 21 and 28 Feb. 1875, CA5/M4, 53, CMS.

[39] Price to Kirk, 7 Apr. 1875, CA5/M4, 79, CMS. Price, who regarded Nasur as a "thorough Anglophobist," got on less well with the governor than other CMS missionaries.

[40] Ibid; N. R. Bennett, "The Church Missionary Society at Mombasa, 1873-1894," in J. Butler, ed., *Boston University Papers in African History* (Boston: Boston University Press, 1964), I, 165-6.

[41] Price to Kirk, 7 Apr. 1875, CA5/M4, 79-80, CMS. Khamis's clan identity ("el-Mandiri") is given in 3rd Cert. in David to Price, 2 Jan. 1880, FO 541/48, 438. See also Berg, "Mombasa under the Busaidi," 50-2,97, 113-7,156-7; Pouwels, *Horn and Crescent*, 117-8. The Mazrui and Mandhry were by no means united against the

been *liwali* since that year and had maintained equilibrium among the diverse clans and moieties in and around Mombasa. He prevented ambitious outsiders, such as the Mazrui, from exploiting local differences to advance their political fortunes. Nasur had acquired a deep distrust of Rashid b. Salim and Mbaruk b. Rashid, the exiled leaders of the Mazrui, living in Takaungu and Gasi, respectively, and he wished to keep Price and the CMS unacquainted with both. Price, under pressure of time and with no knowledge of local politics, built the mission with support from the top rather than on any popular foundation. With the land in his possession, Price forged ahead, knowing that despite local enmity, he would enjoy the protection of the Busaidi authorities.

Price's immediate task was constructing buildings for the September arrival of "condemned" (newly freed) slaves sent from Zanzibar. Of the Bombay Africans who had been arriving in small groups since January, roughly half had no practical skills to speak of and were sent to farm at the Rabai mission station, where they were expected to live "under Christian rule and discipline." Price employed the skilled and educated as staff members on the new mission station at Kisauni. In May they commenced building "Frere Town," named by Price in gratitude to Sir Bartle Frere for his interest in the freed slaves of Bombay and for his role in combating the slave trade in East Africa.[42] By July, Price reported that "all were employed and doing well." Price later stated that without the Bombays' "willing and valuable help....I know not how I could have surmounted the difficulties I encountered in the early days of the colony."[43] In September the station was ready when the British consul in Zanzibar sent to Frere Town its first two consignments of freed slaves, totaling 280 adults and children. Almost all of them were Makua who, Price wrote, "are said to be more susceptible of training than many other tribes. More than 100 are mere children. Here at once is clay for the potter."[44]

Frere Town and Rabai expanded rapidly. By March 1876 Frere Town had a total population of 342, of whom all but a few were freed slaves, including about seventy Bombay Africans.[45] Over sixty Bombays lived at Rabai with Rebmann's four Miji Kenda converts, all men.[46] Before the end of 1876 the

---

Busaidi. The Mazrui under Rashid b. Khamis of Takaungu to the north of Mombasa accepted Busaidi rule, and two leading Mandhry, the brothers Rashid and Mohammed b. Ali, were strong Ibadhis and confidants of sultans Majid and Bargash.

[42] Price to Kirk, 7 Apr. 1875 and Price to Hutchinson, 6 May 1875, CMS CA5/M4, 79-80, 84.

[43] Price to Euan Smith, 16 Jul. 1875, CA5/M5, 105; East African mission report, 6 Oct. 1882, G3A5/01(1882), CMS. The Bombays who arrived in 1875 comprised sixty men, thirty-five women, and thirty-five children. Russell to Hutchinson, 30 Nov. 1876, CA5/025, CMS.

[44] Price journal, 4 and 19 Sep. 1875, CA5/023; Kirk to Derby, 14 Sep. 1877, C. 2139, 363.

[45] Price to Hutchinson, 1 Mar. 1876, CA5/023, CMS.

[46] Russell to Hutchinson, 30 Nov. 1876, CA5/025, CMS. The four were Samuel Kango, James Mwachingo, Mark Mlangulo, and Abraham Begonja. Isaac Nyondo,

population on the CMS stations was increased by further additions of raw, captured slaves, plus another twenty Bombays who arrived with Jones. In November the total number of freed slaves at Frere Town and Rabai, Bombays included, stood at 480.[47] Price relied on Bombays as mission police, wardens, teachers,

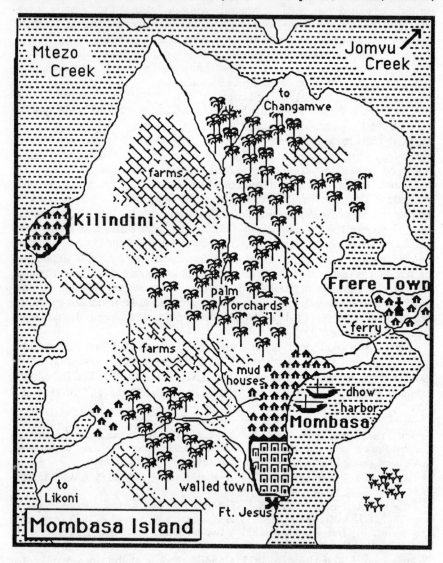

Begonja's son, was in Europe acting as Johann Rebmann's servant.

[47] Figures based on numbers and lists in Russell to Hutchinson, 30 Nov. 1876, CA5/025, CMS.

carpenters, builders, sailors on the mission launch, and as overseers of the station in Rabai.[48]

Within months of the opening of Frere Town, the Bombay Africans became a major source of conflict between Price and other missionaries. J.G. Pearson, who supervised mission construction, complained bitterly to CMS headquarters in London about those in his charge. Pearson called them a continual clog and hindrance to the work," slighting them for their "idleness," "carelessness," and shoddy workmanship.[49] The mission employed slave artisans and laborers from Mombasa to do most of the construction work.[50] E.W. Forster, the mission doctor, was equally critical of his Bombay assistants, Samuel Freeman and Josiah Johnson, and had them demoted to common laborers.[51] Forster wrote discouragingly about the other Bombays, questioning their religious convictions along with their manual skills.

> These natives from India [I think] a failure....We expected great help from them, but we are doomed to disappointment--with a few exceptions I consider them unfit as gospel interpreters. Their Xtianity does not appear to me to be sufficiently intelligent.[52]

Though Price was himself the first to assert that the Bombays included those of "a very low type," he was inclined to forgive their lapses and encourage them in their work.[53] The other missionaries favored punishment, scoffed at Price's leniency, and asked for more authority to deal with the Bombays. Price resisted, and the others regarded his faith in the Bombays as an act of infidelity to themselves. The "levity and indulgence and confidence so often reposed in these poor half-taught Nassickees rather than in the Europeans," wrote Dr. Forster, "has a bad effect upon the former and bred distrust in the minds of the

---

[48] A list of the more prominent Bombays includes Jacob Wainwright (schoolmaster), Polly Christian Nyondo (headmistress), George David (catechist and head of the Rabai mission), Tom Smith (chief engineer of the "Dove"), Henry Williams (shopkeeper, Rabai), and one of Rebmann's disenchanted assistants, Ishmael Semler, who returned to Mombasa in 1873 and after Price's arrival was appointed a catechist in Frere Town.

[49] Pearson to Wright, 17 Apr. 1876, CA5/01, CMS.

[50] In December 1875 the mission was employing 150 slaves for building work. Price journal, 24 Dec. 1875, CA5/023, CMS.

[51] Forster to Wright, 30 Dec. 1875, CA5/M4, 177, CMS. Johnson and Freeman were charged not only for incompetence, but because, as Forster later admitted, for "their bad morals." Forster quarterly report, 30 Apr. 1876, CA5/010, CMS. James Ainsworth, Forster's other assistant, earned the doctor's full confidence. "He has proved a faithful friend, a conscientious Christian, and an intelligent learner.... He seems to have been sent in the Providence of God to supply a place which probably could not otherwise have been filled."

[52] Forster to Wright, 30 Dec. 1875, CA5/M4, 177, CMS.

[53] Price journal, 11 Sep. 1875, CA5/023, CMS.

Europeans."[54] Forster bemoaned Price's "infallible and unlimited power" and his failure to consult other missionaries. Pearson, the angriest of Price's opponents, was more to the point:

> The Europeans under Mr. Price are blackened and the boys from Nassick whitened at every turn.[55]

Frere Town was also hard put in coping with the first arrivals of freed slaves, or *mateka*, who immediately became a source of concern.[56] Price described the first group as "nearly all covered with itch; and two of them are emaciated and otherwise suffering. When they arrived they appeared very sullen."[57] Other groups arrived in even worse condition. The twenty-five who landed in February 1876 had "all more or less a starved appearance. Many are pitiably emaciated."[58] The change of diet, climate, and home compounded their problems. Even the health and morale of those in sound condition deteriorated rapidly.

> Nostalgia, or *maladie du pays* began to tell a tale, so that diarrhea, dysentery, fevers, and various dyspepsias, also melancholy or at any rate mental dejection showed themselves among the adults, whilst diarrhea, anaemias, and misintine disease have been prevalent amongst the children; very many cases of ulcers, many of a strongly and phayoedemic character came to notice.

Soon after their arrival several of this group died from what Forster diagnosed as "permanent melancholia," and seven deaths occurred among the children who, after showing similar symptoms, wasted away from diarrhea and complete exhaustion. Within one year 13 per cent, or 36 out of the original group of 279 at Frere Town, had died.[59] The setting was too new for the *mateka*, the missionaries too impatient. The older ones particularly exasperated Price, who had been expecting them to show gratitude. "The children we could easily manage, but the adults," he wrote, "are simply a lot of idle savages, and until they can be

---

[54] Forster to Wright, 24 Mar. 1876, CA5/M4, 225, CMS. The term "Nassickees" was commonly used by Europeans when referring to the Bombay Africans. It is derived from Nasik, the large town near the Sharanpur Industrial Mission where the African Asylum was located.

[55] Pearson to Wright, 17 Apr. 1876, CA5/O1, CMS.

[56] *Mateka* is KiSwahili for "booty," or "captive," referring to those slaves captured by the British from Muslim traders in the Indian Ocean and "condemned" in the British Vice-Admiralty court in Zanzibar. For a romanticized account that ignores the hardships *mateka* suffered after reaching Frere Town, J. Mbotela, *Uhuru wa Watu-mwa (The Freeing of the Slaves)*, 2nd ed. (Nairobi: East African Literature Bureau, 1967).

[57] Price journal, 4 Sep. 1875, CA5/O23, CMS.

[58] Ibid, 28 Feb. 1876.

[59] Forster quarterly report, 31 Dec. 1875, CA5/O10; Russell report, Nov. 1876, CA5/O25, CMS.

made to understand their position and our kind feelings towards them we shall have something to do to keep order."[60]

3. *Frere Town and Coastal Slavery*

Frere Town's development was also challenged by runaway slaves seeking refuge. Soon after Frere Town was established, slaves from Mombasa streamed into the station begging for asylum. Price cooperated with authorities and returned them to their masters.[61] His decision to stay within Islamic law created an obvious moral dilemma for the head of a freed slave settlement, and he attempted to resolve it by championing the legal rights of slaves. Quick to use the law for the protection of slave interests, he took masters of ill-treated runaways to court and sometimes landed them in jail. "It is becoming pretty well known both to slaves and masters, that the muzungu [European] at the Mission House has some power to protect oppressed slaves, and bring brutish masters to punishment, but as I always take care when I do interfere, to do so thro' the authorities the latter have no just ground of complaint; of course, they don't like me any more for that...."[62] Price's most celebrated triumph followed his appeal to Zanzibar against the actions of the sheikh of Takaungu, Rashid b. Salim, who had confiscated property from his client, Yaa wa Medza. As a result of the appeal, Sultan Bargash ordered Rashid to appear before the *liwali* of Mombasa, Ali b. Nasur, and return the property (which included several slaves) to Yaa. Not long thereafter, Rashid was succeeded by his brother, Salim. In April 1876 Salim sold Price land adjoining Frere Town, perhaps as a gesture of friendship to the missionary, but more likely as a slight against Ali b. Nasur, who opposed the mission's expansion (the governor's own slave had tried to seek refuge at Frere Town.). When Salim travelled to Zanzibar to pay his respects to Bargash, he was imprisoned for six months.[63]

---

[60] Price to Wright, 5 Oct. 1875, CA5/M4, 125-6; Price journal, 1 Oct. 1875, CA5/023, CMS.

[61] "It goes sadly against the grain, but as the law stands, I fear there is no alternative." Price journal, 10 Oct. 1875, CA5/023. For other references to runaways, see ibid, 8-10 Oct. 1875, 15 Dec. 1875, 22 Apr. 1876; Price to Hutchinson, 1 Mar. 1876, CA5/M4, 198; Handford quarterly report, 25 Mar. 1876 and 2 Feb. 1876 enclosure, CA5/011; Russell to Hutchinson, 6 Nov. 1876, CA5/M5, 11, CMS. For mission policy on fugitive slaves, see chs. 4 & 5.

[62] Price journal, 25 Mar. 1876, CA5/023.

[63] Kirk to Derby, 25 Dec. 1875, and encl., C. 1829, 186-7; Price journal, 22 Apr. 1876, CMS. Hardinge memorandum, 26 Aug. 1896, C. 8274, 32. In April 1876 Nasur also tried to obstruct the Methodist mission from purchasing land in Jomvu by imprisoning the Swahili who were prepared to sell. A year later, the Methodists received permission to build at Jomvu after the intervention of Kirk. Wakefield to Barton, 31 Jan. 1876, UMFC *Magazine* (Apr. 1876), 251; Price Journal, 23 May 1876, CA5/023, CMS; Wakefield to Barton, 21 Apr. 1877, UMFC *Magazine* (Oct. 1877), 637; Wakefield, *Thomas Wakefield*, 150.

Price had become a skilled, though unpopular, politician. And his fellow
missionaries were not pleased. The medical missionary, E.W. Forster, used his
quarterly report to London to condemn Price, alleging that the CMS was con-
tinuously mixed up in political matters and thereby making the Swahili and
Arabs strongly antagonistic toward the mission. "I am surprised," he wrote
sarcastically, "at [the] mere civilisation and secular concerns occupying the
supremacy." [64]

Price's involvement in civic affairs also extended to the slave trade. After
1873, slaves had been smuggled into the Kenya coast or trekked overland from
the major outlets of the southern hinterland supply routes. Traders marched their
slaves to Pangani and Tanga, from which they supplied Pemba, Mombasa and
other points north. Vice-consul Frederick Holmwood, dispatched from Zanzibar
in 1874 to investigate, estimated that 32,000 slaves annually were sold as a
result of the new land traffic.[65] Mombasa became an important way-station and
brokerage point on the land route. Slave owners in Takaungu depended partly on
Mombasa agents for their slaves, and Mombasa traders sometimes went directly
to Kilwa and marched their own slave purchases north.[66] Holmwood estimated
that 12,000 slaves arrived in Mombasa for sale or reshipment.[67] This traffic
was legal, but by 1875 Kirk pressured the sultan for a new proclamation.
Probably as a result, the trade in the Mombasa area became surreptitious and the
missionaries' attention unwelcome. Price nevertheless made it his business to
uncover the local traffic, publicize it at CMS headquarters, and provide the CMS
Intelligencer with stories and sketches of caravans.[68] The mission embarrassed
local Asian traders, who were secretly dealing in slaves despite being banned
from the slave trade since 1845. Holmwood found the Asian chief customs
master in Zanzibar to be involved in the Mombasa traffic, and Frere Town
sleuths pinpointed the farm of the local customs master, Khimji, as an important way-station.[69] Mombasa Asians and older Arab families were connected
to this trade, as the sheikh of the Mombasa Arabs had married the daughter of a
Hindu trader.[70] These connections were uncovered through the vigilance of the
Bombay Africans, who were then assisting the sheikh's slave to purchase her
freedom.[71]

---

[64] Forster quarterly report, 30 Apr. 1876, CA5/010, CMS.

[65] Holmwood report, encl. in Holmwood to Prideaux, 17 Nov. 1874, C. 1588, 4-16.

[66] Holmwood report, encl. in Prideaux to Derby, 8 Feb. 1875, ibid, 64.

[67] Ibid., 7.

[68] Price to Hutchinson, 12 Aug. 1875, CA5/M4, 116, CMS; CMS *Intelligencer*, 2
(1875), 42-3.

[69] Ibid.

[70] The sheikh was Majid b. Jabiri al-Rijeby. FO 541/48, 437-9.

[71] George David to Price, 2 Jan. 1880, ibid. The slave was actually owned by sheikh
Majid's wife, who was herself the Hindu trader's daughter by his African slave
concubine. The trader's name was not given, though George David, who was raised in
Bombay and spoke Hindustani and Gujarati, would be certain of his religious identity.

By this time, Price's African staff members had become outspoken critics of slavery within Mombasa town itself. On the 19th of June, 1876, several Bombays were involved in a row with some Mombasans over the ill-treatment of a slave girl.[72] This incident, coupled with rumors that Frere Town was harboring runaways, convinced Ali b. Nasur that the Bombays were the root of all the troubles between the mission and the townspeople. "These negroes," he wrote Bargash, "are arrogant, finding themselves supported by the missionaries and are reckless as to consequences."[73]

When news reached Mombasa that Bargash had banned the land trade, Frere Town became the target of a threatened attack by several hundred townspeople. According to Price's Arab friends, the group was led by the son of the *qadi* of Mombasa, sheikh Ali b. Abdallah al-Mazrui, an old ally of Mbaruk b. Rashid of Gasi and opponent of the sultan. Preparing to cross the creek to Frere Town, the crowd declared themselves in rebellion "against the Wazungu [Europeans] and Said Bargash." *Liwali* Nasur sent troops to break up the crowd and prevent them from crossing. Baluchi troops were sent to guard Frere Town, and Price's Arab friends, Khamis b. Saad and Mahomed b. Said, supplied fifty of their personal retainers. Meanwhile Hamis b. Kombo, the *tamim* of the Mombasa moiety, Tisa Taifa, met the rebels at the crossing and discouraged the attack. The night at the station lasted without incident, and by next morning the crisis had passed.[74]

Price's Frere Town experiment had thus far survived with the sultan's protection and the help of Mombasa Arab and Swahili leaders who identified the mission as part of the new political order. In the following months, the station's influence in coastal affairs steadily declined. Price's wife had been ill for months and was traumatized by the attempted raid, so Price resigned his position and returned with her to England in July 1876. The missionary colleagues who had helped him found the station had already left following personal wrangles with Price. Their replacements arrived with opposite notions about the purpose of a freed slave settlement and the role of a Christian mission in a Muslim land. None, including the new head of mission, Rev. James Abner Lamb, had Price's flair for local politics or the personal connections in Zanzibar which appear to account for so much of his assertiveness. They also lacked his tolerance. Unlike Price, they were unacquainted with India and uncommitted to the graduates the graduates of the African Asylum. And they soon came into conflict, almost without exception, with the Bombay Africans.

Under Price Bombays had occupied all but the very highest religious and secular positions in the CMS mission. Church administration depended on George David, Ishmael Semler, and William Jones, who visited families and

---

[72] Price journal, 19 May 1876, CA5/O23, CMS.

[73] Nasur to Bargash, 27 May 1876, C. 1829, 263.

[74] Price journal, 24, 27, and 28 May 1876, CA5/O23, Price to Wright, 18 Jun. 1876, CA5/M4, 256, CMS; Kirk to Derby, 7 Jun. 1876 and encls., C. 1829, 261-3. For sheikh Ali b. Abdallah, Pouwels, *Horn and Crescent*, 117-8; Berg, "Mombasa under the Busaidi," 155-7.

single adults, instructed catechists, interpreted at worship services, did written translation work, and oversaw the Bombay farming community in Rabai. They also were in touch with Miji Kenda enquirers settled in the hills north of Rabai and had travelled in many parts of the Mombasa hinterland. Jacob Wainwright, Moses Willing, Henry Williams, and William Isenberg served as teachers (as did Robert Keating and Jonah Mitchell from 1878) in the church schools set up for *mateka* and Bombay children. Bombay couples, such as Polly and Isaac Nyondo, oversaw the children's dormitories and organized their daytime activities. Elsewhere on the station, Bombay Africans assisted as record keepers, clerks, messengers, policemen (under Sergeant Major Richard Dowman), nurses, doctor's aides, mechanics, sailors (under Tom Smith, captain of the Frere Town steamer), shopkeepers, and farming overseers. Their salaries made the ranking Bombays persons of means. George David, Tom Smith, and Ishmael Semler purchased land of their own adjoining the station, and others would later follow suit. The influence of these conspicuously well-to-do freed slaves was felt in Mombasa, along the Muslim coast, and among the Miji Kenda of the hinterland.

4. *The Regimes of Lamb and Streeter*

Rev. Lamb opposed Price and the Bombays' wish to make the CMS a coast-wide power in its own right and favored raising religious and moral standards within Frere Town. Lamb, who had arrived before Price's departure, was critical of the "business aspect" of the mission and of the delays in evangelizing the *mateka*.[75] He began by punishing *mateka* found guilty of unchristian behavior and, with his wife, took a personal hand in seeking out moral offenders for summary beatings. A prison was built for the worst violators and placed in charge of Samuel Morris, a Bombay African. Lamb's net soon snared Bombay Africans. Lamb had a low opinion of Price's staff, whom he thought conceited as well as irregular in their attendance at worship.[76] His efforts to punish Bombays along with the *mateka* were tempered by the Frere Town superintendent, W.F.A.H. Russell, who opposed jailing moral offenders even though he was personally distressed by their behavior.[77] Lamb persisted in his campaign, nonetheless, unmindful that it had become a threat to the very people who ran his mission. Within several months a crisis erupted that challenged Lamb's control.

In March 1877, with Russell in Zanzibar, the Bombays seized control of Frere Town. Trouble began when the Nyassa *mateka* defied the authority of the Frere Town police, made up of Bombays. The Bombays had imprisoned the wife of a *mateka* to force the husband to join a group leaving Frere Town for Saadani

---

[75] Lamb to Wright, 16 Jun. 1876, CA5/M4, 263, CMS.

[76] Lamb to Wright, 28 Jul. 1876, ibid, 273.

[77] "Mr. Lamb is annoyed at my not sending men to prison whenever a charge is made against them of immorality.... Mrs. Lamb has lodged complaints against different people at times some of which upon investigation have turned out utterly frivolous." Russell to Wright, 1 Jan. 1877, CA5/M5, 30. See also Russell to Hutchinson, 1 Jan. 1877, CA5/M4, 29a, Russell to Wright, 1 Jan. 1877, CA5/M4, 30; and Russell to Wright, 21 Jun. 1877, CA5/M4, 2116-7, CMS.

opposite Zanzibar where they had been contracted to do road work. The Nyassa *mateka*, armed with knives and machetes, then staged a revolt and retreated into the nearby coconut plantations. The unarmed Bombays then convinced Lamb that Frere Town was about to be attacked by Arabs and thereby secured the mission's Snider rifles, which they used against the Nyassa settlers. During the ensuing fight, Joshua King, one of the Bombays, shot dead a Nyassa man. The principal Bombays in this affair included Ishmael Semler, Tom Smith, George David, and Richard Dowman, all leading men in the Frere Town community since its inception. Isaac Nyondo was also involved.[78]

The March incident led to another overhaul of Frere Town. Kirk, who travelled from Zanzibar to investigate, criticized Lamb's administration and urged that the station be placed under a "judicious secular head" who would "restore the order and discipline that up to the departure of Mr. Price...made the mission so promising as a means of improving the people of Eastern Africa."[79] The CMS acted quickly, though not in conformity with Kirk's request. Like the British consul in Zanzibar, they wanted order and discipline on the station, but for their English lay subscribers they desired a greater religious emphasis and more converts than Price had been able to achieve. The CMS Lay Secretary, Edward Hutchinson, supported Lamb's policies, although he was embarrassed by Lamb's failure to control Russell and the Bombay Africans. The CMS sent out J.R. Streeter, whose ideas agreed with Lamb's, to replace Russell. Streeter and Lamb worked closely. They enforced mission rules strictly through harsh punishment and the curtailment of privileges, especially so if the offenders were Bombay Africans. On Lamb's return home in 1878, Streeter took full command of the settlement and prosecuted with even greater intensity. Other missionaries acquiesced, and for the next three years morality in Frere Town was upheld by imprisonment, confinement to stocks, and flogging. Most victims of the new regime were Bombay Africans, and Streeter reserved the harshest punishment for those he found guilty of drunkenness, carousing, wife-beating, and adultery. Streeter retained in position of authority Bombays willing to participate in meting out strokes.[80]

After 1877 the Bombays steadily deteriorated as a community. Desire for marriage and children, which initially had been strong, gave way to neglect and

---

[78] Russell to Hutchinson, 29 Mar. 1877, CA5/M4, 73-4; Lamb to Wright, 23 Mar. 1877, CA5/017; Praeger to Wright, 29 Mar. and 21 Apr. 1877, CA5/022; Kirk to Derby, 30 Mar. 1877, C. 2139, 303-4. This incident suggests that the Bombays, if not Lamb's missionaries, were touting *mateka* labor up and down the coast.

[79] Kirk to Derby, 30 Mar. 1877, C. 2139, 304.

[80] For example, the role of Ishmael Semler and Tom Price in the flogging of Charles Farrar, Streeter to Wright, 22 May 1878, CA5/027. In the same letter, Streeter quoted George David as saying "the Bombay Boys were a bad lot and it was a pity they were ever sent here." Many missionary letters following Price's departure refer to Bombay offences.

indifference.[81] Incidents of wife-beating and adultery became commonplace in missionaries' reports, and a marked drop in the childbirth rate after 1876 is indicated in the census data.[82] Streeter and the other missionaries, who thought Africans naturally unfaithful, regarded adultery and marital violence as causes rather than symptoms of marital distress. He aggravated the problem with punishments and forced reconciliations. Missionaries also regarded drunkenness, which increased among Bombays after 1876, as proof of natural depravity rather than a symptom of recent despair. By 1877 palm wine had become popular on mission grounds, and Bombays frequented neighboring Swahili-owned coconut orchards, where slave tappers sold wine openly. By 1879, missionaries reported that Bombays were indebted to tappers and even dying from alcoholism, concluding that Africans were unable to curb their instincts.[83] Flogging was the prescribed cure for those caught drinking. Preventative treatment, insofar as it was applied, consisted in encouraging open-air dancing as a harmless release for libidinous energies.

> Twice a week outside they have their 'ngoma' or Tom Tom. [It] keeps them from the shambas [coconut orchards] which are their ruin. These East Africans have an amount of steam in them which must escape they won't give it off in work, and the ngoma is their safety valve (or rather destructive valve as conducted outside) but here it is a treat to see them. [It] beats the Christy Minstrels.[84]

The Bombays were subjects of missionary rulers who, with the exception of Price, took no trouble to know them. Lamb and his fellow missionaries acted on preformulated, negative assumptions and remained deaf to the meaning of words uttered by the Bombays and blind to the value of secular tasks they performed. Bombays continued as teachers, carpenters, overseers, masons, and farmers, but without direction, encouragement, or reward. Missionary criticism of their work helped to make it shoddy. Some Bombay Africans labored under these under these constraints and managed to earn praise from missionary superiors, but the large majority lost their place in the CMS mission.

For a time, most preferred remaining on the mission rather than try living somewhere else. Moving into Mombasa or another part of the Muslim coast was

---

[81] Among the first generation of Bombays, only two remained single. One was William Isenberg, who suffered from recurrent mental disorders. Jacob Wainwright, the other, left Frere Town in 1877.

[82] Between 1874 and 1876 eighteen children were born to sixteen of the twenty-four married Bombay couples living in Frere Town. Between 1876 and 1881 a total of seven children were born among the twenty-two couples still resident. Compare Russell to Hutchinson, 30 Nov. 1876, and "Statement of Freed Slaves received by the Church Mission [sic] Society Mombasa East Africa," n.d., CA5/025, with Frere Town "Rough Plan" Map, Jan. 1881, G3A5/01(1881), CMS. See also Bombay list in Append. 1.

[83] Streeter to Venn, 28 Dec. 1878, CA5/027; Binns to Wright, 29 Nov. 1879, CA5/M6, 105, CMS.

[84] Streeter to Wright, 5 Dec. 1878, CA5/027, CMS.

out of the question, because the status of freed slaves off mission grounds was unprotected.[85] Also the Bombays had developed an intense dislike for coastal Muslims in general and slave owners in particular.[86] Some tried to live in Zanzibar, twenty having settled there by 1882, a few others following.[87] Of this group, some joined caravans or went to South Africa to work as servants.[88] Those with jobs in Zanzibar clustered on the Universities Mission to Central Africa's station at Mkunazini, where they were welcome but not content. In the 1880s Price twice visited this group. They were fretting about their wayward children and hoping for the chance to return to Frere Town.[89]

The Bombay Africans would no sooner live among the Miji Kenda. The Bombays referred to these residents of the Mombasa hinterland with the standard Swahili pejorative "Wanyika" (bush people), and like coastal Muslims saw them as uncivilized. The Bombays' own clothing, western education, Christianity, and aversion to full-time agricultural work stood them in contrast to the poor Miji Kenda farmers and contributed to their notions of superiority.[90] With the exception of William Jones, Bombay Africans were unwilling to deal open-handedly with the Miji Kenda around the mission station at Rabai. They shared the view of catechist George David, a popular figure among the Bombays, who thought of the Miji Kenda as a "wretched and degraded race--no learning, no civilization, but gloomy and barbarism."[91] As inferiors on a white-ruled mission station, David and other Bombay Africans looked down on blacks outside. They behaved like the Islamized slaves who despised Wanyika pagans.[92] Bombay Africans were susceptible to missionary doctrines of supremacy which elevated them, in company with their hurtful masters, above non-Christians on the coast.

Religious militancy inside the station, where Streeter battled offenders of the faith, had its counterpart in confrontation with Muslims outside. Streeter set aside Price's policy of working with the *liwali* and using Islamic law to protect the mission and abused slaves. Rather than visit Ali b. Nasur to pay respects or make requests, Streeter went to the governor's to threaten and lecture. Streeter

[85] George David to Wright, 10 Oct. 1878, CA5/M5, 246, CMS.

[86] Price journal, 19 May 1876, CA5/023, CMS; Ali b. Nasur to Bargash, 27 May 1876, C. 1829, 263.

[87] Price to Wigram, 14 Dec. 1881, G3A5/01(1882), CMS.

[88] Menzies to Hutchinson, 29 Jan. 1880, CA5/M5, 46; Lane to Lang, 2 Apr. 1882, G3A5/01(1883), CMS.

[89] Price to Wigram, 14 Dec. 1881, and "Report on the East Africa Mission," 6 Oct. 1882, G3A5/01(1882), CMS; Price, *Third Campaign*, 42, 85.

[90] Price's dream of a Bombay agricultural community, to which the Miji Kenda around Rabai would be attracted, was a failure. By 1878 the Bombay men had become dependent on wage labor for the mission. Binns annual letter November 1878, CA5/03, CMS.

[91] David to Wright, 10 Oct. 1878, CA5/M5, 246. In the 1870s, David supervised the CMS mission in Rabai during the absences of H.K. Binns. For Jones, see chs. 5 & 6.

[92] New to UMFC, 25 Oct. 1864, UMFC *Magazine* (1865), 345.

saw himself as a soldier fighting for souls endangered by Islam, a natural enemy of Muslim temporal or legal authorities, and a self-appointed defender of territory where Islam was not in control. He intervened on the side of the Miji Kenda in their disputes with the Mombasa Swahili, opened mission stations to slaves who had run away from Muslim and Miji Kenda owners (while assuring Kirk in Zanzibar that the CMS had not done so), and encouraged slaves to revolt against their masters.

In June 1880, Streeter helped runaways in Frere Town plan a general slave rising. For three days, the runaways and slaves from Mombasa met on a farm near the mission where they feasted, fired guns, and discussed insurrection. At the time Streeter hoisted on the main mission house a flag emblazoned with the word "Freedom," in Swahili characters. When the meeting broke up inconclusively, Streeter tried to keep the movement alive. In August, he sent messages into the hinterland asking runaway slaves to lend their support. And while he waited, Streeter turned Frere Town into an armed camp: sand bags and timber were stacked, Snider rifles issued, and twelve-pound war rockets placed in position.[93] No slaves or runaways joined this exercise, which was patently suicidal, and Streeter's call for revolt was not taken seriously by either the governor or the Muslim town folk. In Mombasa, however, the popular desire increased greatly to be rid of this pest. The British consul in Zanzibar, still supporting the sultan's law on the coast, concurred.

After receiving worried letters from Streeter's colleagues, Kirk intervened.[94] In early October he and his assistant arrived in Mombasa to investigate. As his vessel steamed into the harbor, Kirk looked across the creek at Frere Town and observed the "freedom flag" flying in plain view. At a public meeting in Mombasa Kirk heard complaints about the harboring of fugitive slaves, particularly at Rabai, and later interrogated CMS missionaries. Then, in a public statement in Mombasa town, Kirk admonished the missionaries to obey the local laws, which recognized the right of slave owners to recover their slaves. Fugitive slaves were to be regarded as trespassers on mission ground and entitled to no protection. If the mission harbored runaway slaves, it would in the future be opposed in any resulting outbreaks by the Sultan's troops.[95] Kirk impressed the Mombasans

---

[93] Menzies to Wright, 18 Jun. 1880, CA5/M6, 133; Streeter to Wright, 17 Jul. 1880, CA5/027; Binns to Hutchinson, n.d.[early 1881?], CMS; Kirk to Granville, 22 Sep. 1880, with encls. and 19 Oct. 1880, FO 541/48, 520-2, 529-530; Kirk to Granville, 4 Apr. 1881, FO 541/49, 247; Binns diary 1 Sep. and 9-16 Sep. 1880, KNA.

[94] Kirk to Granville, 22 Sep. 1880 encls, FO 541/48, 520-2. The letters, dispatched on 10 Sep., were most likely sent by Rev. R.W. Felkin, then visiting Frere Town.

[95] Kirk to Granville, 19 Oct., 1880, FO 541/48, 530-1. The Parent Committee of the CMS responded to these events immediately by instructing their missionaries not to retain runaways "save where claims of humanity require it, but they will either induce the slave to return to his master or inform the Wali [liwali] of the event." Resolutions of the General Committee, 16 Nov. 1880, in Hutchinson to Granville, 14 Jan. 1881, FO 541/49, 201.

and, before returning to Zanzibar, convinced the CMS to limit their activities to mission work and disengage with runaway slaves.

When Streeter's imprudence continued, the British consul conducted another investigation. Apparently Kirk's visit to Mombasa incensed Streeter, who became even more a tyrant within the mission. Perhaps he held the literate freed slaves responsible for sending word to Kirk. At any rate, Streeter's anger was directed at the few Bombays active in religious work. In February 1881, five wrote a letter of protest to CMS headquarters.[96] Alongside a long catalog of complaints against their work made by Streeter and the other missionaries, the authors listed their achievements and those of other Bombay Africans, asking for an apology or relocation to their own settlement. When a letter of apology arrived, Streeter was enraged.[97] He accused headquarters of circumventing him and accepting the word of the Bombays, whom he suspended or imprisoned. In July, Zanzibar vice-consul Frederic Holmwood visited Mombasa to hear charges made by the elders of Mombasa that in Frere Town Streeter had detained and flogged several townspeople, including some slaves. Given the previous year's events, Streeter's actions caused widespread indignation, and Holmwood found relations between the mission and Mombasa "still full of danger." After a hearing with Mombasa elders, Holmwood was approached by Tom Smith, "a well-dressed and educated member of the station," who made "complaints of undue severity" regarding Streeter's methods of enforcing discipline in the Frere Town settlement. The vice-consul, who had already heard similar accusations from the Mombasa elders, decided to visit the mission.

Holmwood's subsequent investigation of Smith's charges provided a damning indictment of Streeter and his fellow missionaries.[98] Tens of Frere Town residents, some of whom bore the marks of extreme brutality, testified that Streeter had used the stick frequently to punish them. Eleven women came forward with complaints, all of whom had been flogged, as well as men whose "cases [were] too numerous to go into fully." Holmwood examined many who had been whipped with the *bakora*, a limber stick capable of producing horrifying results. One man, punished with sixty lashes, had scarcely survived, and another, flogged two years previously, was still suffering from the effects.

> His body was fearfully scarred across the side and partly over the stomach, where the scar of a large ulcer, which had formed in the wounds presented a ghastly appearance. His health was completely shattered by the effects. Anything approaching this in the way of severity I had never before witnessed.

Though Holmwood did not identify them as such, his report makes it clear that most of Streeter's victims were Bombay Africans. Of the eleven women who

---

[96] G. David, I. Semler, T. Smith, J. Ainsworth, and R. Keating to CMS, 28 Feb. 1881, G3A5/01(1880-81), CMS.

[97] Hutchinson to David, Semler, Smith, Ainsworth, and Keating, 19 May 1881, ibid.

[98] Holmwood to Kirk, 7 Jul. 1881 in Kirk to Granville, 21 Jul. 1881, FO 541/49, 294-8.

came forward to testify nine "were Christians and spoke English," and of the five men referred to by name, at least three were Bombays. Holmwood mentioned several others whose complaints place them in this group. Several wanted to accompany Holmwood to Zanzibar, because "since they had forwarded a petition [to the CMS headquarters]," Streeter's "harshness towards them had so increased that they lived in constant dread of it."

After a copy of Holmwood's report reached mission headquarters in London, the CMS Parent Committee recalled Streeter and sent W.S. Price to Frere Town for six months to patch up relations with the Muslim community and reinvestigate the Streeter scandal. Price exonerated two missionaries, Alfred Menzies and W.E. Taylor, but confirmed the charges against Streeter in Holmwood's report.[99] To his dismay Price learned that since the scandal other missionaries were still flogging freed slaves for some offenses and using the stocks.[100] He removed the stocks ("this relic of barbarism"), abolished flogging, compensated victims, and reaffirmed Bombay Africans in positions of authority.[101] His stay was nonetheless too brief to alter the missionaries' attitudes or stay the exodus of Bombay Africans.

The Streeter scandal merely increased missionary intolerance of misconduct. Upon Price's departure they became more dogmatic in favor of Streeter's discredited policy: that Africans must lead Christian lives to be full members of the church and to take part in mission work. After 1881 the missionaries stopped beating sinners to create saints. Instead, they cut them off from the church or dismissed them from the settlement. Less inclined to win back errant Christians, they as well demanded more of church members. They spurned industrial training and emphasized spiritual concerns. In the 1880s they were inclined, in effect, to become pastors, who saw as their primary responsibility the upholding of moral and religious standards for others to follow.

Apart from the period under Price's administration, Frere Town failed as an experiment in serving the aspirations of freed, much less runaway, slaves on the Kenya coast. The emergence of wealthy Bombay Africans indicates that some Christian ex-slaves had more economic opportunities than Muslim slaves, but the Christian community under Lamb and Streeter's rule held few other comparative attractions. Mombasans asserted to Holmwood that their own slaves were treated more humanely than Streeter's subjects, and their claim has the ring of truth.[102] The British consulate itself, except for the years when Price was there, sent few redeemed slaves to Frere Town. But apart from physical treatment, which was bad enough, or even the fact of their dependency on the mission for

---

[99] Price to Hutchinson, 4 Feb. 1882, G3A5/(1882), CMS.

[100] Price to Miles, 24 Jan. 1882, ibid. See the code of punishments drawn up by the Frere Town Finance Committee after the Holmwood investigation, Minutes, 9 Sep. 1881, G3A5/01(1880-81), CMS.

[101] Price journal, 6 Jan. 1882, Price to Miles, 24 Jan. 1882, and report, 6 Oct. 1882, G3A5/01(1882), CMS.

[102] See remarks of Mohammed b. Khamisi, Holmwood to Kirk, 7 Jul. 1882, FO 541/49, 289.

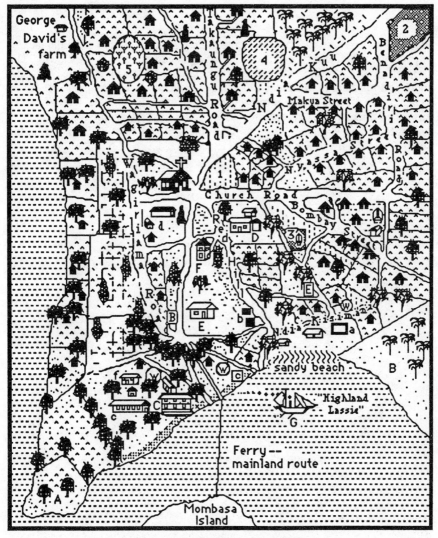

Frere Town, 1881

[based on 'Rough Plan', Jan. 1881, G3A5/01(1880-81), CMS]

A M. Isenberg's farm (own)	1 Cricket field	a Washing place
B I. Semler's farm (own)	2 Cemetery	b Carpentry & forge
C Wright House	3 Prison	c Girls' dormitory
D Hutchinson House	4 Swamp	d Boys' dormitory
E Venn Cottage	5 Rice swamp	f Matron's house
F Chichester House	B Bell	E Engine house
G CMS Steamer	C Boat house	W Well

land and income, the ex-slave residents in Frere Town suffered from the lack of support in establishing families and creating a community of their own. The drop-off in the birth rate and breakdown of marriages among the Bombays amidst increased physical punishment was the consequence of Christianization at any cost. Because Frere Town remained under white missionaries with outlooks similar to Streeter's, it retained only submissive freed slaves, mostly youngsters, and attracted no voluntary settlers. Until the establishment of British rule, the resident community at Frere Town remained effete.

4

Missionaries and Fugitive Slaves

Missionaries on the Kenya coast encountered few Africans hungrier for Christianity than fugitive slaves, or converts readier to "die for the Book." Maroons stood in marked contrast to coastal Muslims, who were indifferent if not hostile to the mission, and to the Miji Kenda, only a handful of whom had responded to the Gospel message. Their fervor also outshone those many freed slaves in Frere Town who regularly violated the Christian code. Fugitive slave converts lived disciplined lives and devoted themselves to building and farming rather than to idleness and drink. Maroons looked to the mission, which was opposed to slavery and connected to powerful political interests, to provide them the security they so desperately craved. Once Frere Town was established and the CMS looked inland to expand its enterprise, missionaries and maroons were drawn strongly toward one another.

The match was ill-starred for reasons obvious to both. Missionaries who yielded to the desire for these eager Christians risked attacks on missions by slave owners, the loss of innocent lives, and angry protests from Busaidi and British officials. Maroons who likewise pressed their affections on missionaries remained blind to the practical role of the mission, which was to conform with the interests of Zanzibar and Britain and to remain on good terms with coastal, Muslim, slave-owning communities. In spite of attempts by missionaries and maroons alike to sidestep these realities, both eventually concluded that their mutual survival depended on maroons staying off mission ground.

Relations were conducted therefore on the sly at inland settlements run by Miji Kenda converts. Hundreds of maroons attached themselves to Daniel Koi's village of Fuladoyo, and developed it into a prosperous, Christian, agricultural community. Slaves from Malindi, Takaungu, and Mombasa, as well as from parts of Miji Kenda took refuge there, and Koi's contacts with Frere Town drew freed slaves into their network. To European missionaries Fuladoyo was the ideal tryst, where they could steal the odd visit, take inspiration from the Christian zeal so pronounced there, and relish the phenomenon without assuming any responsibility.

Fuladoyo ultimately attracted the wrath of coastal slave owners, particularly the Mazrui of Takaungu. Maroon settlements made it harder for the Mazrui to control their plantation slaves, to trade in the hinterland, and to maintain their position on the coast as a quasi-independent sheikhdom. Eventually, in 1884, the Mazrui sent an army to destroy Fuladoyo and stamp out marronage throughout the hinterland. Maroons hoped that the mission connection would prevent slave owners' attacks, but when the Mazrui arrived, missionaries were nowhere to be seen. The maroons had to face them alone.

1. *Early Contacts*

Since the mid-1860s, slaves from the new grain plantations at Malindi and Mambrui had been escaping into the bush. Flight had its risks. The area they entered was controlled by the Oromo, who captured fugitives for sale on the coast or made them pay tribute and grow their food.[1] In the late 1860s, however, when the Oromo moved their herds north to escape Kwavi cattle raiders, maroon settlements sprang up. One of these was located at Jilore, twenty-five kilometers west of Malindi. Another, forty kilometers further west at Makongeni, likely came into existence at this time.[2] Pinned in as they were by arid bush north and west, and by the plantation belt on the east, the maroons looked south for friends and allies.

Their first contacts were with the Oromo's old Miji Kenda trading partners based in the hills west of Takaungu. Among the most familiar with the trans-Sabaki area was Yaa wa Medza, a Giriama Muslim, who lived at Kazi ya Moyo and served as a middle-man in the Oromo-Takaungu ivory trade. Since 1860 and probably before, Yaa and other Miji Kenda traders had conducted regular trading expeditions into Oromo country and in the process set themselves up as heads of their own little villages made up of wives, children, and slaves. Their contacts extended to the southern Miji Kenda as well as to Mombasa, and included the early CMS and United Methodist Free Church (UMFC) missionaries. In 1865 Thomas Wakefield, the first missionary to travel in the hinterland north of the Sabaki, used Yaa wa Medza as his guide.[3]

It is from this group of traders that Johann Rebmann at Rabai obtained a convert, Mwaringa wa Bengoa of Godoma, through whom the CMS became involved with fugitive slaves. Mwaringa and his slave wife, Mwadze, came to Rabai in 1861 after the Giriama banished him for some reason, probably because of his eccentricities. Rebmann taught Mwaringa to read, baptized him Christian and, after Mwaringa tried unsuccessfully to return to his people, Rebmann made him keeper of the CMS house in Mombasa. There Mwaringa fatally wounded Mwadze with an axe and, after being sent to India by Rebmann to get a "fresh start in life," returned to Mombasa only to incur the wrath of the Mombasans. After he bought a slave to be his wife and then sold her, Mwaringa returned to Giriama in 1870 and built himself a house in a tree at Petanguo near Godoma. This bizarre little man, who spent his days reading St. Luke's gospel above ground, eventually attracted a small group of Christian enquirers. Mwaringa's son, Mark Mlangulo, took instruction from Rebecca Wakefield at

---

[1] David and Nyondo to Lamb, 22 Feb. 1877, CA5/017; Lamb to CMS, 19 May 1877, CA5/M5, 91, CMS.

[2] Ibid; The first reference to Makongeni is in 1871, when it was used as a retreat by Mbaruk b. Rashid after his defeat by Ali b. Nasur's troops. Hinawy, *Al-Akida and Fort Jesus*, 35.

[3] T. Wakefield, *Footprints in Eastern Africa, or Notes of a Visit to the Southern Galas* (London: W. Reed, 1866), iv, 65, 79; Krapf journal, cv 13 Aug. 18[65?], UMFC *Magazine* (Feb. 1866), 70-1; Wakefield journal, cv 5 Sep. 1865, Ibid.(Mar. 1866), 210.

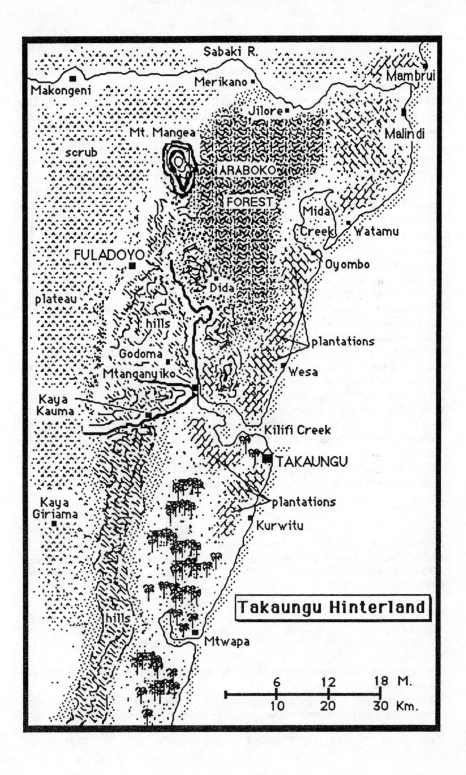

Takaungu Hinterland

Ribe.[4] Mwaringa's group also included a recent convert of Rebmann, Koi wa Besidi, son of the headman of Fuladoyo near Godoma. In 1870 or 1871 a Jilore maroon named Abdullah met Koi and thereby became known to the CMS. The maroons hoped that by befriending the Godomaites and adopting Christianity they would gain "British protection." Out of curiosity Rebmann sent Isaac Nyondo, a Miji Kenda convert at Rabai, to meet the Jilore maroons.[5] Nothing appears to have resulted from Nyondo's visit. Rebmann had little personal interest in runaway slaves, and at the time the maroons were busying for war.

In 1872 Jilore was attacked by slave owners. After regrouping at Merikano, Abdullah's people launched a series of retaliatory raids on plantations around Malindi and Mambrui over the succeeding months, killing a number of slave laborers.[6] Planters were forced to keep their slaves in stockades by night, and the sultan's troops were garrisoned east of Jilore to prevent the maroons from entering Malindi district.[7] For the next two years Abdullah's people moved into yet more remote areas, but security eluded them. They also began to split up. Abdullah and at least eight of his followers joined Mbaruk. Others moved to Makongeni, sixty-five kilometers west of Malindi, while others returned to Jilore. The latter had the more difficult time and by 1875 were kidnapping and selling children in order to feed themselves.

Soon after they arrived to build Frere Town, Price and the Bombay Africans learned of the plight of the maroons from Koi and the Giriama trader, Yaa wa Medza. The latter had recently moved to Godoma, where he had agnatic kin. What seems likely is that Yaa had come to regard Godoma as a base from which to develop new ivory trading contacts between the maroons, who occupied an area thick with elephants, and the southern coast now firmly controlled by the British-backed Busaidi, thereby breaking the ivory monopoly of the Mazrui of Takaungu. This would explain why in early 1875 sheikh Rashid b. Khamis of Takaungu confiscated Yaa's property, including his slaves, as well as why Price took a personal interest in Yaa's case.[8] At any rate, after Yaa attached himself to

---

[4] Rebmann to Venn, 2 May 1863, 27 Feb./ and 16 Nov. 1866, CA5/024; Jones to Hutchinson, 16 Apr. 1870, CA5/01; Chancellor to Hutchinson, 12 Apr. 1874, CA5/05, Parker to Lang, 21 Dec. 1886, G3A5/04, CMS. Mark received instruction as well in Zanzibar from Bishop W.G. Tozer of the UMCA. Tozer to Rebmann, 8 Sep. 1865, in Rebmann to Venn, 27 Feb. 1866, CA5/024, CMS; Price, *Third Campaign*, 159.

[5] David and Nyondo to Lamb, 22 Feb. 1877, CA5/017, CMS.

[6] Deimler report, *Mombasa Diocesan Magazine*, 1, 1(Oct. 1903), G3A5/016, CMS. A.M. Champion, "History of the Wa Giryama," 23 Jan. 1914, DC/MAL/2/3, KNA. The attacks on Jilore were led by Suleiman b. Abdullah, alias Kimenya ("hateful one"), a wealthy owner in the Mambrui area.

[7] Kirk to Granville, 6 Nov. 1873, C. 1064, 802; Fitzgerald, *Travel*, 121; Lugard, *Diaries*, I, 243.

[8] See "Frere Town and Coastal Slavery" in ch. 3. In the 1860s the Oromo attempted to break the Takaungu monopoly and establish trading relations with Mombasa, with the help of Yaa wa Medza and Thomas Wakefield. Wakefield, *Footprints*, 57, 67. For Yaa's agnatic kin in Godoma,Wakefield journal, cv. 5 Oct. 1865, UMFC *Magazine*

the Miji Kenda Christians, Frere Town initiated direct contact with Godoma and Jilore. In June 1875, George David and Jonah Mitchell visited Godoma, then journeyed north to Jilore, via Dida Ga(ra)licha, once inhabited by maroons but abandoned since 1874. At Jilore, David and Mitchell were disappointed to find the "area devoid of people."[9]

Several months later three Jilore maroons appeared in Rabai and asked Price, then spending several weeks there, for protection for themselves and their fellow maroons.[10] Price permitted the men to stay in Rabai on a month's probation, but they and the Mombasa slaves seeking refuge in Frere Town at this time were confronting Price with the dilemma of harboring fugitive slaves in defiance of local opinion and Muslim law. To protect the mission, Price asked the maroons to leave Rabai.[11] Contacts with the maroons remained active nevertheless. In 1876 Christian Mwaringa left Godoma and resettled at Jilore. None of the other Godomaites followed him, perhaps because Mwaringa soon died.[12] Mwaringa's place as head of the Godoma Christians was taken by Koi, recently baptized in Frere Town as David. By late 1876, Yaa wa Medza established a village to the north, near a maroon settlement and within reach of his old trading partners, the Oromo, who had returned to the area.

Yaa and Koi's Christian and maroon affiliations interested missionaries surveying the hinterland for new stations. In February 1877 Harry Binns, newly arrived in East Africa and stationed at Rabai, hiked to Jilore with Yaa and Koi as his guides. Binns considered establishing a station there for the Godamaites until he found Christians and maroons living in an area still controlled by the Oromo, who were themselves maintaining contacts with the UMFC in Ribe.[13] Six months later, Thomas Wakefield journeyed from Ribe through this same area, known to the the Oromo as Dida Galicha ("land of the slaves"), and was told by the Oromo that he could establish a mission "on condition that the missionaries would abstain from interfering with the settlements of runaway slaves."[14] They exacted a "protection" fee from coastal slave owners in return for not raiding their plantations.[15] Oromo also received payment for returning runaways, but they also profited by allowing maroon settlements to sprout in their territory. The Oromo extorted grain and ivory from the maroons and

---

Yaa's agnatic kin in Godoma,Wakefield journal, cv. 5 Oct. 1865, UMFC *Magazine* (March 1866), 215.

[9] David report of Godoma visit, n.d.[1875], CA5/06, David to Price, 21 Jul. 1875, CA4/M4, 108-9, CMS

[10] Their visit followed within days the arrived in Frere Town of Godomaites David Koi and his wife. Price journal, 17 and 23 Oct. 1875, CA5/023, Price to Wright, 5 Oct. 1872, CA4/M4, 128, CMS.

[11] See "Frere Town and Coastal Slavery" in ch. 3.

[12] Price journal, 23 May 1876, CA5/023, CMS.

[13] Binns Jilore report, Feb. 1877, CA5/03, CMS.

[14] Wakefield, "Fourth Journey," 371.

[15] Holmwood report, in Prideaux to Derby, 8 Feb. 1875, C. 1588, 65.

placed on them, as Binns later recalled, a "yoke which had become as galling as the Slavery of the coast."[16]

2. *Return to Rabai*

During 1878, Kwavi raids drove the Oromo north of the Sabaki River for good, and coastal masters immediately began scouring the countryside for maroons. They marched in force into the Malindi hinterland, destroyed Makongeni, and drove maroons from the area.[17] In the following year armed parties of slave owners returned to break up other settlements, and maroons scattered.[18] Many fled south and joined Koi's settlement at Fuladoyo or appealed for sanctuary at the mission stations in Rabai and Ribe. When maroons started arriving in Rabai sometime in mid-1878, the station was under the care of the Bombay African catechist, William Jones. He let them stay. By the time Binns returned from leave in November, they were well settled.

> When I went home in the summer of 1877 I left a comparatively small village formed of one square, containing from twenty to thirty houses. On my return I find a long street, extending away to the northwest, another to the northeast, another to the south. All the houses have been built entirely by the natives themselves, and their inmates are runaway slaves from the Giriama country.

By Giriama country, Binns meant Makongeni.[19] Binns found forty-four maroons in Rabai, where they continued arriving at the rate of one per day.

Binns allowed the maroons to remain in Rabai and later arrivals to settle, because Streeter had reversed Price's policy on runaways. Binns was also eager for fresh converts to supplement the few Rabai Christians that remained on the station since Bombay African farmers had abandoned Rabai during Lamb and Streeter's administrations. Newcomers lived with friends until they built their own houses and supported themselves by raising crops or with the earnings received for repairing mission buildings and for cultivating the mission's farm. By January 1879 one hundred had settled on the mission, their houses clustered on the west side of the station, and the Rabai Christians on the east. Runaways from Giriama owners also began to come in. Binns appointed Enoch Tosiri as headman of the Makongeni maroons, and they took an active part in mission life by joining the daily prayers and attending scripture, catechism, and singing classes. By mid-1879, their number had increased to three hundred.[20]

---

[16] Binns to Lang, 15 Feb. 1888, G3A5/05, CMS.

[17] Kirk to Salisbury, 12 Nov. 1879, C. 2720, 237.

[18] Menzies to Wright, 15 Jul. 1880, CA5/018, CMS.

[19] Jones to CMS, 10 Oct. 1878, CA5/014: Binns to Wright, 2 Nov. 1878, CA5/M5, 255; Binns annual letter, Nov. 1878, CA5/03, CMS. Binns' diary, 22 Nov. 1878, 30 Apr. 1879, 22 Nov. 1879, KNA; Kirk to Salisbury, 12 Nov. 1879, C. 2720.

[20] Streeter to Wright, 30 Jan. 1879, Binns to Wright, 23 Apr. 1879, CA5/M6, 19, 45, resp; Binns diaries, 9-10 Jan. 1879; Binns to Hutchinson, 21 Feb. 1881,

Slave owners soon forced the issue of CMS policy. In September 1879, fifty armed Giriama demanded that Binns hand over their runaway slaves. He refused, and the mission settlers prepared to fight. When the missionaries at Frere Town received word, they informed *liwali* Ali b. Nasur, who sent troops to Rabai to disperse the Giriama. By the time they arrived, the Giriama had already left, having received reports that Kwavi were in the area raiding cattle.[21] Binns and Streeter suspected that Nasur and the Mombasa Arabs were using the Giriama against the maroons as a way of creating an incident that could be reported to the sultan and result in the disclosure that Mombasa slaves had recently tried to gain refuge in Rabai. Binns was convinced that Majid b. Jabiri, whom the sultan had appointed on Nasur's recommendation as protector of the Rabai and Giriama, was the principal instigator. Over the past several years Jabiri had lived intermittently in Rabai, and many individual Rabai had complained to Binns that Jabiri had extorted their property.[22] Jabiri, who was also sheikh of the Mombasa Arabs, was regarded by the CMS and the Bombay Africans as an archenemy. In the months surrounding the September incident in Rabai, Jabiri had been embroiled in a court case brought by George David and J.W. Streeter against him charging cruel treatment of one of his slaves.[23] When the Rabai incident was put before the sultan for judgement, Jabiri was there bearing credentials from Nasur and representing the Giriama.[24] Kirk advised Binns, who also travelled to Zanzibar, to close his station to new runaways and tell everyone settled there to move elsewhere for their own safety.[25]

For some time, the maroon issue remained a source of conflict between coastal Muslims and the missions. The CMS promised to receive no more, but Binns continued admitting new runaways at Rabai, and at Jomvu, much closer to Mombasa and already the scene of Muslim-Christian confrontation, the Methodist mission started doing the same. When the Jomvu mission was established in 1877, protesting Muslims were told by Nasur, who accompanied the first missionary, that the plot of land in question had been given to the Methodists by the sultan of Zanzibar.[26] Any remaining good will in Jomvu toward the UMFC ended after the missionary-in-charge, R. C. Ramshaw, admitted runaways. In 1880 close to fifty, from Mombasa and Giriama, were settled on mission ground

---

G3A5/01(1880-81), CMS; CMS *Intelligencer* (Jan. 1881), 40-1; ibid, (July 1881), 440.

[21] Binns to Wright, 5 Oct. 1879 and Streeter to Wright, 1 Nov. 1879, CA5/M6, 83-4 and 86-7, resp., CMS; Knight to Wright, Nov. 1879, CMS *Intelligencer*, (1880), 167-9.

[22] Binns to Hutchinson, n.d. [continuation of 29 Dec. 1880 in the same file?], G3A5/01 (1880-81), CMS.

[23] See encl. in Pauncefote to Kirk, 21 Apr. 1880, FO 541/48, 437-38.

[24] Nasur to Bargash, 16 Mohurrum, FO 84/1574.

[25] Kirk to Salisbury, 9 Jan. 1880, ibid.

[26] Nasur "also made a speech...handing me over to them as the Sultan's friend, and urging them all to show me proper respect." Wakefield to Barton, 21 Apr. 1877, UMFC *Magazine* (Oct. 1877), 637.

and cultivating large plots.[27] Like Streeter and Binns, Ramshaw was prepared to defy local laws as long as he had the sultan's protection. Jomvu and Rabai were often visited by slave owners in search of runaways, but such visitors received no cooperation from the missionaries or residents. Missionaries were emboldened by Streeter's militancy and excited by the Christian propensities of runaways. They also found they could challenge Muslims in plantation areas without risk. Slave owners tried to recover runaways on the stations, but no missionary was ever threatened in the process. The slave owners could not complain to Zanzibar,

---

[27] Kirk to Granville, 19 Oct. 1880, FO 541/48, 530-1.

as the sultan's governor was unwilling to represent them. Nasur disliked the missionaries as much as did his subjects, and disliked the British even more, but unless the missionaries threatened British interests neither he nor the sultan could act. His only choice was to wait for the missionaries to overstep themselves and cause the British consul to intervene.

Streeter's abortive slave rising in July-September 1880 was Nasur's opportunity. For more than two months after Streeter hoisted his "freedom" flag over Frere Town, Nasur remained quiet and sent not a word to Zanzibar. Calm on the part of the townspeople also continued these many weeks. That was until, in early September, a Mombasa man trying to trace his runaway slave was murdered by the mission dwellers of Rabai.[28] In the past, other enquiring slave owners had merely risked a beating. When a vocal vigilante group was formed to go to Rabai and investigate, Frere Town's missionaries anticipated a bloodbath and sent a message to Kirk in Zanzibar. Nasur also took this opportunity to write the sultan. The sultan's promise of an investigation by Kirk cooled emotions. In early October Kirk and his assistant arrived in Mombasa and received complaints from the townspeople and then toured the missions. Kirk publicly asserted the right of the sultan's troops to use force against runaways on mission ground in the future, admonished missionaries to turn back runaways or return them to their owners, and required them to turn out those already settled.[29] The CMS in London, when apprised of events, instructed their missionaries not to retain runaways in future.[30]

At the end of the crisis, the Giriama slaves and Makongeni maroons remained on the station. Giriama owners received no assistance from Kirk, who was unwilling to "consider [any] claims from Pagans of the interior."[31] Few of the Makongeni group feared that their distant Malindi owners would travel in force to claim them. Runaways from the nearby coast, however, quickly left Rabai and Jomvu and travelled southwest into Duruma country where they built a settlement.[32] They did not resettle far enough away, because the following month Nasur dispatched his troops to break up the town. The inhabitants then scattered, some moving north into the Takaungu and Malindi hinterlands out of reach of Nasur's troops.[33] At this point many found their way to Fuladoyo, recently established by the Godoma leader, Daniel Koi.

---

[28] Binns to Hutchinson, 29 Dec. 1880, G3A5/01, (1880-81), CMS.

[29] Kirk to Granville, 22 Sep. 1880, and encls., 19 Oct. 1880, FO 541/48, 520-32.

[30] Resolutions of the General Committee, 16 Nov. 1880, in Hutchinson to Granville, 14 Jan. 1881, FO 541/49, 201.

[31] Kirk to Granville, 4 Apr. 1881, FO 541/29, 247. See also Binns diary, 12 Oct. 1880, KNA.

[32] Binns diary, 15-6 Sep. 1880, KNA.

[33] Ramshaw to Felkin, 25 Nov. 1880, G3A5/01(1880-81), CMS; Kirk to Granville, 14 Nov. 1880, FO 541/48, 544; Binns to Lang, 15 Nov. 1888, G3A5/05, CMS.

3. Fuladoyo

In 1878 the Godomaites quarrelled when Koi was in Frere Town receiving instruction and broke up soon after his return. Some moved north and joined the Jilore maroons, and in 1879 Koi took the remaining few of his followers and re-settled in the southern foothills of Mt. Mangea at Fuladoyo, near his father's village. Fuladoyo had excellent water and was situated in a fertile area. Streeter, who knew personally both Koi and his principal follower, Jeremiah Mwangi, visited Fuladoyo months before the September 1880 crisis, and was visited by them as the crisis developed. Streeter learned from Koi that the maroons were located in the Takaungu hinterland and he became enthusiastic about recruiting converts among runaways. After his meeting with Streeter, Koi returned to Fuladoyo and began admitting runaways, including fourteen slaves belonging to Rashid b. Salim who had recently run away from Takaungu.[34]

Months later, following the Kirk investigation and the Rabai-Jomvu exodus, Fuladoyo began to swell with maroon additions from the south. In April 1881 one hundred ninety-seven maroon settlers were counted, and their number continued to rise. By the end of 1883 between six and seven hundred runaway slaves were living in Fuladoyo, making its population larger than any of the mission stations.[35] Fuladoyo became as prosperous and orderly as it was large. Daniel Koi made residence conditional on Christian observances, providing the first example of an indigenous, evangelical Christian movement in East Africa. Koi's CMS connection was reinforced by visits to Frere Town by himself and Mangi, and by visits to Fuladoyo by missionaries, Bombay Africans, and *mateka* schoolboy instructors. Even though Frere Town and Rabai missionaries had adopted a non-harboring policy since the Kirk investigation, their involvement with Koi provided maroons the shelter they required.

Although Streeter was required to turn away runaways from CMS stations, Koi's maroon followers at Fuladoyo kept alive Streeter's hopes of gaining converts. After the crisis, Streeter sent two Frere Town schoolboys to Fuladoyo to help instruct the children and adults under Koi.[36] But Streeter was not supported by the other missionaries and in March 1881, when Binns visited Fuladoyo, he tried to break the connection. Binns was disturbed that Koi was risking Fuladoyo's destruction by allowing in t he maroons. He found the Fuladoyans

---

[34] Binns to CMS, 27 Mar. 1879 and Handford to Wright, 2 Dec. 1879, CA5/M6; Streeter to Wright, 17 Jul. 1880, CA5/M6, 136-9; Handford to Wright, 8 Sep. 1880, CA5/011, CMS.. His contact with Koi explains how and why Streeter's issued his summons to the maroons to join the slave revolt during the September 1880 crisis. Se ch. 3.

[35] Binns to Hutchinson, 6 Apr. 1881, G3A5/01(1880-81); Price to Miles, 23 Jan. and 7 Mar. 1882 and Price journal, 9 Jan. 1882, G3A5/01(1882); Parker to Lang, 21 Dec. 1886, G3A5/04, CMS.

[36] Binns to Hutchinson, 8 Apr. 1881, Streeter to Menzies, 21 May 1881, G3A5/01(1880-81), CMS. The boys were Adam Krapf and Christopher Boston, In 1882 Boston helped in the establishment of the CMS mission in the Teita Hills. Wray, *Kenya*, 21-2. Boston appears, seated at Wray's right, in an engraving in the CMS *Gleaner*, January 1885.

"armed to the teeth" and anticipating an attack from the Takaungu Mazrui. He rejected Koi's request for a missionary. "I would soon get into difficulties with the Arabs," Binns reported to London, "and would simply be outlawed by [my] own consul."[37] Binns' visit occurred several months prior to the Frere Town scandal, which ended Streeter's administration and returned W.S. Price to the Mombasa scene.

Upon his arrival at Frere Town, one of Price's first acts was reconsideration of CMS relations with Fuladoyo. During the months surrounding the Frere Town crisis, the mission had been out of touch with Koi, and Holmwood had not delved into the maroon question. Price wanted badly to resolve it, however, lest another incident on the heels of the Streeter disaster risk destroying the mission. In January 1882 after meeting Koi in Frere Town, Price wrote to acting consul S.B. Miles, seeking advice on what the CMS should do about the maroons, who "were settling down near our branch mission station in Fuladoyo." Price was concerned about the "continual, fresh additions to the colony" which if they continued would place the mission in a "perplexing position." He claimed the CMS had warned the maroons against entering Fuladoyo, "but it is highly probable and not unnatural that Arabs, and others whose slaves have taken refuge there, should come to the conclusion that we have connived at, if not actually encouraged, the movement."[38]

Before receiving Miles reply, Price decided to see Fuladoyo for himself. In late February he traveled, by way of the old Giriama Christian settlement in Godoma, and reached Fuladoyo on the 27th.[39] Price arrived with the anxieties which had occasioned his letter to Miles. He expected the maroons to be the worst sort: "a large number of half-wild and desperate men--the scum of the population--herded together in wretchedness and confusion." The people whom the missionary encountered were instead the stuff of reverie.

> They had only a few days notice of our intended visit, and must have set to work at once and with a will to prepare for it. Several large trees had been felled, and laid from bank to bank to form a bridge for us to cross the river, and a splendid wide road had been cleared through the thick wood which leads up thence to their village. A great crowd was collected on the opposite bank, and as we stepped from the bridge on to Fulladoyo ground, a shout of joy rang thro' the forest, and echoed among the Hills, which produced sensations in me which I shall never

---

[37] Binns to Hutchinson, 6 Apr. 1881, G3A5/01(1880-81).

[38] Price journal, 9 Jan. 182, and Price to Miles, 23 Jan. 1882, CA5/01(1882), CMS.

[39] Price, "Notes of a visit to Godoma and Fuladoyo," 23 Feb. 1882, G3A5/01(1882), CMS. Of the original Godoma Christians, only two families, headed by the brothers Petros and Daniel Muchanje, remained. Paulos Menza, Andreas Randu, Johannes Wanje, Phillipos Masha, and Mark Mlangulo, had broken from Christianity and moved away. The CMS attempted in 1882 to revive the Godoma Christians by relocating their settlement on Mwaiba hill, and by posting an African catechist there to teach and minister to the community. Of the original group, only Petros moved to Mwaiba, and the site attracted few followers. Price report, 6 Oct. 1882, part 3 (Kamlikeni), G3A5/01 (1882), and Handford to Lang, 29 Dec. 1883, G3A5/01(1883), CMS.

forget, but which I cannot describe. Then came the shaking of hands. Men and women crowded upon us, each one eager for a shake, and yambo yambo sana [Hello! Hello! Good to see you!) greeted us on all sides.

On emerging from the wood we came at once upon a large village, or rather a small town: the best built and most orderly kept of any I have seen in this country. I found a comfortably settled and well ordered community, meeting together morning and evening in a place or worship which they have put up at their own cost, to hear the Word of God, and join in Prayer and Praise. I saw, too, on all sides the signs of industry and prosperity. There was altogether an air of uncommon respectability about the place. The homes are neatly and strongly built, and the shambas [fields] are well cultivated and rich with Indian corn, and other grain and fruits.

In the evening religious services were held in an open shelter in the center of town, the congregation overflowing onto the veranda. Koi delivered the sermon

and in simple and earnest language set forth Jesus as the true Ark of refuge, provided by a merciful God for perishing sinners. Then followed the Prayers: a selection from the Book of C. Prayer, of which now, thanks to Bishop Steer, we have a fair translation; and very touching and soul stirring it was to hear them all as with one voice joining in the Confession, Lords Prayer and General Thanksgiving. I never witnessed greater decorum and attention in any congregation, which is much to say when we consider who and what these poor people lately were, and what in fact they still are: runaway slaves.

Price left Fuladoyo the following morning:

I turned my back on Fulladoyo with a feeling of intense thankfulness to Almighty God for all I have seen and heard. I cannot help feeling that here we have the beginning of a great movement and one that bids fair to do more to give a death blow to the wretched slave system of this country than all your Treaties and men of war.

These vivid impressions failed to prevent the CMS from withdrawing its support from Fuladoyo. On his return to Frere Town Price was handed Miles's letter advising the mission not to intervene in affairs between the maroons and their owners.[40] Though in strong sympathy with the maroons, Price promised Miles that the CMS would observe a hands-off policy.[41]

With the British consulate opposing CMS support for maroons, the sultan's liwali of Mombasa, Muhammad b. Suleiman, put greater pressure on the CMS to declare a clean break. Until April, Price had been on good terms with the governor, but in May, relations soured. Muhammad, seizing an opportunity to place the CMS on the defensive, used the occasion of Price's visit to the Shimba hills, where Price hoped to establish a mission among the Digo, to accuse him

---

[40] Miles to FO, 31 May 1882, FO 84/1621.
[41] Price to Miles, 7 Mar. 1882, G3A5/O1(1882), CMS.

of being in league with Mbaruk b. Rashid, then in revolt.[42] Muhammad ordered
Frere Town blockaded and despatched 250 soldiers into the Shimba hills. The
governor then sent complaints to Zanzibar alleging that Price and his fellow
missionaries had been luring slaves away from their Mombasa masters. "They
never cease to injure your people residing in this town," wrote Muhammad, "and
seduce their slaves and entice them by what pleases them, so that many lately
have fled to Fordo [Fuladoyo]."[43]

The charges were groundless, but they unsettled Price, then preparing to return to England. When passing through Zanzibar en route home, Price persuaded
Sultan Bargash that the missionaries were innocent of any wrong-doing and
forced Muhammad to withdraw his statements and tender an apology.[44] Nevertheless Muhammad, who had been trying to break relations between the CMS
and Fuladoyo rather than prove mission complicity with Mbaruk, had pinned the
runaway stigma on Price. To remove it, Price wrote to Frere Town admonishing
his colleagues to have nothing further to do with maroons.[45] In July the Frere
Town Finance Committee voted to break all connections with Fuladoyo and ask
Koi to "relinquish his position as chief."[46] In October Binns and his wife,
Anna, traveled to Fuladoyo and asked Koi to leave the settlement and thereby
demonstrate that the CMS had no connection with the maroons.[47] The CMS
turned its attention to the Giriama Christian settlement at Mwaiba, twelve miles
southwest of Fuladoyo, in the hopes of siphoning off the Giriama and other non-
maroons at Fuladoyo under Koi.

Daniel Koi remained at Fuladoyo. George David, catechist at Mwaiba, for a
while believed that the maroons were leaving and that Koi was attracting converts among the Giriama and Kauma. In June 1883, however, the runaways were
still in Fuladoyo, and Koi was still their leader.[48] Koi's "conduct for some time
has been a perfect enigma to me," wrote an exasperated Binns in August 1883.
"I can only account for it by the fact, that years ago before he became a
Christian, he was afflicted with insanity, for a time, and it seems that the trouble
of having so many people to look after, has brought on the same again."[49]

Rising insecurity in Fuladoyo may account for Koi's indecisiveness. Since
1880 the maroons had lived in an uneasy peace with the Giriama and the Mazrui
of Takaungu. To reduce provocation for attack, the Fuladoyans refused to admit
runaways from nearby areas. By 1882 most of the maroons were from the more

---

[42] Price account, n.d.[Jun. 1882], G3A5/01(1882), CMS.

[43] Muhammad b. Suleiman to Bargash, 21 and 22 May 1882, FO 84/1621.

[44] Miles to Granville, 24 Jun. 1882, ibid; Price account, n.d.[Jun. 1882],
G3A5/01(1882), CMS.

[45] Price to East African missionaries, 19 Jun. 1882, G3A5/01(1882), CMS.

[46] Minutes, 5 Jul. 1882, ibid.

[47] Binns to Lang, 21 Oct. 1882, ibid; diary, 4 Oct. 1882, KNA.

[48] David report, 27 Dec. 1882, Binns to David, 18 Jun. 1883, G3A5/01(1883),
CMS.

[49] Binns to Lang, 3 Aug. 1883, ibid.

distant points of Malindi and Mombasa.[50] The chance of open hostilities between Fuladoyo and its neighbors nevertheless remained. In 1882 Fuladoyo was
nearly attacked by some coastal Muslims incited by Salim b. Khamis of Takaungu, and in 1883 the Giriama and the Fuladoyans came close to a scrap.[51]

The maroons, hoping for missionary intercession, were putting pressure on
Koi to remain at Fuladoyo. The missionaries may have believed they were disentangling themselves from the maroon settlement, but their exchange visits
with Koi and posting teachers there were conveying the opposite impression.
Though the CMS broke formal relations following its July 1883 Finance
Committee meeting, Binns kept in touch with Koi, and George David became
personally involved in Fuladoyo, the people of whom David regarded as
"Mzungu's [the British's] people"[52] Koi seems to have been willing to respond
to the missionary request to move away with his Giriama converts, but the maroons considered him irreplaceable.[53] Perhaps under threat or merely trying to
buoy up hopes, Koi yielded and postponed repeatedly his departure from the settlement. Vacillation cost Koi his life.

4. The Fuladoyo Wars of 1883-84

With the CMS cleanly distanced from Fuladoyo in the British consul's eye,
slave owners prepared an attack from the coast. In August 1883, Binns planned
to travel once more to Fuladoyo and talk to Koi about moving with his followers to Jilore, where the CMS had acquired some land.[54] Word had come that Koi
was serious about leaving. The move was considered too late. Before Bins arrived from Rabai, an three thousand armed men stormed Fuladoyo. Composed of
slave owners and followers from Malindi, Takaungu, and Mombasa, the force
met runaways in a pitched battle, eventually driving the maroons into the bush.
The attackers burned Fuladoyo to the ground, pillaged the area, and carried away
the grain stored from the recent harvest.[55] Casualties were light on both sides,
but one captive was taken. Koi, who had not taken up arms, was turned over to
the slave owners by the Giriama. Koi was then taken to the coast, where he
"reportedly died a horrible death."[56]

---

[50] Price to Miles, 23 Jan. 1882, G3A5/01(1882), CMS.
[51] Price journal, 8 Feb. 1882, G3A5/01(1882); Binns to David, 18 Jun. 1883,
G3A5/01 (1883), CMS.
[52] Binns to David, 18 Jun. 1883, ibid.
[53] Koi's only possible replacement, Jeremiah Mwangi, left Fuladoyo in late 1882,
to become a catechist for the CMS in Rabai. Shaw to Lang, 23 Jan. 1883, G3A5/
01(1883), CMS.
[54] Binns to Lang, 31 Aug. 1883, ibid.
[55] Kirk to Granville, 9 Nov. 1883, C. 3849, 128; Binns to Lang, 27 Nov. 1883,
G3A5/01 (1883), Parker to Lang, 21 Dec. 1886, G3A5/04, CMS; Lugard, Diaries, I,
94.
[56] Stock, History of the CMS, III, 91-2; Binns to Lang, 27 Nov. 1883,
G3A5/01(1883), CMS; Handford report, n.d., CMS Intelligencer, New Series, 10
(Mar. 1885), 167;

The attack touched off an all-out war between the maroons of Fuladoyo and their former owners. In December and January parties of slave owners moved through the countryside to capture renegade runaways.[57] Maroons retaliated with ferocity. "There is a war to the death between the *watoro* [runaway slaves] and the Waswahili," wrote missionary John Handford from Frere Town. "The *watoro* are roaming all over the country killing every Swahili they meet. Three have been killed only a short distance from us."[59] They committed many atrocities. The hands and feet of their enemies were severed. Sometimes their palms were cut out and jammed into the victims' mouths. At least one Arab was flayed.[58] The effects of the Fuladoyo attack and the subsequent raiding by slave owners kept the maroons on the move and made it difficult for them to get food. The entire area from Malindi to Mombasa was affected. "The country is filled," reported Kirk, "with armed bands of men forced to subsist on plunder."[60]

In some ways the spreading turmoil worked to the maroons' advantage. Depredations by roving Swahili and maroon raids in the Takaungu area weakened Salim b. Khamis's hold on his territory. In January 1884 his rule was undermined further by the sudden appearance of Mbaruk b. Rashid, who began pressuring the maroons to join his group.[61] In order to counter Mbaruk's bid for influence in the Takaungu hinterland, Salim tried to entice the maroons into joining him instead. He offered the maroons the goods that Mbaruk had--guns, powder, and protection--and included grain stores as well. In exchange, Salim wanted the Fuladoyans to cease raiding, give him their allegiance, allow Arab traders to pass through Fuladoyo, and stay clear of the Mazrui grain exporting centers of Mtanganyiko and Konjora.[62]

Despite these pressures, most Fuladoyans avoided alliances with coastal Muslims while rebuilding their settlement. Perhaps they feared the protection of slave owners as much as, if not more than, their armed attacks. A few joined Mbaruk after the destruction of Fuladoyo.[63] Others joined raiding parties or simply resumed living in Fuladoyo. Koi's settlement sprouted once more. Old townsmen returned from the bush, and new runaway slaves came to settle. The new Fuladoyo grew even larger than the old. By early March 1884 eight hundred lived there, some two hundred more than before the attack. The new Fuladoyans

---

[57] Kirk to Granville, 21 Jan. 1884, C. 4523, 47; Handford to Lang, 29 Dec. 1883, G3A5/01(1884), CMS.

[59] Handford journal, 29 Jan. 1884, in Handford to Lang, n.d.; and Shaw to Handford, 19 Feb. 1884, ibid; Kirk to Granville, 31 May 1884, FO 541/26, 190.

[58] Handford to Lang, 19 Apr. 1884, quoting an undated letter from G. David, G3A5/01 (1884), CMS.

[60] Kirk to Granville, 21 Jan. 1884, C. 4523, 47.

[61] Handford journal, 19 Jan. 1884 and David to Handford, 10 Feb. 1884, as in Handford journal, G3A5/01(1884), CMS. Mbaruk was interested in getting the runaways of Makongeni on his side and reportedly promised to move his capital from Gasi to Mt. Mangea in order to protect Fuladoyo and Makongeni.

[62] David to Handford, 10 Feb. 1885, as in Handford journal, ibid.

[63] Kirk to Granville, 9 Nov. 1883, C. 3849, 128.

followed the old ways, keeping to themselves and avoiding contact with the Takaungu Mazrui. They continued, too, to "follow the Book" and to seek British protection.[64] The fate of the maroons was of particular concern to the Bombay African catechists in Mwaiba, where George David reported on their activities. In March 1884 he was replaced by Ishmael Semler, who learned that the Fuladoyans had received another proposition from Salim. They would be allowed to live in the Takaungu area under his protection on condition that they give up Christianity. Salim tempted them with the assurance that they would be able to marry more than one wife.[65] Semler was impressed by the Fuladoyans, who, apart from the few prepared to accept Salim's offer, "prefer dying for the Book."

> We believe that it was the Book that saved us from our enemies last time, and it is the foundation of our settlement in that place. The people say, shall we leave the book and join him to be slaves again? We said no.[66]

As they renewed the missionary connection, the maroons sought other allies to challenge the slave owners. In late March the Fuladoyans joined the northern Giriama in an effort to defeat Salim's troops and to obtain better guarantees of peace from Takaungu. On 22 March Salim's troops, under the command of his nephew, Mubarak, attacked the Giriama in the neighborhood of Fuladoyo. Salim was angry with the Giriama for an alleged violation of an agreement giving the Mazrui a monopoly of the Giriama grain trade. The Mazrui also needed slaves for their plantations. With support from the Fuladoyans, the Giriama defeated the Mazrui forces. They lured the enemy into the dry plain west of Mt. Mangea region and, when their pursuers wearied, laid an ambush. Disaster ensued for the Mazrui, at the battle scene and along their path of retreat. Hundreds were slain by Giriama poison arrows and by Fuladoyan guns probably obtained from the Mazrui themselves under the old peace terms. One estimate placed Mazrui losses at 568 killed, as opposed to ten Giriama.[67] Salim sued for peace, promising that henceforth he would regard the Fuladoyans as free people.

Maroons had learned how to bargain for protection. As Christians in a Muslim land, the Fuladoyans like the early Rabai settlers had drawn the missionaries to them. The CMS connection stayed the hands of the sultan's forces, while the maroons built up their settlements, prospered, and made alliances with other Africans. The Bombay Africans kept them informed of CMS and British plans,

---

[64] David to Handford, 10 Feb. 1885, as in Handford journal, G3A5/01(1884), CMS.

[65] Semler to Handford, n.d., as in Handford journal, 27 Mar. 1884, ibid.

[66] Ibid. Semler encouraged the maroons: "I told [them] that as you think that it is the book, wh. is the foundation of our settlement you had better die for the Book. The Lord will guard you and protect you, but if you leave the Book the Lord will leave you and you will be slaves again."

[67] Handford to Lang, 17 May 1884, ibid. See also Handford journal, 27 Mar. and 5 Apr. 1884, ibid; Hardinge to Salisbury, 17 Feb. 1896, C. 8274, 61; Macdougall, "Notes on the History of the Wanyika," 31 Mar. 1914, DC/MAL/2/3, KNA: Koffsky, "History of Takaungu," 108-11 (this last source mis-dates the battle to "1881-82").

passed on gossip from Mombasa, and hid them from missionary view on their visits to Rabai. Under William Jones, Rabai became a refuge for runaways in its own right.[68] The Fuladoyans also attracted the attention of Mbaruk b. Rashid, proverbial rebel against Zanzibari rule. Potential support for Mbaruk gave the Fuladoyans leverage with Salim b. Khamis, who had accepted the sultan's authority in order to guarantee his position among the Mazrui. The maroons were becoming important, too, to the Giriama and other Miji Kenda expanding north in the wake of the retreat of Oromo pastoralists. Fuladoyo was situated in a fertile area coveted by grain farmers moving up from the south. Grain had export value because of the markets developed by coastal slave owners, and Giriama and Kauma sold in the ports controlled by the Mazrui of Takaungu. Miji Kenda-maroon cooperation reduced Mazrui control over the grain export trade, enabling the Giriama to colonize the Malindi hinterland and gradually supplant slave production there. The alliance was less a formal arrangement than part of an ongoing process. As slave-based production competed with Miji Kenda farmers in the hinterland, the numbers of runaway slaves increased. Within ten years after Fuladoyo's resurrection, the number of maroons occupying the hinterland totalled an estimate three thousand.[69]

5. The Impact of Marronage on Takaungu

Fuladoyo's survival also helped to ease conditions of servitude on the many Mazrui plantations in the Takaungu neighborhood. Takaungu town and the surrounding district had been developed by the junior Zaheri branch of the Mazrui family, after Seyyid Said drove them out of Mombasa in 1837.[70] They established scattered slave plantations north and south as far as twenty-five kilometers inland. Around Takaungu, center of cultivation in the south, plantations were located at Mnarani on the Kilifi creek, Makonde, Mikinduni, and Kurwitu. North of Kilifi creek, where most slaves were located, plantations were concentrated at Konjora, Mtondia, Roka, and Watamu. The domain of the Zaheri ultimately extended from Kurwitu to Mtataje, a distance of nearly eighty-five kilometers with plantations totalling 160,000 acres.[71] Until mid-1884, the district's annual

---

[68] See ch. 5.

[69] Macdougall quarterly report, 8 Apr. 1901, CP 71/25, KNA.

[70] The Mazrui of Mombasa were descendants of Mahomed b. Othman of the Ghafiri clan in Oman, from whence he came in 1730 as the Imam's governor of Mombasa. For the final years of Mazrui rule in Mombasa, see Gray, *The British in Mombasa*, 173-92; S.A.b.A. Al-Mazrui, "History of the Mazrui Dynasty of Mombasa," J.R. Ritchie, trans.(typescript, n.d.), 55-70. The senior Uthmani branch of the Mazrui settled at Gasi on the coast forty-two kilometers south of Mombasa.

[71] Gissing to Kirk, 14 Sep. 1884, FO 541/26, 239; Weaver to Craufurd, 23 Jul. 1896, CP 75/46, KNA; Hardinge, *Diplomatist in the East*, 158. For more description of Mazrui expansion in and around Takaungu, based mainly on accounts of Ludwig Krapf and Charles New, see Koffsky, "History of Takaungu," 31-95. Also Morton, "Slaves, Fugitives, and Freedmen," 57-60.

exports of millet, maize, sesame, rice, and beans totalled an estimated fifty-five hundred tons.[72]

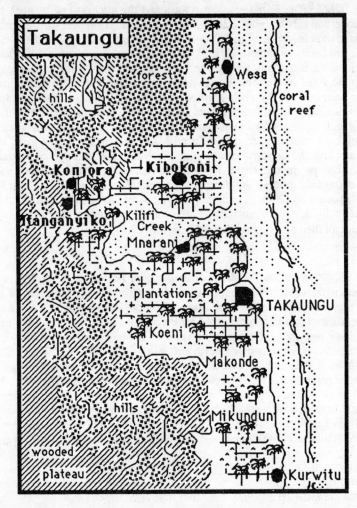

C.E. Gissing journeyed through this district in 1884 soon after the Zaheri Mazrui had conceded defeat to the maroons of Fuladoyo. He noted of the slaves that "many run away and join bands of Watoro."[73] At Mtondia plantation Gissing also found that the slaves were:

---

[72] Gissing to Kirk, 16 Sep. 1884, FO 84/1679.
[73] Gissing to Kirk, 14 Sep. 1884, FO 541/26, 240.

kindly treated by the Arabs; each one has a 'shamba', or garden of his own; they have one Friday, which is their Sunday, to themselves, also the next day is given them to cultivate their 'shambas' or do as they like in; the remaining five days they work for their masters; they receive two meals a day, and special pay during the time of harvest; the ordinary pay of a labourer during harvest is one basket each day of the produce he has been collecting in; the basket is as large as our ordinary market basket; the produce is given in in the ear not beaten out; the man beats it out at home, and either sells it or takes it back to where his house is.

Growing restraint toward slaves was an important consequence of the rise of Fuladoyo and its success in repelling attacks launched from Takaungu and other coastal towns. The Zaheri could no longer afford to mistreat their slaves, therefore, or sustain control over their agricultural production. If an owner "claimed too oppressively large a share," Hardinge later observed of the Zaheri's slaves, "they would prefer to run away into the bush...subsisting...on grain stolen from their former village, or else join one of the Watoro Settlements."[74]

Slave plantations in Takaungu district contained as many as three or four hundred people, each governed by a resident senior member of the Zaheri or, as occasionally happened, placed in charge of a ranking slave. At least Shaka and Makonde had at times a slave as principal overseer, and Koeni, or Choeri, took its name from the head slave of one of the sultans of Takaungu, Khamis b. Khalfan.[75] Serving as small commercial and social centers, the plantations drew visitors from the surrounding area. All had year-round wells, a decided attraction in an area lacking fresh surface water. Several plantations were market centers for Oromo, Liangulo, and Miji Kenda who traded their cattle, grain, or ivory for cloth, iron implements, and palm wine. Religious and social life probably centered around the mosque, built by the Takaungu sultans primarily for Arab owners and visitors, but used by slaves, many of whom were converted to Islam. European passers-by often referred to these plantations as "Swahili villages."

Giriama expansion during the 1880s also limited Mazrui power in the hinterland and eased plantation slavery. The retreat of the Oromo together with improved fighting techniques enabled the Giriama to expand north from their capital, Kaya Giriama.[76] Together with the Kauma, who were also expanding, the Giriama converted what had been rangeland for the Oromo into a grain belt for themselves. The Zaheri Mazrui monopolized the Giriama and Kauma export trade until the Giriama and Fuladoyans defeated the Zaheri in 1884. Thereafter, increasing quantities of Giriama grain were sold to Swahili and Hindu traders, who traveled from Mombasa to Mtanganyiko (under the nominal authority of the sultan of Zanzibar) at harvest time. Swahili traders often visited Giriama and

---

[74] Hardinge to Salisbury, 12 April 1896, FO 403/226, 180.

[75] Greffulhe, "Voyage de Lamoo," 341; Pigott diary, 14 Sep. 1889, FJL; Handford journal, 7 Mar. 1884, G3A5/01(1884), CMS. For a partial, unsourced list of outlying villages and their clan founders, Koffsky, "History of Takaungu," 68-9.

[76] C. Brantley,"Gerontocratic Government: Age-Sets in Pre-colonial Giriama," *AJIAI*, 49, 2(1979), 112-33; idem, *The Giriama*, 27-32.

eventually gained control of the hinterland ivory trade from the Oromo and Takaungu Mazrui.[77]

Giriama traders also settled along the fringes of Takaungu district. In the 1880s some moved into the Rare river valley north of Mtanganyiko and stimulated the growth of Mazrui markets at Mtondia, Konjora, Roka, Araboko, and Oyombo by selling grain, especially eleusine.[78] The Giriama founder of Dida, Ngonyo wa Mwavua, became wealthy through his trade in slaves, ivory, and cattle.[79] Ngonyo, the most powerful figure north of Mtanganyiko, accepted as blood brothers two of the most influential Zaheri of Takaungu: Aziz and Mubarak, the nephews of Salim b. Khamis.[80] In 1887 Salim himself acknowledged the growing importance of his neighbors by gaining admission, at great personal expense, into the fraternity of Giriama elders.[81] The level of economic self-interest in these alliances is suggested by the growth at this time of Takaungu as a major slave trading outlet for slave caravans traversing Giriama territory en route from the interior to the coast.[82]

Giriama farmers, as converts to Islam, also settled inside Zaheri territory on or close to many slave plantations.[83] They were called *mahaji*, the term used

---

[77] Taylor diary, 17 Oct. and 22 Nov. 1887, G3A5/05, CMS; Fitzgerald, *Travels*, 138, 144, 154; Barrett, "Customs of the WaSania" 15 Oct. 1908, and n.a., "Notes on the Wasanye," 13 May 1931, "Native Tribes and Their Customs," I, 2, KNA; Maclean to PC, 4 Apr. 1909, CP 62/43, KNA; Hobley political report, "Trade," 29 Jul. 1913, DC/MAL/2/3, KNA.

[78] Fitzgerald, *Travels*, 144; Hardinge to Salisbury, 12 Apr. 1896, C. 8274, 87.

[79] Ngonyo was the son of the first wife of Abraham Begonja, a Rabai slave of probable Digo origin, who converted to Christianity in 1861. Abraham's second wife bore him Isaac Nyondo, who became the husband of Polly Christian Nyondo, among the first Bombay Africans to work at Rabai. Ngonyo wa Mwavua was a blood brother to a prominent local ivory and slave trader, Mwinga wa Kivinga. When the Giriama expanded north, Ngonyo traveled with his adoptive Digo father to Rare, became involved in trade, and eventually established his own settlement in Dida. Through his numerous followers, economic power, and personality, Ngonyo eventually assumed the leadership of one of Giriama's largest clans, Akiza. Rebmann to CMS, 22 Apr. 1861, Ca5/024, CMS. CMS *Gleanrer*, 8(1881), 71; Interview with Tuguu wa Baya, Rabai, 19 Sep. 1973; Hardinge to Salisbury, 17 Feb. 1896, and encl., C. 8274, 63, 65; A.M. Champion, "Report on Illicit Ivory Trade in Giryama Country," 31 Mar. 1913, DC/MAL/2/1, KNA; Hobley inspection report, 10 Aug. 1915, CP 17/61, KNA; Brantley, *The Giriama*, passim.

[80] Macdougall to Pigott, 3 Dec. 1895, CP 75/46, KNA.

[81] Taylor diary, 19 Oct. 1887, G3A5/05, CMS; Hardinge to Salisbury, 12 Apr. 1896, C. 8274, 87.

[82] See ch. 6.

[83] References to *mahaji* re Konjora, Koeni, Kibokoni, Majajani, Mavueni, Sokoke, Tezo, Roka, and Araboko from Pigott diary, 4 Dec. 1889, FJL; Macdougall to Pigott, 20 Aug. 12 Oct.[two letters], 24 Nov. and 13 Dec. 1895, CP 75/46, KNA; Hardinge to Salisbury, 2 Dec. 1895, FO 403/211, 219; Hardinge to Salisbury, 17 Feb. 1896, encl. C. 8274, 64; Macdougall to Nairobi, 17 Jun. 1910, CP 64/62, KNA; Palethorpe

along the southern coast with reference to Islamized Miji Kenda.[84] At Kibo-koni, *mahaji* accepted the authority of the slave governor, Akida Bakari. Bakari was himself the proprietor of several estates, having acquired title from the Zaheri to the produce thereof, terms perhaps extended to these new settlers and to plantation slaves themselves.[85]

The Mazrui, who had lost the means of coercing their slaves, used incentives to keep their allegiance. Slave plantations were becoming usufruct properties, while agricultural slaves were becoming tenant farmers. *Mahaji* were welcome on underutilized land in order to stimulate productivity near the ports. The Zaheri's new economic strategy, which made slaves and *mahaji* dependent on the Zaheri for their land, also enabled Salim b. Khamis of Takaungu to supply large quantities of labor to the IBEACO on terms that, for the sultan, were very favorable.[86]

Takaungu's attempt to destroy Fuladoyo and end marronage formed part of its effort to reassert hegemony in its immediate district and its influence in the adjoining hinterland. Mazrui ambitions were achieved in the sense that until 1895 Takaungu remained free of Busaidi and British interference in its internal affairs and unfettered as an exporter in the clandestine slave trade.

---

settlement by *mahaji* in Mavueni, near Takaungu, Koffsky, "History of Takaungu," 112-21. Koffsky claims that Digo were among the settlers (113), which agrees with accounts heard by myself in Rabai, of Digo resettlement among northern Miji Kenda following the Mwachisenge famine.

[84] Mathews's notes in Hardinge to Salisbury, 12 Apr. 1896, CP 67/13, KNA; Mbotela, *Uhuru wa Watumwa*, 78.

[85] *Mahaji* farmers settled with the permission of the Mazrui. Macdougall for Ali b. Salim, Said b. Abdullah, and Musa b. Saad, 13 Apr. 1910, and Macdougall to Nairobi, 17 Jun. 1910, CP Serial No. 3, KNA. *Mahaji* settlement seems to have been a result of resistance to full Islamization in the densely settled foothills of Miji Kenda country and in Northern Giriama, where Islamic anti-sorcery medicines were very popular.

[86] See ch. 6.

5

Rabai and William Jones

Mission stations had special appeal to runaways who coveted the protection enjoyed by converts. Missionaries received constant pleas for refuge from runaway slaves, but as a rule they turned them away. They could not harbor fugitives without endangering relations with the Muslim community and losing the support of the British consul. Yet, despite their closed-door policy, which came into effect in the early 1880s, hundreds of determined runaways slipped inside the CMS mission station at Rabai, built homes on mission ground, started families, tilled the soil, and took part in mission life. They succeeded in gaining protection because African converts quietly admitted them into their community. At the time, the CMS station Rabai was administered by one of the Bombay Africans, William Jones.

The Christian settlement of Rabai stood as one of nineteenth-century coastal Kenya's more striking anomalies. Located in the hills west of Mombasa, this community took root and flourished amidst the wars, slave raids, famines, and civil strife of the 1880s. Consisting of a cluster of neighborhoods built around the CMS station at Kisulutini, Rabai managed to grow while other coastal communities fragmented or declined. Between 1882 and 1888, its population increased tenfold, from three hundred to three thousand. Rabai's inhabitants transformed a once-abandoned plain, extending west from the Rabai Hills, into a "broad belt of prosperous plantations."[1] Almost overnight Rabai became East Africa's largest Christian settlement, quickly surpassing Frere Town in size and population. For every Christian at Frere Town in 1886, four were counted at Rabai.[2] And whereas Frere Town's residents were dependent on grants from the CMS Parent Committee in London, Rabai's residents contributed the entire cost of maintenance of their church, schools, and resident missionary. As a mission station Rabai was also exceptional in that it attracted Miji Kenda enquirers. In contrast to earlier years, when at most a handful of Miji Kenda entertained conversion, hundreds began to settle at Rabai alongside ex-slaves from other parts of eastern Africa. In the 1880s Rabai was more than a mission. It was, as much as anything, a busy meeting ground. Caravans proceeding to the interior often used Rabai as a staging point and as a recruiting site for porters. Rabai was also the coast's major producer of palm wine, which attracted buyers from distant parts of the hinterland, paid for imported grain even in drought years, and contributed to Rabai's reputation as something of an entertainment center.

---

[1] Taylor to Lang, n.d.[Jul.?, 1886], G3A5/03, CMS.
[2] CMS *Proceedings*, 1886-87.

As much as any factor, however, Rabai's development was the result of the administration of clergyman William Henry Jones, missionary in Rabai from 1882 and sole missionary-in-charge between 1884 and late 1888.[3] Though more energetic than most as an organizer and as committed an evangelist as any, Jones was exceptional for his respect of mission dwellers and their neighbors who retained non-Christian values. African religious beliefs and Islam existed alongside Christianity at Rabai. Jones created alliances with the non-Christian Miji Kenda off the mission for the purpose of joint defense against attacks of the Kwavi, the Mazrui, coastal slave owners, and the sultan's troops. He knew how to communicate with and control persons of all sorts, a rare quality in the jumbled and rapidly-evolving coastal environment of the nineteenth century. His linguistic skills played a central role. He was the only missionary, perhaps the only person, on the Kenya coast who could converse in Swahili, English, Marathi, Hindustani, Nyassa, Yao, Galla, and several Miji Kenda dialects. Jones's greatest talent lay, however, in uniting disparate, otherwise weak, individuals under his leadership. He was a shrewd and devious man, braver than most, and one who took chances.

Jones built Rabai by protecting fugitive slaves when other missionaries and British officials would not. Harboring runaways violated the 1880 accord between the CMS, coastal slave owners, and the British consulate in Zanzibar.[4] Under Jones's authority, Rabai welcomed over five hundred slaves from the Muslim coast, a fact Jones concealed from his superiors and visiting officials. Eventually, the risks he ran resulted in the threatened destruction of the settlement by the slave owners of Mombasa. This crisis, erupting in October 1888, also challenged the fragile authority of the Kenya coast's first European rulers, the Imperial British East Africa Company (IBEACO). Jones's sympathies for runaways, in other words, jeopardized the interests of the CMS and the British Crown. Jones did not caste his lot with the growing establishment. He possessed an independent frame of mind, to be explained best, perhaps, by the fact that before he was appointed as missionary to Rabai and before he was ordained as the first protestant clergyman born in East Africa, William Henry Jones had been a slave.

1. *Jones's Early Years*

Jones was born a Yao, in the area east of Lake Malawi in ca. 1840. As a boy, he was pawned by his stepfather to his stepfather's brother for a debt. Eventually he was sold in Kilwa to an Arab trader, who took him to Zanzibar. After several months, during which the trader failed to find a buyer for Jones, the

---

[3] Jones was ordained an Anglican deacon in 1885 and a priest in 1895.

[4] See ch. 3. In November 1880 the CMS Parent Committee instructed its missionaries not to retain runaways "save where claims of humanity require it, but they will either induce the slave to return to his master or inform the Wali of the event." Resolutions of the General Committee, 16 Nov. 1880, in Hutchinson to Granville, 14 Jan. 1881, FO 541/49, 201.

boy was taken on a caravan to Nyamwezi, for use as exchange capital, but was never sold, and returned to Zanzibar. There he was bought by Muscat Arabs, whose vessel was seized by the British anti-slave patrol off the coast of Oman, in 1853.[5] Jones was then taken to Bombay and handed over to Mr. and Mrs. Theodore Zorn, who had just established the Asylum for African boys at their house on Waverly Hill. The following year, the Asylum lapsed with Mrs. Zorn's death, and Jones and others were handed over to the Indo-British Institution, where they remained until 1856, when Jones and another Yao freed slave youngster, Ishmael Semler, were placed in the care of CMS missionary James Gottfried Deimler. Deimler, friend of the first CMS missionaries in East Africa, Ludwig Krapf and Johann Rebmann, trained the two lads with a view to their becoming assistants in the East African mission.[6] In the meantime, they attended the African Asylum at the CMS Sharunpur mission, where Jones trained as a blacksmith and where, a few days before they set sail for Mombasa in 1864, Jones and Semler married Galla freed slaves from the Sharunpur Orphanage.[7]

Jones's first return to East Africa, though unpleasant, was instructive. The story of his mistreatment and that of the other "Bombay Africans" under Rebmann at the CMS station in Kisulutini has already been told.[8] Yet, Jones alone among his fellow mission assistants was accorded some respect from the irascible missionary, who once wrote of Jones's "considerable degree of fitness [as a teacher]."[9] Spared much trauma by taking assignments off the station, where his linguistic skills were useful, Jones spent more than two years in Zanzibar working for the Universities' Mission to Central Africa (UMCA). His experience, already exceptional, grew as he journeyed with Bishop Edward Steere to the new UMCA mission at Magila, Bondei, then under the suzerainty of Kimweri we Nyumbai of the Shambala.[10] Jones's first child, John (Johnny) Edward

---

[5] Jones, "Self-history," copied by C.W. Isenberg, 7 Aug. 1861, together with Isenberg note, CI3/048, CMS. Jones never divulged, in his autobiography or any subsequent writing, his original name.

[6] Ibid.

[7] Deimler to Fenn, 27 Aug. 1874, CI3/035, CMS

[8] See ch. 3.

[9] Rebmann to Venn, 27 Feb. 1866, CA5/024, CMS.

[10] A.E.M. Anderson-Morshead, *The History of the Universities' Mission to Central Africa, 1859-1909* (London: UMCA, 1909), 57, where Jones is referred to as "a layman." Jones was employed by Bishop Tozer of the UMCA to instruct three Miji Kenda boys, Samuel Kango, Mark Mlangulo, and Peter Mwamba, sent by Rebmann to Zanzibar for instruction. Deimler to Venn, 10 Jun. 1865, CI3/035, and Tozer to Rebmann, 8 Sep. 1865, CA5/024, CMS. Tozer and Rebmann, whose wives were sisters, were accustomed to trading favors. According to Jones, his three scholars soon abandoned their studies and returned to Rabai. Jones to CMS, 16 Apr. 1870, CA5/01, CMS. But Jones remained in Zanzibar until the end of 1868 working with Steere, most probably because of his knowledge of Yao. The UMCA mission in Zanzibar was established in 1864 after an unsuccessful attempt by Tozer to launch a mission in the Shire highlands. Eventually, in 1876, Steere established Masasi village in Yaoland for the resettlement of freed slaves.

Jones, was born in Zanzibar. In 1868 Rebmann posted Jones to the CMS house in Mombasa, where he worked alone and later assisted Rev. T.H. Sparshott. While based in Mombasa, he acted as messenger to the Giriama in the hinterland, as well as to the *liwali* of Mombasa, thereby increasing his personal contacts and knowledge of coastal languages and geography.

In 1870 Jones resigned and returned to India. His wife's death, coming one month after the birth of their second child, was certainly a factor, but Jones left East Africa convinced that the CMS mission under Rebmann lacked purpose or direction. And he did not hesitate making his opinion known. In his letter to Henry Venn, CMS Lay Secretary in London, Jones asserted that the mission was failing because its leader lacked any pastoral or evangelical ambition.

> Many have fallen away.... I am not surprised if they do, but I am rather surprised at those that are still remaining.... Without any means of spiritual grace, without s[e]rmons, without any atom of any kind of instruction imparted to them, no meetings, no lectures, in short we are like sheep in the wilderness that has no shepherd so that we live and act as our hearts would have us to live.[11]

Most of all, Jones was angered by Rebmann's indifference toward slavery. He related the story of a Miji Kenda convert, who bought a slave to marry and then later sold her away. Both transactions were taken, Jones alleges, with Rebmann's knowledge and without his disapproval.

> I told [Rebmann] that the Committee would be very much displeased to hear such a thing being done or allowed by one of their missionary of the Gospel in Africa. After shewing him much the] evil of allowing one of his baptized man [sic] to sell and to buy a woman,... he answered me thus: 'So far as your letter about Abe Ngowa's affair is the expression of your abhorrence of slavery I am pleased with it. It was a case in which I could not interfere. The matter is however settled now.' It is evidently [sic] from the above circumstance how far we are from the Gospel spirit of love. If a pastor will not 'interfere' when his converts go wrong, who else can? If the Gospel missionary sanctions his converts to sell and buy slaves, we that are no missionary[sic] will go farther than that and the work of all the mighty ships of war which go about in quest of slave dhows is vain.[12]

Six years later, Jones returned to East Africa, this time as part of Price's effort in realigning the coast mission to include the care of freed slaves.[13] Before he left India, Jones, who had remarried, served as a catechist among African Christians in Bombay (performing the Sunday afternoon catechumen service "in a mixture of languages") and visited others working for the railway.[14] In large measure because of Jones's itinerating efforts, almost this entire congregation was recruited by Price for the building of Frere Town. As much as

---

[11] Jones to Venn, 16 Apr. 1870, CA5/01, CMS.
[12] Ibid.
[13] See ch. 3.
[14] Deimler to Fenn, 22 Feb. 1875, CI3/035, CMS.

anyone, Jones supported the experiment and had confidence in Price, whom he had known since 1861. In late 1874 and early 1875, as parties of "Bombay Africans" shipped for Mombasa with Price, Jones remained behind to Christianize a group of Islamized freed slaves--18 men, 12 women, and 13 children-- and induce them to repatriate to Africa. He needed only ten months to accomplish his purpose. Then, in December 1875, when Price summoned him to set up a mission among the Giriama, Jones and his family set sail for Mombasa with his new converts on board.[15]

By his arrival the following March, the Frere Town experiment was already turning sour.[16] Several missionaries had left following disputes with Price, who was himself about to return to England. The plan for Jones to evangelize among the Giriama was scrapped by Price's successor, J.A. Lamb, after it was learned that Jones was quarrelling with his wife.[17] He was then assigned to Rabai under the young and inexperienced missionary, Henry Binns, while the task of overseeing spiritual work in Frere Town and making contact with the Giriama was given to George David. In Rabai, Jones soon talked about resigning, and Binns wrote Frere Town that he wanted "rid of" Jones.[18] Jones was experiencing the rapid demotion suffered by other leading Bombay Africans. Having but months before stood near the center of the East African mission enterprise, Jones found himself on the periphery. With the departure of Price, the mission was governed by those without experience of East Africa and without appreciation for its India connection. The struggle between the missionaries in Frere Town and the Bombay Africans was about to begin.

Jones, though no follower, was a fighter. Shrewd enough to disassociate himself from the Bombays involved in the March 1877 plot to wrest control of the mission, he helped the missionaries identify the leading conspirators.[19] Jones was taking his first opportunity to work his way back to a position of authority. While Streeter carried out his brutal shake-up in Frere Town, Jones remained unaffected in Rabai, his reputation slowly recovering. Binns went on leave in June, and Jones was left in charge. Fifteen months later, on the eve of Binns's return, he was recommended for ministerial training.[20] Never an institutional climber, Jones was a solitary, African clergyman wanting to lead on his own terms. His only realistic opportunities nevertheless lay in remaining acceptable to the powerful. As such Jones deferred to his seniors, but was jealous of his delegated authority and charted his own policy when left alone. In Between mid-1877 and November 1878 when left in charge of Rabai while Binns

---

[15] The group were based on the Government Model Farm at Bhargam in Kandeth, Deimler to Fenn, 17 Jan. 1876, CI3/035, CMS.

[16] See ch. 3.

[17] Jones claimed that she was barren. Lamb to Wright, 12 Aug. 1876, CA5/M4, 278.

[18] Lamb to Wright, 4 Nov. 1876, CA5/M5, 2, CMS.

[19] Praeger to Wright, 29 Mar. 1877, CA5/022, CMS. See ch. 3.

[20] Bishop of Mauritius to Wright, 4 Oct. 1878, CA5/M5, 243-4, CMS

was on leave in England, Jones allowed forty-four runaway slaves to settle.[21] Many were refugees from Makongeni, recently attacked by Malindi slave owners.[22] Jones revealed sympathies which in future would involve the CMS deeply in the runaway slave question. It was left for Binns to decide what to do. In March 1879, Jones was given leave, once again, to find a third wife in India.[23]

When he returned the mission had undergone a second, and more fundamental, transformation. The Streeter scandal had ended hopes for Frere Town as center of the CMS's future in East Africa. Frere Town increasingly confined itself to the care of young freed slaves, while the Mombasa hinterland and East African interior, particularly Buganda, received greater attention. As many Bombay Africans were eased out of the mission, the running of Frere Town became almost entirely the affair of white missionaries. Rabai, the CMS's oldest and for years moribund station, began to expand. After 1880 all adult freed slaves were transferred to Rabai, where they proved capable of supporting themselves. Freed slave teachers in Rabai were also used to staff schools among the Miji Kenda, who at the time were showing greater interest in the mission. Their work was the more important after 1881, when Rabai station was often without a capable white missionary or without any at all. In short, Rabai was becoming dependent on African mission workers. When Jones arrived in Mombasa in February 1882, he was met by Price, his old and respected mentor, who had returned briefly to patch up the damage that had occurred since his departure for England six years prior. Price, who believed that "to get the best out of Jones, we must put responsibility upon him," assigned his charge to Rabai to take Binns's place.[24] Jones was returning to the center of mission enterprise.

2. Rabai under Jones

Jones did not assume full control of Rabai at the outset. Until September 1882 he was subordinate to Binns and, until mid-1884, to A. Downes Shaw. In 1883 Jones also spent time away from the settlement assisting Alfred Wray establish the new CMS station in the Teita hills.[25] At Rabai Jones's responsibilities were left undefined, but it gradually fell to him to tend to the Christian community settled around the Kisulutini church, while Shaw concentrated on converting the neighboring Miji Kenda. This arrangement proved unsatisfactory because it implied an equality of rank that Shaw was unwilling to grant. In January 1884 Shaw had a spat with Jones as to who was in charge. Shaw

---

[21] Binns annual letter, Nov. 1878, CA5/03, CMS. See also Jones to CMS, 10 Oct. 1878, CA5/014, CMS.

[22] See ch. 4.

[23] Sally, Jones's second wife, died of consumption in late April/early May 1877. Lamb to Hutchinson, 19 May 1877, CA5/M5, 91, CMS.

[24] Price journal, 13 Feb. 1882, G3A5/01(1882), CMS.

[25] Binns to Lang, 3 Aug. 1883, G3A5/01(1883), CMS.

accused Jones of giving "the people of Rabai to understand that he is the head there, and that all matters of whatever kind must first be brought to him." Shaw wanted Jones put straight. "He ought to be told," Shaw wrote to his superior in Frere Town,"that he is to be under not at all equal with the head of this mission."[26] Jones became effective head at Rabai anyway. After June, with Shaw on leave, the responsibilities for the Christian community and the evangelization of the Miji Kenda fell entirely on Jones's shoulders.[27]

Once under Jones's charge Rabai changed rapidly, as it had when Jones took over from Binns in 1878. But this time Jones had much greater scope to exercise his authority. Shaw was transferred to Frere Town soon after his return from England, leaving the eccentric and incompetent Taylor at Rabai.[28] Binns, based in Frere Town, was in Rabai from October 1886 to March 1887 engrossed with the completion of Rabai's new stone church. Until late 1888 Jones ran Rabai single-handedly, while the Rabai mission community expanded at an enormous rate. From 1884 to 1888 the number of baptized Christians and unbaptized adherents quadrupled from 510 to 2,090.[29] Two 1888 estimates of the Rabai population put the total number close to three thousand.[30] Some of this rapid increase is to be accounted for by the movement of adult freed slaves from Frere Town to Rabai, where land was fertile and abundant.[31]

---

[26] Handford to Lang,, n.d., with journal extract, 29 Jan. 1884, G3A5/01(1884), CMS.

[27] Of the four catechists who helped Shaw to evangelize the Miji Kenda none continued their work long after Shaw's departure. Isaac Taylor and Edward Cantella were dismissed in December 1884 for immoral acts, and soon thereafter Jeremiah Mangi and Cecil Mabruki were transferred to Mwaiba and Teita, respectively.

[28] Bishop Hannington regarded Taylor as a "complete episcopal puzzle" and incapable of managing a station. "He is pious and moral and upright....but at the same time upsets almost everything he puts his hands to. One day he is late for prayers and the next day forgets all about it. For two days he will nurse and doctor a patient almost to death and the third day never go near...I delivered him 60 dollars to pay wages with. He goes up to Rabai and forgets to pay the wages and spends it on sundries and not one dollar can he account for. Misses an orange and orders his two boys to be beaten on the spot. The next day remembers that he told the catechist to take it for a sick child. Can a man of that sort manage a station?" The Bishop considered his recall. Hannington to Lang, 29 May 1885, G3A5/02. See also Shaw to Lang, 25 Jun. 1886, G3A5/03, CMS. Taylor, whose talents lay in linguistic research, published several works on coastal languages of high quality.

[29] CMS *Intelligencer* (1884-85), 45; Ibid.(1887-88), 63.

[30] Churchill to Euan Smith, 25 May 1888, FO 403/105, 113; Price memo, 3 Nov. 1888, G3A5/05, CMS.

[31] The farms at Frere Town were hemmed in by Swahili land, and there was no room for expansion. "The people who are here," wrote Binns at Frere Town, "are desirous of getting away and are envious of their fortunate brethren who have settled at Rabai." Binns to Lang, 26 Oct. 1885, G3A5/02; Shaw to Lang, 19 Aug. 1886, G3A5/03, CMS.

At Rabai, mission settlers colonized an extensive area unoccupied by the Rabai group of the Miji Kenda, living in forested hills east of the mission station at Kisulutini. West of the mission in locations today known as Mwele, Kaliang'ombe, Mgumopatsa, Kokotoni, and Simakeni, mission settlers brought large acreages under cultivation and planted coconut, mango, and other fruit trees. This territory had belonged to the Rabai, but since the mid-1870s the Rabai had been confined to their hilltop settlements for security. Kwavi and Oromo raids, quarrels with other Miji Kenda, and slave raiding by coastal Muslims discouraged utilizing the fertile plains below. Only a few members of the Amwakamba clan, who were comparative newcomers among the Rabai, accepted the risks of cultivating the land, raising stock, and building their houses in Mgumo wa Patsa and Kokotoni.[32]

As its agriculture expanded, the mission community built a large and orderly settlement. When Rabai reached full growth, visitors were "struck with the great cleanliness, order, and neatness of the place. Each little hut, which in every single instance was neatly kept and very clean, was surrounded by a small plantation in which rice, Indian corn, sweet potatoes, etc. were planted."[33] Rabai, "a huge village, is kept with scrupulous cleanliness, the paths are wide and kept free from grass, and the huts are in the midst of groves of plantain and coconut palms."[34]

Under Jones's direction Rabai became not only a settlement of Bombays, newly freed slaves, and old runaway slaves from Giriama, but of the converts from Miji Kenda. In contrast to Shaw who placed catechists among the Miji Kenda, Jones induced them to settle around him. Until 1884 only small numbers of Miji Kenda had moved into Rabai, but after Jones assumed control of the mission, they settled in large numbers. Within two years Jones reported that three hundred were on the mission roles and attending religious classes.[35] Thus he succeeded where Krapf, Rebmann, and other missionaries among the Miji Kenda had failed. In 1888 visitors noted the large "Wanyika" representation on the station, and Price, returning to East Africa after an absence of six years, was surprised by the "considerable number of indigenous Wanyika" who had attached themselves to the mission during his absence. At the time more than five hundred Miji Kenda lived in Rabai.[36]

---

[32] Mkamba wa Benyoka, interviewed 9 May and 17 Jul. 1973; Tsochizi wa Tsimba, 11 May 1973, Tuguu wa Baya, 5 Sep. 1973. In 1973 many Rabai were settled in these areas, but aside from a few Amwakamba, all family heads interviewed or their fathers had been born in the Rabai hilltop settlements (*kaya*), or in other Miji Kenda locations. With regard to the abundance of available land in Rabai, Price to Hutchinson, 27 Feb. and 3 Jul. 1875, CA5/M4, 31, 92; Russell to Hutchinson, 13 Sep. 1877, CA5/M5, 127; Price report, 6 Oct. 1882, G3A5/01(1882), CMS.

[33] Macdonald to Salisbury, 13 Feb. 1888, FO 541/28, 201.

[34] Churchill to Euan Smith, 25 May 1888, C. 5603, 13.

[35] Jones to Lang, Oct. 1886, G3A5/03, CMS.

[36] Price memorandum, 3 Nov. 1888, G3A5/05, CMS. "WaNyika" is the Swahili reference to Miji Kenda.

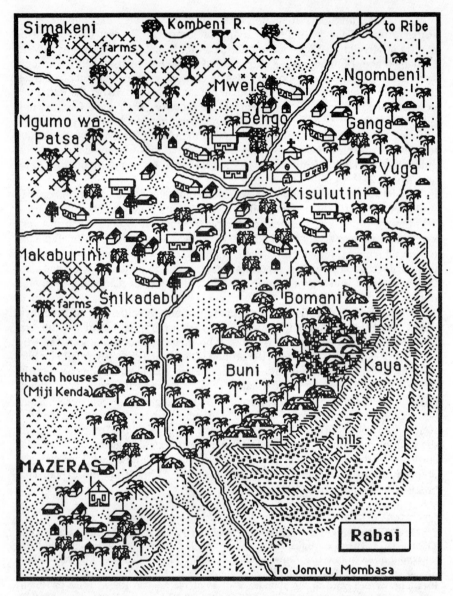

Most Miji Kenda settled at Rabai because they were attracted to Jones, a fact largely unobserved by European missionaries. Price and CMS Bishop Henry Parker were convinced that the Miji Kenda came purely to be converted. William Taylor believed that "in the minds of the natives the prominent idea is that of following the Mzungu [European], not of obeying God."

The contrast between their sparsely populated 'Kayas' with their sordid squalid inhabitants and our own bright, tidy cheerful settlement, with its broad belt of prosperous plantation, is what they chiefly look at: and not at the cause of our peace and plenty. [Taylor emphasis].[37]

Taylor overlooked the real "Mzungu" admired by the Miji Kenda--Jones. For years the Rabai and other Miji Kenda had thought certain mission leaders as endowed with rare mystical powers. They looked on Streeter as a rainmaker, and on Binns as a potent representative of their complaints before the *liwali* of Mombasa.[38] But these two missionaries failed to exploit their popular standing and press for conversion.

Jones promoted himself as a protector of the Rabai by arbitrating internal disputes, entering their clans, and aiding in their defense against hostile outsiders. Oral sources reveal that Jones joined at least three clans--Amwakamba, Tsui, and Kariaka--by sharing blood with clan elders, and that numerous disputes were taken to him for judgment. Mwakoyo wa Chisubi made blood brotherhood with Jones thereby admitting him to his clan, Mwamkamba. From there Jones was able to enter the *kaya*, or council of elders and, in the customary way of paying fees, to reach the *mvaya*, or senior grade.[39] At Rabai he ran the mission settlement as his personal domain and used the pulpit to preach, more dramatically than anyone before or since, to the hundreds of listeners who jammed the church on Sundays. Jones's powerful oratory could rivet a congregation's attention on the hottest and most uncomfortable days.[40] The Rabai, though accustomed to law through the elders, were then as they were nearly a century later, most responsive to the individual with exceptional oratorical and mental gifts. To the Rabai Jones was a seer and a prophet. His presence was the main reason for the station's success.[41]

Jones further expanded the mission community by violating CMS policy and admitting runaway slaves from the Muslim coast. Between 1883 and 1888 over five hundred of them settled in Rabai. In 1883 about forty slipped into the

---

[37] Taylor to Lang, n.d.[1886], G3A5/03; Parker to Lang, 14 Mar. 1887, G3A5/04; Price memorandum, 3 Nov. 1888, G3A5/05, CMS.

[38] Lamb to Wright, 26 Jan. 1878, CA5/017; Jones to CMS, 10 Oct. 1878, CA5/014; Streeter to Wright, 12 Jul. 1879, CA5/027, CMS; Binns to CMS, 23 Apr. 1879, CMS *Intelligencer*, 4(1879), 699; Binns diary, 26 Jun. and 8 Jul. 1879, KNA.

[39] Tsochizi wa Tsimba, Rabai (Mgumo wa Patsa), interviewed 11 May 1973. Discussions with other Rabai residents indicate that Jones cultivated the friendship of many other Rabai Miji Kenda. Jones spoke fluent Rabai. See also Taylor to Lang, 17 Mar. 1885, G3A5/02, and Taylor to Lang, n.d.[early 1886?], G3A5/03, CMS.

[40] Taylor to Lang, 15 Mar. 1886, G3A5/03, also Ackerman journal 24 Mar. and 9 Jul. 1895, G3A5/011, CMS.

[41] Tsochizi wa Tsimba, interviewed 11 May 1973; Tuguu wa Baya, 5 Sep. 1973. Parallels exist between Jones, who achieved his influence when the Kaya elders were declining in ritual importance, and Kajiwe, a young Rabai who in 1966 led an anti-sorcery campaign among the Rabai and other Miji Kenda. D.J. Parkin, "Medicines and Men of Influence," *Man*, 3,3(Sep. 1968), 431-7.

settlement, passing themselves off to Shaw as Miji Kenda slaves.[42] There was little likelihood then that Jones, with his long experience on the coast, did not know from whence these slaves had come. In April 1884 Shaw decided to shut Rabai's doors to all runaways after the new Mombasa vice consul, C.E. Gissing, visited the station.[43] When Jones assumed charge in June, the policy was quietly abandoned. In 1884 a total of 129 runaways from the coast settled in Rabai, and others followed: 91 in 1885, 126 in 1886, 44 in 1887, and 147 in 1888, totalling at least 524 slaves while Jones headed Rabai.[44]

The Rabai admixture of Miji Kenda, freed slaves, and runaways gave ex-slaves unprecedented social opportunities. Rabai, though a mission community, contained strong elements of indigenous African culture. Miji Kenda who settled on the mission in the 1880s, in contrast to earlier converts, had not come as social rejects. Retaining traditional ways, they shunned cultural transformation. They lived in their own quarter, wore traditional clothing, and performed customary dances on mission ground.[45] Ethnic divisions within the mission community were allowed to persist, but individuals established personal ties across such boundaries. Freed slaves of Rabai, unlike those at Frere Town, and the runaways from the coast, had the means to acculturate themselves without taking the risk of leaving the mission.

The most common form of interaction was for ex-slaves to adopt a Rabai clan and take Rabai wives.[46] Today many persons who call themselves "Arabai" are descended from ex-slaves.[47] Foremost among the clans with ex-slave representation are the Amwakavyo and Tiga, whose members in the 1880s appear to have predominated among the Miji Kenda settled on and near the mission church

---

[42] Shaw believed that allowing in the runaways from Miji Kenda ameliorated conditions for those who remained with their masters: "The owners know that if they are cruel the slaves will run away to us and get protection, so they treat them more as members of the family." Shaw annual letter, 22 Dec. 1883, CMS *Intelligencer* (Apr. 1884), 244. Shaw broke no rules by allowing Miji Kenda slaves into Rabai. See pp. 52-3 above.

[43] Shaw to Lang, 14 Apr. 1884, G3A5/01(1884), CMS.

[44] Minimum figures based on the detailed lists of runaway slaves present in Rabai in late 1888 and according to date of settlement. Mackenzie summary, 13 Nov. 1888 in Euan Smith to Salisbury, 20 Nov. 1888, FO 541/28, 443-4.

[45] Churchill to Euan Smith, 25 May 1888, C. 5603, 13; Price Memorandum, 3 Nov. 1888, G3A5/05, CMS. See also Ackerman journal, 26 Dec. 1894 and 11 Mar. 1895, G3A5/011, CMS. The Rabai were concentrated primarily in the Vuga and Ganga sections of the mission.

[46] Remarks on clan entry and marriage are based on cases corroborated in the field and on general remarks made by numerous Rabai and ex-slave descendants in the Rabai area.

[47] It is difficult to gather precise information from the Rabai about lines of descent from ex-slave ancestors. Admission of ex-slave origins leads to embarrassment, and the younger generations are often kept ignorant on the subject. It so happened in 1973 that one of my assistants learned to his chagrin during an interview that his male ancestors were not Rabai, but Nyassa.

at Vuga and Ganga. Marriage and clan entry, though not widespread among ex-slaves, took place often enough to show that a significant minority desired to become part of a community that extended beyond mission boundaries. As one Rabai told me, "when the ex-slaves joined our clans, it meant that they had accepted the fact that they were here to stay."[48]

Clan entry was a simple, inexpensive process that occasioned long-term benefits and obligations for both parties. Normally, two men were joined through the process of blood brotherhood, or *kurya tsoga* ("eating the cut"). In so doing the ex-slave acquired the patrilineal clan name of his ceremonial partner along with, in theory, full status among the partner's patrilineal co-equals. On occasion fees were paid to the elders of a Rabai patriclan whereupon the ex-slave was entitled to the privileges and obligations of all other clansmen. In both cases, the ex-slave could call on the support of his Rabai fellows to gain and hold land, raise capital for feasts, pay for curative medicines sold by local doctors, and acquire Rabai wives. Clan and agnatic entry did not absolve the ex-slave of ex-slave status, which was a barrier to social mobility within Rabai society. But if his wife were a Rabai, his offspring could become full members by virtue of their dual clan inheritance.[49] For the Rabai, the acceptance of ex-slaves into formal association allowed brothers or clansmen to retain a measure of control over the offspring of ex-slave/Rabai marriages and to draw upon the resources of ex-slaves in times of need.

Though means to acculturate among the Miji Kenda existed, some ex-slaves preferred to retain their exclusiveness. In the 1880s the mission settlement at Rabai assumed form along much the same ethnic lines that characterized Frere Town. Most people lived in their own neighborhoods, had their own social groups and dances, and identified their offspring by their father's ethnicity.[50] Ex-slaves who perpetuated old ethnicities tended to intermarry (especially true of the "Nyassa" folk) and assume appearances that set them apart as a community from the Miji Kenda. They dressed in western-style clothing, built coast-style houses, conversed in Swahili, and used Christian names for themselves and their

---

[48] Mbogo wa Kinda, interviewed 26 Jul. 1973.

[49] Among the Rabai, a person received through birth the father's patrilineal clan (*kulume*) and the mother's matrilineal clan (*kuche*). Other than defining, with the patrilineal clan, member status as a Rabai, the matrilineal clan served primarily as a group which administered oaths (*vyapo*) to its members who suffered from spiritual afflictions. Female descent and inheritance, which operated effectively among the Digo and the Duruma in the nineteenth century, were not present among the Rabai. *Kurya tsoga* was common in the coastal region. T.J. Herlehy, "Ties that Bind: Palm Wine and Blood Brotherhood at the Kenya Coast during the 19th Century," *IJAHS*, 17, 2(1984), 298-307.

[50] In the 1880s the four major groups were, together with locale, Nyassa (Mbarakani, Mwele Adzomba), Makua (Kalungoni), Mgindo (Kavirondo), and the Bombay Africans (Puna, Bengo). With the exception of Puna and Bengo, dances were held in each of these quarters at places set aside for the purpose. Matrilineal descent was the traditional rule among the Nyassa, the largest of the four groups, but patrilineal descent was adopted in order to continue ethnic identity to subsequent generations.

children.[51] The Rabai called them *Ajamaa* ("those from another land"), or used other, sometimes derisory, terms that identified them as aliens.[52]

Many ex-slave men made their living through caravan work. After 1884 Rabai became one of the principal recruiting centers, first for travelers and missionaries, later for British imperial officials, all of whom required large parties to carry goods to Uganda. Beginning a pattern that continued until the building of the Uganda railway (1897-1902), hundreds of ex-slaves from the Rabai mission signed on as porters, cooks, guides, and servants.[53] As a staging center, Rabai gained the reputation as a kind of Sodom, where recently-paid porters from all parts were serviced by women and wine-sellers.[54] Since mid-century, Rabai had been a major palm wine producing center of a regional network of exchange, which channeled grain and stock to the Rabai people, who produced little of their own food. The ex-slaves around the Rabai mission--the "WaMisheni" as they were coming to be known--strengthened the palm wine trade with their porterage and agriculture.[55]

Jones's rule, and his example, also reinforced the economic and social ties binding the WaMisheni and Rabai. He devoted much time to secular affairs and

---

[51] Rectangular houses with mud walls and a high, palm-thatched roof with pole supports is a design common in Mombasa town and in other areas of the Muslim coast. The Miji Kenda lived in low oblong huts, without mud walls, built instead with a wicker frame covered with thatched grass.

[52] *Atumia a Azungu* ("slaves of the Europeans") and *koroboi* ("call a boy"), which exaggerated ex-slave dependence on the mission, and frequently *Adzomba*, which the Rabai also used with reference to dark, coastal Muslims. The term used in Rabai today for surviving ex-slave descendants, *Ahendakudza* ("newcomers") has been in circulation since the late 1930s.

[53] Handford to CMS, 22 Jul. 1885, CMS *Intelligencer* (1885), 753; Shaw to Lang, 28 Aug. 1885, G3A5/02, CMS; Dawson, *James Hannington*, 391; Taylor to Lang, 28 Jun. 1886, G3A5/03, CMS; J. Thomson, *Through Masailand: a Journey of Exploration among the Snowclad Volcanic Mountains and Strange Tribes of Eastern Equatorial Africa* (London: Sampson Low, Marston, Searle, Rivington, 1887), 28; H.H. Johnston, *The Kilima-Njaro Expedition* (London: Kegan, Paul, Trench, 1886), 43; A.D. Shaw, *To Chagga and Back: an Account of a Journey to Moshi, the Capital of Chagga, Eastern Equatorial Africa* (London: Church Missionary House, 1887), 10-1; Parker to Lang, 8 Jul. 1887, G3A5/04, CMS; Price, *Third Campaign*, 68, 79, 155, 157, 182-3; Finance Committee Minutes, 18 Aug. 1888, and Price to Lang, 28 Nov. 1888, G3A5/05, CMS; J.C. Willoughby, *East Africa and its Big Game: the Narrative of a Sporting Trip from Zanzibar to the Borders of the Masai* (London: Longmans, Green, 1889), 38-9; Drummond to Holmwood, 31 Jan. 1887, FO 84/1851.

[54] Ernest Gedge, who worked for the Imperial British East Africa Company in 1889, regarded Rabai as a "curse to all caravans. As what with drink and women the men become simply fiends incarnate, and ours were no exception to the rule." Diary, 20 May 1889, MSS.Brit.Emp. s.290, Gedge 6/4, RH.

[55] Herlehy and Morton, "WaMisheni of Rabai," 262-4.

ruled the settlement with something of an iron hand.[56] His strict enforcement of mission rules governing worship, school attendance, and baptism maintained a Christian veneer over the community, but underneath non-Christian activities flourished. Jones himself owned palm trees, hired tappers, and sold wine.[57] Traditional doctors were known to practice on mission ground, including visits to Jones's house.[58] As well, the mission settlement held frequent dances, or *ngoma*, in the evenings as a form of entertainment for WaMisheni and Rabai alike.

The WaMisheni exposed the Rabai to new and often dazzling distractions. Some ex-slaves, such as Brown Baraka and Bemaasai, achieved notoriety as magicians who could transmogrify themselves, set fingers on fire, and travel great distances in seconds.[59]

3. *Keeping Slave Owners Away*

While Rabai flourished, Jones had to perform a regular magic act himself. In order to conceal the true state of affairs at Rabai it was necessary that he hoodwink CMS missionaries and British officials and keep at bay slave owners and other unwanted intruders, often armed.

In 1882, when Mbaruk b. Rashid pressured Rabai into joining him and then left his new allies to face the Sultan's troops alone, the mission's Snider rifles had to be used in aid of the Rabai's defense. Jones himself appears to have joined in the firing.[60] Jones also condoned the use of force, or threats thereof, to discourage slave owners from approaching the settlement. In January 1884 three Swahili were murdered near the station, a fact Jones kept from Shaw (then in charge at Rabai) in order to obtain ammunition in preparation for what the WaMisheni perceived as an imminent retaliatory attack. When news of the murders surfaced, Jones persuaded his fellow missionaries that they had been committed by people off the station.[61]

---

[56] Gibson Ngome, interviewed Rabai, 3 May 1973. Ngome, who died in 1974, told me that Jones "could not have been a priest today."

[57] Tuguu wa Baya, interviewed Rabai, 5 Sep. 1973. According to Tuguu, Jones maintained a private depot on church ground where the wine was traded.

[58] Ibid.; Binns to Lang, 3 Dec. 1891, G3A5/07, CMS.

[59] Herlehy and Morton, "WaMisheni of Rabai," 266. See also ch. 8.

[60] See ch. 3. According to troops interviewed by Zanzibar vice consul W.B. Cracknall, they had been fired at by "one of the missionaries, and produced Snider rifle shells to support their case (the Arabs did not use Snider rifles)." Cracknall to Miles, 4 Aug. 1882, FO 84/1622. During these events, which took place in July, Jones was in sole charge of the mission. Shaw and Binns were in then Frere Town. See Binns to Lang, 7 Jul. and 10 Aug. 1882, and Shaw to Lang, 28 Sep. 1882, G3A5/01(1882), CMS.

[61] Extracts of Handford journal, 29 and 31 Jan., 1 Feb. 1884, G3A5/01(1884), CMS. The new vice consul at Mombasa, C.E. Gissing, conducted an inquiry into the affair

Then, and for the next four years, the CMS did not suspect that Jones was allowing coast runaways to settle at Rabai. Jones confided in no one, nor was there any hint from the slave owners to suggest that Jones had something to hide.[62] After mid-1884 the Mombasans were governed by *liwali* Salim b. Khalfan, in whom they had no confidence as a guardian of their interests. In contrast to his predecessors, Salim squelched complaints against the CMS and took a hard line against the slave owners, in large part to curry favor among the British. In June 1887 the townspeople used the opportunity of a British consular inquiry into Muslim-mission affairs to accuse the CMS of harboring their slaves in Rabai. Ernest Berkeley, the vice consul, made arrangements for the owners to go to Rabai and identify their slaves, but Berkeley then left Mombasa and the *liwali*, "not wishing to stir up more bad feelings," refrained from helping the owners.[63]

Soon two British officials visited Rabai but uncovered nothing to implicate Jones or the mission. In November 1887 when reports of Salim's obstruction reached Zanzibar, C.M. Macdonald, British acting consul-general, decided to investigate. In January 1888 he traveled to Mombasa, met with Binns at Frere Town, and made a surprise visit to Rabai. Jones took Macdonald around the settlement, the size and neatness of which greatly impressed Macdonald, and talked with him at length. Admitting that it was common for runaways to pass through, Jones claimed that no runaways were there. He also confessed he had been uncooperative with two Arabs demanding their slaves be returned to Mombasa, bound and tied, but this, sympathized Macdonald, "Mr. Jones had, I think, very properly refused to do." Jones's performance was convincing. Macdonald came away believing that there was no runaway danger in Rabai, and in his report to the Foreign Office, he stated that "it would be very unadvisable if

---

. and obtained the confession of a mission resident, Hassani, whereupon he and several others were arrested and put into the Mombasa fort for trial. However, Shaw then made his own enquiry [how it was conducted he does not report] exonerating the Rabai people and then wrote Frere Town that he was "quite upset today to be hearing [from Jones?] that a number of people had left Rabai" because it "was being given over to the consul," therefore making it unsafe. Two days later, Gissing concluded "after careful examination" that the prisoners were innocent and that "for some unexplained case," Hassani "was foolish enough to confess to a murder of wh. he was not the perpetrator." Ibid., 25 and 27 Feb. 1884; Shaw to Handford, 19 Feb. 1884.

[62] In May 1884 consul John Kirk wrote to the Foreign Office and the CMS Parent Committee in the belief that many runaway slaves from the coast were being harbored in Rabai. Kirk's position was unsupported by evidence, and the matter was dropped. Kirk to Granville, 31 May 1884, FO 541/26, 190; Kirk to CMS, 4 Aug. 1884, G3 A5/01(1884), CMS.

[63] Macdonald to Salisbury, 16 Nov. 1887, FO 541/27, 138. The Berkeley inquiry was occasioned by cross-accusations between the mission and the townspeople over incidents in which several Swahili kidnapped some mission people, killed another, and burned several houses in Frere Town. The Swahili complained that mission folk harassed them, stabbed a Mombasan in the back, and had used the governor of Mombasa to jail illegally several townspeople. For the inquiry, Berkeley to Holmwood, 24 Jun. 1887, in Holmwood to Salisbury, 10 Jul. 1887, FO 403/102, 75-9; Holmwood to Salisbury, 14 Sep. 1887, FO 541/27, 113-4.

1. "Rescued from a slave gang" [near Mombasa, ca. 1875]

2. Mombasa mission house of the Church Missionary Society and
the United Methodist Free Church, ca. 1875

3. Jacob Wainwright, George David, Priscilla Christian David, Polly Christian Nyondo, and Henry Williams (standing), ca. 1876

4. Polly and Isaac Nyondo, ca. 1876

5. J.R. Streeter and the Frere Town Police, ca. 1876-77

6. Armed Rabai (Miji Kenda) at the Rabai mission, ca. 1876

7. William Henry Jones and family, ca. 1876
Sally Jones (Jones's second wife, who died in 1877), William Henry
Jones, and his eldest son, Johnny

8. Mbaruk b. Rashid seated between his Takaungu nephews, Mubarak (l.) and Aziz, 1896 (identities of men standing unknown)

From the Bodleian Library, Oxford, R.H. Ms. Afr. 1494. Reprinted by permission.

9. Godoma Christians at their baptism in Rabai, August 1875
Sarah Muchanje, Martha Masha, Mariamu Wanje;
Andreas Randu, Petros Muchanje, Phillipos Masha, Johannes Wanje

10. Christian Bengoa Mwaringa, ca. 1875

11. Mombasa slave women, ca. 1890
"Outrageous are the decorations of the girls in the streets of Mombasa,
by the insertion of brass discs in the lobe of the ears, and the disfigure-
ment of the protruding and distended lip by the flat discs thrust in it."
(Newman, *Banani*, 43)

12. Mombasa street scene, ca. 1895
Muslim trader (center), customs clerk (left center), upcountry
porters (seated left), and ivory tusks (rear center)

13. IBEACO granting freedom papers to 1,421 fugitive slaves at Rabai, 1 January 1889

settlements such as Rabai were interfered with."[64] In May Harry Churchill, the new vice consul in Mombasa, visited Rabai and reached the same conclusion. Jones assured Churchill that "as far as [he was] aware, there were no runaway slaves in the settlement."[65]

Binns later claimed that, when the above events transpired, he was already aware of Jones's involvement with the runaways. In late 1886 Binns went to Rabai to complete the large stone church, which was needed to accommodate Rabai's burgeoning Christian community. At the time he related nothing unusual about the settlement.[66] Two years later, however, Binns alleged that he had found Jones harboring runaway slaves "well knowing them to have come from Mombasa." One problem at Rabai, Binns wrote, "is having a native like William Jones in charge, as I have found that he will not give up a slave under any conditions whatever, if he can possibly help it." In retrospect Binns excused Jones from having full knowledge of the numbers of runaways in the settlement. "It is impossible to tell who is and who is not living there, runaways are constantly coming and going and it is impossible for Jones or anyone to know who is on the settlement at night. The place is like a Rabbit Warren."[67]

Binns's two-year silence over Jones and the runaways is difficult to explain. He made his remarks when a full investigation had already uncovered Jones's complicity. If Binns had full appreciation of the situation in 1886 there would have been good reasons to approach the British consul and arrange to get all runaways off the station. It is unlikely that he was shielding Jones, for whom the missionary long had held a low opinion.[68] Perhaps he simply feared to tell his fellow missionaries, the British authorities, or his own Parent Committee, who might have held him in some way responsible. What seems more likely is that in 1888 Binns remembered more than he had been actually aware of in 1886. His memory had failed him on other occasions.[69] Moreover, he told Macdonald

---

[64] Macdonald to Salisbury, 13 Feb. 1888, FO 541/28, 201-2.

[65] Churchill to Eaun Smith, 25 May 1888, C. 5603, 13.

[66] Before Binns completed his task, he was visited by Bishop H.P. Parker who after inspecting the station was so taken by Jones's work that he planned to make him the official head of the station when Binns completed the church. "I doubt whether the [Parent Committee] realise what an important work is going on there." Parker to Lang, 14 Mar. 1887, G3A5/04, CMS.

[67] Binns to Lang, 15 Nov. 1888, G3A5/05, CMS.

[68] Binns got on poorly with Jones and other catechists, whom he regarded as "not sufficiently motivated in their work and that there was too much love of money." Binns thought Jones the most unfit of the catechists for ordination. Conference Minutes, Rabai, 24 Sep. 1883, G3A5/01(1883), also Price journal, 13 Feb. 1882, G3 A5/01(1882), CMS. Binns's dislike of Jones may be traced back to 1876. Lamb to Wright, 4 Nov. 1876, CA5/M5, 2, CMS.

[69] In the very letter which he implicated Jones, Binns made four substantive errors related to incidents in which Binns himself had been involved with runaway slaves. Other of his letters dealing in retrospect with questions of slavery in Kenya contained wrong or misleading information. Among the larger lapses occurred in 1897, when

in January 1888 that if runaway slaves were found in Rabai, the settlement ought to be destroyed, hardly a suggestion to be made by someone who knew runaways to be there. Binns said that perhaps runaways spent a short time in Rabai before going on to Fuladoyo or other runaway settlements in the interior.[70] This seems to have constituted his, as well as the other missionaries', understanding of the situation in Rabai at the time, because when all the facts surfaced in October 1888, the CMS missionaries were caught completely, and not pleasantly, by surprise.

4. The Reckoning
In October 1888 George S. Mackenzie established the Imperial British East Africa Company (IBEACO) in Mombasa amidst growing discontent. On the 15th he arrived in Mombasa to meet formally with the town elders and to hoist the company's flag. Weeks before Mackenzie's arrival, the advent of the Company had caused alarm. A rebellion in the south had already broken out against the new German East Africa Company, and the Mombasans, angry with the Sultan of Zanzibar for reportedly "having sold them to the English Co.," looked ready to take up arms.[71] Frere Town missionaries, headed again by Price, feared being mistaken as IBEACO accomplices and anticipated attack.[72] On the night of 11 October several IBEACO porters died in a fight with the townspeople, and the row was followed by an armed demonstration against the Company.[73] Three days later Mackenzie arrived in Mombasa without incident, but he found "a large and influential number of the community in a very critical frame of mind" toward the Company. "It would," he judged, "take very little to set the whole thing in a blaze."[74] In an attempt to reduce tensions Mackenzie met with Mombasa elders on the 17th, explained the Company's intentions, and listened to the town people's complaints.

Protesting elders had Mackenzie's sympathy on the issue of runaway slaves on mission stations. The first condition they placed on assent to Company rule

---

Binns wrote that only lazy or criminal slaves, or those running away with a spouse, made up runaway slaves, rather than victims of cruelty. "I hardly ever came across a case of a slave having been cruely beaten, although I have heard of cases." Yet in 1878 Binns was convinced enough of the cruelty of the owners to prevent a slave from being taken by force at Rabai. "The poor slaves of course would not return to their master for he would kill them." Binns diary, 10 Dec. 1878, KNA. Binns to CMS *Intelligencer*, 25 Mar. 1897, FO 403/214, 18. For the witnessing of owner cruelty by Binns' missionary contemporaries, see ch. 1.

[70] Macdonald to Salisbury, 13 Feb. 1888, FO 541/28, 201.

[71] Price, *Third Campaign*, 161.

[72] Ibid., Price to Lang, 29 Sep. 1888, G3A5/05, CMS. Price returned to Frere Town in March 1888.

[73] Salim b. Khalfan regarded Hamisi b. Kombo, of Mtwapa, as the principal leader in the outbreak. Price, *Third Campaign*, 174-6; Price to Euan Smith, 16 Oct. 1888, G3A5/05, CMS; Euan Smith to Salisbury, 22 Oct. 1888, FO 84/1910.

[74] Mackenzie to Euan Smith, 18 Oct. 1888, FO 403/107, 157; Euan Smith to Salisbury, 22 Oct. 1888, FO 84/1910.

was that Mackenzie "demand for us our domestic slaves which have taken shelter in the hands of the missionaries." Other demands were made, but after talking at length with the elders Mackenzie concluded that this one alone held the "possibility of conflict or danger." He held missionaries responsible for "harboring slaves who leave their masters on the most frivolous pretext," and was ready to act on the owners' behalf. As the Company charter obligated him to uphold local law, Mackenzie felt that as the Sultan's representative he had the "indisputable right to demand the giving up of slaves." He was worried, too, that should he do otherwise the Company would suffer. "The question is a grave political one," he wrote to the British consul in Zanzibar, "and on the manner in which it is handled depends the success or failure of the Imperial British East Africa Company."[75]

Price, of the CMS, was convinced that all the fuss was unnecessary. The Mombasans' complaints were exaggerated, he felt, and based in most cases upon false suspicions. "It is quite possible that a runaway or two may steal in and find shelter [at Rabai]," he admitted, "but it is quite contrary to our Rules, and I have over and over again strictly charged Mr. Jones to keep a sharp look-out and to expel at once any suspicious interlopers."[76] In the past Price had made the offer of assisting owners to identify their slaves, and was prepared to repeat it. On 20 October Price and Mackenzie agreed that a commission should inquire into the state of affairs at Rabai and that Price himself should go before the sheikhs of Mombasa to express the mission's willingness to cooperate.[77]

Price was acting in good faith. On his return to East Africa the previous March he had uncovered nothing while investigating allegations against Rabai station, and had talked with Jones and Salim b. Khalfan on runaway matters. This time the *liwali* advised Price to drop the matter, and Jones led Price, like Macdonald and Churchill, to believe that no runaways were living at Rabai.[78] Price, nevertheless, stressed to Jones the need to refuse entry to any slaves, and on 22 October, before the sheikhs of Mombasa, Price once more drew attention to this fact. "I have already given strict orders to Mr. Jones not to allow any of your slaves to remain in hiding in our mission settlements," he announced, "and I have every reason to hope that these orders will be obeyed."[79] Of course, his orders had been ignored, and not until the morning after the meeting did Jones finally let him know the serious state of affairs at Rabai. On Tuesday, 23 October, Price recorded his shock:

---

[75] Mackenzie to Euan Smith, 18 Oct. 1888, with enclosures, FO 403/107, 157-60.

[76] Price to Euan Smith, 16 and 19 Oct. 1888, G3A5/05, CMS.

[77] Mackenzie to Euan Smith, 18 Oct. 1888(postscript 20 Oct), FO 403/107, 159; Price, *Third Campaign*, 189.

[78] Price, *Third Campaign*, 203; Price memorandum, 3 Nov. 1888, G3A5/05, CMS.

[79] Price address to Mombasa sheikhs, 22 Oct. 1888, G3A5/05, CMS; Price, *Third Campaign*, 190-1. The day before he addressed the sheikhs, Price learned from Jones that some runaway slaves were at Rabai, but there was no indication that they were numerous. Price urged Jones to get them off the station. Jones to Price, 21 Oct. 1888 and Price to Jones, 21 Oct. 1888, in ibid., 195-6.

Startling news reaches me from Rabai. The 'watoro' there--numbering to my
intense astonishment some four hundred--refuse to leave. They are determined
to make a stand. They are desperate, and will fight for their homes and liberty,
and many freed slaves and others will join them.[80]

Price was just as surprised to learn that few of the runaways were newcomers.
Many had families, homes, and farms. A large portion Jones had baptized and
confirmed.[81] The runaways wanted to stay where they were, and they camped
with their arms on Buni Hill, which overlooks the coast, awaiting the enemy's
approach.[82]

For Jones, too, the moment of truth was near. Over the previous four years
he had allowed the runaways to settle at Rabai and had made them members of
the community. As long as their presence remained a secret, he could ignore
mission policy without taking any personal risks. In October 1888, with Rabai's
runaways suddenly a public issue, he had to decide whether to take full responsibility or not. If he did, Jones placed in jeopardy not only his standing with
the mission, but his life. If he did not, he would be guilty, in Price's words, of
"allowing our Mission Station to be converted into a trap, whereby these
unfortunate men and women may be caught and handed over again to the cruel
bondage from which they have escaped."[83]

According to his own account of the events of October, Jones was prepared
to join cause with the runaways.[84] His Christian duty gave him no alternative.
The IBEACO decided to "aid the Arabs and the Swahili," he argued, "and thereby
condemn the missionaries['] work of love in sympathizing with the ill treated
and down trodden slaves of Mombasa and the other parts of the coast." He had
no desire to help the Company, which he blamed for "seeking its own interests,"
any more than the slave owners. "Our motto was no giving up, but rather to die
than give up our people who have been brought to the knowledge of the truth as
it is in Jesus."

In contrast, his letters to Price at the time suggest that Jones, although
sympathetic, was not prepared to make a personal sacrifice. When the threat of
attack became real, Jones moved to uphold, rather than continue to defy, mission
policy. On the 20th Jones wrote that he was trying to carry out Price's orders to
get the runaways off the station.[85] In subsequent messages he gave Price no
reason to doubt that, in spite of his feelings, he would remain loyal to mission
interests. When the runaways refused to leave Rabai, Price wrote home that they
were "beyond the control, even of Jones, for whom they have the greatest

---

[80] Price, *Third Campaign*, 191.

[81] Ibid, 191-2.

[82] Jones to CMS, 27 May 1889, G3A5/06, CMS.

[83] Price, *Third Campaign*, 183.

[84] Jones to CMS, 27 May 1889, G3A5/06, CMS.

[85] Price, *Third Campaign*, 195.

respect."[86] On the 24th, moreover, Jones sent a "touching reply" to Price stating that, when the time came for Mackenzie and the slave owners to take their slaves, he would be absent from the spectacle. "How could I bear to see these poor baptized Christians, and communicants, pass by me with the hands fastened--beaten--abused--and dragged through the village where they have lived and sung praises to the God of Heaven?"[87]

It is quite possible that these sentiments would have impelled Jones to take up arms and join the runaways when the moment came to face the owners and defy the IBEACO. At root, he was made of action: impetuous, resolute, and capable of great courage.[88] Over the years Jones had clashed with European missionaries who preventing him from using arms when the security of Rabai was at stake. The incident most revealing about Jones's behavior during the crisis took place on 2 November 1895, during the Anglo-Mazrui war, when guerrillas attacked Rabai in the predawn darkness. Arthur Smith, then in charge of the settlement, refused to allow the mission guns to be issued on grounds that a small party of Zanzibar soldiers was charged with the defense of Rabai. Jones, over Smith's strong objections, entered his house, removed the guns, and issued them to the men ready to return the fire of the Mazrui force. One of the qualities which most endeared Jones to Africans in Rabai was his readiness to stand up to white people, European or Arab.[89] These circumstances were similar to those of October 1888, when Rabai's security was also threatened by armed slave owners. To suppose that Jones, then in sole charge of the station, would have stayed out of the fray, casts him out of character.

The question became moot on 25 October, when Mackenzie averted a collision by offering to redeem the slaves. Price had informed Mackenzie that hundreds of runaways, prepared to fight, were at Rabai. The two agreed that an armed party going to Rabai would spark off not only a battle, but a war pitting runaways everywhere against their owners.[90] Mackenzie, greatly upset with

---

[86] Ibid., 191-2.

[87] Ibid, 197.

[88] In 1885, when he traveled with Bishop Hannington through Maasai territory on the way to Uganda, Jones chased a group of Maasai, who had stolen a load of wire. Jones, unarmed and alone, rushed into their midst, disregarded their raised spears, and walked away with the bundle. Dawson, *Hannington*, 407. After Hannington's murder, Jones led the caravan, from Kavirondo to Rabai, on a forced march of two months, at the end of which Jones arrived in a "fearfully emaciated" condition. Handford to Lang, 15 Jan.[Feb.], 1886, G3A5/03, CMS.

[89] Gibson Ngome, interviewed Rabai, 3 May 1973. The surviving reports of Smith and Jones do not mention their quarrel, but it is significant that Smith made no reference to the part played by the mission people in turning back the attack, whereas Jones emphasized that "our men of the settlement" were among Rabai's defenders. Smith to Baylis, 11 Nov. 1895, and Jones to CMS, 15 Nov. 1895, G3A5/011, CMS. Solomon Foster Mwingereza, who was a boy at the time, distinctly remembers that Jones and other mission people used guns in the affray. Interviewed at Chaani, Mombasa, 4 Oct. 1973.

[90] Mackenzie to Euan Smith, 26 Oct. 1888, FO 541/28, 437-9; Price, *Third*

Price but obliged to protect the mission, saw no alternative but to compensate the owners. The owners accepted the Company's offer and allowed Mackenzie time to negotiate terms and compile a list of runaways and their owners. On 30 October Mackenzie, Price, and Lloyd Mathews traveled to Rabai, where for the following week they took the names of all the runaways living at Rabai, as well as those settled on the neighboring Methodist mission stations of Jomvu and Ribe, and the Lutheran mission at Jimba. A total of 1,421 names were recorded, 907 of which were those of runaways from the coast. Of the latter, 656 lived at Rabai.[91]

During November and December Mackenzie completed arrangements with the owners and the missionaries for manumission of all the runaways. On 22 November the owners agreed to accept MT$25 for each slave in exchange for a signed certificate renouncing any future claim.[92] Mackenzie restricted claims to Muslim owners living in the coast ports, and he entitled unclaimed slaves and the runaway slaves of the Miji Kenda to a freedom certificate issued by the Company.[93] As for the missionaries, they agreed to permit only those with freedom papers or permits signed by Mackenzie to remain on their stations. At Rabai, the major source of concern, Price posted John Burness, an English missionary, to fill the new post of Lay Secretary, and he placed under Burness four patrolmen to keep out other runaway slaves.[94] By the end of December the long and costly task of compensation was completed, and on 1 January 1889 at Rabai the Company issued freedom certificates to 1,421 runaway slaves.[95]

Campaign, 194.

[91] 416 of the 656 coast runaways were from Mombasa. Mackenzie to Euan Smith, 15 Nov. 1888, and enclosures, FO 541/28, 441-6. The coast runaways at the other stations were as follows: Ribe, 208; Jomvu, 28, and Jimba, 40. The Ribe station acquired most of its runaways while under the direction since early 1888 of Rev. F.J. Heroe, an African ordained minister from Sierra Leone. See ch. 8.

[92] Mackenzie to Euan Smith, 23 Nov. 1888, FO 541/29, 25-6.

[93] Ibid. The runaway slaves of the Miji Kenda totalled as follows: Rabai, 264; Ribe, 103; Jomvu, 102; and Jimba, 20.

[94] Price to Burness, 26 Dec. 1888, G3A5/06, CMS.

[95] Mackenzie to Euan Smith, 5 Jan. 1889, FO 403/117, 151. The cost of compensation amounted to £3,500 of which £1,300 came from the Company. The rest was contributed as follows: British Treasury, £800; CMS through Fowell Buxton, £1,200; and the United Methodist Free Churches, £ 200. P.L. McDermott, *British East Africa, or IBEA: a History of the Formation and Work of the Imperial British East Africa Company* (London: Chapman and Hall, 1893), 30.

6

The Imperial British East Africa Company

Even for a philanthropic enterprise pledged to fight slavery and the slave trade, the Imperial British East Africa Company's redemption of 1,421 runaway slaves in Rabai within weeks of receiving its lease to govern the coastal strip was a dramatic opening act. Company director George Sutherland Mackenzie also wanted to make it the Company's last public performance as far as freeing slaves was concerned. He would have nothing further to do with runaways. "I have found no practical gratitude in the redeemed slave," he wrote a local missionary, "and beyond the peaceful settlement of a difficult question the Company derives no benefit whatever by my action.[1] The British consul-general in Zanzibar, C. B. Euan Smith, who looked on runaways as "idle, indolent fellows, merely anxious to avoid work" and who complained about the "wrong inflicted on the Arabs" helped Mackenzie clamp down on mission stations and impose a non-harboring policy.[2] At Mackenzie's request, Euan Smith issued a circular to all missionaries "in the British Sphere" requesting them to "take advantage of the present state of good feeling" to turn away all slaves not possessing a "paper of freedom" or, in cases of ill-treatment, to send them to the *liwali* of Mombasa.[3] When a local Methodist missionary took exception, the IBEACO forced compliance by putting pressure directly on the home mission office.[4] Within one year, the Company committed itself to restoring runaway slaves to their owners, by force if necessary.[5] This policy remained in effect until IBEACO rule ceased on the 30th June 1895 with the establishment of the East Africa Protectorate.[6]

---

[1] Mackenzie to Price, 24 Jan. 1889, FO 541/29, 76C.

[2] Euan Smith to Salisbury, 20 Nov. 1888, FO 541/28. 436.

[3] Euan Smith circular, 19 Feb. 1889, FO 541/29, 134-5. "I believe that, if these measures are carried out loyally and humanely, the Arab and Swahili slave-owners will soon relinquish their present undoubted fears as to the *bone fides* of the missionaries, and that the domestic slaves themselves will, except in cases of real ill-treatment, cease to attempt to find an asylum within the Mission stations."

[4] Carthew to Euan Smith, 10 Mar. 1889, FO 403/118, 39-40; Buchanan to Portal, 19 Jul. 1889, FO 403/119, 118-9; IBEACO to United Methodists' Free Churches Home and Foreign Missions, 24 Sep. 1889, FO 403/119, 586.

[5] As per the IBEACO director's notice of February 1890. Mackenzie to Foreign Office, 21 Jan. 1896, FO 403/225, 70.

[6] In January 1895, the IBEACO helped capture and restore two slaves who had run

The IBEACO needed the support of slaving interests, and to secure it the Company assisted in the capturing of runaways and the destruction of maroon settlements. They also employed slave laborers. Company officials often saluted the humanitarian ideal, but they were commanded by self-interest and fear.[7] Particularly dreaded was a revolt against European rule by the Mazrui factions in Gasi and Takaungu, whom the Company attempted to assuage through protection and pay-offs. Mbaruk of Gasi was granted a substantial retainer and supplied with arms, while his armed slaves were employed as mercenaries.[8] Salim b. Rashid of Takaungu was accorded full control of his territory, from which a slave export trade to the northern coast operated unmolested until 1895.[9] The Company ignored, if not entirely hushed up, the existence of the trade (one 1892 Melindi-Takaungu district report alleged that the slave trade was "stamped out," even though that same year Salim was selling Giriama slaves on the northern coast[10]) and was in 1890 accused by the British vice-consul in Zanzibar of "being on the [Arab slave-owners'] side in this important matter."[11] The IBEACO needed Salim b. Khamis to discourage the German East Africa Company, which operated a trading station near Takaungu. In return he was expected to control the "disaffected Arabs" of Malindi district, outspoken in their dislike of the Company and suspected of being in league with Witu.[12]

---

away from their owner, Mbaruk b. Rashid of Gasi. Mbaruk to Pigott, 6 May, 13 Jul., and 23 Dec. 1894, and n.d.[received 26 Jan. 1895], CP 67/14, KNA.

[7] M.J. de Kiewiet, "History of the Imperial British East Africa Company, 1876-1895" (London: University of London Ph.D. Thesis, 1955), 261, re "inconsistency" in the IBEACO's humanitarian policies; see also Berg, "Mombasa under the Busaidi Sultanate," 301-4.

[8] The salary of Mbaruk and his staff was 1,940 rupees (£190) per month. Mackenzie to IBEACO, 1 Dec. 1888, FO 403/138, 209-10. This salary was still being paid in late 1890, and his men were employed by the IBEACO at least through 1894. Euan Smith to Salisbury, 2 Sep. 1890, ibid., 208; Hardinge to Kimberley, 1 May 1895, C. 8274.

[9] Salim, whom the British vice consul praised in 1885 as the coast's "best and most energetic governor," was notorious among CMS missionaries in Mombasa months prior to IBEACO rule as the "slave trading governor of Takaungu." Takaungu was acknowledged as a slave trading center by the IBEACO as early as June 1890. Taylor diary, 17 Oct. 1887, G3A5/05, CMS; Simons to Euan Smith, 24 Jun. 1890, FO 403/138, 192, de Winton to Euan Smith, 7 Aug. 1890, ibid., 141-2; A caravan route from the interior to Takaungu, via the Sabaki river, was still "much used" in 1895. Ainsworth to Pigott, 31 Jan. and 20 Feb. 1895, FO 403/209, 35, 41, resp.

[10] Dec. 1892 report of J. Bell-Smith, Superintendent of Melindi-Takaungu Districts, FO 2/57. Macdougall to Craufurd, 11 Mar. 1898, CP 75/46, KNA.

[11] Euan Smith to Salisbury, 2 Dec. 1890, FO 403/139, 23.

[12] de Winton to Euan Smith, 4 and 9 Oct. 1890, ibid., 137. The Germans had maintained a trading post at Mtanganyiko since February 1887 and abandoned their claim in April 1891, after receiving a payment from the IBEACO of 1,000 rupees. Macdonald to Salisbury, 21 Nov. 1887, and encl., FO 403/103, 36-7; Foreign Office to IBEACO, 30 Apr. 1891, FO 403/158. The IBEACO also depended on Salim to hire

Most slaves, maroons, and other African groups seeking parity and protection understood the Company's pro-slavery policies and resisted accordingly. Maroons distrusted IBEACO officials, and the maroons of Witu resisted Company authority to the point of declaring war. True, Witu participated in the slave trade, but so did the Company's political allies. Maroons fought for independence, not for the slave trade, and against fealty to British interests. Only the Gosha of the distant Juba river, where news had reached of the Rabai redemptions and where Zanzibar had established good relations, looked on the IBEACO as a potential ally.

In fairness, the Company did serve to undermine slave owners' authority, long challenged by runaway slaves, by enforcing slave and slave trade laws in the few towns under its effective authority. In Mombasa, Malindi, and Lamu slave owners were unable to coerce their slaves in the presence of the Company and loyal *maliwali*; the law forced them instead to negotiate with their slaves and acknowledge their right to market labor and acquire property. Slaves were not prepared to accept anything less. The consequence was, to use Cooper's term, "independence under slavery," at least in Mombasa. Cooper describes the considerable mobility and economic activity of Mombasa slaves during the 1890s, though without recognizing that such "personal initiative and ability" had arisen but recently as a consequence of marronage and legal enforcement.[13]

Marronage ameliorated slavery and obliged the Company to do the same. Maroons were obstacles to smooth administration that Company officials were at pains to remove; and restricting the increase of maroon settlements entailed restricting slavery itself. Maroons and maroon communities on the southern and northern coasts challenged the authority of IBEACO officials and tested their limits as self-professed humanitarians, governors, and businessmen.

1. *Lugard's Fuladoyo Scheme*

The moment the IBEACO intervened in Rabai, the maroon settlement of Fuladoyo became part of the controversy between the CMS and angry slave owners.[14] Although initially included in Mackenzie's redemption scheme, the Fuladoyans were not freed in Rabai along with the mission-based runaways, because their list was not completed in time. For much of 1889 the IBEACO and the missions put off the matter, but late in the year the Company was forced to act. Slave owners, angry that slaves continued to flee into the hinterland after the mass redemption at Rabai, were planning an attack on Fuladoyo. Company

---

out his slaves for caravan work to Uganda, giving him cash in advance. Hardinge to Salisbury, 12 Apr. 1896, FO 403/226, 176.

[13] Cooper, *Plantation Slavery*, 228-42 and passim. Cooper argues, without evidence, that these conditions appertained along the entire Kenya coast throughout the nineteenth century. Cooper often paints broad chronological and geographical murals with a brush dipped in a tiny time and place. For other comments on Cooper, see chs. 1 and 8, and the conclusion.

[14] For an earlier mission-owner controversy involving Fuladoyo, see ch. 4.

officials had no soldiers to prevent hostilities, yet they could not allow , as Frederick Lugard later put it, "a sanguinary war to spring up at the very gates of their headquarters, while they posed as the administrators and paramount power of the country."[15] Mackenzie was prepared to redeem the Fuladoyans in order to avoid trouble. The missionaries, too, were ready to cooperate. In late November and early December, Jones traveled around Fuladoyo district to resume work on the list begun the previous year.[16]

In January 1890 Lugard persuaded Mackenzie to drop his plan for wholesale redemption.[17] Lugard, who had recently joined the Company, believed strongly that runaways should purchase their own freedom. They could work for the Company as porters or laborers to earn the money. Lugard opposed repeating the Rabai offer because the freedom papers issued in Rabai had acquired a "market value," thus depreciating the legal and moral values for which he believed they had been issued. Papers were sold, freed runaways sold themselves back into slavery, and slave owners cooperated to take a share of the profits. Rather than solve the question of runaway slaves, the scheme made it worse. "It is a direct inducement to slaves to run away and augment these gangs of fugitives." The Company would get better results, argued Lugard, if it advanced to the runaways the cost of their redemption in return for a fair share of work. "Those willing to work out their own freedom," he concluded, "will be worthy of it."[18]

Lugard's idea met with approval from maroon and owner alike. On 2 January 1890 Lugard met with the Fuladoyans, led by Uledi Mwachinga and Mandevu. Jones had completed registering their names, and Lugard discovered that the Fuladoyans "are expecting their freedom daily." He proposed that the runaways work out their redemption as protected employees of the Company. The Fuladoyans, he wrote, "jumped at the idea."[19] On the 16th Lugard discussed his scheme with maroons at Makongeni. Lugard returned to Mombasa where he conferred with Mackenzie and Mandevu of Fuladoyo.[20] Soon Mackenzie met with the slave owners, who agreed on the redemption price of MT$16 (later revised to MT$15), a sum considerably less than the MT$25 paid by the Company for the Rabai runaways.[21]

[15] Lugard, *Rise of Our East African Empire*, I, 224.

[16] Pigott Malindi diary, 4 Dec. 1889, FJL; Mackenzie to Euan Smith, 12 Feb. 1890, MSS. Brit. Emp. s. 18, C68/123, RH; Lugard, *Diaries*, I, 60-1.

[17] Lugard, *Diaries*, I, 86-7.

[18] Ibid, 56-7. Lugard's experiences with the Fuladoyans and his understanding of coastal slavery were to play an important role in his proposals for dealing with the institution in Nigeria and in his formulations of Indirect Rule once he became High Commissioner of Northern Nigeria (1900-1906) and Governor of Nigeria (1912-18). J. Hogendorn and P. Lovejoy, "The Development and Execution of Frederick Lugard's Policies toward Slavery in Northern Nigeria," *Slavery and Abolition*, 10, 1 (1989), 1-43.

[19] Lugard, *Diaries*, I., 61-2

[20] Ibid., 86-7.

[21] Mackenzie to Euan Smith, 12 Feb. 1890, FO 403/136, 173-4. The Maria Theresa

Within months, Lugard's scheme ran into trouble. After traveling up-country he found on his return that the IBEACO had made little progress toward the redemption of the Fuladoyans. Work for them had not been provided. Many had left their settlement on account of drought, hunger, and fear of attack. When Lugard passed through Fuladoyo on 7 May he found that the "Fuladoyo fields were mostly waste land overgrown with grass, half the men they said [with Uledi Mchinga (Mwachinga)] had gone to settle at Rabai." Some had moved to Ribe, others to Makongeni, while some had joined groups of marauding bands--and, as some had done in the Mwachisenge famine, turned to slave trading.[22] The

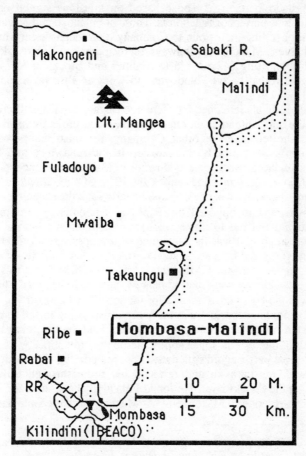

dollar, or "Black dollar," served as the currency of the East African coast throughout the mid- and late-nineteenth century. According to Sheriff, £1 equalled MT$ 4.75. *Slaves, Spices, and Ivory*, xix.

[22] When Lugard arrived in Makongeni from the interior on 5 May, he learned that two Fuladoyans had recently tried to sell two Kisauni women as slaves to the people of Makongeni. *Diaries*, I, 214-6.

Fuladoyans who remained behind continued working for their redemption, but, noted Lugard, "all were disheartened at nothing having been done."[23]

Lugard, who had returned to the coast to organize a caravan to Uganda, worked alone and against the clock to revive the redemption scheme. He journeyed to Fuladoyo, Mwaiba, Rabai, and Ribe in order to determine how many of the Fuladoyans in each location remained interested, and he compiled a detailed list of Mombasa and Malindi owners to assist the Company after his departure. More than 150 were living in Rabai with Uledi Mwachinga. Others were drawn from Mwaiba (20), Ribe (where almost 100 Fuladoyans were settled), and Fuladoyo itself.[24] Those based on missions signed on with the Company either as porters or as laborers. Those at Fuladoyo and Mwaiba had the added option of selling their grain to Company representatives at Mnarani after the August harvest. Makongeni runaways, on the other hand, were asked to work on the road connecting Makongeni to Malindi and Stockade No. 2. In July Lugard put the Rabai-based Fuladoyans to work at Taru on a road-building project.

Company officials remained indifferent to Lugard's scheme. Tactlessness on the part of the superintendent in charge of the Taru project contributed to its failure. The shortcomings of other Company men also hampered Lugard's efforts. Officials were plainly uninterested in the runaways, and Francis de Winton, who replaced Mackenzie as director in May, was no exception. Lugard claimed that, in the July meeting among the IBEACO, the *liwali* of Mombasa, and the Mombasa slave owners, de Winton nearly sank the scheme by encouraging those owners who opposed the February agreement.[25] In spite of such setbacks, Lugard hurried to make workable arrangements before he left for Uganda. Most important was the launching of a properly supervised work project. De Winton refused to spare anyone to run it. In late July, however, Lugard received assistance from the CMS, who released William Jones to superintend the runaways in railway construction near Mombasa. Jones, well known to the runaways, was the best man available for the job.[26] Yet Lugard was convinced two weeks before his departure that the scheme was going to fall through. "The Watoro and the Arabs are suspicious," he wrote, "and, by nature, apathetic. The Company is not interested. Jones appears to be the only hope."[27]

For the most part Lugard's prediction proved correct. On 6 August he left Mombasa with his caravan and retraced his route through Fuladoyo and Makongeni on the Sabaki river. He found Fuladoyo abandoned, the inhabitants for the most part gone to Makongeni. At Makongeni the people had lost their

---

[23] F. Lugard, "The Watoro of Fuladoyo," 23 Jul. 1890, MSS. Brit. Emp. s. 99, East Africa 1888/92 Letter Book, RH; Lugard, *Diaries*, I, 214-6.

[24] Lugard's final total of Fuladoyans committed to the scheme was 280. *Our East African Empire*, I, 298.

[25] Lugard "Watoro of Fuladoyo," Lugard, *Diaries*, I, 235.

[26] Lugard, *Our East African Empire*, I, 297-8; Lugard to Fitch, 29 Jul. 1890, MSS. Brit. Emp. s. 99, East Africa 1888/92 Letter Book, RH.

[27] Lugard to Waller, 26 Jul., 1890, ibid.

earlier enthusiasm for the redemption scheme. K. Anstruther, for a time stationed at Makongeni to supervise workers on the Malindi-Makongeni road, was absent. Lugard heard that the Makongenites were in touch with Salim b. Khamis of Takaungu, who wished to recruit them as followers. The people, Lugard noted in his diary, "have lost heart because Anstruther has been withdrawn from the Sabaki and they think it best now to temporize with the other side."[28] Before setting off into the interior, Lugard made a brief trip to Malindi to meet *liwali* Said b. Hamed and to make some last-minute attempts to keep the scheme alive. He left feeling he had persuaded Said, until then misinformed about the scheme, of its value. Again, Lugard's problem proved to be less local opposition than failures on the part of the IBEACO. The detailed runaway lists, which had arranged for dispatch to Malindi, had never been posted. Lugard's apprehensions resurfaced. "Once I am out of the way the [redemption scheme] will be shelved." He blamed de Winton. "I don't believe Sir Francis cares a curse about it."[29]

Jones did achieve a degree of success after Lugard's departure. Numbers of runaways from Makongeni and the Fuladoyans, both from Fuladoyo and the missions, signed on for the railway project. By early September between two and three hundred were at work, many of whom earned the price of redemption.[30] The work scheme encountered problems from the first, however, and eventually broke down.[31] No statistics appear to have survived, but Robert Cust in Rabai reported in December that "our population has [been] largely increased by people from Fuladoyo and elsewhere, who have either bought their freedom with corn, etc., or else worked it out at the railway works of the Company."[32] Likewise people from Fuladoyo and Makongeni were preparing to settle at the new CMS station in Jilore, near the Sabaki, once their freedom had been purchased.[33]

Nevertheless most maroons had lost faith in redemption schemes and concentrated on reviving their old settlements. W.W.A. Fitzgerald, who visited Makongeni and Fuladoyo in September 1891, found both thriving and populous, with abundant fields of crops. Makongeni appeared to be growing. Fitzgerald noted that runaway settlements "were scattered about the country on both sides of the Sabaki. I visited two large and substantial villages, the inhabitants of which

---

[28] **Diaries**, I, 239.

[29] Ibid, 245-6

[30] de Winton to Euan Smith, 3 Sep. 1890, FO 541/36, 10.

[31] Lugard, *Our East African Empire*, I, 299. It appears that Jones's supervision of the scheme stopped before February 1891. de Winton to Jones, 2 Mar. 1891, G3A5/07, CMS. Hogendorn and Lovejoy's account of Lugard's scheme ends at the point when Jones took over. "Frederick Lugard's Policies," 4.

[32] Cust letters, Dec. 1890, *Anti-Slavery Reporter*, Series 4, 11, 2(Mar./Apr. 1891). Those who sold grain had arranged to sell their harvest to the IBEACO. Lugard, "The Watoro of Fuladoyo" and Lugard to Fitch, 29 Jul. 1890, MSS.Brit. Emp. s. 99, East Africa 1888/92 Letter Book, RH.

[33] Shaw to Lang, 24 Jan. 1891, G3A5/07, CMS. A few Fuladoyans settled on the Methodist mission station at Ribe. Carthew report, in UMFC *Magazine*, January, 1891.

looked well-fed and contented."[34] For the next five years, Makongeni and Fuladoyo continued to receive fresh additions of runaway slaves from Malindi and other districts on the coast.[35]

For these maroons, little had changed. They still feared raids from slave owners and other hostile intruders. When J.R.L. Macdonald passed through Makongeni in 1891 he found the people "in constant dread of raids by the natives beyond the Sabak," much as they had been when Lugard first arrived there in early 1890.[36] The maroons were worried, as well, about attacks from the coast. So they pulled down Lugard's stockade to prevent parties of slave owners and others from using it as a base, and let their sector of the Tsavo road revert to bush. "The Watoro discourage its being kept open," wrote Arthur Hardinge in 1896, "not caring for the visits of Arab or Swahili caravans, some of which might bring up their former owners, and prefer to be encompassed on every side by miles of dense bush into which they can run for refuge if attacked."[37]

IBEACO officials, the runaway's erstwhile emancipators, were responsible for many of their subsequent troubles. In early 1890 during deliberations over Lugard's redemption scheme, George Mackenzie tried to influence the owners by issuing a proclamation which made the Company liable to recapture and return all slaves who ran away.[38] De Winton reaffirmed Mackenzie's actions, which also had the backing of Lugard.[39] Soon after, forays against Makongeni and Fuladoyo were launched by slave owners with the consent of the IBEACO. They carried the Company's flag and, in some cases, used the Company's soldiers. And on behalf of owners, the Company captured runaways from these districts and threatened to burn villages harboring fugitive slaves.[40] Some justification may have existed for attacking the maroons, who were known for slave raiding in the hinterland and on the coastal plantations. They employed the captives themselves or traded them away to the Miji Kenda.[41] Company-sanctioned raids on the maroons invariably failed to destroy their settlements. And in their wake

---

[34] Fitzgerald, *Travels*, 119-26, 136-7.

[35] Weaver to Craufurd, 24 Jul. 1896, CP 75/46, KNA. Hardinge report, C. 8683, 12.

[36] *Soldiering and Surveying in British East Africa, 1891-1894* (London: Edward Arnold, 1897), 20-1.

[37] Hardinge to Salisbury, 17 Feb. 1896, C. 8274, 63.

[38] Hardinge to Salisbury, 13 Nov. 1895, and encls., FO 403/211, 172-5.

[39] de Winton to Malindi sheikhs, 28 Sep. 1890, FO 403/211, 174; Lugard to de Winton, 31 Jul. 1890, MSS Brit. Emp. East Africa 1888/92 Letter Book, RH. In spite of his work on behalf of the runaways, Lugard cared little for them personally. He regarded the people of Makongeni with contempt: "a set of cowardly, thieving rascals--the refuse of Malindi, etc." Lugard, *Our East African Empire*, I, 304.

[40] Hardinge to Kemball, 26 Nov. 1896, MSS. Brit. Emp. s.22, G5, and Hardinge to Mackenzie, 16 Jan. 1898, s. 18 C59/134, RH.

[41] Fitzgerald, *Travels*, 131; Hardinge to Kimberley, 25 Jun. 1895, FO 403/210, 60-1; Hardinge to Salisbury, 29 Aug. 1895, ibid, 261; A.M. Champion, "History of the Wa Giryama," 23 Jan. 1914, and O.S. Knowles, "Kauma History," n.d., KFI/13, KNA.

maroons became more hostile toward the coast and the British.[42] When the Mazrui rose up against the East Africa Protectorate in 1895, maroons fought on the rebel side.[43]

2. The Destruction of Witu

On the northern coast, where it also took over the administration of the Sultan's dominions, the IBEACO for a while competed with a German company for control of the Lamu mainland. But their bane was the Witu sultanate, which after recognizing the German protectorate during its tenure from 1885 to 1890, withstood Company rule until 1893. Though the Witu-German alliance certainly frustrated the IBEACO's plans, the strongest resistance to British [and for that matter, European] rule emanated from Witu's *watoro* forest communities, as became apparent when the Germans pulled out. Not until 1894, when British troops destroyed Witu's forest strongholds, and placed its territory under British, as opposed to Company, administration, may the period of imperial rule over the northern coast be said to have begun.

Witu was too weak to pose as an independency inside a British sphere of influence. Its defiance invariably crumbled when confronted by a few hundred troops. Britain preferred to destroy Witu and its satellite villages rather than negotiate a peace and recognize the sultan of Witu as a ruler in his own right, as they had done with the Mazrui. Witu's destruction was justified on the grounds that Witu opposed the end of the slave trade and that it was plotting an anti-European revolt along the entire Kenya coast. Yet, if such charges were valid--and evidence was provided--they could have been levied as well against Salim b. Khamis of Takaungu, whom the Company preferred to keep as a "friend." The sultan of Witu's downfall was brought on by his followers, who were responsible for those acts which directly challenged the authority of Zanzibar, the IBEACO, and Great Britain. Company and British officials thought of Witu, not as the prosperous agricultural district ripe for trade, which it was, but rather as a "den of lawless robbers and outlaws." The sultan of Witu was a criminal who "had gathered round him a following of felons, malcontents, and runaway slaves who had lived by plundering...and selling [slaves]...for cattle."[44]

After the establishment of the German-Witu protectorate, the sultan of Zanzibar withdrew his garrisons from the old boundaries of Witu territory and flew his flag only at Kipini and Kau, and on Lamu and Pate islands.[45] The

---

[42] Ibid., Frederick Burt of the CMS station at Jilore told Hardinge that the maroons at Makongeni became hostile toward British rule and Europeans in general as a result of the IBEACO-sanctioned raids.

[43] See ch. 7.

[44] Hardinge, *Diplomatist in the East*, 130; Jackson, *Early Days*, 26.

[45] Holmwood to Salisbury, 4 Feb. 1887, FO 403/100. Holmwood to Salisbury, 2 Mar. 1887, FO 403/101. The Anglo-German Agreement of 1886 deferred the question of rights to Manda and Pate islands. For the German period in Witu, Ylvisaker, *Lamu*, 129-49, and for events leading to the German protectorate, see ch. 2 above.

Germans entitled Simba the "Sultan of Swahililand" and recognized him as sovereign of an area stretching from the Tana river to Kiwaiyu. Where the sultan of Zanzibar's control was uncertain, allegiance of local leaders wavered. In the *watoro* district, Avatula b. Bahero, who had expressed loyalty to Zanzibar until the sultan accepted the Anglo-German agreement, hauled down the Zanzibar flag at his Jongeni headquarters.[46] Then Mzee Seif, head of the Bajuni on Pate island and the opposite mainland, led a delegation to Witu to swear loyalty to Simba.[47] With the loss of the Bajuni, support for Zanzibar's came only from Lamu island and a few traders and farmers settled in Kau, Kipini, and Siu. Even there it was unclear to the inhabitants who would be ruling in the near future. In 1888 the German Witu Company increased uncertainties by establishing a post office in Lamu, demanding the cession of Lamu to the German sphere, and persuading the German government to press its claim in Europe.[48]

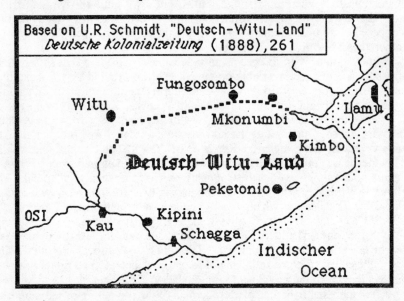

Based on U.R. Schmidt, "Deutsch-Witu-Land" *Deutsche Kolonialzeitung* (1888), 261

Ultimately, Zanzibar turned to the IBEACO to challenge Witu and the Germans. Though only incorporated by royal charter in April 1888, the IBEACO had obtained in May 1887 as the British East Africa Association a concession from Sultan Bargash to administer the ten-mile strip from Vanga to Kipini. In 1888 the concession was reaffirmed by Bargash's successor, Khalifa, with the promise of a future arrangement for the administration of the sultan's dominions north of Kipini. The German Witu Company disputed this concession and

---

[46] Simons to IBEA, 24 Oct. 1889, in Alexander to FO, 19 Nov. 1889, FO 403/120, 149.

[47] Denhardt statement, 9 Apr. 1890, FO 403/137, 122.

[48] McDermott, *IBEA*, 34-6.

presented its own claim with the backing of the German government, but after arbitration the award went in August to the IBEACO. Khalifa then issued the IBEACO a new concession, which included Lamu, Pate, Kismayu, Mogadishu, and the other towns of the Benadir coast. [49]

By then IBEACO officers and directors, eager to drive out the Germans and take full possession of the northern coast, had anticipated the award and were pressuring the German Witu Company. In July 1889 it publicized its treaty with Avatula, who had deserted Witu and signed over to the IBEACO his jurisdiction over the territory from north of Lamu to Kismayu.[50] In the closing months of

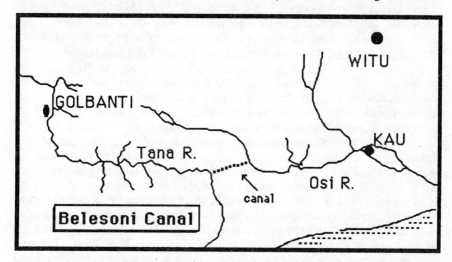

the year, the IBEACO used the threat of force to get the soldiers of Witu and the German Witu Company to vacate their important stockade on the Belesoni canal, which connected the Tana and Osi rivers.[51] The German Witu Company, already in serious financial difficulty, began to collapse when confronted by the IBEACO challenge. Germany, which was losing interest in the northern coast, then abandoned the Witu Protectorate and its other claims north of the Tana in the Anglo-German agreement of July 1890.[52]

As the German Company withdrew, Witu became more militant and came closer to conflict with the IBEACO. In January 1889 Simba died, and Fumo

[49] Ibid, 31-44; E. Hertslet, *The Map of Africa by Treaty*, 3 vols. 3rd ed. (London: His Majesty's Stationery Office, 1909), I, 350-61; de Kiewiet, "IBEA," 128-77.

[50] Portal to Salisbury, 29 Jul. 1889, and Sandys to Portal, 21 Jul. 1889, FO 403/119, 120. See also map in Alexander to Salisbury, 31 Oct. 1889, FO 403/120.

[51] McDermott, *IBEA*, 48-53; Euan Smith to Salisbury, 1 Dec. 1889, FO 403/120, 249; Euan Smith to Salisbury, 11 Jan. 1890, and encls., FO 403/136, 108-11.

[52] Coupland, *Exploitation of East Africa*, 484-5.

Bakari, Simba's outspoken and forceful cousin and son-in-law, took his place.[53] Fumo Bakari's succession led to the departure of Gustave and Clemens Denhardt, Simba's old advisors, and the rise of the German Witu Company manager, Kurt Tüppen, who supplied Fumo Bakari with arms and encouraged Witu to resist IBEACO's attempts to secure a position on the Tana and take the Belesoni canal stockade.[54] Bakari's succession also unleashed the old Witu militants, most notably *watoro*, who had remained quiet under Simba while Germany was enlarging Witu's sphere on the northern coast. From May to October 1889, bands of Witu soldiers roamed the IBEACO's territory on the Tana river, where they levied heavy taxes, removed people to the north bank, planted flags, and threatened those suspected of wanting to sign treaties with the IBEACO.[55] In late November the soldiers crossed over to Lamu town unchallenged and frightened the public with what Euan Smith called "their riotous and insulting manner."[56] The IBEACO then issued an ultimatum to Bakari to rein in his troops and abandon the Belesoni stockade, and when it became apparent that the Company would act on their threats and that Tüppen would produce no support, Fumo Bakari's forces withdrew. Bakari then asked to be place under the IBEACO's protection, but the Company not trusting him declined.[57]

In August 1890 Sultan Khalifa's successor, Ali b. Said, proclaimed the abolition of all slave trading. He placed restrictions on slavery in his dominions, which, since July and with the signing of the Anglo-German agreement, once again included Witu. Promulgation of the decree caused resentment all along the Kenya coast; the British were especially concerned about Witu, where rumors circulated that Fumo Bakari was planning a coast-wide rebellion against Zanzibar and the IBEACO.[58] In September, a party of seven Germans met a bloody death at the hands of Fumo Bakari's men within the town walls of Witu. The next day, people from Witu looted and destroyed German estates in the neighborhood and killed two other Germans.[59] The British Foreign Office was convinced these acts were directed at Europeans in general and decided to dispatch a punitive force. In late October a large body of troops under Admiral E.R. Fremantle marched on

---

[53] Euan Smith to Salisbury, 2 Feb. 1889, FO 403/117. Fumo Bakari was the eldest son of Ahmed b. Bwana Sheikh, the brother of Simba's father. Fumo Bakari was Simba's son-in-law by virtue of his marriage to Simba's only child and daughter, Binti es Sultan. They had no issue.

[54] Simons to IBEACO, 24 Oct. 1889, in Alexander to FO, 19 Nov. 1889, FO 403/120, 148.

[55] Sandys to Portal, 7 Jun. 1889 and Buchanan to Portal, 7 Jun. 1889, FO 403/119, 30C-D; Alexander to FO, 5 Jul. 1889, ibid., 13; Sandys to Portal, 21 Jul. 1889, ibid. 120; Simons to Portal, 5 Oct. 1889, FO 403/120, 165; McDermott, *IBEA*, 46.

[56] Euan Smith to Salisbury, 1 Dec. 1889, FO 403/120, 249.

[57] Ibid, 248; Euan Smith to Salisbury, 11 Jan. 1890 and encls., FO 403/136; McDermott, *IBEA*, 52-4.

[58] Simons to Euan Smith, 24 Aug. 1890, 202. At the time Witu was involved deeply in the slave trade. Simons to Euan Smith, 24 Jun. 1890, ibid., 192.

[59] Euan Smith to Salisbury, 3 Oct. 1890, and encls., FO 403/139, 98f.

Witu, drove out the inhabitants, and razed the town. More than half the estimated supporters of Fumo Bakari appear to have been *watoro*.[60]

Britain ignored the evidence of Mazrui involvement in Witu's resistance. After the Mazrui ouster from Mombasa, the Mazrui were assisted by the Nabahani from their new base in Witu.[61] During the 1880s, Mbaruk of Gasi and Simba of Witu were in frequent association, a fact known to the British up to Witu's acceptance of the German protectorate.[62] As of June 1890 the IBEACO was aware of slave trading between Takaungu and the Witu-controlled port of Mkonumbi, and prior to Fremantle's advance on Witu, Company officials heard constant rumors that Witu, Takaungu, and Gasi were communicating with one another.[63] More incriminating were substantive allegations that the Mazrui had committed as many as one thousand troops to the defense of Witu. After the battle letters between Witu, Takaungu, and Gasi, dating to the previous April, were also captured.[64] Yet, following the battle, the consul-general of Zanzibar, Charles Euan Smith, even though he had been in Lamu at the time, made no mention of Mazrui troops to the Foreign Office and stressed instead the "loyalty and good behaviour" of Mbaruk of Gasi and Salim of Takaungu."[65] Euan Smith's timidity in the face of Mazrui defiance was underscored in Takaungu a few days after the battle at Witu. As an IBEACO official recalled:

> [Euan Smith] went himself, without any previous negotiations, to overawe, as he thought, the redoubtable Salim bin Hamis of Takaungu, who was 'in' with both Fumo Bakari and Mbaruk [of Gasi]....What induced him to seek an interview with Salim...no one knew, but he went in a small cruiser, and on anchoring within a couple of hundred yards of the landing-place, sent his interpreter with a message to tell him to come aboard. Salim's reply was to send one of his men down to the landing-place, who, by order, turned round and smacked his bare sit-upon, as Sir Charles, surrounded by the ship's officers, stood on deck, and looked on in amazement and no small degree of chagrin![66]

---

[60] Fremantle to Admiralty, 1 Nov. 1890, and encls. FO 403/161, 1-25. In one estimate, 4,500 of 8,800 defenders of Witu were labeled Wazigua, Katawa, and Watoro, all *watoro* designations. Ibid, 25.

[61] G.S.P. Freeman-Grenville, "The Coast, 1498-1840," in R. Oliver and G. Mathew, *History of East Africa, vol. I*, (Oxford: Clarendon, 1963), 149; Sparshott to CMS, 12 Jan. 1871, CA5/026; Greffulhe, "Voyage de Lamoo," 337-8.

[62] Haggard to Kirk, 25 Aug. 1884, FO 541/26, 231; Kirk to Granville, 3 and 7 Jul. 1885, FO 403/94, 40.

[63] Simons to Euan Smith, 24 Jun. 1890, FO 403/138, 191; de Winton to Euan Smith, 4 Aug. 1890; ibid., 140; Simons to Euan Smith, 5 and 24 Aug. 1890, ibid., 201-2; Pigott to Euan Smith, 21 Sep. 1890, FO 403/139, 100.

[64] Encl. no. 13 in Fremantle's report, FO 403/161, 25; Euan Smith to Salisbury, 8 Nov. 1890, and encls., FO 403/139, 179-80.

[65] Euan Smith to Salisbury, 8 Nov. 1890, FO 403/139, 179.

[66] Jackson, *Early Days*, 351. Jackson writes about this incident in such a way that it can be confused with the period following the destruction of Witu in 1894, but his reference to Fumo Bakari dates the Salim incident clearly in 1890. Bakari died in

The British neither lodged a protest over Salim's actions nor attempted to reprimand him, lest a revolt be provoked on the southern coast. The IBEACO director, Francis de Winton, was convinced Salim and Mbaruk were on the verge of colluding with the Mombasans to set the coast in flames. Euan Smith was persuaded of the "standing danger" posed by the two Mazrui leaders, who might, "if roused to hostility, form a powerful combination against the Sultan's authority which would be beyond the control of the Company's forces."[67]

The British chose instead to make an example of a rebellious Muscat Arab with few followers. He was Suleiman b. Abdullah (alias "Kimenya"), who owned extensive grain plantations and many slaves in the Malindi district.[68] Like Mbaruk and Salim, Suleiman's armed retainers took part in the defense of Witu. But Suleiman had the rashness to join the fighting and the misfortune of getting captured. He was already a marked man. In the weeks prior to the attack on Witu, when Company nerves were most sensitive to signs of revolt, Suleiman had a confrontation at Malindi with de Winton. After his capture, the Admiralty convicted Suleiman of aiding the Witu rebellion and deported him to Muscat. His slaves and plantations were confiscated and turned over to the IBEACO.[69]

In March 1891 the IBEACO assumed authority over the entire Witu district. The Company signed a treaty with Fumo Bakari and granted him a stipend. At the same the Company refused to recognize Bakari as sultan in Witu district and placed their administrative headquarters in Witu town, complete with an armed garrison. The effect was to frighten Fumo Bakari away into the recesses of the Utwani forest. Considerable possibilities of commerce were thereby squandered, because Witu's long-established communication links with the rest of the coast were essential for tapping the plantations operated by the maroons of the forest settlements. IBEACO officials were aware of the forest's agricultural potential. The company's agronomist, W.W. A. Fitzgerald, attested to the rich soils of Witu district, and other officials had remarked on the flourishing plantations of bananas, millet, red peppers, plantains, Indian corn, and rice in the vicinity of Pumwani and Jongeni, where rubber was also being harvested.[70]

January 1891. See note 74.

[67] Euan Smith to Salisbury, 17 Aug. 1890, FO 403/138, 166-7. De Winton exaggerated the strength of Salim and Mbaruk whom he alleged could "bring from 2,000 to 4,000 men each into the field, armed with guns." de Winton to Euan Smith, 14 Aug. 1890, ibid., 160.

[68] He was also heavily in debt to the *liwali* of Mombasa, Salim b. Khalfan, an old friend of the British. Cooper, *Plantation Slavery*, 88, 91, 146.

[69] Suleiman owned 261 slaves, valued at MT$13,050, land worth MT$12,000, and other grain and property worth MT$2,500. His debts totalled MT$15,000. Bell-Smith to de Winton, 5 Jan. 1891, FO 84/2146. Also Smith to Salisbury, 31 Jan. 1891, ibid; de Winton to Euan Smith, 4 Oct. 1890, FO 403/139, 137. W.W.A. Fitzgerald, the IBEACO manager of Suleiman's confiscated estate at Magarini, provides a detailed account of the Malindi hinterland and coast for the 1891-93 period in his *Travels*.

[70] Fitzgerald, *Travels*, 352f; Rogers and Jackson report, 20 Jul. 1891, FO 403/159, 86; Berkeley to IBEACO, Jul.[?] 1892, FO 403/172, 56. See also Peters, *New Light*

Fumo Bakari based himself at Jongeni, Avatula's home in the center of the *watoro* district. From November 1890 to July 1893, the IBEACO regarded Jongeni and Pumwani as the sources of numerous raids launched for slaves and food.[71] With the exception of the early months of 1891, when Fumo Bakari died and his eventual successor, Fumo Omari, made a temporary peace with the IBEACO, raiders kept the Lamu mainland and the Tana river districts in turmoil.[72] Apparently little notice was taken that, for all the time allegedly devoted to raiding and plundering, the forest maroons somehow managed to harvest considerable amounts of cash crops. Adopted policy dictated control before commerce. Company officers led several attacks on Jongeni, captured some raiders in the outlying districts, but were unable to secure the entire area under their jurisdiction.[73] Meanwhile many of the sultan's subjects abandoned their mainland farms and remained on the islands for security, and some, such as Mzee Seif, dealt clandestinely with the forest maroons while voicing loyal sentiments to the Company and the Sultan of Zanzibar.[74]

When the IBEACO announced in May 1893 that it would abandon Witu's administration, the Foreign Office once again decided to intervene. In late July, just before the Company's Witu garrisons withdrew from their stations, a 250-man force led by the consul-general of Zanzibar, Rennell Rodd, disembarked at Lamu with orders to place the Witu territory effectively under the control of the British protectorate of the sultan's dominions. Action was being taken because, in Rodd's words, the runaway slave subjects of "this unmanageable Chieftain" have used Pumwani and Jongeni as "fortresses...[for]...raiding and stealing slaves, while plentiful cases of relentless mutilation of women have been laid to

---

on Dark Africa, 66. The German Witu Company had hoped to develop Witu as one, vast plantation. For German agriculture in Witu, Ylvisaker, *Lamu,* 129-32.

[71] Jackson to Euan Smith, 21 Nov. 1890, FO 84/1910; Jackson to de Winton, 31 Dec. 1890, FO 84/2146; Fitzgerald, *Travels,* 328, 332-3, 352; Portal to Salisbury, 3 May 1892, FO 84/2231; Rogers to Pigott, 21 May 1893, FO 403/183, 49; Rodd to Rosebery, 5 Aug. 1893, ibid, 22.

[72] Fumo Bakari died on 4 January 1891. Bwana Shehe, Fumo Bakari's brother, was next in line for succession, but two days after his nomination he was chained and imprisoned because he advocated making peace with the IBEACO. Avatula was reportedly behind the move. Fumo Omari, the younger brother of Bwana Shehe, then succeeded to the sultanship of Witu. In March Fumo Omari and Avatula concluded a peace agreement with E.J.L. Berkeley, British vice consul, and George Mackenzie, director of the Company, but it soon became clear they had no intention of abiding by its terms. Euan Smith to Salisbury, 29 Jan. 1891, FO 84/2146; Berkeley to Euan Smith, 25 Mar. FO 403/158, 40-3; Hardinge to Kimberley, 9 Feb. 1895, FO 403/208, 180-82.

[73] Rogers to Pigott, 13 and 21 May 1893, FO 403/183, 48-9; Rodd to Rosebery, 5 Aug. 1893, ibid., 222; R. N. Lyne, *Zanzibar in Contemporary Times* (London: Hurst & Blackett, 1905), 165.

[74] For a glimpse of Mzee Seif playing the double game at this time, see Fitzgerald's account of his journey on the Bajuni coast in 1892. Fitzgerald, *Travels,* 379-500.

their charge [and] Lamu farms "have gradually fallen out of cultivation."[75]

> The Chiefs have consistently refused to give up any of the delinquents, even
> where their guilt was obviously established, and have continued to defy the
> authority of the Company's officers until the present day, so that within a few
> miles of Witu [since its destruction] there exists at least two cities of refuge
> where the murderer and the mutilator can secure immunity from arrest.

On 7 August Rodd and his men stormed Pumwani, and sacked and burned
the town along with the surrounding farms. His force then proceeded to Jongeni.
On approach, Rodd was struck by the abundance of food grown around the
stockaded village. "The plantain groves were very fine, and the rice-fields mag-
nificent, and the necessity of destroying all these food stores was consequently a
painful duty. But these people can neither be reached by fair words nor by force."
On the 13th Jongeni fell. Fumo Omari fled with his followers, but in the
coming months small parties flushed out scattered rebels and eliminated the
remaining pockets of resistance.[76] On 16 June 1894 Fumo Omari surrendered,
and the resistance of Witu and the maroons of the Utwani forest came to an end.
Over Ali b. Said's objection, the new consul-general, A.H. Hardinge, allowed
Fumo Omari to reside in Witu and receive a small pension. In November,
however, Omari was caught plotting another rebellion and was removed to
Zanzibar, where he died in August 1896.[77] The Witu district, which was noted
for its cash crops and agricultural prosperity, was abandoned by the maroons as a
result of the campaigns of 1890 and 1893. Where they went has not been recorded, though it is likely they receded into the interior before returning several
years later. As of 1896, when the first report on this and other parts of the
Lamu District of the East Africa Protectorate was filed, it was, in Hardinge's
words, "to all intents and purposes,...a wilderness; its inland boundary is still,
and must for many years to come, continue undefined."[78]

3. *The Gosha of Juba River*

Whereas the *watoro* of Witu actively resisted IBEACO rule, the maroons of
the Juba river welcomed it. The Gosha, as the maroons and their many river
villages were known, were first contacted by R.T. Simons, IBEACO superintendent in Lamu in April 1890. He brought their representatives to Kismayu to
meet director George Mackenzie. This delegation had already heard of Mackenzie
on account of his redemption of runaway slaves at Rabai (which "made a very

---

[75] Rodd to Rosebery, 5 Aug. 1893, FO 403/183, 222.

[76] Rodd to Rosebery, 5, 11,15, and 17 Aug. 1893, and encls., FO 403/183, 220-31;
Mathews to Hardinge, 22 Jun. 1894, FO 403/195, 109; Rogers to Mathews, 24 May
and 5 Jul. 1894, ibid., 153-4; Rogers to Mathews, 7 Aug. 1894, ibid., 308.

[77] Hardinge to Kimberley, 13 Nov. and 3 Dec. 1894, with encls., ibid., 180-5, 211-
7; Hardinge, *Diplomatist in the East*, 131.

[78] C. 8683, 15.

favourable impression"), and they "readily assented to place themselves under the administration of the Company." After hearing their reports of Christian Galla beyond the Gosha "also ready to welcome the advent of European," Mackenzie felt he had at last found the allies needed to deal with the troublesome Somali, who had defied Zanzibari and Company laws as far south as the Tana river. The Galla and Gosha, thought Mackenzie, would act as "a powerful lever at hand to hold the lawless Somali in check, and bring him rapidly under civilizing influences." Such breakthroughs would entail, logically speaking, the Company's advance into the northern interior.

The opening up of the River Juba to navigation is, I consider, second only in importance to the construction of a railway to the Victoria Nyanza.[79]

As discussed in chapter two, the Gosha maroons were the past possessions of the Somali and had established their villages in the 1850s, and possibly earlier. At the time of IBEACO contact, the Gosha population was estimated at 40,000 in 160 villages.[80] They had developed the river banks into an extended, prosperous agricultural strip that produced grain, cotton, and tobacco for trade. The Gosha also manufactured cloth. Their villages were run by councils and headmen, some of whom, such as Nassib Bunda and Songollo Mafula, exercised authority over many villages. They had successfully defended themselves against the Somali and were even manufacturing their own, albeit crude, gunpowder.[81] Since the 1880s Zanzibar supported the Gosha maroons as one of their allies against the Somali of the Webe Shebelle. The Gosha acquired guns from Zanzibar traders, and sultan Bargash's British military advisor, Lloyd Mathews, helped to strengthen Gosha's defenses by donating five hundred Enfield rifles.[82]

Thus, the IBEACO were building on an old alliance, and the Gosha readily entered into treaty arrangements. The Gosha leaders agreed to pay one-third of their annual crop and half the ivory captured in return for arms, ammunition, agricultural tools, and seed. Monthly cash stipends were also provided to the Gosha signatories and their headmen.[83] Soon the IBEACO sent a reconnaissance team up the Juba by steam launch, which returned with glowing reports of the potential of the "Gusha district." Other visits underlined prospects for future trade.[84] The Company was also spared competition with the Royal Italian East

[79] Mackenzie to Euan Smith, 24 Apr. 1890, FO 403/137, 163-4.

[80] Simons to IBEACO, 26 May 1890, FO 403/138, 31.

[81] Cassanelli, "Bantu Former Slave Communities," 216-38; Dundas, "Expedition up the Jub River," 214-7; Craufurd to IBEACO, Report of Kismayu District to 31 Dec. 1893, CP 68/19, and Jenner to Craufurd, 21 Jul. 1895, CP 74/45, KNA.

[82] Hardinge to Salisbury, 1 Oct. 1897, FO 403/244, 79; Cassanelli, "Bantu Former Slave Communities," 229-30.

[83] The treaties were officially signed in Sep./Oct. 1891. Hertslet, *Treaties*, I, 378. See also Salisbury to Portal, 22 Mar. 1892 and encls., C. 6555, 20-2.

[84] Dundas to Berkeley, 25 Sep. 1892, FO 403/173, 257-8; Dundas, "Expedition up the Jub River" and "Exploration of the Rivers Tana and Juba"; Craufurd report, Jan.

Africa Company (RIEACO), which confined its activities to the Benadir coast and deferred to the Company on Juba matters. R.T. Simon, the IBEACO's man in Lamu and head of the treaty delegation, was happy to negotiate on behalf of his employers with the Gosha on the west bank, and provide the same service for the RIEACO on the east bank.[85]

The Company, strapped for funds and understaffed in hostile Kismayu, could not press its advantage. As of 1892, the resources of the IBEACO had been overextended by the struggle to administer Witu district, and the Company was limited to a lone agent in Kismayu, where Somali harassment became daily routine. The Herti Somali, under Ali Naar, were irritated by the IBEACO's interference with the overland slave route via Jongeni. The Company compounded their labor problems, too, by protecting the Gosha, who since the treaties were admitting runaway slaves. The Company received complaints on this account as well through the Italian consulate in Zanzibar, because the RIEACO feared Somali reprisals.[86] For a time the Company agent in Kismayu, J. Ross Todd, calmed matters by convincing Nassib Bunda and Songollo Mafula to return runaways to the Somali. But then, to the anger of the Somali, Todd requested additional arms for the Gosha and began issuing freedom papers to slaves who escaped from the Somali and reached the fort at Kismayu.[87] Todd had also landed himself in trouble with the IBEACO. The Company had no intention of encouraging more slaves to run away after its experiences at Rabai and Fuladoyo. Todd was replaced, and a treaty for the return of runaway slaves was negotiated with the Somali in May 1893.[88]

Two months later, the Company's administration along most of the northern coast collapsed. Effective 31 July it withdrew its authority from the mainland, except for the ports, much to the dismay of the British government.[89] Company salaries to the Gosha leaders soon came to a halt. Responsibility for payment devolved to the British consul-general in Zanzibar but was not assumed until the following year.[90] The IBEACO agent at Kismayu continued reporting a modest level of exports from the Gosha district and maintained "friendly relations" with Gosha leaders.[91] But effective contact had ceased.

1894, CP 68/19, KNA.

[85] Simons to IBEACO, 26 May 1890, FO 403/138, 31; Treaty 81, IBEACO, 19 Sep. 1891, C. 6555, 21.

[86] Berkeley to IBEACO, 13 Aug. 1892, FO 403/173, 54-5.

[87] Todd to Pigott, 1 May 1893, FO 403/182, 206-7.

[88] Farrant to IBEACO, 29 Jul. 1893 and Craufurd to IBEACO, 20 Mar. 1894, CP 68/19, KNA.

[89] Foreign Office to IBEACO, 15 Jun. 1893, FO 403/182, 272-4.

[90] IBEACO to FO, 19 Jan. 1894, FO 403/193, 46; Craufurd to AgAdmin, Mombasa, IBEACO, 8 Feb. 1894, CP 68/19, KNA.

[91] Craufurd to Pigott, 28 Nov. 1893, Ibid; Craufurd to IBEACO, 21 Nov. 1894, CP 68/19, KNA.

The Gosha did well enough on their own. In 1894 they repulsed a Somali attack and afterwards destroyed their enemy's stronghold.[92] By the following year, nearly all the Somali's slaves were reported to have joined the Gosha, who were resettling on the western bank.[93] Nassib Bunda and Songollo Mafula kept in touch with the British, but when the East Africa Protectorate was established in 1895, most of the Gosha were residing inside the Italian sphere.[94]

4. *Slavery under the IBEACO*

Like other representatives of external powers on the coast--the sultan's governors, the British vice-consuls, the missionaries--IBEACO officials were, apart from paroxysmal gestures, unwilling and incapable of assisting individuals in their transition to freedom.[95] The Company was chartered to "abolish by degrees any system of slave trade or domestic servitud," and slavery was eroded in some areas of the coast by the Company's enforcement of the Sultan's law. At the same time, the Company wanted the cooperation of slave traders and slave owners, whose interests IBEACO officials repeatedly placed above those of slaves and maroons. The indifference displayed toward the Children of Ham by the Company is consistent within the policies of all outside powers, apart from a few sanguine officials. Though portraying slavery as evil, all gave priority to the extension and maintenance of control and power.

As a rule the IBEACO issued certificates of freedom in bulk, during crises, rather than as routine observance of the law. Of the 3,200 slaves freed between 1888 and 1895, nearly 75 per cent were made up of Rabai redemptioners and the condemned property of Witu rebels. A breakdown of individual cases for the coast as a whole appears not to have survived, but the records of the Lamu superintendent, which account for nearly half of the coast's redemption certificates, reflect a passive Company policy. Of the 247 Lamu cases recorded, 164 (or two-thirds) were freed because their owners had died. Only 41 received their certificates "by order of the Administrator of the Court."[96]

---

[92] Jenner to Hardinge, 28 Jul. 1895, FO 403/210, 228; Hardinge to Salisbury, 1 Oct. 1897, FO 403/244, 79.

[93] Jenner to Hardinge, 28 Jul. 1895, FO 403/210, 227.

[94] In 1897, only an estimated 12,000 were reported still living "on our side of the river." H.S. Newman, "East Africa Protectorate," in J. Scott Keltie, ed., *British East Africa* (London: Kegan Paul, Trench, Trübner, 1901), 286. For Gosha during the Protectorate period, ch. 8.

[95] In Swahili, *ungwana*, the "state of being a free man, in general freedom, civilization ...as opposed to *tumua*, slave; politically free as opposed to *shi*[e]*nzi*..., to be subjected, vassals." Krapf, *Dictionary of Suahili*, cv unguana. Also W.E. Taylor, *Giryama Vocabulary and Collections* (London: Society for Promoting Christian Knowledge, 1891), cv freedom.

[96] In Lamu no slaves were freed by the Company prior to 31 Mar. 1891. MacLennan to Hardinge, 16 Aug. 1895, FO 403/210, 267.

Slaves freed by IBEACO

1,421	Rabai, 1 Jan. 1889
158	Slaves of rebels Sul.b.Abdullah, Nasur b. Suliman, 1890.
800	Witu slaves freed, 1894
200	Lugard's work scheme(est.)
621	Other (individual cases)
3,200	Total[97]

The Company, as well as the Foreign Office and the missions, had a vested interest in stabilizing the slave population, whose labor was badly needed for porterage. Initially, the slave owners were extremely sensitive to the hiring of slave porters. They made their point in Mombasa in October 1888, when porters hired by the Company were set upon with swords and knives. Many were seriously wounded. Slave owners then extracted a concession from Mackenzie that the Company would obtain the owners' permission before employing slaves.[98] This agreement, together with the Company's runaway policy, which ignored redemption-through-work schemes such as Lugard's, made finding porterage work more difficult for maroons and mission dwellers. Also, CMS missionaries tried to prevent its station residents, including freed slaves, from joining caravans because caravan life "unsettled" the men, who thereafter found it hard "to submit to the usual restraints and discipline of the mission station."[99] Many mission men signed up anyway, though their numbers were insufficient to meet the demand, and their reputation among employers was not good. Demand for porters, which increased dramatically during the IBEACO period, was filled instead with legally-owned slaves, from Zanzibar and the Kenya coast.

Both the Company and the CMS employed many slaves as porters. In 1891, the Company hired 1,300 Zanzibari slave porters throughout East Africa, the CMS, 300 for caravans to Uganda.[100] Company policy was to adhere to the law by paying the slave rather than the owner, but Company practice, as Lugard learned, was apt to "pay the master, not the man."[101] And, in cases where a large number of slaves could be contracted through a single owner, cash was paid

---

[97] Mackenzie to Euan Smith, 5 Jan. 1889, FO 403/117, 151; Smith to Salisbury, 31 Jan. 1891, FO 84/2146; MacLennan to Hardinge, 16 Aug. 1895, FO 403/210, 267; Pigott to Allen, 28 Aug. 1895, Brit. Emp. MSS. s. 18 C66/10, RH.

[98] Mackenzie to Euan Smith, 19 Oct. 1888; Mackenzie's list of demands of Mombasa people, FO 403/107, 160-1; Euan Smith to Foreign Office, 22 Oct. 1888, FO 84/1920; Price, *Third Campaign*, 174-6; Price to Euan Smith, 16 Oct. 1888, G3 A5/05, CMS.

[99] Frere Town Committee minutes, 18 Aug. 1888, G3A5/05, CMS. See also Price, *Third Campaign*, 182-3.

[100] Portal to Salisbury, 12 Sep. 1891, FO 84/2149; Lugard, *Our East African Empire*, 481.

[101] Lugard, *Diaries*, I, 235, 246.

in advance. The Company made an undetermined number of such arrangements with Salim b. Khamis of Takaungu, who contracted his slaves for caravan and railway work with the IBEACO. The "fiction of a free contract" described by Mackenzie in Salim's case was understood by the Company and defended by its successor, the East Africa Protectorate. "You must have caravans," explained Hardinge in 1896, "and it is difficult to make them up without slaves."[102]

Legal obstacles to the hiring of slave porters, in place as of late 1889, were simply ignored. Sultan Khalifa b. Said, under pressure from Britain to restrict the slave trade, issued a proclamation with effect from 1 November 1889 declaring free all slaves arriving in his dominions. When it was noted, a few hours after the decree was made public, that slave porters returning to the coast would henceforth be entitled to claim their freedom, the sultan attempted to rescind the decree.[103] Consul-general Euan Smith then telegraphed the Foreign Office putting the question "as to whether the slaves and others similarly situated will have the right to claim their freedom upon re-entering the Sultan's dominions under the provisions of the Decree. Decree says nothing about raw slaves, but simply all slaves." London declared immediately that the decree "distinctly liberates all slaves entering after 1st November."[104] Yet, of the slaves who gained their freedom on the Kenya coast during the Company's time, there is no evidence that any porter returning from upcountry while employed by the IBEACO was among them. The Company employed many slaves it had freed, principally from Rabai, but no one appears to have acquired a certificate of freedom under the sultan's 1889 decree by virtue of having been a porter in the employ of the Company.[105]

Rather than liberate slaves, IBEACO officials confined their duty to the amelioration of slavery. And in this regard, the Company depended on loyal Busaidi bureaucrats hired on from Zanzibar, foremost among which was Salim b. Khalfan Walad Sheba al-Busaidi, *liwali* of Mombasa. Long before the Imperial British East Africa Company assumed control of the coast Salim had already become a faithful servant of the British. Posted to Mombasa by the sultan of Zanzibar when the first British vice consulate was opened there in 1884, Salim and a succession of vice-consuls enforced anti-slave-trade proclamations. "The

---

[102]Hardinge to Kemball, 26 Nov. 1896, Brit. Emp. MSS. s. 22 G5, RH; Hardinge to Salisbury, 12 Apr. 1896, FO 403/226, 176; Hardinge report, 53. Also de Winton to Euan Smith, 18 Nov. 1890, FO 403/139, 220.

[103] Euan Smith to Salisbury, 8 Jan. 1890, FO 403/136, 13.

[104] Euan Smith to Salisbury, teleg. 16 Jan. 1890, Salisbury to Euan Smith, teleg. 17 Jan. 1890, FO 403/136.

[105] High wages offered by the IBEACO lured many Rabai freedmen. Cole to Lang, 30 Dec. 1889, G3A5/006, CMS. In June 1890 some Fuladoyan maroons signed up as porters as part of Lugard's redemption scheme but soon withdrew because their families appeared to be in jeopardy. Lugard to de Winton, 24 Jun. 1890 and notice, Brit. Emp. MSS. s. 99, East Africa Letter Book. 1888/92, RH; Lugard, *Diaries*, I, 239. Sixty of the slaves freed on the Magarini estate of Suleiman b. Abdullah in 1890 (see ch.2) then became caravan porters. Fitzgerald, *Travels*, 34.

Governor has acted most loyally throughout," remarked Mombasa vice-consul C.S. Smith (later consul-general in Zanzibar), "in spite of the dislikes and intrigues which are being excited against himself."[106] Smith commended Salim for "zealous behaviour" in dealing with kidnapping. Salim "has always left the accused to be tried by me, and has always awarded the punishment which I advised. Indeed I feel I cannot speak too strongly of the willingness of the Governor to follow my exact wishes."[107] Salim's work against kidnapping made him popular among CMS missionaries, who estimated the *liwali* had done more "to check the slaver's traffic than several gun-boats." In 1886 they honored him with a watch and an Arabic Bible.[108] Salim, whose "friendly feelings towards the British are well know," was *liwali* of Mombasa when IBEACO offi-cials arrived to establish their headquarters in 1888, and he was there to see them off in 1895.[109]

During the IBEACO period Salim, together with three other anglophile *maliwali*--Salim's son, Ali b. Salim (*liwali* of Mambrui), and Salim's in-laws, the brothers Said b. Hamed (*liwali* of Malindi) and Sud b. Hamed (*liwali* of Lamu)--made it possible for the Company to establish its authority and enforce new laws restricting slavery. "During my whole residence there," recalled George Mackenzie, the Company's first administrator, "[the above men] did everything they could to to establish the Company on a firm basis at the several ports...and openly threw in their lot with the Company against all malcontents."[110] By virtue of the confidence placed in them by the British, Salim and the other three handled all slave cases, enforced Sultan Ali b. Said's decree of 1890, and eliminated cruelty toward slaves. In the process Salim usurped many judicial powers of the local judges (*makadhi*), who traditionally handled civil mat-ters.[111] In part, he and the others acquired such power by being both appointees of the sultan and the de facto judicial arm of the Company, the officials of which were too burdened with administrative work to take any legal initiative. The IBEACO as well depended on the governors to mediate between themselves

---

[106] Smith to Kirk, 31 May 1885, C.4776, 123.

[107] Smith of Kirk, 18 May 1885, and 31 May 1885, ibid., 122.

[108] Shaw to Lang, 25 Jun. 1886, G3A5/03, CMS; Price, *Third Campaign*, 25. In 1884 while *liwali* of Malindi, Salim had received a gold watch from the British Admiralty for his help to the anti-slave patrol. Gissing to Kirk, 14 Sep. 1884, FO 541/26, 242.

[109] Churchill to Euan Smith, 25 May 1888, FO 403/105, 112; Salim was, during the first three months of IBEACO rule, away from Mombasa while his duties were performed by Said b. Hamed and the Sultan's personal representative, Hamed b. Suleiman.

[110] Mackenzie to de Winton, 28 Aug. 1890, FO 403/138, 124.

[111] Berg, "Mombasa under the Busaidi," 297-8. Pouwels argues that the principle theme of this period in legal history was change caused by "cultural misunderstanding and patronization" on the part of Europeans and overlooks the use *maliwali* made of the IBEACO presence to increase their power at the expense of the *makadhi*. Pouwels, *Horn and Crescent*, 172-4.

and leading townspeople and to help the Company control unrest. They presided over all important public meetings and enforced their authority with IBEACO police.

The *maliwali* nevertheless took their directions from the Company. They had been transferred from the sultan's payroll to that of the Company, which also acquired the power of dismissal. Initially the Company accorded slavery low priority and preferred to act as "custodian of [its] commercial and financial interests in East Africa and only secondarily as the viceroy of the coast" so as "to arouse the least popular distrust and resistance."[112] Avoidance of slavery issues for fear of encountering public resistance led to slaves being treated as cruelly as they had been prior to 1884. In Mombasa and Lamu, many instances of open cruelty, forced prostitution, and gross neglect were reported. According to IBEACO official Lugard, the legal rights of slaves were of little concern or even knowledge on the coast, and the decrees subsequent to 1873 were not upheld in the courts. What was usually the issue was whether a slave was legally held, not legally acquired.[113] But as of May 1890, the IBEACO began to commit itself to tighter restrictions. That month it proclaimed that the possession of any Miji Kenda, Kamba, Sanye, Teita, or Pokomo was henceforth illegal.[114] Francis de Winton, administrator in Mombasa (and successor of Mackenzie, who had served as director), also insisted that *maliwali* protect slaves' legal rights. Underlining the point by sacking the *liwali* of Lamu, Abdulla b. Hamed, for neglecting them, he replaced him with his brother, Sud b. Hamed, who immediately reversed matters.[115] De Winton's action marks the turning point in the institution of slavery on the Kenya coast, though it was quickly overshadowed by Sultan Ali b. Said's 1890 decree.

The 1890 decree was the result of the efforts of Charles B. Euan Smith, who had pressed for tougher slavery laws since becoming consul-general in Zanzibar in 1888. His campaign was strengthened by the Brussels Conference of 1888-89 on slavery and the slave trade. With the support of the Foreign Office, Euan Smith put pressure on Sultan Khalifa to institute measures that, though avoiding the issue of abolition, served to increase the protection and security of slaves in Zanzibar and the rest of the sultan's dominions. Khalifa agreed to the decree before his death, and his successor, Ali b. Said, ratified it. Euan Smith anticipated that slavery conditions would be "immensely ameliorated by the provisions of the Decree" and that "the entire abolition of slavery and the emancipation of

---

[112] Berg, "Mombasa under the Busaidi Sultanate," 297.

[113] Lugard, *Our East African Empire*, II, 226-7. Price, *Third Campaign*, 311; Simons to Euan Smith, 24 Jun. and 28 Jul. 1890, FO 403/138, 164-6, 191-4; Howe to Carthew, 7 Jul. 1890, ibid., 195-6.

[114] Proclamation re slavery of "friendly tribes," 1 May 1890, G3A5/07, CMS; McDermott, *IBEA*, 353-4.

[115] Mackenzie, incidentally, protested de Winton's action. Mackenzie to de Winton, 28 Aug. 1890, FO 403138, 124. For Abdulla's conduct, Simons to Euan Smith, 24 Jun. and 27 Jul. 1890, ibid., 164-6, 191-4.

all slaves must...be the inevitable outcome"[116] Among its provisions, the proclamation prohibited the exchange or sale of slaves, restricted inheritance to lawful children, required forfeiture in cases of ill-treatment, entitled slaves to full rights in courts of law, and provided for purchase of freedom.[117]

The announcement of the decree on 1 August, the day it was supposed to go into effect, disturbed the IBEACO. De Winton was convinced that as news of the decree spread, a general revolt would occur which the Company's small police force would be incapable of suppressing. De Winton also sympathized with the slave owners. After the decree was read in a public *baraza* in Mombasa, he immediately conveyed to Euan Smith the complaints of the Mombasa elders and expressed concern that the decree would eliminate the use of slaves as legal security against loans. For these and other reasons, de Winton argued, the law, "while framed for a good and proper purpose...may turn out to be productive of injustice and wrong." He therefore instructed his officers to post the proclamation only after cutting off the English translation. "This will make it appear as if it were, as it is, an order direct from the Sultan, and not as having emanated from the Company." De Winton also informed the consul-general that his Company wished "to avoid any active part as regards the Proclamation."[118] Euan Smith's first reaction was that de Winton and the Company superintendent in Malindi, J. Bell-Smith, were attempting to scuttle the decree.[119] But he was soon persuaded that the Company was threatened by resistance unless the sultan of Zanzibar himself publicized the new anti-slavery law. A special envoy, Hamed b. Suleiman, was therefore sent to the port towns to promulgate the sultan's decree, a task he completed by early September.[120] And, as talk of revolt over the decree led the Company to pull its administration out of Witu, the British stepped into the breach and destroyed the Nabahani town in October.

Thereafter the Company took responsibility for enforcing the decree, with profound results.[121] Prohibiting exchange or sale reduced the cash value of slaves and confined their utility to labor. Liability to punishment of owners for ill-treatment or cruelty, moreover, all but eliminated the efficacy of coercion.

---

[116] Euan Smith to Salisbury, 3 Aug. 1890, FO 403/138, 112. Euan Smith also gained from Khalifa an agreement freeing children born to slaves after 1 Jan. 1890, but it was not promulgated. Euan Smith to Salisbury, 8 and 9 Jan. 1890, FO 403/136, 13, 104-5; Currie to Euan Smith, 7 Mar. 1890, ibid; Agreement, 30 Sep. 1889, FO 403/158, 105. See also "Defending Slavery" in ch. 7.

[117] FO 403/1158, 106.

[118] de Winton to Euan Smith, 7 and 11 Aug. 1890, de Winton to Simons, 5 Aug. 1890, FO 403/138, 142-3.

[119] Euan Smith to Salisbury, 2 Sep., 1890, ibid., 211. Euan Smith heard that Bell-Smith had assured slave owners in Malindi that the Company "would protect their interests as against the Decree." See also Bell-Smith to de Winton, 21 Aug. 1890, ibid., 213; Lugard, *Diaries*, I, 246.

[120] de Winton to IBEACO, 28 Aug. 1890, FO 403/139, 61; Foreign Office to IBEACO, 4 Sep. 1890, FO 403/138.

[121] Hardinge to Salisbury, 12 Apr. 1896, FO 403/226, 11-2.

The rights of slaves, who previously had been denied access to the courts, became equal to those of free persons before the law.[122] The "whole institution of slavery" wrote the IBEACO director in 1892, "has been shaken...[because] the owners feel that their tenure over those [slaves] who still remain is insecure.... Many Mohammedans, so far from wishing to maintain slaves, consider those which they possess a burden...."[123] By the end of IBEACO rule, cases of cruelty had become rare, and East Africa Protectorate governor, Arthur Hardinge, was struck by "the far greater ease with which the various anti-slavery decrees could be enforced in the towns really ruled by the Company as compared with the difficulties to be met with in Zanzibar."[124]

Success was achieved at a price. As compensation for restrictions placed on slavery by the Decree of 1890, the Company pledged to recover, with force if necessary, all runaways. Before the decree, in February 1890, Salim b. Khalfan proclaimed in Mombasa on behalf of the Company a pledge to recover all future runaways, though director George Mackenzie offered all runaways the opportunity of purchasing their freedom for MT$15.[125] In September, however, following the promulgation of the 1890 decree, de Winton abolished the provision for self-redemption and publicly committed the Company to the recovery of runaways and the destruction of maroon settlements.

> The masters will be allowed to send for [runaways] with Askaris (police) of the Company, and all the Watoro will be told that if they resist, the Company will take all their Headmen and burn their village.

De Winton's pledge, made without reference to Company directors, was known officially in Britain only after IBEACO rule on the coast had ended.[126]

The Foreign Office may or may not have been aware of the pledge, but it had known from the beginning the Company's runaway policy, and endorsed it. Within months of de Winton's pledge, for example, the new consul-general in Zanzibar, C.S. Smith, advised the Foreign Office that the status and rights of fugitive slaves were protected by the Brussels Act recently signed by Britain. If enforced, the Brussels Act would

> embody a complete change in the status and rights of a fugitive slave....The right of the slave to get away if he can, is now acknowledged to the fullest extent. In every case a fugitive slave applying for freedom to the proper

---

[122] MacLennan to Hardinge, 16 Aug. 1895, Rogers to Hardinge, 28 Aug. 1895, FO 403/210, 266-9.

[123] Mackenzie to the *Scotsman*, 6 Dec. 1892, in H. Waller, *Heligoland for Zanzibar* (London: Edward Standford, 1893), 48-9.

[124] Hardinge to Salisbury, 12 Apr. 1896, FO 403/226, 12.

[125] Notice of 19 Rejab 1307 [Feb. 1890], FO 403/211, 174.

[126] De Winton to "Uzee" of Malindi and Mambrui, 28 Sep. 1890, ibid., 174-5; Mackenzie to Hardinge, 21 Jan. 1896, FO 403/225, 70-1; Hardinge to Kemball, 26 Nov. 1896, MSS. Brit. Emp. s. 22, RH.

authorities is immediately to receive it... [In the case of a fugitive slave where slavery exists] a slave is entitled to freedom on reaching the frontier.[127]

The matter appears to have ended there, because violations of the Act later occurred in areas under Company jurisdiction. Frederick Lugard alleges that in 1892 a new sultan's decree directed against manumission and freedom-by-purchase was being secretly implemented on the Kenya coast.[128] And, in 1893, in an incident involving a slave concubine who had run away from her master and settled with her husband on the Methodist mission station at Mazeras, the Company's police went to the mission, seized the woman, and restored her to her owner, all without protest from the Foreign Office. The Company upheld its actions on the basis of a policy formulated in early 1889 by the British consul-general, Company director George Mackenzie, and the missionaries regarding the non-harboring of runaways on mission stations. This agreement and de Winton's pledge to slave owners were rendered null and void by the Brussels Act, but none of the missionaries invoked it.[129]

By then, the Company's days on the coast were numbered. In 1893, its withdrawal from Uganda had provoked Britain into declaring the Uganda Protectorate, and its declining commercial fortunes elsewhere had by 1894 led to negotiations between IBEACO director G.S. Mackenzie and the British Government over the outright purchase of the Company. By early 1895, Mackenzie surrendered the charter, together with all IBEACO assets in East Africa and the sultan's lease of the coast for £250,000.[130] Britain then "bought out" the sultan of Zanzibar's "rights" to his mainland dominions. In June 1895 the Kenya coast became part of the East Africa Protectorate, subject to the administration of the consul-general of Zanzibar. Since late 1894 this post had been occupied by Arthur H. Hardinge, sympathetic to slave owners, who expected that British rule on the coast would nevertheless "incur the dislike of the native population by measures aimed at the destruction of slavery."[131]

---

[127] Smith to Salisbury, 2 Apr. 1891, FO 84/2147.

[128] Waller, *Heligoland for Zanzibar*, 31. Accusations that the colonial administration was quietly supporting slavery while claiming that its policy was designed to eradicate it were also made with regard to Lugard's policy in Northern Nigeria. See Hogendorn and Lovejoy, "Lugard's Policies toward Slavery" and a full treatment in their forthcoming volume (Cambridge University Press).

[129] FO 403/182, 98-105.

[130] M.P.K. Sorrenson, *Origins of European Settlement in Kenya* (Nairobi: Oxford University Press, 1968), 16-7; de Kiewiet, "IBEA."

[131] Hardinge, *Diplomatist in the East*, 132.

7

The East Africa Protectorate

Arthur Hardinge, consul-general of the East Africa Protectorate from 1895 to 1899, was determined to allow the institution of slavery to die out gradually rather than abolish it and to guarantee owners full use of their slaves. Put into practice, Hardinge's policy continued the arrest of runaway slaves, opposed the abolition of the legal status of slavery, left unenforced the decree freeing all children born after 1889, and used the courts to compel obedience from slaves. The Protectorate, as slave owners' guardian, was the Company all over again. Continuity resulted from Hardinge's wish to preserve large slave owners as a governing elite, from the Protectorate's demand for labor, and from the control of key administrative positions by ex-IBEACO employees. Hardinge's fight against abolition was aided, too, by several CMS missionaries and until late 1897 had the support of the British foreign office secretary, Lord Salisbury.

From the beginning, Hardinge's plan to shore up slave owners' interests was actively opposed. In Britain, the British Anti-Slavery Society lobbied against all of Hardinge's measures, and their campaign was supported by two noted old East Africa hands, Frederick Lugard and John Kirk. On the Kenya coast the CMS bishop of East Africa, Alfred Tucker, acted as the abolitionists' voice and spur. The Bishop kept his British friends informed, and his efforts to gain legal protection for slaves and runaway slaves pitted him against members of Hardinge's administration and his Frere Town staff. While abolitionists at home pressured Salisbury to prohibit Hardinge from stalking runaways and to see that the consul-general was enforcing existing laws, Tucker won a case in Mombasa that promised immediate freedom for most adult slaves. In practical terms, however, the abolitionist campaign brought few changes. With each restriction placed in the way, Hardinge and Protectorate administrators devised means of circumventing it. They had the advantage of operating largely unsupervised; Tucker was more often in Uganda than on the coast.

Slaves were much more successful than abolitionists in undermining Hardinge's policy. Despite the Protectorate's attempts to discourage fugitive activity, slaves fled their masters at increasing rates. The vast majority did so without assistance or encouragement from abolitionists. In a land where missionaries and administrators befriended slave owners, hope of salvation through Europeans continued to be rare among slaves. They ran away instead for the reasons that had become common over the past quarter century--fear of harm, resentment of owners, desire for survival, longing for escape from slavery, and because the opportunity presented itself.

Rather than lift the hopes of slaves and runaways, the Protectorate weighed like a bane. In contrast to the Company, which began its brief tenure by emancipating 1,421 runaway slaves at Rabai, the Protectorate commenced with an eleven-month war that caused the deaths of hundreds of slaves and brought misery to thousands. As with earlier struggles for supremacy on the coast, the 1895-96 war between the British and the Mazrui was conducted without reference to innocent bystanders and was often directed against slaves and runaways presumed to be in league with the enemy. Fought in the Takaungu district and in the Shimba hills, the war not only caused widespread suffering but destroyed the agricultural areas where slaves had based their livelihood.

1. *Origins of the Anglo-Mazrui War*

Before the Protectorate assumed authority over the Kenya coast, all towns save two were governed by pro-British *maliwali*. The two upstarts -- Mbaruk b. Rashid of Gasi, and Salim b. Khamis of Takaungu--were both slave dealers who had led or supported rebellions against the sultan of Zanzibar and the IBEACO. Because the IBEACO feared to challenge them and because, in Salim's case, he could provide the laborers the Company so desperately needed, they had retained their posts. Between 1888 and 1894 the Company left the sultan's law in their districts unenforced, employed Mazrui slaves as porters, paid Mbaruk of Gasi a healthy stipend, and served other Mazrui interests to avoid conflict.[1]

In early 1895, Salim b. Khamis's sudden death gave the Company, then in its concluding months of rule, an opportunity to influence the succession. Normally, authority would have passed to Mubarak b. Rashid, eldest male in the direct Zaheri line. Mubarak was the son of Salim's brother and predecessor, Rashid b. Khamis. Company officials, however, regarded Mubarak as anti-British. Thus, when the Takaungu Mazrui delayed in confirming Mubarak's succession, the Company intervened in what it termed a "quarrel" to impose their own candidate. Kenneth Macdougall, the Company officer present in Takaungu during succession deliberations, favored Salim's eldest son, the affable Rashid b. Salim, who "is about 28,...[and is] said to bear a good character, and to be well-disposed to English rule."[2] Macdougall then forced the matter through by asserting the Company's power as appointer of governors and, over the protests of Mubarak, by installing Salim. Mubarak yielded momentarily and recognized Salim, but he soon stormed out of Takaungu and based himself with his supporters at Konjora. At this point the IBEACO, having alienated a sizeable portion of the Mazrui against the British, withdrew from the scene leaving Hardinge, then poised to establish the Protectorate, to deal with the threat of armed Mazrui resistance. Though the Protectorate was more than a month away from being proclaimed, Hardinge decided to intervene in order to prevent Mubarak from overthrowing Salim.

Half-hearted attempts to negotiate were made by both sides while each prepared to fight. Mubarak and his spirited young brother, Aziz, raised a force

---

[1] Hardinge to Salisbury, 12 Apr. 1896, FO 403/226, 179. The Company collectors were stationed at the outlet of the Kilifi creek, 6 km.. north of Takaungu, and at Shimoni, 25 km.. south of Gasi. For the IBEACO and the Mazrui, ch. 6.

[2] Hardinge to Salisbury, 13 Feb. 1895, C. 8274, 1. Koffsky, "History of Takaungu," 175-8.

of roughly one thousand armed slaves, inherited from the late Salim. When rumors reached Hardinge in Zanzibar that the dissidents were planning to attack Takaungu, he dispatched a gunboat to discourage the attack and hurried over himself. On 13 June, less than three weeks before the Company formally handed over authority to the Protectorate, Hardinge arrived with his forces, pronounced Mubarak and Aziz rebels, and on the 16th marched to Konjora to demand an unconditional surrender. Mubarak expressed a wish to talk. But before he could appear a scuffle and a gunshot sparked open fighting. Hardinge's forces routed their opponents, but in winning this skirmish he lost an opportunity to avert war.[3]

2. The War

In the aftermath of the Konjora affray, Aziz was harbored by the Arabs of Araboko and the maroons of the hinterland. In May the Fuladoyans had supplied arms to the Mazrui, and after Konjora they remained in league with Aziz. On the 17th after burning Mtanganyiko and looting the town's Indian shops, Aziz marched north through the Sokoke forest and encamped at Araboko, the home of Salim b. Husein, alias Jembea. Jembea, head of the Muscat Arabs of Malindi district and an old ally of Suleiman b. Abdullah (executed for his part in the Witu resistance of 1894), was the dominant figure in a town regarded by the British as a nest of outlaws and bad characters. More than likely Jembea had been involved with the Fuladoyo and Makongeni maroons in recapturing runaway slaves for the Malindi market. He now acted as a conduit between the maroons and Aziz's forces.[4] With new strength, Aziz launched raids on several coastal towns and pulled down wire on the Mombasa-Lamu telegraph line to convert

---

[3] Hardinge to Kimberley, 25 Jun. 1895, FO 403/210, 58-61. Published accounts of the Anglo-Mazrui war, or Mazrui Rebellion as it is often termed, are numerous. All rely heavily on British administrative and military dispatches, most of which appear in C. 8274. The best general accounts are Cashmore, "Sheikh Mbaruk bin Rashid bin Salim el Mazrui," 111-37, and Chiraghdin, "Sheikh Mbaruk bin Rashid," 150-79. Hardinge's own version is in his *Diplomatist in the East*, 155-86. Other general accounts include Salim, *Swahili-speaking Peoples*, 71-4; R.W. Gregory, *Foundation of British East Africa*, reprint (New York: Negro Universities Press, 1969), 144-61; Koffsky, "History of Takaungu," 181-91; G.H. Mungeam, *British Rule in Kenya, 1895-1912: the Establishment of Administration in the East Africa Protectorate* (Oxford: Clarendon Press, 1966), 21-5. For details of British military movements, H. Moyse-Bartlett, *King's Africa Rifles: a Study in the Military History of East and Central Africa, 1890-1915* (Aldershot: Gale and Polden, 1956), 106-11. For Giriama involvement, Brantley, *The Giriama*, 43-51.

[4] Pigott to de Winton, 12 May 1893, FO 403/182, 177; Hardinge to Kimberley, 24 Jun. 1895, FO 403/209, 288; Hardinge to Kimberley, 25 Jun. 1895, FO 403/210, 60-1; Hardinge to Kemball, 16 Dec. 1896, MSS Brit. Emp. s.22, G5, RH. Koffsky renders his name, Salim b. Hoseif. "History of Takaungu," 181. Koffsky's discussion of the war (181-91) overlooks the slave factor.

into gunshot. After the British destroyed Araboko on 24 June, the Mazrui shifted to Fuladoyo and resumed their activities.[5]

Help for the Takaungu dissidents then came from Mbaruk b. Rashid of Gasi. For almost a generation, Mbaruk's attempts to force the Zaheri of Takaungu to accept his leadership had kept them loyal to Zanzibar. But British meddling in the succession and the Konjora affray stood Takaungu politics on its head. The principal menace to Zaheri independence now came from Zanzibar, and the Takaungu militants, threatened with destruction by Britain, turned to Gasi for support. After Konjora, Mubarak fled south with the women and children to Gasi and appealed to his uncle, Mbaruk, to join cause.[6] For a month, the aging Uthmani leader sent expressions of loyalty to the British, though already indulging his zest for pure, unbridled revolt.

Warfare then escalated. By early July Mbaruk's son and heir, Eyub, had joined Aziz in Fuladoyo, and on the 8th they led five hundred men into battle against the British forces at Takaungu. There the Mazrui suffered a major defeat and, a month later, another at Mwele. Aziz and Eyub, with help from the Takaungu townspeople, surprised the British in a pre-dawn assault. They captured a mosque and held off the British for nearly two hours, but a counterattack led by Capt. Raikes dislodged the Mazrui and drove them out of the town.[7] During the following months the Mazrui refrained from attacking enemy strongholds, and the British gradually took the offensive.

On 22 July Hardinge marched toward Gasi to demand that Mbaruk hand over his nephew. Hardinge's approach forced the hand of Mbaruk, who had not yet declared his sympathies. Before Hardinge arrived, Mbaruk left Gasi, moving south. On the 26th he attacked Vanga, looted Indian shops, and burned down most of the town. From there his forces marched inland to Mwele, located deep in the Shimba hills, and prepared to attack. On 12 August after waiting to collect his forces, Hardinge set off from Gasi, and three days later reached Mbaruk's fortress. On the morning of the 16th, the British overran Mwele and inflicted heavy casualties on the defenders, who fled in disarray. Mbaruk, Mubarak, and Eyub, who had returned south to aid his father, escaped unharmed.[8] The battles of Takaungu and Mwele exposed the Mazrui's inferior military position. They had failed to penetrate their opponent's strongholds and had been unable to defend their own.

These defeats were paid for with the lives of many slave followers. In both the Zaheri and Uthmani forces slaves made up the rank and file, which varied in

---

[5] Hardinge to Kimberley, attached note, 27 Jun. 1895, FO 403/210, 61; Hardinge to Salisbury, 6 Jul. 1895, C. 8274, 11.

[6] Ackerman journal, 21 Jun. 1895, G3A5/011, CMS; Hardinge to Salisbury, 6 Jul. 1895, C. 8274, 10.

[7] Macdougall to Pigott, 9 Jul. 1895, CP 75/46, KNA.

[8] Cashmore, "Sheikh Mbaruk bin Rashid," 129-31. At the time of the battle, Aziz and his forces were in the north in the Sokoke forest, where they had been since the battle of Takaungu. Macdougall to Pigott, 13 and 26 Jul. and 20 Aug. 1895, CP 75/46, KNA.

these early months from five hundred to one thousand men. Perhaps as many as three hundred were traditional fighting slaves; the remainder, domestic servants, town laborers, and farmers, were probably bearing arms and risking their lives for the first time. They participated, perhaps as Hardinge believed, out of loyalty created through years of contact with their masters, some of whom, such as Akida Bakari, were slaves themselves.[9] Many, nevertheless, deserted the Mazrui in the confusion following the defeats at Takaungu and Mwele.[10] Their escape suggests that some Mazrui slaves were conscripts, rather than volunteers, in the war effort.[11] Until Mwele, casualties in the war had been confined to the slaves involved directly in the fighting. After Mwele when the Mazrui moved north once more, the slave civilians of Takaungu district began to pay the dearer price for the second, and final, Mazrui campaign.

In September the Mazrui attempted to revive their chances of victory by resorting to guerrilla tactics. They planned to concentrate their forces in the Sokoke forest and direct raids against vulnerable food and population centers, thereby placing the British on the defensive and leading them to spread their forces. In the long run, they hoped as well to marshall broad support among the non-Muslims of the hinterland and the Swahili of the coast. Before Mbaruk departed from the south, he sent ahead a section of his men to make gifts of cloth to the Giriama settled on the fringes and to the west of Takaungu district. He also let it be known that the Mazrui, rather than the British, had been victorious at Mwele.[12] On or about 10 September Mbaruk and the remainder of his army broke camp near the German East Africa border and marched north toward Sokoke. His propaganda appears to have achieved results, for along the march he and his followers were welcomed and fed by the Duruma and Giriama, and they arrived to find the northern Giriama sympathetic and preparing for war.[13] Mbaruk may have received signs that coastal Muslims were also ready to support him; purportedly upon his arrival he called for a holy war against the infidels. Banners with religious inscriptions were flown in his camp.[14]

Takaungu's agricultural slaves were the pawns in the new campaign. As the guerrillas were in urgent need of food and shelter during September and October, they lived off the slaves' recent harvests, used their plantations as temporary

---

[9] Hardinge to Salisbury, 29 Jan. 1896, C. 8275, 32; Hardinge to Salisbury, 12 Apr. 1896, FO 403/226, 180-1, 183; Hardinge report, C. 8683, 62.

[10] Macdougall to Pigott, 9 Jul. and 6 Aug. 1895, CP 75/46, KNA; Hardinge to Salisbury, 28 Sep. 1895, FO 403/211, 62.

[11] Hardinge reported after the war that, at least in one instance, Mubarak of Takaungu commandeered eighty slaves of a pro-British Mazrui Arab at Mtanganyiko. Hardinge to Liebert, 27 Mar. 1897, FO 403/242, 30.

[12] Smith to Pigott, 25 Aug. 1895, and Jones to Pigott, n.d.(recd. 26 Aug) and 28 Aug. 1895, CP 65/4, KNA.

[13] Jones to Pigott, 9 Sep. 1895, Hoffman to Pigott, 15 Sep. 1895, Smith to Binns, 16 Sep. 1895, CP 65/4, KNA; Macdougall to Pigott, 11 Sep. 1895, CP 75/46, KNA.

[14] Macdougall to Pigott, 22 Sep. 1895, CP 75/46, KNA; Hardinge to Salisbury, 28 Sep. 1895, FO 403/211, 62.

bases, and traded away their grain and animals to the Giriama.[15] In late September, Aziz's forces roamed the Takaungu and Malindi hinterlands, populated by slaves, and seized men and women. Those taken prisoner were pressed into military service as soldiers or laborers in the early months, and later traded in the hinterland in exchange for support.[16] In settlements near Sokoke, slaves were recruited into guerrilla ranks and used to defend the Sokoke base. In this case, as in others, slaves responded according to the strength and proximity of the guerrillas rather than to sentiments of loyalty.[17] Soon after the Mazrui began their campaign from Sokoke, slaves fled Takaungu district and took refuge in British-held territory. Over five hundred entered Takaungu town alone in the first twelve days of October.[18]

The guerrilla strategy neutralized Britain's strength for weeks. They were compelled to position their troops among strategic points over a wide area and depend on small units to counter the Mazrui in the countryside. Garrisoning loyalist towns, mission stations, key points on the caravan route to the interior, and population centers of Takaungu district left at most two hundred men available for patrol work.[19] Guerrilla bands had the run of much of the countryside, enjoyed growing popular support outside the slave areas, and became increasingly aggressive.

---

[15] The many scattered references to guerrilla activity, including trade with the Giriama, in the dispatches of Macdougall (CP 75/46, KNA) make no direct reference to food confiscation from slaves, but since the beginning of the growing season in May the guerrillas had been in no position to cultivate and raise their own. They had been either south with Mbaruk or moving about the north with Aziz. During this time the non-combatant slaves of Takaungu district were the only active cultivators and their harvests in September the only food supply available to the guerrillas for the taking.

[16] Macdougall to Pigott, 12 Oct. (two letters), 26 Oct., 17 Nov., and 3 Dec. 1895, 19 Feb. 1896, CP 75/46, KNA.

[17] An incident illustrating the fear slaves harbored for the guerrillas occurred in December at Kurwitu, south of Takaungu district. The slaves of the area were owned by Mombasa Arabs who had been loyal to the British from the beginning of the war. Their slaves, too, gave evidence of siding with the government until December. In that month Hamisi b. Kombo of Mtwapa joined the Mazrui, and the guerrillas moved into the Kurwitu area, whereupon the slaves accepted arms from the guerrillas but did not join their bands. Instead they posted sentinels and waited for a British attack, preferring this to guerrilla reprisals. Macdougall to Pigott, 13 and 14 Dec. 1895, ibid.

[18] Macdougall to Pigott, 12 Oct. 1895, ibid.

[19] In the course of operations, garrisons were established at Tezo, Roka, Mtanganyiko, Konjora, Sokoke, Mtondia, Takaungu, Mazeras, Rabai, Ribe, Jimba, Gasi, Vanga, and points in the Shimba hills, in addition to other posts along the caravan route to the interior. Some of the troops were composed of Sudanese and Zanzibari regulars, but the majority were British seamen, who proved unsuitable for patrol work. In December 199 Indian troops arrived from Bombay, but many of these were needed to establish or strengthen garrisons. By February 1896 Hardinge had more than one thousand troops, only two hundred of which could be used for mobile operations. Moyse-Bartlett, *King's African Rifles*, 109.

In late October British patrols managed to drive Mubarak out of the Mtwapa area and to dislodge Aziz from Sokoke. By early October Mbaruk of Gasi and his son, Eyub, had returned south to establish a base at Mwareni in the Duruma country from which to command and supply the northern guerrillas.[20] Soon thereafter Mubarak became active south of Takaungu and received support from Hamisi b. Kombo, resident of Mtwapa and head of the Mombasa moiety, Tisa Taifa. After the British attacked Mtwapa on 19 October, Mubarak retreated south

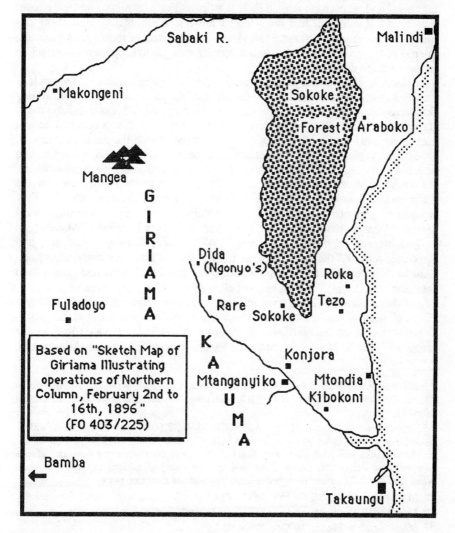

[20] Marx to Bradbridge, 9 Oct. 1895, CP ADD. MS/8, KNA; Hardinge to Salisbury, 24 Oct. 1895, FO 403/211, 111.

to Mwareni.[21] He arrived with many women and children, and it is probable that he had evacuated his dependents and Sokoke civilians. All had come under heavy fire from Macdougall's patrol operating out of Takaungu. On 10 October Macdougall's ninety-five men attacked Sokoke using war rockets and a maxim gun. Aziz would have risked innocent lives by making a stand, and so withdrew his forces immediately.[22] Within days, however, he and his men returned. On the 21st Macdougall attacked again, finding the guerrillas "collected in great numbers" and prepared to defend their positions. Forty extra men and the maxim gun meant Macdougall had the stronger hand, and the guerrillas, low on ammunition, eventually yielded.[23] Having been deprived of their forest base, the guerrillas moved inland and began a desperate struggle to keep their forces active in the northern districts.

Macdougall's campaign caused considerable suffering among bystanders, mostly slaves, and drove them into the arms of the guerrillas. After overrunning Sokoke on the 10th, Macdougall's men burned crops from Sokoke to Kibokoni-- the crops, in other words, of *mahaji* and slaves. Macdougall reported that he was careful to spare the fields of those not in sympathy with the guerrillas, though he omitted explaining how he distinguished between the property of those who had been coerced by the guerrillas and those who had joined them voluntarily. He remarked after the 10 October attack that numbers of slaves escaped from the guerrillas at Sokoke and returned to their plantations, an indication that they wanted no part of the fighting.[24] Yet, in the wake of the crop burning, many slaves appear to have joined the guerrillas. Ten days later when Macdougall staged his second assault, the people of Sokoke, Araboko, Konjora, and Kibokoni returned the fire.[25] Rather than to punish guerrilla supporters, Macdougall dispossessed neutral populations, endangered their lives, and turned them into enemies. He also commandeered slaves to serve as his porters.[26]

Another guerrilla defeat soon followed at Rabai. With the northern forces in disarray, Mbaruk made a bid for a desperately needed victory by sending Eyub from Mwareni to harass the British outposts on the caravan route to the interior.[27] On 2 November at 2 a.m. Eyub's forces successfully attacked the

---

[21] Macdougall to Pigott, 6, 7, and 10 Oct. 1895, CP 75/46, KNA; akida Sherifu to Pigott, 10 Oct. 1895, CP 67/14, KNA; Hardinge to Salisbury, 24 Oct. 1895, FO 403/211, 111.

[22] Macdougall to Pigott, 12 Oct. 1895, CP 75/46, KNA. "The maxim gun and 9-pounder war-rockets were...brought into action, whilst skirmishers were thrown out on either flanks[sic] who fired well directed volleys at their main position, and after a few minutes firing the enemy took to flight in every direction, the cries of their women and children were most hideous to listen to, as they ran away."

[23] Macdougall to Pigott, 26 Oct. 1895, ibid.

[24] Macdougall to Pigott, 12 Oct. 1895(two letters), ibid.

[25] Macdougall to Pigott, 26 Oct. 1895, ibid.

[26] Weaver to Craufurd, 1 Aug. 1896, ibid.

[27] Hardinge to Salisbury, 13 Nov. 1895, C. 8274, 47. Originally Mbaruk may have been responding a request for reinforcements from Aziz, who while en route north

camel caravan camp at Mazeras, near the Methodist mission station. After routing the unprepared and small British garrison, Eyub ransacked the stores and set fire to the village nearby.[28] A second force, led by Mbaruk's slave lieutenant, Akida Sungura, then moved on Rabai, five miles to the north. At 4 a.m. they opened fire and began to burn houses along the main street leading toward the church. Sungura's men, believing that Rabai was temporarily unguarded by British troops, strode together into the settlement center, shouting loudly and terrifying the residents.[29] While enjoying their moment, the guerrillas lost the element of surprise and exposed their position. Rabai had been alerted and was waiting. Sungura's men suddenly encountered heavy fire from thirty-five Zanzibari regulars, mission converts armed with rifles supplied by Jones, and a large gathering of Rabai bowmen. After a heavy exchange, the mission forces trapped a section of the guerrillas in the market place and began to shoot them down. Sungura, who was among them, fell with an arrow in his chest and, along with his wounded men, begged for mercy. He pleaded by offering the only lasting possession his life had given him:

> *Msinue! Msinue! niwe mtumwa wenu!*
> (Spare me! Spare me! I shall be your slave!)

His captors refused. "Sisi hawatutaki watumwa hapa," one man replied ("we want no slaves here"). He turned Sungura on his face, raised his machete, and dispatched him with a single blow across the neck.[30] Remnants of the guerrilla force managed to escape southward, running headlong before the Rabai, who killed others before the pursuit was abandoned. In Rabai and along the path of retreat, the guerrillas left behind nearly forty dead, thirty-five of whom were Mazrui slaves.[31]

After Rabai, the guerrillas continued to lose battles and grow weaker through desertions and increasing shortages of food. By mid-November Macdougall succeeded in driving all of Aziz's forces out of Sokoke district. For the next three months the northern guerrillas moved deep into northern Giriama

---

learned that Mazeras was vulnerable to attack. Macdougall to Pigott, 29 Oct. 1895, CP 75/46, KNA.

[28] Hardinge to Salisbury, 13 Nov. 1895, C. 8274, 48; Muhidini's account, trans. by Jones, 2 Nov. 1895, CP 93/164, KNA.

[29] Jones to CMS, 15 Nov. 1895, G3A5/011, CMS. Solomon Mwingereza, who was a boy of five at the time, remembers hearing the guerrillas shout "Wakristo wa Rabai leo mtwaona Jesu Kristo!" (You Christians of Rabai will see Jesus Christ today!). Interview, Chaani, Changamwe, 26 Sep. 1973.

[30] Mwingereza interview..

[31] Ackerman journal, 2 Nov. 1895, Smith to Baylis, 11 Nov. 1895, and Jones to CMS, 15 Nov. G3A5/011, CMS; Smith to Pigott, 2 Nov. 1895 (two letters), and Hoffmann to Pigott, 2 Nov. 1895(two letters), CP 65/4, KNA; "Arabs killed at Rabai," n.d., CP 93/164, KNA; Hardinge to Salisbury, 13 Nov. 1895, C. 8274, 48.

country and abandoned all attempts to raid in coastal districts.[32] Desertions of
guerrilla leaders and slaves depleted their numbers. In late November Nasoro b.
Hamid turned himself in with a number of his followers, and soon thereafter 150

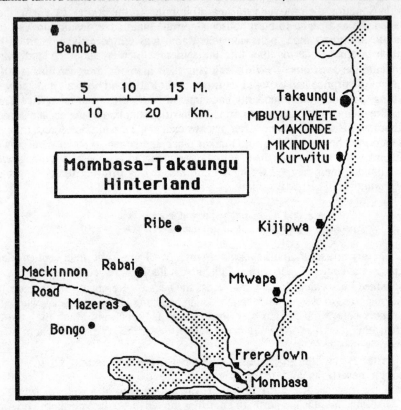

guerrillas, all slaves and *mahaji* attached to Akida Bakari, surrendered at Takaungu.[33] Macdougall then captured Mtwapa and Shimo la Tewa from the
followers of Hamisi b. Kombo, and in early December he drove Mwenye Jaka's
guerrillas out of Mtongwe, from which supplies had been smuggled to the
southern forces.[34] At Mwareni, where Mbaruk continued to direct the Mazrui
war effort, famine had reportedly set in, and Aziz, after going south temporarily,
returned to the northern districts with Eyub in an effort to keep their forces
alive.[35]

---

[32] Macdougall to Pigott, 17 Nov. 1895, CP 75/46, KNA; Hardinge to Salisbury, 2
Dec. 1895, FO 403/211, 219.
[33] Macdougall to Pigott, 5 Dec. 1895(two letters), CP 75/46, KNA.
[34] Ibid.
[35] Smith to Pigott, 1 Dec. 1895, and Jones to Pigott, 2 Dec. 1895, CP 65/4, KNA.

Hopelessly on the defensive, the guerrillas began to lose the support of the Giriama. Since September Giriama in the Takaungu district had supplied grain to the guerrillas and afforded them shelter, though hesitating to join their campaign. Collaboration profited the Giriama, who received cloth, money, donkeys, and slaves in exchange.[36] Their cooperation was also encouraged by the visit of Mbaruk in September. Fearing his vengeance, long notorious among the Miji Kenda, the Giriama also believed in his ability to escape from the British by means of *mazingombwe* ("magical trickery").[37] Once Mbaruk left and the British had demonstrated their strength against the guerrillas at Sokoke, the elders and other prominent Giriama of Takaungu district were quick to express their loyalty to the Protectorate.[38] During November and December the guerrillas moved about the northern and central areas of Giriama territory and received shelter and food in exchange for trade goods.[39] Giriama hospitality nevertheless declined as the British military reputation was more widely recognized. Eventually, all Giriama would fall in line with their fellows in and around Sokoke and assist the British in driving the guerrillas out of their districts.[40]

British military success also persuaded maroons and Muslim townspeople to suppress their anti-European feelings and withhold support from the guerrillas. In the early stages of the war the people of Fuladoyo and Makongeni aided Aziz and Mbaruk. Traditionally at odds with the Mazrui and mindful of their vulnerability to the British, the wary maroons soon broke ties with the guerrillas. In July they struck a truce with the British and moved into Malindi district to settle at a safe distance from the areas of fighting.[41] Like the maroons, the

---

[36] Smith to Pigott, 25 Aug. 1895, and Jones to Pigott, 25 and 28 Aug., 9 Sep. 1895, and Hoffmann to Pigott, 15 Sep. 1895, CP 65/4, KNA; Burt to Baylis, 27 Sep. 1895, G3A5/011, CMS; Macdougall to Pigott, 22 Sep., 12 Oct., 17 Nov., 3 Dec. 1895, and 19 Feb. 1896, CP 75/46, KNA; Hardinge to Salisbury, 2 Dec. 1895, FO 403/211, 219; Hardinge to Salisbury, 17 Feb. 1896, C. 8274, 61.

[37] See esp. the remarks of the Giriama elders at Bale, Hardinge to Salisbury, 17 and 19 Feb. 1896, C. 8274, 61, 70; Hardinge, *Diplomatist in the East*, 186; Chiraghdin, "Maisha ya Sheikh Mbaruk bin Rashid," 173-4. Also remarks of Mzee Ndungu, Macdougall to Pigott, 30 Mar. 1896, CP 75/46, KNA, and Giriama gullibility regarding the Mazrui's "clean escape" at Mwele, Jones to Pigott, 28 Aug. 1895, CP 65/4, KNA.

[38] Macdougall to Pigott, 17 and 22 Nov., 3 and 22 Dec. 1895, CP 75/46, KNA.

[39] Macdougall to Pigott, 17 Nov. and 14 Dec. 1895, ibid; Carthew to Pigott, 12 Jan. 1896, CP 65/4, KNA; Ewart to Pigott, 22 Jan. 1896, CP 93/164, KNA; Hardinge to Salisbury, 17 and 19 Feb. 1896, C. 8274, 62-3, 69; MacLennan to Pigott, 15 Feb. 1896, and Macdougall to Pigott, 30 Mar. 1896, CP 75/46, KNA; Harrison to Hardinge, 22 Mar. 1896, C. 8274, 82.

[40] Hardinge to Salisbury, 17 and 19 Feb. 1896, C. 8274, 62, 70; Harrison to Hardinge, 22 Mar. 1896, ibid, 82; Hardinge to Salisbury, 27 Mar. 1896, FO 403/226, 111-2; Macdougall to Pigott, 30 Mar. 1896, CP 75/46, KNA.

[41] Hardinge to Kimberley, 25 Jun. 1895, and Hardinge to Salisbury, 6 Jul. 1895 and 17 Feb. 1896, C. 8274, 7, 11, 63; Pigott to Hardinge, 1 Sep. 1895, CP 73/37, KNA; Macdougall quarterly report, 8 Apr. 1901, CP 71/25, KNA. See ch. 8 for their sub-

Swahili resented the growth of British power, but they cared little for the Mazrui. Mbaruk's September appeals for a "holy war against the infidels" did elicit a response from one of his old enemies, though also well known as a Europhobe, Hamisi b. Kombo. Hamisi and his son joined the rebels, as did Mwenye Jaka of Mtongwe, but the British had little trouble dealing with the new insurgents. Mtwapa was sacked in October and Khamis's slaves set free. Thereafter Khamis, his son Mahomed, and several of their armed slaves traveled with the guerrillas in the north.[42] Mwenye Jaka, who initially aided the British, rebelled in November. He was reinforced by Eyub and arms sent from Mwareni.[43] British strength, most conspicuous on the coastline, nevertheless increased the ranks of loyalist town dwellers and discouraged conspiratorial activities among the disaffected, even in Takaungu where sympathy for the rebels was the strongest. "The people of Takaungu are in deep sympathy with Mbaruk," observed Macdougall, in charge of the northern forces, "but cannot do anything."

> I do not allow any private shauris[meetings], nor do I allow any one to go outside the stockade except on business to his shambas [farms] and they be inside before sunset. All shauris are discussed on the public baraza before the Liwali and everybody in town must recognize him as their Arab leader which they fully regard.[44]

The townsfolk, like the Giriama, reduced their risks by staying out of the conflict. Compared with the guerrilla's supporters, those outwardly loyal to the Protectorate received much greater protection. Guerrillas were unable to control any one place for more than a few weeks, and their attacks on coastal targets were easily repulsed. From the point in the war at which Britain secured the towns by garrison, only Mazeras was attacked by the guerrillas without heavy losses. In February 1896 they attacked Malindi and before they were driven off had lit a fire that spread throughout the town. Though a partial military success, the guerrillas gained it at the expense of local sympathy. The effect of the attack, reported Hardinge,

> was to excite the people of Malindi. . . into a state of the utmost fury with the rebels. They had believed that if the latter entered the town they would merely attack the Government troops and officers..., and they now found, to their dismay, that they themselves and their property were the only sufferers.[45]

In the contest for popular support, the British gained easily the upper hand

---

sequent history.

[42] Macdougall to Pigott, 20 Oct. 1895, CP 75/46, KNA; Pigott notice 5, 22 Oct. 1895, CP 66/12, KNA; Jones to Pigott, 2 Dec. 1895, CP 65/4, KNA; Macdougall to Pigott, 3 Dec. 1895, 11 Jan. and 30 Mar. 1896, CP 75/46, KNA..

[43] Macdougall to Pigott, 5 Dec. 1895, CP 75/46, KNA; Chiraghdin, "Maisha ya Sheikh Mbaruk bin Rashid," 169, 171.

[44] Macdougall to Pigott, 22 Sep. 1895, CP 75/46, KNA.

[45] Hardinge to Salisbury, 17 Feb. 1896, FO 403/225, 287.

because in the towns they could normally guarantee personal security. In the hinterland, where full occupation was impractical, the British were increasingly able to command respect with the threat of force. The Giriama were too numerous to be coerced by the guerrillas but no match for the maxim guns and armed patrols of the British.[46] Their allegiance, like that of the town people's, was determined by the fear of reprisal.

In contrast, slaves and *mahaji* in Takaungu district remained unprotected. On 21 January 1896, Eyub led two hundred men in an unsuccessful attack on Frere Town and then moved north toward Takaungu.[47] Instead of attacking the town, the guerrillas raided the plantation district of Makonde, seizing and carrying off slaves.[48] Two weeks later, another party began raiding plantations in the north. On 12 February Aziz, who had collected his scattered forces in northern Giriama, made a surprise raid on Malindi. After being driven back, Aziz and his men moved south into the Tezo-Roka area, and on the 13th they set fire to Roka and Oyombo. At Roka they recaptured Nasoro b. Hamed, who had deserted them in December, and journeyed west into Giriama country with, according to Hardinge, "a certain portion of the [Tezo-Roka] population [having] joined them."[49] The "certain portion" were slaves and *mahaji*, who probably accompanied the guerrillas for the reasons shared by the slaves of Makonde. As Macdougall afterwards informed his superior, "the slaves and others raided by the rebels on the coast shambas are all sold into slavery to the Wanyika [Miji Kenda] and Wakamba, or bartered for food."[50]

Though the guerrillas lost followers by resorting to such methods, their mobility prevented Hardinge from using his much larger army to decisive advantage. With approximately eight hundred men anchored to towns and stockades in anticipation of attack, few could be spared to chase guerrillas in the countryside. In early February Hardinge and Capt. E. Harrison marched through the northern Giriama district with one hundred Sudanese and Zanzibari regulars, but aside from prompting shows of loyalty from the Giriama the touring force neither encountered the guerrillas nor curtailed their activities.[51] As they marched about the hinterland, Aziz slipped into Malindi district, attacked Malindi and Tezo-Roka, and escaped once more into the bush. Hardinge was reminded of the necessity of strong garrisons in the towns; still, he became convinced that large mobile columns were needed to flush the guerrillas from the hinterland. He

---

[46] In September the guerrillas coerced the Chonyi and later used their villages as a temporary base of operations. Macdougall to Pigott, 22 Sep. 1895 and 18 Apr. 1896, CP 75/46, KNA.

[47] Binns's account, 21 Jan. 1896, in Binns to Baylis, 31 Jan. 1896, G3A5/012, CMS.

[48] Macdougall to Pigott, 23 Jan. and 2 Feb. 1896, CP 75/46, KNA.

[49] Hardinge to Salisbury, 17 Feb. 1896, C. 8274, 68 (also 66-7); Hardinge to Salisbury, 25 Feb. 1896, ibid., 72; MacLennan to Pigott, 15 Feb. 1896, CP 75/46, KNA.

[50] Macdougall to Pigott, 19 Feb. 1896, CP 75/46, KNA.

[51] Hardinge to Salisbury, 17 Feb. 1896, and itinerary, 19 Feb. 1896, C. 8274, 57-66, 68-70.

therefore wired for reinforcements, while barricades and garrison troops were increased in Tezo-Roka, and Harrison marched inland again to track Aziz.

In March, with Harrison's patrol and the arrival of 830 additional troops, the last brief phase of the war began. After leaving Takaungu on 4 March, Harrison followed Aziz for more than a week deep into northern Giriama territory. On the 14th, at Gabina twenty miles west of Mt. Mangea, Aziz and four hundred men attempted a pre-dawn attack on Harrison's camp, but they suffered heavy losses and retreated. Unaided by the Giriama, who had come to fear the British, Aziz and his men moved south into the Bamba area, where they foraged for grain and fruit and hid during the day in the forests.[52] Meanwhile, 724 officers and men of the 24th Baluchistan regiment and 106 Sudanese troops arrived in Mombasa.[53] With Aziz then in retreat, Hardinge used his reinforcements to mount a two-pronged assault on the southern guerrilla bases. Within a week columns at Mombasa and Vanga were poised to march into the Shimba hills.

Before joining Mbaruk in the south, Aziz's men darted east from Bamba and entered the southern sector of Takaungu district, where they raided slave plantations. On 24 March at Mbuyu Kiwete, the guerrillas under Akida Bakari seized fifty slaves and escaped to the west. Pursued by a small British force, the guerrillas were forced into a skirmish at Mikinduni, where half of their captive slaves were abandoned. Mikinduni was the last confrontation in the war.[54] The guerrillas then divided, with Bakari moving into the forests of southern Giriama and Aziz fleeing southwest. The British chased Aziz. At Bongo in Duruma country, the harried leader rendezvoused with Mbaruk and, before the British caught up, moved quickly on to Mwele. On the next day the British patrol destroyed Bongo and returned to Mombasa. The final push against the guerrillas, now starving in a great huddle at Mwele, was left for the two large columns.

Within weeks the war was over. In early April before the columns converged on Mwele, Mbaruk, Aziz, and twelve hundred followers crossed the German East Africa border near Tanga and asked for asylum. German governor von Wissman demanded the surrender of their arms, promising Mbaruk and other leaders that they would not be extradited to the north.[55] Mbaruk hesitated. According to one source, he had hoped to leave only the sick, wounded, and children in German territory and return north to resume fighting.[56] After two weeks of deliberation, however, he and his men decided to end the war. On the 21st, at Moa, they handed over their rifles to von Wissman.[57]

---

[52] Harrison to Hardinge, 22 Mar. 1896, C. 8274, 81-2.

[53] Hardinge to Salisbury, 27 Mar. 1896, FO 403/226, 111-2.

[54] Ibid, 112; Macdougall to Pigott, 28 and 30 Mar., 6 and 18 Apr. 1896, CP 75/46, KNA.

[55] Hardinge to Salisbury, 17 Apr. 1896, C. 8274, 94.

[56] Macdougall to Pigott, 13 May 1896, CP 75/46, KNA, according to the report of Mahomad b. Ali, who in February at Roka had been captured by the guerrillas and was released by them at Moa in April.

[57] Hardinge to Salisbury, teleg. 22 Apr. 1896, C. 8274, 82. Four hundred rifles were surrendered, all but eighteen of which were muzzle loaders.

Mbaruk's surrender stranded groups of slaves and *mahaji* guerrillas scattered between Mtwapa and Takaungu. During April and early May, British patrols flushed them out of Kurwitu, Mtoni, and Kijipwa and swept down on Akida Bakari's camp at Weruni. Without hope of reinforcements or escape, the guerrillas surrendered in steady numbers. Three hundred followers and their families

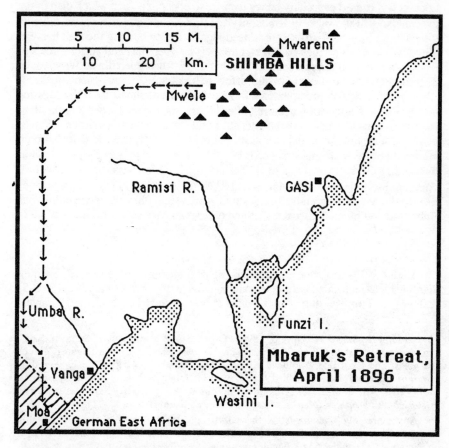

came into Mombasa, Mtwapa, and Takaungu in April, and more than twenty surrendered at Takaungu in the first two weeks of May.[58]

The defeat of the guerrillas ended Mazrui control in Takaungu and Gasi districts. Rather than face imprisonment, Mbaruk, Aziz, and Mubarak remained in exile in German East Africa, where they spent the rest of their lives.[59] Hardinge appointed Ali b. Salim, son of the *liwali* of Mombasa, as the new *liwali* at

---

[58] Macdougall to Pigott, 6, 11, and 18 Apr., 6 and 13 May 1896, CP 75/46, KNA.
[59] Cashmore, "Sheikh Mbaruk bin Rashid," 136-7. Mubarak died in 1898, Mbaruk in 1910.

Gasi.[60] In Takaungu the Zaheri sheikhdom, which they had already placed in the hands of Rashid b. Salim, continued dependent on British, rather than local, support.

Slaves in turn abandoned Takaungu district. The war destroyed their plantations, which had already suffered from drought and locusts in previous months. Locusts had caused especially heavy damage to coconut palms, which died in the thousands.[61] In its wake, in Kibokoni, Koeni, Konjora, and other areas close to the guerrilla base at Sokoke, came Macdougall's forces burning the first harvest. Slaves who remained then had to endure theft by guerrillas and suffer threats to their own lives. In September and October 1895 when guerrilla activity was at its peak, hundreds of slaves fled for safety to Takaungu. Later, guerrilla skirmishes with the British precipitated a large movement of slaves from the Mtwapa area.[62] Further emigration occurred after Mbaruk had spread word that the British would attack everyone who did not reside inside their garrisons. Slaves believed during the war, and continued believing so after, that the British would punish them for their masters' deeds.[63] They attempted to occupy safer land to the south, joined other refugees in Takaungu and Mombasa, or, as others had done, fled to Fuladoyo and Makongeni.[64] When hostilities ended, many slaves left Takaungu district altogether. By mid-April 1896 they were streaming into Rabai and continued to arrive at this and other mission stations for the remainder of the year.[65]

3. Defending Slavery

Like the Mazrui succession crisis, coastal slavery was an issue in which Hardinge was embroiled before he could announce the Protectorate in July 1895; and just as Hardinge immediately went to war against the Mazrui to guarantee

[60] Hardinge to Salisbury, 28 Sep. 1895, FO 403/211, 62. Ali, son of Salim b. Khalfan, was appointed *liwali* on 25 Sep. 1895. He was regarded by Hardinge as "one of the ablest and most liberal-minded Arabs in this country." Ali previously served as *liwali* of Mambrui and would in 1921 succeed his father as head of the Kenya coast's *maliwali*. A.I. Salim, "Sir Ali bin Salim," in K. King and A. Salim, ed., *Kenya Historical Biographies* (Nairobi: East African Publishing House, 1971).

[61] Approximately two-thirds of the coast's plantations were destroyed by this plague. Macdougall to Craufurd, 25 May 1897, CP 68/20, KNA. Also letter of Weaver in Fitzgerald, *Travels*, 639. For descriptions of the plague and its affects in Rabai, Ackerman journal, 28 Dec. 1894, 11 Jan. and 26 Apr. 1895, G3A5/011, CMS.

[62] Akida Sherifu Ali to Pigott, 10 Oct. 1895, CP 67/14, KNA.

[63] Macdougall to Pigott, 17 Nov. 1895, CP 75/46, KNA, regarding his conversations with Miji Kenda elders and slaves captured by Aziz. Of the Mazrui who remained loyal to the British during the fighting, slaves showed greater confidence and a disinclination to run away. In Roka, where the Mazrui opposed the guerrillas, slaves resumed farming as soon as British patrols secured the area in early March. They removed hidden grain stores from the nearby bush and helped their masters rebuild destroyed portions of the town. Macdougall to Pigott, 30 Mar. and 18 Apr. 1896, ibid.

[64] Jones to Pigott, 13 Aug. 1895, CP 65/4, KNA.

[65] Hardinge to Mackenzie, 16 Jan. 1898, MSS. Brit. Emp. s.18, C59/134, RH.

the new Protectorate's right to determine the Zaheri successor, so was he committed from the outset to preserving Protectorate control over the slave population for the sake of his administration. In fact months before the runaway crisis developed during the Anglo-Mazrui conflict, Hardinge had launched his own private campaign against British citizens who were determined to mark the occasion of formal British rule in East Africa with the legal abolition of slavery.

The struggle began in February 1895, when Donald Mackenzie of the British Anti-Slavery Society visited East Africa for the purpose of sounding British officials in Zanzibar and Company officials on the coast regarding slavery. Hardinge had been forewarned by the colonial secretary that public opinion in Britain was "increasingly strong on the subject [of abolition], and complaints are made that...no legislative advance has been made."[66] In a long reply to the foreign office, Hardinge counseled strongly against abolition and, when Mackenzie arrived in Zanzibar, told his visitor the reasons why. The Protectorate intended to uphold the "promise" already given by the Company "to observe local customs," stated Hardinge, who felt "bound in honour to observe it." Mackenzie was informed that "practically all Europeans in Africa take a difft. view from the Anti-Slavery people at home. The slaves themselves wd. not like new legislation for every slave looks forwd. to owning slave.... Slaves [on the mainland]," asserted Hardinge, "now [are] never treated cruelly."[67] Hardinge, whose mother's family estate in Jamaica was ruined following emancipation, was determined either that slavery in East Africa be allowed to fade away under existing laws or that owners receive full compensation.[68]

After Mackenzie's report appeared in May calling for the abolition of slavery in East Africa, Hardinge worked in late July and early August to offset its impact in Britain. Together with his own lengthy dispatches, the consul-general assembled letters from ex-IBEACO officers on his new staff and from CMS missionaries opposed to abolition. All raised the specter of utter social and economic collapse should slavery be brought to an abrupt end. The long list of certain catastrophes included the ruin of the slave-owning class, soaring prostitution and crime rates, and public disorders caused by destitute slaves.

Hardinge's officials magnified the scale of disaster by wildly exaggerating the mainland slave population (140,000), by ascribing present evils only to "bad slaves," and by portraying runaway slaves and freed slaves as fiends. Clifford Craufurd and John Pigott claimed that "all runaways are lazy and thriftless to the extreme....The worst characters on the coast are...either runaway or freed slaves."[69] Hardinge told the Anti-Slavery Society that his administration had

---

[66] Kimberley to Hardinge, 16 Feb. 1895, FO 403/208.

[67] Mackenzie's notes, MSS. Brit. Emp. s. 18, C59/141, RH; Hardinge to Kimberley, 26 Feb. 1895, C. 7707, 27-38. Mackenzie report, 6 May 1895, *Anti-Slavery Reporter*, 4th Series, 15(1895), 69-96.

[68] Hardinge, *Diplomatist in the East*, 194. Hardinge erred in stating that Mackenzie came out to East Africa to investigate slavery only in Pemba. Ibid., 110-11.

[69] Hardinge to Salisbury, 29 Aug. 1895, with encls, FO 403/210, 260-9; Hardinge to Salisbury, 17 Sep. 1895, FO 403/211, 49.

the interests of slaves at heart. "Mahomedan slavery in its present mild form is a lesser evil than that which would...follow a general and simultaneous emancipation.... It is our duty as trustees for the weaker and more backward races of mankind, whose destinies are...in our hands, to do our utmost to bestow on them all the advantages which we ourselves enjoy, and to do so, not for our benefit, but for theirs."[70]

Four CMS missionaries supported Hardinge's position: Harry Binns, William Taylor, Annie Grieve, and Maggie Lockhart. Grieve and Lockhart were newcomers to Frere Town and East Africa, but Binns had served on the coast since 1876, Taylor, since 1881. Taylor's sympathy for slave owners was long-standing; he had abandoned regular mission work in the mid-1880s for the academic study of the KiSwahili language and coastal Muslim culture, of which he was regarded by Hardinge and others outside the mission as an expert. Taylor was popular among Muslims in Mombasa and spent most of his time with town-based scholars. He also had a vicious streak when dealing with freed slaves.[71] In his letter supporting Hardinge, Taylor opposed the liberation of "settled slaves, [who are] unaccustomed to the proper use of freedom," though several years earlier he had also expressed fears that, with abolition, the Christian mission field in the coastal hinterland would dry up because the people would rapidly convert to Islam.[72] Harry Binns opposed abolition because he expected that, apart from leaving slaves destitute, it would "raise the whole of the slave-owning population against the Government." Given the mission's history of being threatened by slave owners and the fact that when Binns penned his letter the CMS was being assisted by the Protectorate in readying its defenses at Rabai and Frere Town in the event of an attack by Mazrui forces, Binns's fears are understandable. Yet, at the time, neither he, nor other missionaries, nor Hardinge's administrators were suggesting that the Mazrui war was in any way connected with a coastal rising against the threat of abolition.[73] When the CMS governing body in England later queried his position, Binns ignored the question of a slave owners' rising and claimed his entire concern was for the plight of older slaves, whom Binns believed the government would not support in the event of abolition. "I have heard some talk," he wrote, "about the masters being

---

[70] Hardinge to Allen, 2 Sep. 1895, MSS. Brit. Emp. s. 18, C59/130, RH.

[71] Binns to Lang, 17 Mar. 1883, G3A5/01(1883) and Hannington to Lang, 29 May 1885, G3A5/02, CMS. For cameos of Taylor, Thomson, *Through Masai Land*, 20; Jackson, *Early Days*, 110; Hardinge, *Diplomatist in the East*, 168.

[72] Taylor to Binns, 26 Jul. 1895, FO 403/210, 264. "The Swahilis will make no effort to propagate Islam among them in the present state of things--because they would close the slave supply lawful to Mohammadans by so doing. When these feelings shall have ceased to act on either side, an era of propagations and wholesale conversion will commence." Taylor to Lang. 3 Dec. 1889, G3A5/06, CMS.

[73] Binns to Pigott, 30 Jul. 1895, FO 403/210, 264. Only during the following year did Hardinge assert that Muslim "fanaticism," sparked by the fear that the British were interfering with laws governing slavery, was a factor in the war. Hardinge to Salisbury, 12 Apr. 1896, FO 403/226, 178, 183.

compensated but I have heard nothing of compensation for the slaves...."[74] Binns appears to have changed his tune to suit his audience. If anything he was disguising the close relationship that had existed between Frere Town and the government since Company days. At the time he wrote his first letter in support of Hardinge, Binns was reprimanding Maria Ackerman and William Jones for trying to prevent Protectorate police from arresting a runaway slave who had alleged that her owner had beaten her and forced her into prostitution. John Pigott, the official who returned the slave to her owner, was also secretary of the Frere Town Finance Committee, which Binns chaired.[75]

Hardinge tried to suppress opinions of missionaries who favored abolition. Maria Ackerman, who worked closely at Rabai with William Jones, protested against the Company's and the Protectorate's treatment of runaway slaves and who opposed Pigott's views on the slavery question, was not invited to make a submission for Hardinge's report to the foreign office. Neither was the CMS bishop of East Africa, Alfred Tucker, though he made one anyway. Tucker had been in East Africa since 1890, spending most of his time in Uganda. Whenever visiting the coast, however, he championed the rights of slaves and freed slaves. In 1892-93 Tucker also disapproved of Binns's Frere Town administration and wrote a scathing report to CMS headquarters alleging mismanagement and abandonment of the Africanization of the church. Their rift over the future of the mission partly explains why Binns and Tucker later took opposing views on Protectorate policy.[76] Months before the Protectorate began, Tucker had persuaded the foreign office to order Hardinge to recognize Christian marriages on the Muslim coast, and on 1 July 1895 when the Company formally handed over to the Protectorate in Mombasa, Tucker was present to request that Hardinge take immediate steps to abolish slavery.[77] A fortnight later, Tucker departed for Uganda in a caravan. Only then did Hardinge begin assembling letters from officials and missionaries, but somehow Tucker received word upcountry and sent Pigott a long letter pressing abolition. It arrived after Hardinge posted his report and was not forwarded. It was filed under "Miscellaneous."[78]

---

[74] Binns to Baylis, 25 May 1896, G3A5/12, CMS.

[75] Ackerman and Jones also argued the runaway slave's case. Ackerman journal, 29 Mar., 7 Jun., and 28 Aug. 1895; Binns to Baylis, 29 Aug. 1895, G3A5/11, CMS; J.W. Gregory, *The Great Rift Valley; Being a Narrative of a Journey to Mount Kenya and Lake Baringo* (London: John Murray, 1896), 381.

[76] Tucker to Wigram, 3 Jun. 1892; Binns to Lang, 13 and 14 Sep. 1892, Binns to Wigram, 7 Nov. 1892, G3A5/08, CMS and Tucker to Baylis, 31 Aug. 1893; Finance Committee report, 19 Sep. 1893, G3A5/09, CMS. For a discussion of Binns and Tucker's opposing views on mission policy, Strayer, *Mission Communities in East Africa*, 23-4.

[77] Tucker to Hardinge, 16 Aug. 1894 and Hardinge to Tucker, 29 Aug. 1894, G3 A5/10 and Kimberley to Hardinge, 15 Nov. 1894, G3A5/11, CMS; Hardinge, *Diplomatist in the East*, 167.

[78] Tucker to Pigott, 19 Aug. 1895, CP 65/14, Miscellaneous Inward, 1894/96, KNA. Tucker wrote his letter ten days before Hardinge sent his assembled dispatches to

In the following year, Hardinge squelched the abolitionist threat and upheld slave owners' rights. The Anglo-Mazrui war eased the pressure on Hardinge in this regard and provided him with additional means of resisting abolition. Two out of every three porters employed by the Protectorate during the war were slaves, and Hardinge argued that abolition would seriously disrupt the transport system. Worse still, slaves would cease working if freed and would not "have the discipline or cohesion required to act in concert" in support of the Protectorate against slave owners.[79] By April 1896, after the war had ended, Hardinge was convinced that Muslim fanaticism was widespread and needed only the provocation of abolition to reignite the coast in the manner of the Bushiri revolt on mainland German East Africa. With the Mazrui now defeated, Hardinge advised that his government be allowed to check all anti-Muslim "propaganda" emanating from Christian missions, to render "scrupulous respect" of all Muslim institutions, and to permit slavery to "die a natural death."[80] In the same month Hardinge's officials committed themselves to recovering those slaves who had run away during the war. At Mombasa senior commissioner John Pigott instructed his officer at Rabai to send all runaways to the port city in order to stop "this tide of runaways...before it assumes much larger proportions."[81] In the Mambrui and Malindi plantation districts, where many slaves had escaped, Macdougall urged Pigott's replacement, Clifford Craufurd, to assist the owners in recovering them. Craufurd responded favorably, promising that "every endeavour will be made to return those that have run away." He had Macdougall compile lists of runaways "with a view to the future return of these people to your district."[82] These decisions, which led to search warrants and seizures, had support from the top. Hardinge himself endeavored to retrieve the slaves who had fled to German East Africa.[83] When privately challenged for having used his powers to restore slaves to their owners, Hardinge defended the runaway policy as part of existing law.

> I have never objected to restoring fugitive slaves where their masters had a legal right under the local law to demand restitution. I have always refused it where they had not. I have regarded it as a question not of sentiment one way or another, but of law.[84]

Anti-slavery pressures increased in Parliament. Since 1895 Lord Salisbury, foreign office secretary, had steadily defended Hardinge's administration against

London from Zanzibar.

[79] Hardinge to Salisbury, 29 Jan. 1896, C. 8275, 32

[80] Hardinge to Salisbury, 12 Apr. 1896, FO 403/226, 177, 183.

[81] Pigott to McClellan, 20 Apr. 1896, also 15 Apr. and 9 May 1896, CP 97/187, KNA.

[82] Macdougall to Craufurd, 3 Feb. and 25 Mar. 1897, CP 75/46; Craufurd to Macdougall, 6 Apr. 1897, CP 97/187, KNA.

[83] Hardinge to Liebert, 27 Mar. 1897, FO 403/242, 30.

[84] Hardinge to Mackenzie, 16 Jan. 1898, MSS. Brit. Emp., s.18, C59/134, RH.

attacks from John Kirk and other members of the abolitionist lobby. Kirk wished to see Hardinge, who was one of Salisbury's favorites, replaced by Frederick Lugard, who was already well known for his views favoring abolition of the legal status of slavery.[85] Lugard's thinking was close to that of Tucker, with whom he became well acquainted while working for the Company in Uganda.[86]

Salisbury tried to stifle the anti-slavery lobby and protect Hardinge by blocking the offer of an East African post to Lugard.[87] But concessions to the abolitionists then had to be made. In April 1897, the legal status of slavery was abolished in Zanzibar and Pemba, where ex-slaves nevertheless continued to supply plantation labor. And, in May or June, the attorney general issued a ruling regarding runaway slaves on the coast that no East Africa Protectorate official could legally assist retaining a person in slavery. Hardinge complained that the ruling would make it impossible for his officials to enforce Muslim laws in areas under Protectorate jurisdiction. Effectively it would abolish laws protecting slavery and undermine the "confidence" of the Muslim population in the new administration. The ruling, too, Hardinge argued, would convert mission stations into "chartered sanctuaries of lazy or vagabond slaves."[88] Hardinge was angered at that moment as much by the return to the coast of Tucker, who wasted no time in ordering CMS mission stations to accept all runaway slaves. In another attempt to rally coastal European opinion against abolition, Hardinge supplied Salisbury with ammunition to defend the Protectorate's runaway slave policy, including a letter from Harry Binns containing one of the more remarkable statements emanating from East African Christendom to the effect that "good slaves" did not run away from their masters.[89]

This time Hardinge's efforts made much less impact in London, where his reputation was slipping. By the end of the year, the foreign office was weary of defending his policy and was beginning to question his reliability.[90] In December 1897 Hardinge was ordered officially to discontinue the issue of search warrants for runaway slaves. "The Courts must, of course, recognize as lawful the detention of a slave by his master," instructed Salisbury, "but the law of Islam may be recognized...without employing the police to assist actively in the

---

[85] Perham, *Lugard: Years of Adventure*, 611; Lugard, *Our East African Empire*, I, 180f; 484-7. The first edition appeared in 1893. For a discussion of the formation of Lugard's views on slavery in East Africa and his early work in promoting abolition see Hogendorn and Lovejoy, "Frederick Lugard's Policies," 1-43.

[86] Lugard, often critical of missionaries, regarded Tucker and Laws of Nyasaland as the two best he had encountered in Africa. M. Perham, *Lugard: The Years of Authority, 1898-1945* (Hamden, Archon, 1968), 423.

[87] In January 1897. Perham, *Lugard: Years of Adventure*, 614-5. Lugard then accepted an offer from the colonial office for a post on the Niger river.

[88] Hardinge to Salisbury, 5 Jul. 1897, C. 8858, 8.

[89] Hardinge to Salisbury, 14 Sep. 1897 and encl., FO 403/244, 14-15, 18.

[90] According to Lugard's recollection of his conversation with George Curzon, parliamentary under-secretary at the foreign office. Lugard, *Diaries*, IV, 350.

work of capturing slaves."[91] Hardinge then ordered his officials to desist from
arresting runaways but at the same time to make arrangements with the runaways for compensating their masters or purchasing their freedom. He also
issued new regulations for the arrest of "vagrants" in the towns and their return
to their "original place of abode." Almost immediately Salisbury quashed the
new policy.[92]

At the time Tucker was on the coast fighting a local court case that he
hoped would produce a ruling abolishing slavery for nearly all persons still held
in bondage. The case concerned a Kamba woman named Karibu who, during the
1884 famine, was enslaved in the hinterland and sold to a man from Jomvu near
Mombasa. In Karibu's defense, Tucker employed an abolitionist argument that
originated with Lugard. In 1893, Lugard argued that most surviving slaves on
the coast had been acquired since the 1873 and 1876 proclamations banning the
slave trade, thus entitling them to their legal freedom without further proclamations or compensation for their owners. Kirk had made this point in 1895, but
Hardinge dismissed it.[93] Now Tucker, said by officials to have become "most
aggressive and pugnacious" after Salisbury's December 1897 instruction to Hardinge, used this line of argument among others to ask a Mombasa court for
Karibu's freedom. Tucker regarded the case as "one which may possibly affect the
position of thousands of slaves."[94]

In April 1898 the court freed Karibu on the grounds that she had been enslaved after the 1876 proclamation, but Hardinge was uninterested in its broader
application; he was reassured, instead, that the presiding judge, Clifford Craufurd,
denied one of Tucker's arguments that the attorney general's ruling of 1897
regarding runaway slaves entitled Karibu, who had run to the CMS mission prior
to the case, to remain free.[95] Tucker took the Karibu verdict as a victory for the
abolitionist cause in East Africa, but by June he was in Uganda, unable to press
his advantage. Hardinge's officials ignored the case and left each slave the task of
taking her/his master to court. Other than Karibu, no slave was freed by the
Protectorate through the enforcement of the 1873 and 1876 proclamations.

The Protectorate also ignored the 1889 agreement freeing children born on or
after 1 January 1890. Hardinge notified the foreign office of a Mombasa court
decision allowing the inheritance of two slave children under Muslim laws

---

[91] Salisbury to Hardinge, 15 Dec. 1897, C. 8858, 26.

[92] Hardinge minute to Craufurd, n.d., regulation dated 12 Jan. 1898; Hardinge to
Salisbury, 16 Jan. 1898 and Salisbury to Hardinge, 25 Mar. 1898, in FO 403/260,
120-3, 215.

[93] Lugard, *Our East African Empire*, I, 186-8; Hardinge to Salisbury, 26 Feb. 1895,
C. 7707, 35.

[94] Hardinge to Salisbury, 16 Jan. 1898, FO 403/260. 123-4; Tucker to Baylis, 25
Jan. and 8 Mar. 1898, G3A5/14, CMS; A. Tucker, *Eighteen Years in Uganda and East
Africa*, new ed. (London: Edward Arnold, 1911), 208-11.

[95] Hardinge to Salisbury, 3 May 1898, FO 403/261, 156-7. For a transcript of the
court hearings and statement of the assessors, see Tucker to Baylis, 8 Mar. 1898, G3
A5/14, CMS.

governing division of slaves, even though the children had been born after the 1889 agreement. Hardinge explained that the decree was regarded in Zanzibar and on the mainland a dead letter because it had never been promulgated.[96] Salisbury ruled that such a course was "illegal and...cannot be permitted to continue" and advised Hardinge to enforce the agreement and make provisions for the children affected.[97]

Hardinge struck the pose of prompt obedience. Though his policy on the mainland had been to "keep the children in slavery," Hardinge promised instantly to respect the 1889 agreement. He noted that responsibility for the consequences, however, belonged not to his administration but with the owners. He expected that emancipation would result in the young ones being turned out, especially by poor owners. But Hardinge was certain that owners who were well off and "given to Eastern hospitality" were likely to look after emancipated children as "the supply of simple wants of native Africans is not a very serious expense; two or three pairs of small black hands more or less in the rice dish will not ruin him."[98] After penning these words to Salisbury in June 1898, Hardinge then waited four months before promulgating the agreement. His instructions to Clifford Craufurd, senior commissioner in Mombasa, moreover, made the enforcement of its provisions dependant on the wishes of slave owners.

> It would not, I think, be necessary for you...to make this notification restrospective in the sense of calling up and emancipating of your own initiative all children who may be effected by it, and for many of whom we have no means of providing, but, in the event of any application being made to you on behalf of such children, you should grant them letters of freedom....[99]

Days prior to receiving these instructions, Craufurd told Harry Binns at Frere Town that slave children "will be declared free I think before very long" and asked if the CMS would be willing to receive them into their care.[100] Yet, after Hardinge's instructions arrived on 17 October, Craufurd's policy toward slave children remained unaltered. As of December 1898 Frere Town had received not a single child, and "it is not likely," understood Binns, "[that] they will be

---

[96] Hardinge to Salisbury, 9 Feb. 1898, FO 403/260, 199-200. See also ch. 6, note 119.

[97] Salisbury to Hardinge, 9 May 1898, FO 403/261, 98-9.

[98] Hardinge to Salisbury, 13 Jun. 1898, FO 403/262, 25-7.

[99] Hardinge to Craufurd, 17 Oct. 1898, CP 90/154 and Hardinge's notification of the agreement on the same date, CP 109/91, KNA; also No. 19 of 1898, Orders-in-Council...in Force in the East Africa Protectorate on the 1st of January 1903, 56.

[100] Binns to Baylis, 6 Oct. 1898, G3A5/014, CMS. Craufurd was not referring to the children the Protectorate had already been emancipating since early 1898 under the decree of 1890 barring the inheritance of slave children by persons other than the deceased owners children. By April 1898, roughly 400 children had been freed under the 1890 decree. See Hardinge to Salisbury, 23 Apr. 1898, C. 8858, 24 and Craufurd's undated returns on freed slaves, CP 93/162, KNA.

received in any numbers."[101] No records related to slaves emancipated during the Protectorate period have yet been found to indicate that any children were freed under the 1889 agreement.

Hardinge had deflected the abolitionist challenge and allowed Salisbury to claim that Britain was dealing with slavery in the East Africa Protectorate under existing laws and decrees as "progressive steps in the direction of its ultimate abolition."[102] For the next nine years on the Kenya coast slavery retained legal status. With Tucker removed permanently to Uganda and Lugard to Nigeria (and Kirk's interests with him), Hardinge's officials were free to protect slave owners' interests without protest.[103] During 1898, the Protectorate condoned the pawning of Miji Kenda children to coastal Muslims, collected "rent" from the Makongeni maroons, established new guidelines for the apprehension of runaway slaves, and encouraged slave owners to make "contracts" with their slaves so that officials could enforce them throughout the Protectorate.[104] Apart from the Methodist missionary protest against the arrest of three runaway slaves at Mazeras by Protectorate-employed African police, Hardinge's policy after mid-1898 went unchallenged.[105]

---

[101] Binns to Baylis, 27 Dec. 1898, G3A5/14, CMS.

[102] Salisbury to Hardinge, 9 May 1898, FO 403/261, 99.

[103] Two abolitionist voices at Rabai, Marie Ackerman and William Jones, were isolated by the Frere Town Finance Committee, chaired by Binns. The committee removed Ackerman from Rabai in 1897 alleging "injudicious conduct" with a young black man (she was not told). Finance Committee Minutes, 20 Apr. 1897; Binns to Baylis, 23 Apr. 1897; Ackerman journal, 30 Apr. 1897, G3A5/13, CMS. Jones was driven out of the mission in 1898 (see ch. 8).

[104] Re pawning, Craufurd to Macdougall, 22 Jun. 1898, CP 86/118, KNA and R.F. Morton, "The Shungwaya Myth of Miji Kenda Origins: a Problem of Late Nineteenth-century Kenya Coastal History," *IJAHS*, 5, 3(1972), 411-17; re Makongeni "rent," Craufurd to Murray, 24 Jun. 1898, CP 86/118, KNA (see also ch. 8); re runaway slaves, Craufurd circular, 8 Sep. 1898, CP 82/93, KNA and note 132 below; re "contracts," Hardinge to Craufurd, 9 Jul. 1898, CP 90/154, KNA.

[105] Craufurd to Howe, 21 Jun. 1898, CP 82/93, KNA; Lloyd to Craufurd, 29 Dec. 1898, and Craufurd to Hardinge, 3 Feb. 1899, CP 76/51, KNA; and Hardinge to Salisbury, 4 Feb. 1899 with encls., C. 9502, 12-26. A study of Hardinge's administration of the coast is needed. Available studies are based only on PRO records and are concerned mainly with the post-Hardinge period: T.H.R. Cashmore, "Studies in District Administration in the East Africa Protectorate, 1895-1918" (Cambridge: University of Cambridge Jesus College Ph.D. dissertation, 1965); Salim, *Swahili-speaking Peoples*; and Mungeam, *British Rule in Kenya*. F. Cooper discussion of Hardinge's slavery policies in Zanzibar creates the mistaken impression that they were applied on the mainland. *From Slaves to Squatters*, esp. 34-46 (for comments on Cooper's treatment of the post slavery period, see ch. 8). The early Protectorate is characteristic of other early African colonial administrations built on working relations with slave-owning elites. Cf. respective comments by D.D. Cordell, R. Roberts, and E.A. McDougall in Miers and Roberts, *End of Slavery*, 151-62, 284; 366-7; and Hogendorn and Lovejoy, "Frederick Lugard's Policies," 10-27.

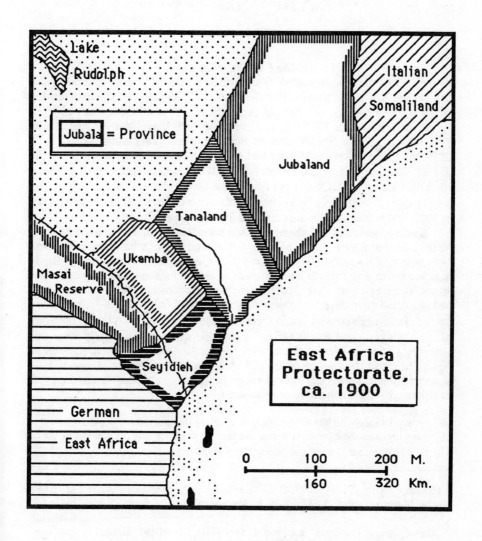

Lake Rudolph

Jubala = Province

Italian Somaliland

Jubaland

Tanaland

Ukamba

Masai Reserve

Seyidieh

German East Africa

East Africa Protectorate, ca. 1900

0   100   200 M.
     160   320 Km.

8

After Slavery

1. *The Last Slave Exodus*

At the end of the Anglo-Mazrui War, Arthur Hardinge, consul-general of the British East Africa Protectorate, reported that 26,259 legally-owned slaves resided on the coast.[1] Hardinge included slaves who had "been scattered in many districts by the disturbances of 1895-96, and...many of them [have] not yet returned to their villages." Later figures revealed that few, if any, ever came back. As of 1899, the entire Takaungu district had only an estimated 500 slaves, Mambrui district, 700, and Vanga district 350.[2] In 1901 Seyyidieh (later Coast) province contained a mere 8,160, or 31 per cent of the slaves claimed by Hardinge to be legally owned in 1897.[3] Following the abolition of the legal status of slavery in 1907, fewer than 7,683 slaves claimed freedom papers.[4]

Hardinge assumed that slaves who had been "scattered...by the disturbances" would return to their masters, because of the benignity of what he referred to as "the system of so-called slavery or, more correctly speaking, serfdom." Hardinge knew that some slaves had run away to mission stations but they had done so not because owners were cruel or slavery was unpleasant, but because owners had neglected their slaves, who were lazy and desired only a life of "comparative ease."[5] Hardinge's convictions in these respects were reinforced by the opinions of local officials and missionaries.[6] However, when slaves clearly were not returning to their masters, British officials used the drop in the slave population figures to credit their policy of gradual abolition and strict enforcement of anti-slave trade laws. Slaves had not run away; they had been "freed." Or, as the 1900 description of Seyyidieh province announced,

> It may be safely estimated that fully 75% of the domestic slave population
> have obtained their freedom within the last ten years, chiefly on account of the
> [1890] Zanzibar Decree abolishing slave markets.[7]

---

[1] Hardinge report, 20 Jul. 1897, C. 8683, 60. In 1897, Mombasa district had 2,667 slaves, Malindi district, 5,442. Ibid, 8; Macdougall to Craufurd, 25 May 1897, CP 68/20, KNA.

[2] "Description of Province," n.a., n.d. [1889-1900], CP 98/191, KNA.

[3] Tritton to Ewart, 16 Dec. 1901, CP 89/146, KNA.

[4] Maclean to Col. Secy, Nairobi, 20 May 1924, CP 47/1123, KNA.

[5] Hardinge report, 20 Jul. 1897, C. 8683, 60-2.

[6] See ch. 7.

[7] CP 98/191, KNA.

District returns of freed slaves, however, show that such was not the case. Between 1895 and 1898, for example, a total of 827 freedom certificates were issued in the districts of Mombasa, Malindi, and Vanga, but of these only fifty-two slaves had been set free by owners. On the other hand, 469 persons, or 57 per cent of the total, were slaves freed under the 1890 decree prohibiting their sale as part of the division of an estate of a childless owner.[8] Manumission rates continued to be slight. In Malindi district, only fourteen were freed in 1900, seventy-nine in 1901.[9] Few were manumitted thereafter. The 1901 coastal slave census figure of 8160, subtracted by the number of slaves freed after 1907, is a mere 477.

Hardinge's "scattered" slaves -- 18,099 to be exact -- had absconded.[10] Amounting to more than two thirds of the slaves legally held when the British East Africa Protectorate was established, they constitute the final, major story in the transition from slavery to freedom. Like the slaves who had already run away from plantations and towns over the previous two decades, slaves under British rule left their masters well in advance of legal status abolition. Thus, the onset of formal colonial rule on the Kenya coast, marked as it was by the Anglo-Mazrui War, was accompanied by a massive and permanent exodus of slaves.

The published literature has portrayed the final years of slavery and the transition to post-slavery as if all of Hardinge's "scattered" slaves returned. Frederick Cooper's central premise in *From Slaves to Squatters* is that slaves in coastal Kenya remained anchored to plantation areas, even after becoming ex-slaves. There, he argues, they were able to

> free themselves altogether from the year-long routine of closely supervised labor and to combine relatively favorable terms as squatters, producing exports as well as food for themselves, with part-time labor for landowners or in the towns.[11]

Cooper refers to a "great exodus" of slaves in the late 1890s to work in Mombasa and on the Uganda railroad, but regards it not as escape from slavery but as one step in the process of altering slave dependency. Cooper's slaves may have worked in town, but they remained tied to the land in and around the plantations, where they became "squatters." To Cooper, the transition from slavery to post-slavery was a "continuum--wage worker to sharecropper to renter to small-scale landowner--shaped by the resources and power that producers and landowners can

---

[8] Craufurd list, CP 93/162, KNA. Thirty-eight slaves had purchased their freedom, and 268 were freed without identification of the means applied.

[9] Murray quarterly report, 9 Jan. 1902, CP 71/25, KNA.

[10] The figure was reached by subtracting the 1901 slave census figure from Hardinge's 1897 total. Cashmore long ago recognized that the drop in slave population figures after 1895 was the result of runaway slave activity. "Studies in District Administration," 171-2.

[11] *From Slaves to Squatters*, 174.

mobilize."[12] His elaborate slave-to-squatter paradigm, based ostensibly on data from old plantation districts, has been used to characterize the experience of virtually all the slaves/ex-slaves of coastal Kenya.

Cooper did not bother to make a head count. In the early colonial period only a handful of slaves/ex-slaves were present and accounted for in the plantation districts. The others had left during, if not before, the first five years of British rule. In Takaungu district, for example, the squatters used for illustration by Cooper were not ex-slaves, but *mahaji* (Islamized Miji Kenda).[13] In Malindi district, where ex-slaves were found in some numbers, most were located not on Arab and Swahili land, as Cooper alleges, but on Crown land, where as *runaways* their fate contrasted sharply with Cooper's paradigmatic "squatters."[14] As the 1920 census revealed, ex-slaves (i.e. both ex-slaves and runaways) made up a small portion of the Malindi district population, two-thirds of which were "pagan Wanyika" (non-Islamized Miji Kenda). Of the remaining adult males, between one-sixth and one-seventh were upcountry "Kavirondo," the balance made up almost entirely of *mahaji*.[15] With reference to Lamu district, Cooper cites official reports that the southern part of the district was settled mainly by ex-slaves, but this area consisted of Witu and the Lower Tana, which had been resorted to by runaway slaves in the nineteenth century, rather than by freed slaves in the twentieth.[16] At any rate, they lived too far away from Lamu's

---

[12] Ibid., 52, 179-80.

[13] Ibid., 202. Cooper's footnote 84, citing the Registrar of Slaves, implies that the squatters referred to are ex-slaves, but they were Miji Kenda *mahaji*. See from the same file quoted by Cooper, Registrar of Slaves to Secy of Admin, Nairobi, 16 Jun. 1910, and Macdougall for Ali b. Salim Said b. Abdalla, and Mussa b. Saad, 13 Apr. 1910, CP 64/62, KNA. In 1915, *mahaji* were living in all the settlements around Takaungu, including Mtanganyiko, Tezo, Konjora, and Roka, where they had been "for many years past" and constituted the "only available labour supply of the District." Vidal to DC, Nyika, 28 Jan. 1915, and Palethorpe to PC, 31 Mar. 1915, CP 18/70, KNA.

[14] Cooper, *From Slaves to Squatters*, pp. 181-2, and note 28. For Crown land squatters, see "Mzee Ali Tete" in this chapter. Cooper quotes Coast provincial commissioner C. W. Hobley as reporting that "large numbers of squatters" were on Arab and Swahili land, but Hobley in fact wrote that ex-slaves were scattered about Kilifi and Malindi districts and that "a few are on the *shambas* of their old masters and a number are squatting on Crown Land." Hobley to Chief Secy, Nairobi, 7 May 1915, KNA CP 20/128a, KNA.

[15] Malindi District AR, 1919-1920, DC/MAL/1/1, KNA. This report uses the term *mahaji* to apply to Islamized Miji Kenda as well as ex-slaves, which on the Mombasa-Malindi coast was not standard usage. For *mahaji*, M.W.H. Beech, *Aids to the Study of Ki-Swahili* (New York: Kegan Paul, Trench, Trübner, 1918), xvi. Until the 1920 census results appeared, Malindi district officials had assumed that "ex-slaves made up a "large and important section of the population" Malindi District AR, 1915-16, CP 22/177, and Fazan to PC, 8 Jun. 1919, CP 25/279, KNA.

[16] See ch. 2 above. Runaway slaves from Lamu and Malindi were entering the Tana river area as late as 1899. Rogers[?] to Craufurd, 31 Jul. 1899, CP 76/51, KNA. The question of maroon settlements on the Tana River, as well as the history of the Tana

old *barani* plantations to qualify as squatters.[17] Even on Mombasa island, site of provincial headquarters, ex-slaves are difficult to find in colonial records. Officials lumped the black population in this bustling port city, swelling to 25,000 people by 1910, under the generic heading of "natives". Cooper's distinctions between ex-slaves and other Africans, even on the adjacent mainland, are, for the most part, arbitrary.[18]

Most ex-slaves are to be found in places other than where Cooper claims them to be. They fled, rather than remained on, plantations and more often than not tried to break free of agriculture rather than "to preserve...occupation rights to small plots of land they had as slaves."[19] The large majority of slaves moved to the coastal hinterland, to the towns, and along routes to the interior. They enlarged older ex-slave settlements, joined Miji Kenda clans, or established new quarters in Lamu and Mombasa. Yet, as a rule, they failed to put down roots. They had few children, and few established extended families. Single men and husbands drifted away into wage-earning careers, single women into petty trading and prostitution. As in the past, before British rule was established, they survived in the crevices and corners of coastal societies, excluded by those around them, even though they adopted predominantly local African, or Muslim, or

---

River area, has awaited detailed investigation since David Miller's death. At least two "watoro villages" on the Tana were reported in 1889, and several Pokomo clans acknowledge slave origins. Pigott Diary, 6 Mar. 1889, and Pigott to Administrator-in-chief, Mombasa, 2 Jul. 1889, FJL.; G. Böcking, "Sagen der Wa-Pokomo," *Zeitschrift fur Afrikanische und Ozeanische Sprachen,* 2(1896), 35; R. G. Darroch, ed., "Some Notes on the Early History of the Tribes Living on the Lower Tana, collected by Mikael Samson and Others," *Journal of the East Africa and Uganda Natural History Society,* 17, 79/80(Sep. 1944), 251, 374, 392.

[17] *From Slaves to Squatters,* 182, note 32.

[18] Cooper's tables (Ibid., 210-12), which are based on Mombasa court records, use "ex-slaves" as a category but do not explain how the records distinguish between ex-slaves and other people. The omission is the more noticeable when Cooper admits (211 note) that the court records do not enable him to distinguish between Swahili and Arab persons appearing before the court, thus accounting for the conflated category of "Arab-Swahili" in his tables. Also, in his extended textual discussion of ex-slaves, Cooper habitually groups ex-slaves with other "squatters," such as *mahaji,* Miji Kenda, and other migrants to the coastal plain, thereby disguising the lack of data as to the ex-slave presence. See, for example, on pp. 14, 61, 174, 183, and 215f, where ex-slaves and migrants are represented as equivalents, and on 174 and 215, for example, where he asserts that ex-slaves were joined by "a new wave of settlers," implying that ex-slaves were already in place and had begun their transition in advance of these non-ex-slave migrants. The archival record abounds with information about Wanyika (Miji Kenda) migrants in the Takaungu and Malindi districts, and it is on this record that Cooper has inferred an earlier, similar process to have occurred among ex-slaves, whom he does not locate separately in space or time for the reader to see. Equating the migrant experience with that of anything more than a small percentage of Kenya's freed slave population is unsupported by evidence. The Cooper paradigm is indeed sublime, but it cannot be put on the ground.

[19] *From Slaves to Squatters,* 202.

Western values, and placed their talents in the service of others. After slavery, they remained the children of Ham.

Ex-slaves and slaves in the early colonial period remained vulnerable to those in power. It has been assumed that the "weakening of slave owners' control" meant that "ex-slaves no longer needed personal protection."[20] Yet, after 1895, slaves and ex-slaves remained liable to coercion. The British, for example, commandeered hundreds of slaves to serve as porters during the Anglo-Mazrui War, though some of those dragooned took the opportunity to disappear.[21] Hundreds of slaves also deserted the war districts, making it difficult afterwards for the government to obtain porters. "Today we can only obtain a few score," lamented the district officer at Malindi, "and that by means of practically arresting them."[22] Porters were commandeered from the fields near Mambrui by the superintendent of telegraphs.[23] The line separating coerced labor from wage labor for the government, insofar as slaves and ex-slaves were concerned, remained ambiguous until after the First World War.[24] Earnings of runaway slaves and slaves in government employ went to slave owners, as payment for their freedom.[25] Slaves and ex-slaves provided the bulk of government porters, as well as laborers in the initial phases of railway construction. In 1900 an estimated 75 per cent of male slaves were working either on the railroad, as servants to Europeans, or on caravans upcountry.[26]

The illegal slave trade also continued. The victims were women and children, stolen by coastal Muslims or the coastal Kamba of Rabai sub district. During the famine of 1898-9, children from the Mombasa hinterland were kidnapped by the Kamba and sold on the coast, via Mtongwe and Jomvu, or traded in German East Africa.[27] As late as 1912, the Kamba were still "trafficking in human beings," reported the assistant district commissioner at Rabai,

---

20 Ibid., 190.

21 Mordwao[?] b. Sh.[?] Mukane and Salim b. Ali Mona to Craufurd, recd. 3 Jun. 1896, and Mahomed b. Abubakar to Craufurd, n.d.[1896], CP 78/63; Weaver to Craufurd, 1 Aug. 1896 and list of porters dated 20 Aug. 1896, CP 75/46; Rogers to Craufurd, 8 Oct. 1896, CP 68/20; Hardinge to Craufurd, 9 Jul, 1898 and 22 Aug. 1898, CP 90/154, KNA.

22 Macdougall to Craufurd, 1 Jan. 1897 and 27 Feb. 1897, CP 75/46, KNA.

23 Weaver to Craufurd, 21 Sep. 1896, CP 75/46, KNA.

24 In 1907, the Malindi district commissioner was preparing to provide "indentured labour" to the new European estates in the district, until "large numbers of AKikuyu [came] to the district in search of work." Malindi district AR, 1906-7, DC/MSA/1/2, KNA. All young men still in the Takaungu sub-district were "drafted" into Carrier Corps service by early 1917. Malindi district AR, 1916-17, DC/MAL/1/1, KNA.

25 Malindi QR, 31 Jul. 1901, CP 71/25 and CP 89/146, KNA, regarding porters used on the Kismayu expedition; and McClellan to Pigott, 30 Apr. 1896, CP 67/15, KNA, re railroad labor recruiting in Rabai.

26 Description of Seyyedieh [Coast] province, 1899-1900, CP 98/191, KNA.

27 Eichert to Craufurd, 15 Feb. 1899, CP 83/98; Craufurd to Hardinge, 5 Jun. 1899, CP 76/51; Johnstone to senior commissioner, coast, 10 Jul. 1899, CP 79/68, KNA.

"but it is very seldom that the offenders can be brought to book."[28] The persistence of slave trading on Zanzibar, Pemba, and the Kenya coast was cited in a lengthy 1901 memorandum as the main risk in using mainland labor on the islands.[29] The illegal slave trade on the Kenya coast has yet to be investigated, but its survival in the twentieth century is not in doubt. Until the 1960s, slavery remained legal in Saudi Arabia and the Sultanate of Oman, both connected to Kenya by the dhow trade.[30]

In the early colonial period, the Kenya coast was a difficult place in which to live, by any standard. Beginning with the Anglo-Mazrui War of 1895-96, general tragedies followed in line like a litany: floods in 1897, famine in 1898-99, smallpox in 1899, then relief until drought and pleuropneumonia among sheep and goats led to the 1909-10 famine, which was soon followed by the 1912-1913 famine, the Giriama rising of 1913-14, and, during the First World War, forced conscription into the Carrier Corps, drought, and influenza. For the children of Ham, such hardships were compounded by the quiet indifference, and open hostility, received from members of established coastal communities, leaders of the self-styled Muslim *waungwana* (freeborn), and officials of the British government. In 1924, the officer summarizing the statistics and results of the 1907 proclamation of abolition, remarked that

> it is quite certain the slaves in no way appreciated their freedom; [that] they neither asked for it nor wanted it and in many cases resented it. They were happier as slaves....[31]

Without realizing it, this official, who happened to be the provincial senior commissioner, conveyed the general despair felt by ex-slaves on the coast. Yet the senior commissioner was just as unaware that he had mis-diagnosed their misery. Where he was wrong, and where his predecessors had erred, was in assuming that ex-slaves misunderstood the meaning of freedom, that they longed for slavery, and that, insofar as their depressed condition was concerned, they had only themselves to blame.

---

[28] Rabai subdistrict QR, 31 Mar. 1912, CP 2/130. See also Rabai subdistrict QR, 31 Dec. 1911, CP 1/37, KNA.

[29] Tritton to Eliot, 26 Mar. 1901, CP 98/192, KNA. See also the case of the dhow, carrying kidnapped children, that wrecked off Wasini island while en route north from Zanzibar. Thirteen children survived. Macdougall to Craufurd, 17 May 1899, ADD MSS/5, KNA.

[30] E.B. Martin, "The Geography of Present-Day Smuggling in the Western Indian Ocean: the Case of the Dhow," *The Great Circle: Journal of the Australian Association for Maritime History*, 1, 2(Oct. 1979), 19. The practice of pawning children to coastal Muslims first came to the attention of colonial officials in 1898, and in 1922 Salim b. Mohamed of Takaungu was charged with trying to ship two Giriama boys by dhow from Kilifi to Arabia. Report of Sale of Children Committee, 22 Sep. 1899, CP 92/157, KNA; Morton, "The Shungwaya Myth," 415-7; Criminal Case no. 779 of 1922, 24 Sep. 1922, DC/MSA/8/5, KNA.

[31] Maclean to Maitland, 20 May 1924, CP 47/1123, KNA.

2. *Mzee Ali Tete*

Mzee Ali Tete, Yao by origin, once the slave of Ali b. Said, was, when the British took control of the coast, the leading elder of the Makongeni maroons. In years past Mzee Ali's people had fended off attackers who tried to return them to slavery. The maroons had also driven back IBEACO troops bent on recapturing them for their previous owners. Direct experience had made Mzee Ali wary of European rulers, who talked against slavery but helped slave owners. It may explain why he distrusted Lugard's redemption scheme. Or perhaps Mzee Ali simply perceived Lugard's personal contempt for his people ("a set of cowardly, thieving rascals," as Lugard confided in his diary, "the refuse of Malindi").[32] The Makongenites shied away from this man and his plan, which looked anyway like another device to capture their labor, and remained where they were, content to defend themselves without outside assistance. When Lugard left Makongeni, they broke up his camp so that no Arabs or Europeans could again use it as a base to harass them. Soon the paths leading to their settlement grew thick with bush, discouraging all visitors and passers-by.

Until the British East Africa Protectorate was established, Mzee Ali Tete's maroons maintained their little republic. Their ranks were augmented by more runaway slaves from the Malindi plantations, as well as by Giriama and Kauma cultivators shifting north from Mangea district. Makongeni grew from a single settlement into a collection of villages stretching across the Sabaki and along both banks. Its people, productive and prosperous, cultivated "fertile plantations of Indian corn."[33]

Ultimately, he had to deal with the coast's new rulers. In 1896, during the Anglo-Mazrui war, Protectorate officials wished to do away with Makongeni. They believed it was involved in the slave trade and providing support to the enemy, though Mzee Ali Tete was thought to be himself "on bad terms" with the Mazrui. Thus Mzee Ali and the Makongeni elders were contacted by the new district officer of Malindi, Kenneth Macdougall (past superintendent of the Melindi-Takaungu district for the IBEACO), who proposed they "throw in their lot with the Government against the rebel chief." Macdougall's assistant, James Weaver, then travelled to Makongeni with an invitation for talks in Malindi, and escorted Mzee Ali and a fellow elder, named Kamtende, to the coast. In Malindi the British gave the two maroon leaders first a demonstration of their maxim gun and then a list of their demands: the maroons must hand in their arms, abandon their settlements, and live close to Malindi. After three days of what Macdougall called "animated discussion," Mzee Ali and Kamtende submitted to the demands.

---

[32] *Diaries*, I, 304.

[33] Hardinge itinerary, 2-10 February 1896, C. 8274, 66. For other sources on Makongeni and Ali Tete, Lugard, *Diaries*, I, 247; Macdonald, *Soldiering and Surveying*, 20-1; Hardinge to Salisbury, 17 Feb. 1896, C. 8274, 63; Fitzgerald, **Travels**, 122, 130-1. See also ch. 3 above.

In return they received two concessions: the maroons would choose their new location, and the British would prevent the slave owners from recapturing them.[34] Mzee Ali Tete left as little as possible to chance. First his people made a grand display of disarmament by coming as a group to Malindi to hand in their old breechloaders. They then moved, as agreed, from Makongeni closer to Malindi, and set to work at planting their new crops. Within months, their settlements of Bura (Kamtende) and Kwa Ali Tete (lit. "at Ali Tete's"), were prospering. In his monthly report for July 1896, Weaver remarked that

> these people are the most industrious in the district; and in addition to the usual crops of grain have considerable areas under tobacco cultivation, they are also making preparation for extensive plantations of coconut trees.[35]

A year later the British noticed that the maroons had conceded less than originally thought. Mzee Ali's people, it appeared, were still armed. And, though Mzee Ali and Kamtende had picked a spot closer to Malindi on which to relocate, they had built their new homes outside the "10-mile strip." Since the 1886 Anglo-German agreement, the strip had defined the limits of the Zanzibar sultan's laws, which recognized slavery.[36] By then, the maroons were causing the British no trouble anyway and having, Macdougall noted, "a peaceful and happy time." So they were left alone.

The new modus vivendi did not rid Mzee Ali of the slave owners, even though the days of slavery were clearly numbered. in 1901, with "no signs [in evidence] of any reconciliation...between master and slave," the British permitted owners to take their runaway slaves to court. As a result, many of Mzee Ali Tete's people (and presumably Ali Tete himself) became defendants in civil suits when their owners claimed "compensation for loss of services." In order to terminate the threat of re-enslavement and gain legal recognition from the British as free persons, Mzee Ali and his people had to pay their owners thirty rupees apiece, plus court costs.[37]

Mzee Ali's troubles had not yet ended. His maroons, a lone group in the hinterland without kinship ties to other Africans, could not prevent the expanding Miji Kenda from overrunning their small territory. The fertility of the maroon area aroused the envy of the immigrants, who began moving in after 1900. Slowly, the Miji Kenda encroached upon Bura, Ali Tete, and another

---

[34] Hardinge to Kimberley, 25 Jun. 1895, FO 403/210, 60-1; Hardinge to Salisbury, 17 Feb. 1896, C. 8274, 63; Macdougall quarterly report, 8 Apr. 1901, CP 71/25, KNA; Macdougall "Notes on the History of Wanyika," 31 Mar. 1914, DC/MAL/2/3, KNA.

[35] Weaver to Craufurd, 24 Jul. 1896, CP 75/46, KNA. Prosperity continued for another decade. See E. Brand report, n.d.[1906], CP 94/166, KNA.

[36] Hardinge report, 20 Jul. 1897, C. 8683, 12; *The Kenya Coastal Strip*, Cmmd. 1585 (1961), 4. Ali Tete's village is located on J.E.Jones's 1904 map, CP 80/79, KNA.

[37] Macdougall quarterly report, 8 Apr. 1901, CP 71/25, KNA.

maroon village, Pumwani. Within a few years the northern banks of the Sabaki and beyond had been colonized completely, and the Giriama were dominating the region's grain trade and intimidating the maroons. Only three of the tens of villages that had sprouted contained maroons, and they were sharing their space with Giriama.[38] Though Mzee Ali was reckoned one of the "zealous adherents" of the colonial government, his people were literally enslaved by the Giriama, and in particular by followers of Ngonyo of Marafa. J.M. Pearson, a British officer, noticed in Pumwani, for example, that the inhabitants "appear to be under the special protection of, and in deep obligation to, Headman Ngonyo"[39]

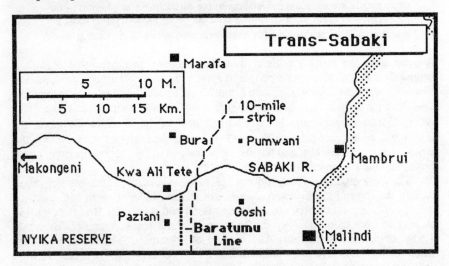

Once at the mercy of the Giriama, the ex-maroons swiftly declined. In 1912, Mzee Ali Tete, thought by the British to be a "very old man" and known to them as the leader of a people who "for many years kept their Arab masters at bay," died at his home. By then the decay was more or less complete. S.L. Hinde, who passed through this area, was struck by the contrast between the ex-maroons and their neighbors.

> [They] appeared to be a feckless lazy lot [and]...an unhealthy community; there were only 3 or 4 children in the whole village; they said that nearly all the children died and several of the villagers were suffering from elephantiasis.... Within a few miles of this settlement we saw Giriama villages full of children and the inhabitants perfectly fit and well.[40]

---

[38] Pearson to Hobley, 11 Dec. 1913, CP 2/154, KNA.

[39] Pearson to Hobley, 22 Mar. 1914, CP 11/101, KNA; Traill report, 17 Jan. 1912, CP 1/37, KNA.

[40] Hinde report, 4 Jul. 1913, CP 64/261, KNA.

Within months, the British dispossessed the people of Bura and Kwa Ali Tete of their farms. In late 1913 officials demanded their withdrawal south of the Sabaki in order, as they claimed, to administer and tax them more effectively. As a matter of fact, their fertile zone had caught the eye of European planters, who were being assisted by the administration. As the district commissioner of Malindi put it:

> Besides the advantages accruing to good government by having these natives concentrated in some more easily administered area, there is also the fact that the left bank of the Sabaki...is very valuable agricultural land which could undoubtedly be made to produce far richer returns if worked by enlightened European planters than at present are in the possession of savages.[41]

Along with the Miji Kenda, the ex-maroons were resettled across the river at Goshi, and their old settlements were destroyed. Three thousand were affected.[42]

Still more tragedy awaited. At Goshi the ex-maroons lived in fear of the Giriama, who had begun to revolt against the British, and paid money to the rebels in order to stay out of the conflict.[43] It was at the hands of the British, however, that the ex-maroons suffered more. Britain's "Giriama Patrol" moved through the area searching for rebels and burning their villages. Ex-maroons were caught in the net, and their houses burned to the ground.[44]

They were then moved to Paziani, west of the Baratumu Line created to delineate part of the new "Nyika Reserve." Through an administrative blunder, they were forced to move back across the line and suffer again the destruction of their newly-built homesteads. The effects were numbing. Mervyn Beech, assigned to aid their permanent settlement, discovered that nearly one hundred heads of families had lost all their worldly possessions: farms, houses, and household goods. "These men," wrote Beech, "are all very old and infirm. I doubt if there will be any left in 10 years time--and this has certainly been a rude upheaval in the winter of their life."[45] Months later, Beech received a pitiful request from the old maroons, asking him to enquire as to promise of compensation for their losses that had been made to them by sheikh Ali b. Salim, the chief *qadi* of the Kenya coast. The ex-slaves reported to the DC that sheikh Ali had not followed through on his promise. "So far they tell me," reported the DC, "that they have received nothing, and they have asked me to enquire on their behalf."[46] Eventually, the ex-maroons were allowed to move back across the Sabaki and settle at Pumwani, under Mzee Moto wa Sheikh Bete, Mzee Ali Tete's successor. Others were given permission to settle on the land of Sheikh Ali's late

---

[41] Skene to PC, 4 Dec. 1913, CP 2/154, KNA.

[42] Bura (1,824) and Kwa Ali Tete (1,170). No figures available for Pumwani. Pearson to PC, 11 Dec. 1913, CP 2/154; Beech to PC, 22 Oct. 1915, CP 20/28, KNA.

[43] Ali b. Salim statement, 3 May 1915, CP 20/128A, KNA.

[44] Beech to PC, 22 Oct. 1915, CP 20/128, KNA.

[45] Beech to PC, 4 May 1915, Ibid.

[46] Beech to PC, 22 Oct. 1915, Ibid.

father, Salim b. Khalfan, near Malindi. It is a sad irony that the latter group, made up of old maroons, were using as their final haven the land owned by the very man, who as *liwali* of Malindi in the early 1880s, had sent the first troops into the hinterland to attack and destroy Makongeni. And there is every likelihood that among these "prodigal slaves" were some who once had been Salim's own.[47]

2. *Freed Slaves of Takaungu District*

For the slaves who remained in Takaungu district after the Anglo-Mazrui war, the delay of abolition carried little significance. Survival presented the greater challenge. During the drought of 1898-99, which eliminated harvests for eighteen months and resulted in thousands of deaths along the coast, the population subsisted on roots, leaves, and rats.[48] Conditions were particularly severe in Takaungu district. Most slaves left altogether and looked for food elsewhere. In Takaungu, where no slaves remained, town dwellers petitioned the government for labor to dig their own graves.[49] Only a few slaves later returned. In 1900 the entire Takaungu subdistrict contained an estimated five hundred.[50] The departure of thousands of others, due to the troubles of past years, had finally severed the connection with land and master. Slave districts which in the 1880s had yielded the greatest share of Mazrui agricultural exports-- Kibokoni, Konjora, and Koeni--at the beginning of the twentieth century stood vacant. After 1900 they were cultivated again, but rather by a new wave of *mahaji* and Miji Kenda farmers pressing down from the hills.[51]

In 1912, the few freed slaves in the area lost their farms. Numbering about four hundred, they were concentrated in and around the towns of Tezo, Roka, and Mtondia.[52] In 1909, O. F. Watkins, assistant district commissioner of

---

[47] Ali b. Salim statements(2), 3 May 1915, Ibid; Gibson report, 4 Jul. 1916, CP 22/177, KNA.

[48] In July 1899 the Seyyidieh Provincial Famine Committee estimated that two million people were seriously affected and that forty thousand children had perished. Committee to Craufurd, 4 Jul. 1899, CP 90/157, KNA. Descriptions of the famine in the hinterland and in Mombasa, where smallpox added to the misery, are to be found in many files of the Coast Province correspondence, CMS archives, and in Hardinge's reports to the Foreign Office.

[49] Petition of the people of Takaungu in Hardinge to Craufurd n.d.[Jul. 1898], CP 90/154, KNA.

[50] Description of province, 1899/1900, CP 98/191, KNA. Also Hardinge report, C. 8683, 6.

[51] See map attached to Fazan, Takaungu sub-district annual report, 1912/13, 17 Apr. 1913, CP 8/157, KNA.

[52] Tezo (195), Roka (129), Mtondia (138). Takaungu subdistrict population, 1908-09, CP 79/72, KNA. Population figures include a small minority of Arab settlers and *mahaji* Traill to Ag senior commissioner, Coast, 17 Dec. 1909 [unnumbered and untitled file, observed on Reel 177, item 7, of the Coast Province Correspondence

Takaungu subdistrict, reported that their

> agriculture is developing very fast.... The slave compensation money in some cases [is] being supplied [by their Mazrui former owners] for clearing new shambas, but more often the freed slave is clearing a homestead for himself.[53]

As the Mazrui sold increasing amounts of their property to cancel debts, the fortunes of freed slaves declined. By 1912 thousands of acres around Takaungu, Kilifi, and Sokoke had been purchased by European rubber, sisal, and cotton companies, and many freed slaves were evicted from the land.

Protectorate attempts to resettle freed slaves on nearby Crown land proved a failure. In October 1912 near Tezo two thousand acres of uncleared government land were set aside as a freed-slave reserve. Families evicted from European plantations or those squatting on government land were encouraged to clear and occupy two acre lots.[54] After two years, however, only fifty-seven families were cultivating inside the reserve, and fewer still had built homesteads. Rather than constructing a new village, they continued to live in the old ones and commute to their plots each day.[55] The loss of their original farms, the lack of water in the reserves, and the normal hardships attending the clearing of new land sapped their earlier enthusiasm. An official who passed through their village in mid-1913 found their condition pathetic. "Roka and Mtondia are small settlements of freed slaves without energy and any kind of enterprise," he remarked. "Their only idea appeared to [be to] gather at my tent and beg for money."[56]

Freed slaves on the land lacked as well the assistance of a younger generation. Ralph Skene, who helped initiate the Tezo scheme, found all the ex-slaves "advanced in age and many of them gray-headed people" and hesitant about shifting from their old farms.[57] The oldest farming generation in the days of slavery had become the only ex-slaves tilling the soil. They had but few children, and the rejection of agriculture by the younger generation increased the burden of the elders to meet their daily needs. Within three years of the establishment of the Tezo reserve, the ex-slave farming community was facing extinction. "The 2,000 acres of the settlement are far in excess of the requirements," noted one report in 1915. The agriculturist ex-slave is rapidly dying out."[58]

Microfilm Collection, Bird Library, Syracuse University].

[53] Takaungu subdistrict AR, 1908-09, DC/MSA/1/1, KNA.

[54] La Fontaine to Skene, 11 Oct. 1912, and Hinde to Skene, 17 Apr. 1913, CP 5/361, KNA.

[55] Takaungu subdistrict AR, 1914-15, CP 16/49; Skene to Hobley, 4 Jan. 1915, CP 20/128A; Hobley to Chf Secy, Nairobi, 9 Aug. 1915, CP 28/350, KNA.

[56] Hinde inspection report, 4 Jul. 1913, CP 64/261, KNA.

[57] Skene to Hinde, 30 Oct. 1912, CP 5/361, KNA.

[58] Skene to Hobley, 4 Jan. 1915, CP 20/128A; also Takaungu subdistrict AR, 1914-15, CP 16/49, KNA.

3. *The WaShenzi of Lamu*

Plantation slavery was established in Lamu earlier than in other parts of the coast, and more slaves were employed there than anywhere else in East Africa, apart from Zanzibar and Pemba.[59] Lamu's importance to slavery research is at least comparable to Malindi, which experienced slavery for a much shorter period, and Mombasa, which had fewer slaves. Yet, Cooper's work on Malindi and Mombasa has been taken--even by Cooper himself--to include Lamu (or, when contradictory evidence from Lamu is cited, to dismiss Lamu slavery as an "extreme" form of Kenya coastal slavery).[60] Revisionists also sidestep the conclusions of Zein, the only scholar to examine Lamu slavery in any depth.[61] Recently Romero has attacked Zein's methodology but has offered no alternative to Zein's view of Lamu slavery, other than Cooper's.[62] Zein clearly does not fit the revisionists' mold. He shows that Lamu society attempted to keep slaves in their place, even as their slaves ran away to Witu and the hinterland forests, even as colonial rule ended the legal status of slavery. *Waungwana* (civilized, freeborn) distanced themselves from slaves and mainland Africans, whom they called *washenzi* (bumpkins, non-free). Fundamental social divisions between free and slave in Lamu, as expressed in religious practice and symbolism, persisted from the nineteenth century into the twentieth.

According to Zein, the WaShenzi of Lamu were regarded by the WaUngwana as a permanently inferior social category distinguished by dress, residence, education, language, access to the mosque, and descent. WaShenzi wore clothing that left arms and upper body exposed in the case of men, arms and shoulders in the case of women. WaUngwana men wore the woolen dress and turban, denied to the WaShenzi men; whereas free women wore the *buibui*, black cloak, WaShenzi women the *kanga*, or wrapper. Apart from concubines, WaShenzi were not allowed into the WaUngwana section of town at night, nor were they permitted into town during the day unless requested by the master. They were regarded as inherently impure and beyond elevation by association with the free-born. Thought incapable of learning, apart from the rudimentary elements of Islamic prayer, they were denied admission into the *madarasa*. WaShenzi were thought to have received their religious knowledge not from the angels, as in the case of the WaUngwana, but from malevolent *majini*, or human spirits. The WaUngwana monopolized the use of Arabic to prevent WaShenzi the use of the language at important religious ceremonies. They were not permitted their own mosque nor were slaves working on the mainland plantations expected to attend Friday mosque or entitled to visitation from a *mwalimu*. When at the mosque, WaShenzi sat at the back, on the left, near the toilets. Upon death, WaShenzi corpses (called *mfu*, the name used for the carcasses of dead animals) were washed

---

[59] See ch. 1.

[60] Cooper *Plantation Slavery*, 197-8.

[61] Zein, *Sacred Meadows*. Ylvisaker's *Lamu* takes no note of Cooper's *Plantation Slavery*, refers to Zein, but hardly touches slavery.

[62] Romero, "Sacred Meadows," 337-46; idem, "Laboratory for the Oral History of Slavery," 859.

only by WaShenzi, and denied the entitlements for WaUngwana, namely perfumes, the *talqin* ceremony, and a mourning period.[63]

The children of slaves were the property of the masters, and their descent was reckoned as *kishenzi*, regardless of the status of the father. Cooper argues that the children of a concubine (*suria*, pl. *masuria*) and a freeborn father became free, whereas Zein distinguishes between the male child of a *suria* and a WaUngwana male owner, to whom freeborn status was accorded, and the female child, who inherited the mother's status. Zein also argues that even male children were regarded as inferior by all children of his father's WaUngwana wives and excluded from their WaUngwana group. The son of a *suria* might mix with his half-brothers, but he ate different food, wore different clothing, and was usually deprived of his father's inheritance. Until the twentieth century, the institution of *mkufu* (marriage among equals) barred a *suria's* son from marrying among WaUngwana groups, all of which were considered superior, and forced to take wives from the daughters of *masuria*. Thus, for all practical purposes, a freeborn father might acknowledge the son of his *suria* as his own, but the Lamu freeborn community confined the child in all important matters to the position occupied by his mother. The inherited low status of *masuria's* sons is related to the belief that a *suria* passed on her malevolent *majini*, which directed hatred, and hostility toward WaUngwana. Thus, her children were regarded as prone to the breeding of conflict in the town, backed as they were by their malevolent *majini*, and to behave in a manner that violated *heshima*, or respectfulness.[64]

Slaves were not part of the recognized community. According to Zein, they were "thought of as inferior to the wangwana in every way. They were the people of the bush, the Wa Shenzi, while the wangwana were the people of the town, the people who alone possess Astarabu [*ustarabu* = civilization, breeding]."[65]

---

[63] Zein, *Sacred Meadows*, passim. The *talqin* involves telling the dead body the words to speak to the angels, but it was withheld from *washenzi*, thought to communicate only with *majini*.

[64] Ibid., 31-3, 73-4. Cooper, *Plantation Slavery*, 197-8. See also Yvlisaker, *Lamu*, 20. Romero ("Sacred Meadows") challenges Zein's conclusions on concubinage and discredits his research methodology on this and other matters. Romero, however, provides no alternative of comparable description of how concubines' children were treated in the nineteenth century. And with regard to the larger question of *waungwana-washenzi* divisions derived from nineteenth century slavery, which underlies much of Zein's analysis, Romero is silent. Instead, she (cf. "Laboratory for the Oral History of Slavery") defers to Cooper ("very thorough and original") on nineteenth-century Lamu slavery and society, and refers to the "comparative benevolence of the system." In Romero's view, Islam reinforced the "continuing belief held by both master and slave that their relationship was sanctioned by God and the Prophet Mohamed and was spelled out in the Koran."(ibid., 859) Romero does not explain how such an assertion may be reconciled with the Witu phenomenon. The same lapses occur in P.W. Romero, "'Where Have All the Slaves Gone?' Emancipation and Post-Emancipation in Lamu, Kenya," *JAH*, 27 (1986), 497-512.

[65] Ibid, 78.

Institutionalized exclusion provoked the WaShenzi and generated support for the opponents of Lamu's leading WaUngwana. The rival sultanate of Witu attracted large numbers of runaway slaves from the Lamu mainland by according WaShenzi a degree of equality with WaUngwana. Its use of armed *watoro* (runaway slaves) to fight the WaUngwana of Lamu underlined the threat Witu posed to Lamu's system of stratification.[66] The rise of Witu effectively crippled the slavery system in Lamu and resulted in de jure and de facto emancipation years before legal status abolition in 1907. WaShenzi nevertheless left Lamu even as abolition approached. Cooper notes that at the turn of the century, Lamu slaves went to Mombasa in search of work, migrated to the Malindi district, or moved permanently to the mainland.[67]

After emancipation, ex-slaves in Lamu remained WaShenzi. The quest for equality, or for recognition as human beings rather than Children of Ham, continued in Lamu long after slavery. Their struggle has necessarily involved the creation of separate institutions of equal purpose (such as the *maulidi* ceremonies), and alliance with religious leaders prepared to invoke Islam as an innovative, egalitarian force. In great detail, Zein traces the rise of a coalition of ex-slaves, *wageni* (Comorians, Hadramis), and Saleh ibn 'Alwi Jamalilil, a fully-licensed WaUngwana sherif, who together created a religious community based around the Reiyadah mosque at which the tenets of religious equality were followed. The state of purity, defined by the WaUngwana as an inherited quality particular to themselves, became under sherif Saleh achievable by anyone through devotion. Opening the gates of paradise to persons regarded by Wa-Ungwana as the servants of the devil was resisted long after sherif Saleh's initiative began in the 1870s. A century later, Zein encountered first hand Wa-Ungwana beliefs in WaShenzi inferiority. He discovered, nevertheless, that Langoni, the largest ward occupied by WaShenzi and *wageni*, had become the economic and religious center of Lamu town. The majority of shops belonged to the *wageni* Hadrami, who supported the sherifs attached to the Reiyadah mosque. Social barriers between those of freeborn and slave descent were lowered by secret marriages, just as the non-WaUngwana population grew to the point where it exceeded that of the WaUngwana and, since independence, enjoyed political power.[68]

Outsiders in Lamu, including ex-slaves, slowly displaced WaUngwana as the dominant element in the local economy and gained social ascendancy through support of sherif Saleh's Islamic reform movement.[69] Sherif Saleh belonged to the small but influential coastal group of learned teachers (*masharifu*) whose popular teachings in the nineteenth century challenged the political elite's hegemony in religious matters and legitimized the social and economic aspirations of those excluded from power. Muslim populism in East Africa reflected social and economic readjustment in towns where the position of

---

[66] Ibid., 82. For the *watoro* of Witu, see chs. 3 and 6.
[67] *From Slaves to Squatters*, 52, 179-80.
[68] *Sacred Meadows*,17-8,103-64; Pouwels, *Horn and Crescent*,112-3,193-9.
[69] Pouwels, *Horn and Crescent*, 192-201.

WaUngwana was eclipsed by the Busaidi and their allies. In Mombasa, for example, populist teaching attracted the WaUngwana trying to challenge the hegemony of the Busaidi, and to destroy the pretensions of the Mazrui.[70]

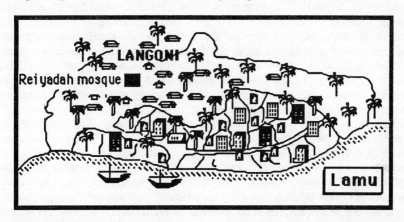

Generally speaking, however, Islam was deployed by freeborn Muslims to elevate their own status rather than that of ex-slaves. Only in Lamu did populism create opposition to WaUngwana, and only in Lamu did ex-slaves become part of the populist movement. Populist Islam contained the message of equality, but outside of Lamu it was not preached to the Children of Ham.[71]

4. *Nassib Bunda*

On the Benadir coast, during the early colonial period, a new Islamic movement attracted many followers, including the Gosha *watoro* leader, Nassib Bunda.[72] The movement, puritanical and militant, was headed by the dervish leader, Mohammad Abdille Hassan, whom the British and Italians labelled the "Mad Mullah." At the time Europeans commonly associated madness, or what they termed fanaticism, with outspoken opposition to European occupation. British officials feared that "fanaticism" lay dormant in all Muslim areas, but on the southern Kenya coast they were spared having to put down a holy war against infidels; Islamic populism in the south merely challenged elitism at the local level while accepting colonial rule. In the north, however, Hassan attempted to unite the disparate clans of Somaliland in order to drive the British and Italians out of the Horn.[73] His movement sprang up in 1899 in the Nagal

---

[70] Ibid., 199. Pouwels refers to these movements as forms of "popularism".

[71] The subject of ex-slaves and Muslim brotherhoods (*tariqas*) in colonial East Africa is in need of research. For some possibilities in this connection, L.V. Cassanelli, "The Ending of Slavery in Italian Somalia: Liberty and the Control of Labor, 1890-1935" in Miers and Roberts, *End of Slavery*, 322-5.

[72] For Nassib Bunda and the Gosha, see also chs. 2 and 6.

[73] R.L. Hess, "the Poor Man of God--Muhammad Abdulla Hassan" in N. Bennett, ed.

valley and reached the Benadir in 1904 and 1905. Among the first in the south to approach Hassan's dervishes was Nassib Bunda.

At first glance Gosha's most energetic *watoro* leader, revered by one colonial author as the "African Spartacus," was the least likely candidate to join a pan-Somali, anti-European cause.[74] He and his Gosha followers had been slaves of the Somali; and as maroons they had received arms from the Busaidi of Zanzibar and had gained recognition from the Imperial British East Africa Company (IBEACO), the Royal Italian East Africa Company (RIEACO), and, after 1895, from the British East Africa Protectorate. By 1897, however, Nassib's relations with Europeans had soured. British and Italian officials were undermining Gosha's economy, discouraging movement across the Juba River (which divided the British and Italian spheres), and were using Nassib and other *watoro* leaders to advance their own ends.

British officials initially feared the "fighting tribes of Gosha," who were well armed and had repulsed Somali raids. Arthur Jenner, Jubaland province's first sub-commissioner, nevertheless hoped that the Gosha's "want of cohesion... will prevent their uniting, even if they want to, against the Government."[75] Loyal service to Britain was to be obtained by recruiting Gosha into the salaried Protectorate bureaucracy and creating Gosha "chiefs" to control their subjects. Sixty eight Gosha regulars were used to man the garrison at Kismayu. They were reckoned "very good material for a native force...besides being very cheap."[76] Gosha soldiers were also placed in "Swahili" units at the Juba river garrison of Mbungu Kizungu and used in campaigns against the Somali.[77] Consul-general Hardinge endorsed Jenner's strategy of reviving old IBEACO treaties with Gosha leaders and placing them on monthly stipends "as a means of attaching these chiefs to our interests and maintaining a hold over them." When Hardinge visited the Gosha in 1897, he pledged to "do all that we can to strengthen their power." Hardinge was convinced that the Gosha *watoro*, who "have the idle, undisciplined habits of runaway slaves...cannot be relied on to obey any orders" from chiefs without British backing.[78] In return, the "chiefs" were expected to provide labor.[79] Within months of the creation of the Protectorate, steamers were picking up men along the Juba river as "free

Leadership in Eastern Africa: Six Political Biographies (Boston: Boston University Press, 1968; B.G. Martin, *Muslim Brotherhoods in Nineteenth Century Africa* (Cambridge: Cambridge University Press, 1976), 177-201; Cassanelli, *Shaping of Somali Society*, 183-5, 243-248, passim.

[74] The honorific was given to Nassib by an Italian colonial. Cassanelli, *Shaping of Somali Society*, 92.

[75] Jenner to Hardinge, 12 Jun. 1895, CP 74/45, KNA; Jenner to Hardinge, 28 Jul. 1895, FO 403/210, 227.

[76] Hardinge to Salisbury, 17 Sep. 1895, FO 403/211, 48.

[77] Jenner to Hardinge, 7 Nov. 1898, FO 403/263, 213.

[78] Hardinge to Salisbury, 1 Oct. 1897, FO 403/244, 77-8.

[79] Jenner to Hardinge, 21 Aug. 1895, CP 74/45, and Hardinge to Craufurd, 31 Dec. 1896, CP 109/89, KNA; Hardinge to Salisbury, 1 Oct. 1897, FO 403/244, 78.

laborers."[80] Others were wanted for work on the Uganda railway; Jenner was instructed as a "matter of extreme importance [to] gather all the men you can that are at all suitable and send them down [to Mombasa]."[81]

Nassib was the key to Britain's Gosha plan. From the outset Jenner regarded him as the "principal [and ablest] chief of WaGosha country" and recommended that other Gosha chiefs be subordinated to him. Jenner was unconcerned that Nassib was living on the "Italian bank." He was reckoned a British subject as he "had people and property on our side."[82] The British overlooked his notoriety in Gosha for pawning women and children, and Nassib was ready to cooperate with the British. By mid-1896 he was living on the "British side" of the river at Mabungu and flew the Union Jack on his flagpole. Jenner located a site north of Mabungu for a British stockade, and had it built the following year. It was called Mabungu Kizungu ("white Mabungu").[83]

Events in the Italian sphere soon concentrated attention on Nassib. Until 1896 the Italian presence was almost imperceptible on the Juba. The RIEACO, under the administration of Vincenzo Filonardi, failed to establish itself other than in several coastal ports, including Merka and Barawa. In 1896, however, when Antonio Cecchi replaced Filonardi, the Italians made concerted steps to assert their influence in the hinterland. They established a garrison in the important caravan trading center of Lugh, located on the Juba river north of Gosha, and Cecchi began to apply pressure on hinterland traders to direct their commerce away from Kismayu in the British sphere and toward Barawa on the Italian Benadir. In November 1896 an Italian force clashed with armed Somali at Lafole, between Mogadishu and Afgoye in the Shebelle valley. The Somali won, and their victory was followed by a spate of anti-Italian incidents in southern Somaliland.[84] Somali fears of European occupation were aroused further by Britain's garrison at Mabungu Kizungu, which stood between the Ogaden Somali west of the Juba and their established trading partners to the east. In the past Nassib's followers had served as middle-men in this east-west trade, which was being upset by the north-south proclivities of the British and Italians. Although they regarded the *watoro* as enemies of the Somali, the British were, in 1897, becoming aware that Bimal and Tunni Somali were residing in the Juba valley with the Gosha, and beginning to learn of Nassib's long-standing trade relations with the Ogaden. Rumors were circulating, too, that Nassib was "intriguing

---

[80] Newman, "East Africa Protectorate," 287.

[81] Craufurd to Jenner, 6 Aug. 1896, CP 109/89, KNA. The use of ex-slave laborers on the Uganda railway is an uninvestigated subject that might bear fruit with further research. In the early months of construction "Swahili" laborers made up the largest segment ahead of other Africans and imported workers from Cutch and other parts of British India. Whitehouse to MMU, London, 18 Jul. 1896 and 6 Nov. 1896, EAR.

[82] Jenner to Hardinge, 28 Jul. 1895, FO 403/210, 227; Jenner to Craufurd, 31 Jul. 1896, FO 403/228, 65-6.

[83] Craufurd to Salisbury, 13 Jul. 1896, FO 403/227, 198-9; Jenner to Craufurd, 31 Jul. 1896, FO 403/228, 64; Jenner to Hardinge, 11 Aug. 1897, FO 403/243, 201.

[84] Cassanelli, *Shaping of Somali Society*, 201-4.

with the Ogaden against the authority of the Government" and that he had been
using "fanatical language respecting Europeans." Nassib was summoned to Kismayu, reprimanded, and warned.[85] Jenner and Perducci, an Italian official, feared
that Nassib would alternate residences across the Juba to avoid direct European
control and agreed they would not allow Nassib to "play off one administration
against the other."[86]

By the time Hardinge visited the Juba river in September 1897, Nassib's
alliance with the British was coming to an end. The British had given up on the
Gosha as a labor source, for reasons yet unknown, and faced the expensive task
of enforcing loyalty among increasingly recalcitrant Ogaden and Herti Somali in
the Kismayu hinterland. Uncooperative "chiefs' such as Nassib, with his large
salary and armed retinue, had become not only financial liabilities but potential
threats to efficient administration. Hardinge met Nassib privately in order to
threaten him, or, as he put it, place Nassib "on good behaviour." Hardinge's report sketched, moreover, the image of a calculating ogre that subsequent official
correspondence obligingly filled in. No longer the "ablest" Gosha leader, Nassib
had become "sterner than most Watoro Chiefs...[and] feared by a large portion of
his people as a wizard as well as a tyrant.... [He was more] addicted to intrigue
than any other native in Gosha."[87] Hardinge relayed no word of Nassib's in their
"private conversation," though the consul-general commented that the *watoro*
leader was "decidedly intelligent." Hardinge was also struck by the fact that Nassib "affected Arab habits" and, "unlike most of the watoro, wore Arab dress."[88]

After launching an expedition against the Ogaden the following year, the
British began easing Nassib out of the Protectorate. His salary was stopped and,
in January 1899, Jenner began filing reports accusing Nassib of trafficking in
slaves, oppressing his people, intriguing with the Ogaden, smuggling ivory, and
committing murder.[89] Whether these charges were based on truth or rumor is
impossible to determine from Jenner's correspondence, but Jenner was ready to
feed Nassib to the lions. At the time, the Italian company officials were
attempting to mend relations with the Somali of the Benadir hinterland by
cooperating with slave owners in recovering their runaway slaves.[90] Jenner
knew of cases of "Italian Somalis" re-enslaving Gosha *watoro*, but neither he
nor any other Protectorate official appears to have protested to Italian officials.
In February 1899 Jenner reported that Nassib was "at war with the Italian
Somalis" but, convinced that Perducci of the Italian company was encouraging

[85] Hardinge report, 20 Jul. 1897, C. 8683, 67; Hardinge to Salisbury, 1 Oct. 1897,
FO 403/244, 78.

[86] Jenner to Hardinge, 24 Jan. 1899, FO 403/281, 24.

[87] Hardinge to Salisbury, 1 Oct. 1897, FO 403/244, 78.

[88] Ibid; Hardinge, *Diplomatist in the East*, 141-2.

[89] Jenner to Hardinge, 24 Jan. and 6 Feb. 1899, FO 403/281, 24-6; Jenner to
Craufurd, 29 Apr. 1899, CP 78/65, KNA.

[90] Cassanelli, *Shaping of Somali Society*, 205, 213.

both sides in the conflict, urged no action. In April Jenner was determined to have Nassib settled in Italian territory.[91]

By then, anti-European militancy had surfaced among the Somali. In 1899 Sheikh Mohammad Abdille Hassan established his dervish movement in northern Somaliland and went into revolt against the British. News of the rebellion spread quickly to southern Somaliland and with it panic among Italian and British officials that dervishes might appear at any time. In 1900 Jenner and his slave servant were murdered while on tour in the Kismayu hinterland; Sheikh Hassan's influence among the Ogaden was suspected, and the British mounted an expedition to destroy Afmadu, the Ogaden capital, at a cost of £20,000.[92] The British administration then abandoned the hinterland and confined itself to the coast.

Nassib was by then allied with the Somali. According to Cassanelli, he supplied food and perhaps firearms to the Ogaden. And, in 1903, he was corresponding with Sheikh Hassan.[93] Nassib was among the first in southern Somaliland to enter Hassan's movement. The reasons were mainly political. Those in the south raising Hassan's standard were indifferent to, if not ignorant of, the ascetic nature of his religious appeal. They responded, instead, to his call for driving out Europeans.[94] In light of his past relations with British and Italian officials, Nassib's desire to join Hassan's militant Salihiya brotherhood seems natural enough. Nassib may have as well wanted Hassan's recognition as a means of keeping Somali slave owners at bay. In 1904 southern Somaliland erupted in rebellion against the Italians. Nassib's old allies and trading partners, the Bimal Somali, blockaded Merka and raided the hinterland. Haji Abdi Abiker Gafle, the Bimal sheikh who represented the Salihiya brotherhood in the Merka district, was conspicuous in clashes with Italian forces.[95] In 1905, however, the violence lapsed, and the Italians regained control.

In 1906 Italian officials claimed that Nassib's sons and followers complained of his tyranny and asked Italian officials to arrest him. The charge rings false, because Nassib, in his seventies, was too old to play the oppressor. More likely the Italians believed that the Gosha had taken part in the 1904-05 rebellion and wished to make an example of Nassib, or that they wished to appease loyal Somali slave owners, who complained that their slaves were gaining refuge

---

[91] Jenner to Hardinge, 18 Dec. 1898, FO 403/280, 115; Jenner to Hardinge, 6 Feb. 1899, FO 403/281, 26; Jenner to Craufurd, 29 Apr. 1899, CP 78/65, KNA.

[92] E.R. Turton, "The Impact of Mohammad Abdille Hassan in the East Africa Protectorate," *JAH*, 10, 4 (1969), 643-5. Jenner's servant was the property of Hardinge's butler. Hardinge, *Diplomatist in the East*, 222.

[93] Cassanelli, "Bantu Former Slave Communities," 230; idem, *Shaping of Somali Society*, 232.

[94] Turton, "Impact of Mohammad Abdille Hassan," 646-9. Cassanelli has speculated that Hassan's appeal in the south was stimulated by Italian policies against slavery in these areas. "Ending of Slavery in Italian Somalia," 319.

[95] Cassanelli, *Shaping of Somali Society*, 196, 226-7.

among the Gosha. He was arrested, taken to Mogadishu, and put in prison. Within months Nassib was dead.[96]

Nassib's life, sketchy as it is, has been preserved as legend rather than history. He is represented, both in accounts recorded by Nassib's British and Italian contemporaries and in oral traditions collected decades after his death, as an epic figure possessing great powers, often evil. Nassib was the wizard *extraordinaire*, wholesale slave dealer, courageous warrior, and tyrant. He ruled, it would seem, through fear.

While ruthlessness and resourcefulness--qualities common among escaped slaves--certainly contributed to his survival as a leader, Nassib also enjoyed the popular support of Gosha villagers along many miles of the Juba river. In the early years of his reign, Nassib helped to establish a tiered system of elected legislative and judicial councils that regulated affairs among the many Gosha villages. These councils survived Nassib and were operating when British officials restored their administration to the area in 1911.[97] The council system helped to integrate thousands of Gosha of diverse origin and supplant ethnic-based governments formed by the first maroons.[98] Nassib and other second generation *watoro* seized control of the Juba from founders who had ruled by controlling land. The shift from exclusive to participatory government under Nassib was apparent when in 1897 Arthur Hardinge met Nassib and other Gosha "chiefs" for the first time. Hardinge, who wanted his chiefs to control their subjects, was exasperated to learn that "few of the Gosha Chiefs have much real authority...over their people.... [The Gosha] cannot be relied on to obey any orders from their chiefs, unless they themselves approve of them."[99] A census conducted the same year shows 74 Gosha villages, 3,705 Gosha "huts," and the names of 69 village heads operating under Nassib's system. Mabungu, Nassib's village, at 45 "huts" was one of the smallest Gosha villages.[100] Nassib's reputation as the most important figure on the Juba derived from his presidency of the main council, which met at Mabungu to issue laws for all of Gosha and to serve as Gosha's highest court of appeal.[101]

5. Servants of the People

In the early colonial period, several ex-slaves acquired governing authority over hinterland communities made up of freeborn persons. In the nineteenth

---

[96] Cassanelli, "Former Bantu Slave Communities," 231.

[97] Lamb report on Gobwen sub-district, 25 Sep. 1914, CP 61/133, KNA; Cassanelli, "Former Bantu Slave Communities," 228-31.

[98] For a summary of the ethnic-based system of Gosha government, which Cassanelli argues continued well into the twentieth century, see his "Former Bantu Slave Communities," 219-26, and "Ending of Slavery in Italian Somalia," 322.

[99] Hardinge to Salisbury, 1 Oct. 1897, FO 403/244, 78.

[100] Jenner to Hardinge, 11 Aug. 1897, FO 403/243, encl. 2, 202-3.

[101] Lamb report on Gobwen sub-district, 25 Sep. 1914, CP 61/133, KNA.

century such individuals ran most of the scattered mission stations of the United Methodist Free Church (UMFC), which evangelized among the Ribe, Kambe, Duruma, and Oromo. Willing to work for Europeans, these ex-slaves assisted the Methodists in the manner of the Bombay Africans who developed Rabai and Frere Town; however, the UMFC did not resettle liberated slaves, using its stations instead to attract coastal peoples (the UMFC also depended on African administrators longer than did the CMS establishment, because it sent fewer missionaries from London and because whites on UMFC hinterland stations suffered higher mortality rates).[102] Administrative opportunities off the mission arose in the colonial period, when a few ex-slaves gained appointments as salaried headmen and chiefs in the Nyika Reserve. Ex-slave administrators remained only briefly at any post. They were dismissed for incompetence or violating rules, lured away by desk employment, or driven out of office. As a rule they failed to win acceptance from people under their authority. In cases where European superiors were satisfied with their performance, ex-slave administrators were liable to be opposed at the local level, where they had no standing. As more freeborn aspired to move into such positions, ex-slaves were pushed aside.

John Mugomba, "first native minister to the Duruma people," was a Duruma-owned slave taught by Ludwig Krapf and baptized in 1870 by Thomas Wakefield, UMFC missionary. In the late 1870s he opened the "Mawsonville" station in Duruma, in 1885 took charge of the UMFC's main mission station at Ribe, and in 1887 founded a station at Tsunga ("Duruma No. 2").[103] Before Wakefield left the coast for good in 1886 he, Mugomba, and Tofiki b. Mwidhani, another ex-slave attached to the mission, authored a document that was used by the UMFC to acquired a land title from the Ribe people in 1893. Mugomba later settled in Mazeras.[104] Many years later in Ribe, however, John Mugomba's name was notorious. The Ribe remembered him as a European agent ("Muhendakudza"--lit., a foreign porter, newcomer) who testified that the Ribe had sold Methodist missionaries their land.[105]

---

[102] For early UMFC mission history, Morton, "Slaves, Fugitives, and Freedmen," 233-5.

[103] References to Mgomba from Krapf diary, 9 Aug. 1865, UMFC *Magazine* (1866), 69; Wakefield to UMFC, 28 Aug. 1867, ibid (1868), 205; missionary notices, ibid (1870), 613; missionary notices, ibid (1871), 339; Wakefield to UMFC, 15 Mar. 1887, ibid (1887); Mgomba to Wakefield 10 Apr. [1879?] and note, *Welcome Words*, 14 (1880), 4; W.A. Todd, "Missionary Life in East Africa" in ibid (1890), 78; A.J. Hopkins, *Trail Blazers and Road Makers* (London: Henry Hooks, 1928), 35; Yates, *Dado*, 59; Wakefield, *Thomas Wakefield*, 196. For a sketch of Mgomba, ibid, 104 opp.

[104] The undated document signed by Wakefield, Mgomba, and Tofiki, together with a bill of sale of land dated August 1893, also containing Mgomba's signature, Ribe mission. Mgomba's presence in Mazeras is attested by the Ganjoni Methodist baptism register, which lists his daughter, Maggie, on 6 Mar. 1910. The register was inspected at the Ribe mission in November 1970.

[105] Interview with Chimwenga wa Ndoro, Chauringo, Ribe. 30 Nov. 1970.

Tofiki b. Mwidhani, who remained in Ribe, detached himself from the running of the mission. In the 1860s UMFC missionary Charles New employed Tofiki, then a slave, as a cook and as a companion on his extended hikes to Teita and Mt. Kilimanjaro.[106] After New's death and Wakefield's departure, Tofiki began farming some of the mission land acquired with his and Mugomba's assistance. Tofiki had already begun cultivating a reputation, however, as a man of coastal values rather than as a mission stooge. He remained, as he had been since his employment with New, a practicing Muslim. In addition to his first wife (an "Mswahili" from Mombasa), Tofiki married a daughter of the Mwanadzombo clan of the Ribe. Tofiki's sons of this second marriage, Hamadhi and Mwidhani, were accepted as Mwanadzombo members. Both married locally and farmed the land their father had acquired from the mission and through marriage. In 1934 the Ribe elected Mwidhani as chief of their sub-location, a position he held until retirement in 1943.[107] Thus, Tofiki's ex-slave status proved no barrier to his son's ascendancy to elected office among the Ribe, though establishing distance over time between the colonial establishment and personal wealth and political connections would appear to have been essential.[108] In contrast to the name of Mugomba, that of Tofiki was later remembered fondly in Ribe.

The Ribe mission, tiny as it was, was also the base of three ex-slaves each of whom the Ribe called Muzungu Mwiru ("black European"), or more quaintly, Amerikani ("American"). Their names were William H. During, F. J. Heroe, and John Walker. Scarcely anything about them is recorded, though for a time at least During and Heroe played pivotal roles in the history of the UMFC mission on the Kenya coast. During and Heroe were Sierra Leonean ministers brought to East Africa to maintain the UMFC mission during the 1880s. Like William Jones, these men assumed authority over ex-slaves and freeborn mission dwellers, but neither remained in post long enough to oversee the development of a new community.[109] Walker remains something of a mystery. William During administered Ribe and occasionally Jomvu between 1880 and 1884, when his wife died, and then established the Golbanti station on the Pokomo river where he remained until 1889. He learned to speak fluent Oromo. During

---

[106] New, *Life*, 287 et. seq. An engraving of Tofiki and his wife appears on 59 opp.

[107] I am extremely grateful to Thomas J. Herlehy for his notes on Tofiki's male descendants,based on his 1980 Ribe interviews, particularly with Tofiki b. Mwidhani, grandson of his namesake.

[108] Intermarriage and blood-brotherhood were common methods used by ex-slaves to attach themselves to Miji Kenda peoples, including the Ribe. See ch. 5 above. Also W. Frank, *Habari na Desturi za Waribe* (London: Sheldon Press/Macmillan, 1953), 2; Herlehy, "Ties That Bind," 285-308; idem, "An Economic History of the Kenya Coast: the Mijikenda Coconut Palm Economy, 1800-1980"(Boston: Boston University Ph.D. dissertation, 1985), 137-45; and Brantley, *The Giriama*, 52, 62. In the nineteenth century slaves were absorbed into families and clans over two and three generations, shedding their slave identity in the process. Morton, "Slaves, Fugitives, and Freedmen," 90-2.

[109] For Jones see ch. 5 and "The Rabai WaMisheni" in this chapter.

resigned the ministry after impregnating the fiance of an Oromo evangelist, married the woman, became an IBEACO interpreter, raised two children, and sometime after 1905 died in Mombasa.[110]

The Reverend F.J. Heroe, product of Fourah Bay College, was transferred from the UMFC Sierra Leone mission to East Africa in 1887 and ran the Ribe mission from 1887 until 1890. During this time the runaway slave crisis culminated in freeing 1,421 slaves at Rabai on 1 Jan 1889, which Heroe attended. Of those receiving freedom papers, 311 had been domiciled at Ribe with Heroe's permission. After the brouhaha died down, Heroe resumed admitting runaways at Ribe.[111] Heroe was an abolitionist cut from West African English tradition, who struck William Price as being "as much a foreigner here as a European would be."[112] In 1891 he resigned from the mission and entered IBEACO service. The Heroe name, with initials "F.A." appears in various civil posts in the Protectorate administration, from 1895 to 1907. The person referred to was probably F.J.'s son.[113] According to Chimwenga wa Ndoro of Ribe, Heroe married a Ribe woman named Amiriri.

To date Chimwenga is the only source on the third "American" in Ribe, John Walker, whose actual origin is unknown. Walker, perhaps a friend or relative of the Heroes, settled in Ribe and, like the Tofiki group, married into the Mwanadzombo clan. His wife had lived for years among the Duruma before Walker married her. They had no children. Walker, who died in Ribe, nevertheless left behind the name "Mudzungu Mwiru" with his homestead.[114] In the 1970s, when the bus travelled on the dirt road from Mazeras to Kaloleni through Ribe, the conductor shouted "Mudzungu Mwiru" at the crest of the first hill south of Ribe for any passengers wanting to drop there.

Among many ex-slaves in government service, a handful were made "chiefs" or "headmen." Some of these titleholders, such as Mzee Ali Tete, were ex-*watoro* leaders who retained positions of authority over their original followers.[115]

---

[110] Biographical data and Parsons to Beetham, 24 Aug. 1956, N/T 46, Methodist Missionary Society Archives, London (MMSA); see also Jackson, *Early Days*, 43. During's name appears on a list of firearm owners in 1905. CP 89/144, KNA.

[111] For the crisis, ch. 5 above. For details of runaways admitted at Ribe under Hero, Mackenzie to Euan Smith, 15 Nov. 1888, FO 541/28, 444-5. For runaways admitted after the crisis, Pigott diary, 30 Jun. 1889, FJM; Lugard, "Watoro of Fuladoyo," 23 Jul. 1890, Brit. Emp. s.99, East Africa 1888/92 Letter Book, RH; Lugard, **Diaries**, I, 216.

[112] Price, *Third Campaign*, 12. For similar comments, Baskerville journal, Apr. 1890, G3A5/06, CMS.

[113] Note from F.A. Heroe, 29 May 1895, CP 85/114; Tate to Tritton, 4 May 1900, CP 72/34; Seyidieh province staff list, 1905, CP 89/144; Hinde to Adm. Sec., 4 Dec. 1907, CP 85/112, KNA. Material on Heroe is also taken from N/T 105, MMSA.

[114] Interview with Chimwenga, 30 Nov. 1970.

[115] Five ex-slaves are listed as village headmen in the Malindi district in 1909. Trail to AgPC, Mombasa, 17 Dec. 1909, CP Miscellaneous Correspondence (no cover), KNA. Also in the Coast Province Microfilm collection, Bird Library, Syracuse

Others were placed over freeborn Miji Kenda in expectation that they would remain loyal to the Protectorate. Such men appear to have been tested first as government policemen. The IBEACO and the Protectorate employed slaves as *askari* ("policemen," "soldiers"), even if it meant remitting part of their salaries to their owners.[116]

One slave who rose from policeman to government headman was Kalama wa Rua. His origin is unknown, but he had been the slave of Rashid b. Salim, *liwali* of Takaungu, and at some point had run away. Most likely he settled at Fuladoyo, because his subsequent career, insofar as it is known, was tied to the Giriama of that area. During IBEACO days he was hired as an *askari* and assigned to the headman of Bamba, Kalama wa Sada. He was retained in the same position by the Protectorate. Kalama wa Rua had by then adopted the first name of the Bamba headman and had probably concocted a Giriama father, Rua, through blood-brotherhood. Kalama's post was nevertheless an opportune one, because the Protectorate regarded Kalama wa Sada as one of the three leading elders of the Giriama. Sometime between 1908 and 1912, Kalama wa Sada died, and Kalama wa Rua was attached to the successor, Kaguma wa Ndoro. In 1913 discontent grew among the Giriama against the government and, when suspicions arose as to Kaguma's loyalty, Kalama managed to have himself installed in Kaguma's place.[117] The new appointee served the British well, being one of the few headmen who remained loyal when the Giriama rebelled in 1913-14. Kaguma proved useful as well after the rebellion, when he deployed his *askari* in collecting goats levied by government as fines and conscripting young men into the Carrier Corps. Francis Traill, Nyika district commissioner, regarded him as "undoubtedly the strongest personality (Ngonyo excepted) among the Giriama headmen."[118] Kalama then ran into difficulty when his personal secretary, Jonah Nicolas, a Frere Town ex-slave, murdered two men.

The Giriama petitioned for Kalama's removal. Instrumental in drafting the petition were Hamis b. Juma (alias Mwasoke), a Muslim Giriama shopkeeper at Bamba, and Samuel B. Kuri, a Miji Kenda Christian who as the new CMS deacon at Rabai had just ended four decades of European and ex-slave administration.[119] In the hearings that followed many Giriama lodged complaints

---

University, Reel 177, item 7.

[116] Hedenstrom to Macdougall, 13 Jul. 1899, and Omari b. Faraji statement before Craufurd, n.d., CP 81/85, KNA. Colonial recruitment of ex-slaves into the police and military was common practice elsewhere in Africa. R. Roberts and S. Miers, "The End of Slavery in Africa," in Miers and Roberts, *End of Slavery*, 35, 43.

[117] "Headman Kalaama wa Ruwa of Bamba Division, Nyika District," CP 108/74, KNA. For an account of events in Giriama leading up to and including the 1914 rebellion, Brantley, *The Giriama*. For Kalama wa Sada, Murray to Tritton, 16 Dec. 1901, CP 71/25; amended Takaungu sub-district headmen list, 18 Feb. 1908, CP 62/13; and for "Mzee" Kaguma, La Fontaine to Hobley, 13 Dec. 1912, CP 6/409, KNA.

[118] Traill report, 13 Nov. 1915, CP 20/136, KNA. In her list of loyal headmen, Brantley mistakenly refers to Kalama wa Rua as Kalama wa Sada(99).

[119] Champion summary of events, n.d., cv 18 Aug. 1915, CP 5/336, vol. 5; "Record of complaints. Oct. 1916" and Pearson to Lightbody, 6 Nov. 1916, CP

against Kalama. They accused him of having people beaten by his *askari*, extorting goats and cattle through fines, forcing youngsters to herd his cattle without pay, and taking women and children as pawns against the payment of fines. One elder even accused Kalama of taking his own wife. Kalama admitted to this charge ("His wife wishes to live with me"), but denied most of the others. Pearson thought Kalama was being attacked because he had remained loyal during the rebellion. The petition, however, struck at Kalama's identity rather than his politics.

> We have noticed...that all tribes have their own tribe man to rule them, why [are] we given a Swahili man to rule us. His home is in Takaungu to Salim bin Rashid, and his mother and brothern[sic] are in Roka even to this day. We humbly beg the Government to give us back Kaguma....If the Government do not like to restore Kaguma let him give us someone else but not this man.[120]

Eventually the government decided on Kalama's removal, presumably to generate good will among the Giriama. Kalama's name then disappears from the record.

6. *The Rabai WaMisheni*

When William Jones governed Rabai, many of the ex-slaves began the process of absorbing, and being absorbed by, the Miji Kenda surrounding the mission.[121] Following the crisis of 1888, this process was halted as control was transferred back to Jones's European superiors. The IBEACO and the missions cooperated to prevent runaways from using the missions as refuge, so that the Company would not have to face another 1888 crisis and jeopardize its tenure on the coast.[122] Until 1898, the Protectorate adhered to the policyinitiated by the IBEACO. In such a context, Jones was regarded by missionaries and colonial administrators alike as "untrustworthy."[123] Jones was retained at Rabai, and even ordained a priest in 1895, but his responsibilities and powers were progressively stripped. As of 1895 he had lost all but his religious role. His property, acquired through admission into two Rabai clans, was impounded by the colonial government. He had developed coconut palms on one and rented plots on the other to Indian merchants.[124]

108/74, KNA; Herlehy and Morton, "WaMisheni of Rabai," 270 and note.

120 "Record of complaints. Oct. 1916" and Pearson to Lightbody, 6 Nov. 1916, CP 108/74, KNA

121 See ch. 5.

122 For IBEACO runaway policy, see ch. 6.

123 Hardinge to Salisbury, 10 Aug. 1897, FO 4043/243, 162.

124 Tucker to Baylis, 11 Feb. 1895, G3A5/11, CMS; Binns to Baylis, 3 Nov. 1898 and Smith to Baylis, 11 Nov. 1898, G3A5/13, CMS; Hollis to Craufurd, 3 and 25 May 1898, Jones to Hollis, 21 May 1898, CP 67/15, KNA.

In 1898, forty five years after he began his attachment to the CMS as an inmate of the African Asylum in Bombay, Jones resigned.[125] From Jones's perspective, he had been driven out. "My persecution," he wrote the CMS headquarters months later, "began long time." In a lengthy list of real, and partly imagined, grievances, Jones emphasized the distrust he felt that missionaries had for him and their unwillingness to defend him against the appropriation of his land by the colonial government. "I appealed to Mr. Binns to settle the [land] matter before going to law but he seemed very indifferent about it. I saw at once that evil was determined upon me..." He concluded with a more basic grievance:

> The natives [of the station] have seen that, and have come to the conclusion that this white man has no interest in their being at Rabai where they have been settled peacefully all these years. The Church sad though it is to speak of it; is left empty. O Lord have mercy upon us....[126]

Jones's losing battle with the mission, however, is a minor factor in accounting for the fundamental changes that took place Rabai in the 1890s. Jones ceased to be a dominant influence in Rabai the day the IBEACO redeemed its runaway slaves.[127] Thereafter the Company became the moving force by converting Rabai overnight into one of the coast's principal recruiting stations for transport laborers. Freed slaves responded with alacrity to the Company's call for porters to supply its upcountry stations and continued to do so until the Uganda Railway reached Nairobi in 1898. At Rabai, Company and later Protectorate officials signed on hundreds of freed slaves as porters, cooks, guides, and servants. Pay was attractive. By 1889 missionaries were bemoaning "the tide setting in towards the Company work to the neglect of the necessary work here.... The Company's high wages have enticed nearly all the able-bodied men away from the mission." As a result, the CMS had difficulty raising enough porters to make up a caravan for their mission in Buganda and were under pressure from their own freed slave employees to increase wages.[128] Rabai supplied men to all the upcountry points, including Teita, Chagga, and Uganda. As many as six hundred men were absent at a time, and before the railroad displaced human transport, Rabai had one thousand readily available for porterage work. In 1897, Rabai was the coast's largest recruiting center.[129]

[125] Binns to Baylis, 29 Aug. and 6 Oct. 1898, Finance Committee minutes, 6 Sep. 1898, G3A5/13, CMS. Jones took a job as cashier in the government service, but was regarded as "inefficient." He resigned his job in 1900, returned to the pastorate in 1902, and died in July 1904, at the approximate age of 64. His eldest son, Johnny, was the Senior Interpreter of the Mombasa High Court. Johnny predeceased his father by ten months.

[126] Jones to CMS, 9 May 1899, G3A5/13, CMS.

[127] See ch. 5.

[128] Edwards to Lang, 5 Oct. 1889; Cole to Lang, 30 Dec. 1889; Smith to Lang, 25 Sep. 1889, Smith address, 22 Oct. 1889, G3A5/06, CMS.

[129] Shaw to Baylis, 11 Sep. 1896, G3A5/12, CMS; Hardinge report, 20 Jul. 1897,

The Company and the Protectorate also hired the mission's school products. From the outset, the IBEACO employed English-speaking Africans as clerks and interpreters. As the colonial establishment expanded, more WaMisheni resided and worked in the towns. Soon after jobs in the Protectorate became available, Rabai youths streamed into Mombasa for work, and Africans employed by the mission were among them.[130] By 1900 they were employed as clerks, interpreters, telegraphers, registrars, and messengers in many departments. Some received salaries equal to the pay of an ordained African deacon. The names of some of the freed slave employees appear in the few extant records of the early Protectorate period, in departmental lists and the correspondence of customs, courts, printing, posts and telegraphs, and transport, among others. In certain cases they were the only Africans in their respective departments.[131]

Access to cash income and the things money could buy allowed the wage earners in town to set standards for youth still at the mission. "Our mission boys can all get so much higher wages at the coast now," wrote one missionary, "that unless they really stay with us for the love of the work we can't expect them to be long without going further. Once they get away we seem to lose a hold over them."[132] Schoolchildren dismissed the idea of a mission or teaching career and thought of becoming clerks and dressing in western clothes. Gibson Ngome, who grew up in Rabai at the turn of the century, recalled that "like other boys, I wanted to be a clerk, because these Africans lived better than other Africans and dressed in trousers, shirts, and shoes."[133] In the late 1890s African mission workers combined and agitated for increased wages, instruction in English, and European-style dress. Sunday itself became a ritual of display, a wage earners' promenade.

> It is a beautiful sight to see the numbers gather.... A fine lad from here is now a head clerk in Mr. Bailey's office; he comes up regularly for the Sunday with his wife and family. I am continually seeing parties of nicely dressed young men in black suits, coloured ties and dazzling white cuffs and collars--they hold good posts....[134]

C. 8683, 52-3. Platts report, Rabai Sub-district, [1909], CP 65/4, KNA. The first assistant collector for Rabai, A.C. Hollis, recruited between four and five thousand porters to convey military stores to Uganda alone. Hollis introduction, Lemenye, "Life of Justin," 33.

[130] Ackerman journal, 11 Mar. 1896, G3A5/12, CMS.

[131] Macdonald to Pigott, 1 Apr. 1895, CP 85/114; Ahmed to Mabruki, 4 Aug. 1895, Mabruki to IBEACO, 19 Aug. 1895, CP 93/164; Binns to Craufurd, 7 Jun. 1898, CP 83/100; Craufurd to Marsden, 27 Nov. 1899, CP 83/101; Customs to Tritton, 7 Feb. 1900, CP 72/34; Tate to Tritton, 4 May 1900, CP 72/35; Customs to Gilkinson, 14 Feb. 1903, CP 72/35; Seyyidie staff list, 1905, CP 89/144; Grenville to sub-commissioner, 18 Apr. 1906, CP 73/40; Osborne to AgPC, 3 Sep. 1907, CP 87/127; La Fontaine to AgPC, 3 Aug. 1912, CP 1/60, KNA.

[132] Ackerman journal, 16 Jan. 1897, G3A5/13, CMS.

[133] Interview in Rabai, 28 May 1973.

[134] Higginbotham journal, 23 Nov. 1909, G3A5/18, CMS.

Christianity lost steady ground among the WaMisheni. Between 1888 and 1900, even though the population of the settlement remained stable, the number of "Christian adherents" in Rabai dropped from 1,887 to 644.[135] Correspondingly, belief in the curative powers of Christianity subsided. During Jones's rule, the existence of witchcraft was acknowledged and the use of *waganga* was legitimized, while attendance at baptism classes was mandated.[136] After Jones's temporal authority in the community was terminated, and religious classes and worship became voluntary, WaMisheni placed less faith in the power of Christianity to cure their illnesses. Of particular concern was the practice of *uanga*, a particularly pernicious form of sorcery. The *waanga*, or practitioners of *uanga*, were thought to be predominantly old women who formed secret societies for the perpetration of murder, exhumation, and eating cadavers. Children made up most of their victims.[137] The removal of Jones, sensitive to these fears and beliefs, accelerated the drift away from Europeans and their narrower approach to healing. Maria Ackerman, stationed in Rabai from 1894 to 1897, noted that

> often the beginning of going astray here is [when] some sickness comes and they go off into a heathen village for medicine which is given with a great deal of witchcraft combined and they forget entirely God alone has the power to heal.[138]

Ackerman noted other incidents related to witchcraft and its practitioners, who "are thought to be many in and around Rabai."[139] Belief in the designs and powers of *waanga* may well have been more a consequence than a cause of internal discord among the WaMisheni, but its presence signifies that potentially unifying forces--Christianity and Miji Kenda culture--were losing strength on the mission.

Growing indifference toward Christianity was especially pronounced among the youth. By the 1890s nearly all the youngsters who had earlier studied under Handford and served as teachers and catechists in Frere Town and Rabai, had either left or been turned out of mission work. Of the eighteen lads who entered special training in 1877, only one, James Deimler, proved himself as a catechist. By 1900 the Africans entering CMS mission work were nearly all Miji Kenda, whose children made up the majority attending school.[140]

---

135 Based on annual returns in CMS *Proceedings*, 1887-88 to 1899-1900.

136 Jones himself publicly consulted *waganga* to determine if his wife's illness was the result of sorcery. Binns to Lang, 3 Dec. 1891, G3A5/07, CMS; Interview with Tuguu wa Baya, Rabai, 5 Sep. 1973.

137 In 1973, when interviews were conducted in Rabai, a few residents were willing to discuss *uanga* but only in private.

138 Ackerman journal, 15 Mar. 1897, G3A5/13.

139 Ackerman journal, 26 Jun. and 28 Sep. 1895, G3A5/11; 13 Feb. and 7 Mar. 1896, G3A5/113; 2 Apr. 1898, G3A5/14, CMS.

140 Binns to Hardinge, 7 Dec. 1898, C. 9502, 19. In 1889 ex-slaves' children outnumbered Miji Kenda by more than two to one. Burness to CMS, 31 May 1889,

Further indication of the estrangement unfolding in the 1890s is the increased rate of Muslim conversions. Islam had been present at Rabai from the time Muslim runaway slaves settled there. Islamization among the WaMisheni paralleled the waning of Jones's influence and that of his syncretic version of Christianity. By 1902, a mosque was erected within a few minutes walk of the CMS church, and not far away stood a Muslim cemetery. By then it is likely there were more practising Muslims in Rabai than Christians.[141] A growing number of persons, many of them single women, left the mission altogether to live in Mombasa, where they converted to Islam. Dormitory girls in Frere Town were prone to leave the settlement and, according to the missionaries, forced to live with Swahili men as a defense against impoverishment. By 1892, the movement of Christianized ex-slaves into town was being noted as a serious problem by the missionaries.[142] In 1896 women missionaries began to visit these "lapsed Christians," as they were called, and to attempt reviving them as a Christian community. The effort failed. Ex-Rabai women, noted Maria Ackerman, "forget all the teaching they had had and just do as the Swahili do." Trying to meet them "is difficult for they...have in most cases lost their love for good things by their contact with evil Mohammedans."

> Our mission people. . .when they come here have left off wearing their skirts and visibau and have taken to the Swahili leso wearing one round their body and one thrown over their heads and shoulders and have bored their ears in Swahili fashion and wear all sorts of borrowed ornaments so as to hide themselves from the laughter of the Swahili and Mahommedan people this they did when they first came to the town: ....by the skirt and kisibau they were known as coming from a Mission station where the book was taught.[143]

Efforts to draw them back into the church continued for another decade, without results. In 1906, the conference report confessed that "pastoral affairs [in Mombasa] have been decidedly depressing." The ex-Christians are "harder to deal with, and are more bigoted, than the Mohamedans."[144] In spite of their struggle to merge with Swahili culture, ex-slaves remained an unwanted element. Both the government and the *qadi* applied Islamic law enabling Christians to dissolve previous Christian marriages by being married by Muslims, yet many of the Ismalized ex-Christian women lived alone with their children after having been

---

G3A5/06, CMS.

[141] Interview with sheikh Mwidadi b. Johari, Rabai, 1970. The cemetery is located in "Kavirondo" section in Rabai.

[142] Tucker to Wigram, 3 Jun. 1892, Binns to Lang, 15 Aug. and 13 Sep. 1892, G3A5/08, CMS.

[143] Ackerman journal, 19 Jun. 1897, G3A5/12, as well as entries 10, 12, 23, and 29 May and 5 Jun. 1897, idem, CMS. *Kisibau* (pl. *visibau*) = waistcoast.

[144] Conference report of 1906, 1 May. 1907, G3A5/17, CMS.

deserted by their husbands. They supported themselves as water carriers, palm wine sellers, and prostitutes.[145]

In Rabai ex-slaves survived as little more than a resident group. Though successful in entering the colonial cash economy, they lacked the resources to create a community. Rabai was merely a base from which to function economically in the East Africa Protectorate (and later Kenya Colony). Having cash made them a distinct type in Rabai, where they set themselves apart from the Miji Kenda in their dress, housing, and use of KiSwahili. And those with the highest incomes stood out there and on the coast at large as English-speakers in western clothing. The surrounding Miji Kenda called the Rabai ex-slaves *WaMisheni* ("mission people"), not because they were Christian adherents, though some were, but because they had emerged as a new coastal group that chose to reside on and around mission ground.

Most first generation WaMisheni men worked as porters and trickled back to Rabai only in their declining years. The colonial government overlooked the negative impact that porterage had on community life, preferring to project this form of labor as wholesome and fulfilling.

> [The ex-slave] settles in a small village on the outskirts of town, builds a hut on [his own] land,...cultivates...and enters into an agreement with a railway contractor or with one of the Government transport headmen. He then goes, from time to time, to railhead or to Uganda, and after an absence of from three to six months, returns to Rabai to greet his family and spend his earnings. Thus, he becomes, in every sense of the word, a free man.[146]

A few WaMisheni probably fit this description, but the life of porters, and especially those with families, was less generous. Porters' wives suffered the hardship of providing for themselves and their children and lived with the fear of being left alone through the death or desertion of their husbands. Porters' deaths, and the corresponding misery they caused in Rabai, were common in the 1890s. On one safari alone, twenty-four men from Rabai perished. "You may imagine," noted one missionary in her diary, "the widows and orphans in their sorrow."[147] Young women, especially those just out of school, greatly outnumbered eligible bachelors on the station and faced a life alone.[148] Male absenteeism turned Rabai very much into a women's settlement. Porters derived from caravan work the independence women lacked, while they denied the community a vital supply of agricultural labor. Their absence was an important

---

145 Jenner to AgAdmin., Mombasa, 31 Aug. 1894, G3A5/10; Ackerman journal, 8 Jul. 1897, G3A5/12; report of 1-6 Apr. 1901, G3A5/15, CMS.

146 Hollis to Craufurd, 9 Oct. 1898, CP 67/15, KNA.

147 Ackerman journal, 16 Aug. 1895, G3A5/11, CMS. For similar incidents, Handford to Lang, 15 and 18 Feb. 1886, G3A5/03; Ackerman journal, 25 Dec. 1896, G3A5/13, CMS; Binns to transport supt., Uganda Railway, 8 Feb., n.d., 26 May, 18 Jun., and 3 Jul. 1896, and Binns to Craufurd, 20 Jul. 1896, CP 66/9, KNA.

148 Binns to Baylis, 4 Dec. 1896, G3A5/12, CMS.

factor in inducing women, some of them married, to move to the towns.[149] Predominate among caravan workers were farmers who abandoned cultivation, family men who left wives and children to fend for themselves, and bachelors who put aside plans for marriage. Youths fresh from school spurned farming, and, without other means of self-support, drifted into caravan work like their elders. By the 1890s Rabai had become for many males a temporary home.[150]

Porterage and other forms of male absenteeism had particularly disastrous consequences for the WaMisheni birth rate. As of the early twentieth century, Rabai contained many bachelors who had already grown old. "If [they] had produced another generation they would outnumber the [Miji Kenda of the Rabai area] today," remarked an old man in 1973. "But so many died without children there was no one to inherit their lands."[151] The drop-off in WaMisheni birth rates even among married couples is apparent in genealogies collected in the course of field work carried out in 1973. In a comparison of forty-seven first generation and forty-one second generation marriages for which corroboration was possible, the average number of children per couple declined from 2.02 to 1.65. These figures include couples of which one partner was Miji Kenda. In cases where both spouses were WaMisheni, the drop-off was much greater, from an average of 1.97 in the first generation to 1.3 in the second. Of twenty all-WaMisheni second generation marriages recorded, only eight produced any children. When asked for reasons why the WaMisheni had so few children and why a very noticeable segment produced none at all, the most common reply among WaMisheni descendants was that men married late in life or not at all, because of caravan work.[152]

The WaMisheni who did marry were also choosing one another. The rate of ex-slave entry into Miji Kenda clans, high in Jones's day, dropped as those who had resisted assimilation became the predominate element in Rabai. The anti-assimilationists were mostly of *mateka* origin, i.e., ex-slaves without any exposure as slaves to coastal culture who had been handed directly to CMS missionaries by the British naval patrol. In spite of ready means for acculturation among the Miji Kenda, the *mateka* generally maintained a high degree of exclusiveness, which was partly encouraged by the missionaries at Frere Town, where ex-slaves were settled in ethnic neighborhoods. After moving to Rabai, *mateka* established ethnically defined wards, intermarried, and promoted their

[149] Binns to Lang, 15 Aug. 1892, G3A5/08, CMS.

[150] Finance Committee minutes, 18 Aug. 1888, G3A5/05, Pruen to Lang, 8 May 1889, G3A5/06; Ackerman journal 28 Jun. 1896, and Binns to Baylis, 4 Dec. 1896, G3A5/12, CMS.

[151] Interview with Joseph Tinga, age 72, in Rabai, 1973. The same was said by other old-term residents. Interviews with Stanley Saburi, Gibson Ngome, Bemkoka Morris, and Edward K. Binns, all in 1973.

[152] Others argued that mission people grew sterile from venereal disease and elephantiasis of the testicles, both common afflictions in earlier days. Miji Kenda informants, however, were unanimous in saying that the WaMisheni killed one another off by *uanga* and other forms of witchcraft.

social uniqueness through such cultural expressions as language and dance. These and other conscious efforts to maintain social distance, such as the taking up of caravan work by many *mateka* men, contributed to the WaMisheni image as a distinct, alien group. What had started in the 1880s as a move toward accommodation between WaMisheni and Miji Kenda became thereafter a drift toward conflict. The story that ensued, with its dual motifs of land disputes and cultural arrogance, persisted through the entire colonial period.[153]

SAMPLE FAMILY SIZES AMONG WAMISHENI, RABAI

	Couples	Children	Av. no. children	Childless couples
1st Generation				
WaMisheni	28	67	1.97	6
Miji Kenda spouse	11	28	2.15	2
TOTAL	39	95	2.02	8
2nd Generation				
WaMisheni	8	26	1.3	12
Miji Kenda spouse	16	43	2.04	5
TOTAL	24	68	1.65	17

---

[153] Herlehy and Morton, "The WaMisheni of Rabai," 267-76.

Conclusion

If freedom may be defined as laboring without coercion and enjoying citizenship at least in a parochial society, then freedom was beyond the reach of nearly all Children of Ham in nineteenth century coastal Kenya.[1] Freed slaves and maroons escaped the abuse and compulsory duties endured by slaves, but they lived in constant danger. Necessity drove them to produce, while enemies plotted to destroy their proceeds along with themselves. Few who escaped slavery gained entry into an established coastal community except as exploitable inferiors, and only the Gosha remained self-governing long enough even to outlast legal slavery itself. Nor did the path of flight away from slavery lead to higher standards of living. Apart from a small group of mission-educated wage-earners who became something of a coastal economic elite during the late pre-colonial and early colonial period, there is little in the way of material fortune to distinguish between ex-slaves and slaves. By the 1890s, in fact, slaves in certain parts of the coast were probably better off economically than most ex-slaves, with the possible exception of Rabai's residents.[2]

Thousands chose nevertheless not to be slaves. They did not wait on freedom papers before leaving their masters. The typical resident of Rabai, as much as of Fuladoyo or Witu, was an escaped, as opposed to a liberated, slave. By 1890 only a few hundred ex-slaves at most had been removed from their owners by the British or the Busaidi.[3] The British, moreover, freed only those slaves taken from vessels in the Indian Ocean. On the Kenya coast, even after the overland slave trade became illegal in 1876, the number of slaves apprehended and freed is small. Before Britain abolished the legal status of slavery in 1907, slaves who wanted to break with their masters had already done so.

---

[1] Igor Kopytoff's suggestion--that "freedom" is a western concept purporting "autonomy and detachment from binding social relations" making possible the "pursuit of happiness," and is therefore inappropriate to the discussion of slavery in Africa and its abolition--is not accepted here. Practically speaking, a normal free person anywhere belongs to one society or another and accepts a higher authority. "The Cultural Context of African Abolition," in Miers and Roberts, *End of Slavery*, 488. For a comprehensive definition of slavery, see P. Lovejoy, *Transformations in Slavery: a History of Slavery in Africa* (Cambridge: Cambridge University Press, 1983), 1-8.

[2] Cooper cites many examples of slaves' economic gains in the 1890s to demonstrate their "independence under slavery." Nearly all of his Kenya coastal data in this respect is derived from Mombasa. *Plantation Slavery*, 228-42.

[3] The CMS, which was the only missionary agency to care for freed slaves on the Kenya coast, received a total of 119 Bombay Africans and 657 "raw," or "condemned" slaves in the 1870s. Of these a relatively high, though undetermined, number died within a few years, emigrated, or survived without issue. See ch. 2. As of 1892 the *mateka* element in Frere Town had greatly dwindled. Tucker to Wigram, 3 Jun. 1892, G3A5/08, CMS.

Controls, and the punishment for resisting them, are much greater in slave societies than in free societies; only a minority of slaves on the Kenya coast were prepared to run away and lead a life of fear, loneliness, pain, and violence. Extreme risk was the price of resistance to slavery, just as slavery was the cost of submission. The dynamics of marronage and freed slave activity on the Kenya coast were not governed by the expectation of safety and material gain, though the quest for both played a role in shaping the ex-slave experience. The odds against obtaining freedom in any protected or profitable sense were always much greater than the chance of escape itself. After the decision to run had been taken, the driving ambition was to remain only, somehow, free of slavery.[4]

Geography was there to aid their escape, and also to test their will. Thick foliage and bush next to plantations and coastal towns provided cover, even in daytime, while hills paralleling the southern coast and forests along the northern coast promised sanctuary. Yet, with every kilometer travelled away from the coastline, the difficulties of life increased. Rainfall, fickle even in adequate years near the ocean, became progressively unreliable in the interior. Somewhere between twenty and forty kilometers inland, depending on location, thornscrub and desert began. Thus, having escaped the comparatively lush and productive plantation zone, fugitive slaves in search of sanctuary were trapped in a narrow strip of terrain that was scarcely habitable. Even established residents such as the Miji Kenda, with generations of experience behind them, were still ill-matched for the sterner contests nature held here regularly in the form of droughts, famines, epidemic diseases, locust plagues, and rat invasions. In the very neighborhood where runaway slaves were struggling to survive, Miji Kenda were either malnourished, starving, or desperate enough to pawn their own children for food.[5]

From the beginning, ex-slaves of the hinterland, whether freed or fugitive, developed a callous streak. They were capable of great cruelty, particularly toward the helpless. Maroons captured and traded slaves and became slave owners themselves. After overwhelming the attacking forces of enemy slave owners, Fuladoyans took no prisoners. Their executions were quick and grisly. Repeated deeds of the *watoro* match, if not exceed, the terror inflicted by any slave owner or slave trader. Their indifference to the lives of others, including slaves and even

---

[4] "A poor creature came to us at night in a pitiable plight [having] made her way from Malindi, she said,--distant about fifty or sixty miles,-- with the fetters on her feet! How she could have walked, one could scarcely imagine; for, connecting the two iron anklets was a bar not more than ten or twelve inches long, impeding her steps, and preventing her from putting one foot much in advance of the other." This account was written by Elizabeth Wakefield, of the Ribe UMFC mission station, sometime before her death in 1873. E.S. Wakefield, *Koona Koocha: Dawn upon the Dark Continent* (London: A. Crombie, 1892), 13.

[5] Missionary correspondence contains many examples of such ordeals. For rats, see especially Brewin, *Memoirs of Rebecca Wakefield*, 103-4. When I did research in Rabai in 1972-3, rats still menaced farmers' crops and entered their home-steads after dark. As a matter of nocturnal routine, rodents scaled my mosquito net and, after being kicked off, climbed back on.

other groups of runaway slaves, was a common characteristic, just as their reputation as murderers and thieves was often earned. During the Anglo-Mazrui War, innocent slaves and *mahaji* were attacked and killed as often by the Mazrui forces as by the British. And, at the same time, when the long-standing conflict between Mbaruk's *watoro* and Jones's ex-slave WaMisheni reached its denouement at Rabai, *watoro* captives, begging for mercy, were beheaded by ex-slaves on the spot.

Such acts symptomatize paranoia. Living among other refugees in communities without security or recognition, ex-slaves were apt to attack the least threatening targets. Lacking forbearance that comes from inner strength, ex-slaves and their communities committed random acts of violence and imitated the strong. Even Rabai, a freer and more peaceful enclave than most, was administered by William Jones in an authoritarian manner typical of the CMS missionaries in Frere Town. And even Jones, with his singular qualities, trafficked in the kaleidoscopic counterfeit common among the Children of Ham. He, as much as any Christian maroon at Fuladoyo, Muslim forest dweller of Utwani, or Gosha chief on the Juba river, covered his vulnerability and sense of inferiority with adornments of power and rank. Jones wore European clothes weekdays and a deacon's robe on Sunday, bought the title of elder from the Rabai Miji Kenda, and chose his three successive wives exclusively from the Abyssinian Galla, prized by wealthy Muslims as concubines.[6]

Eclecticism suited the Children of Ham, who after all were persons of diverse backgrounds, known but recently to one another, and bound together mainly by the desire to avoid re-enslavement. Without loyalty to any single tradition, and distrustful of single solutions, their communities were patchworks of borrowed ideas and competing influences, rather than blueprints of new societies. It would be too much to expect that, under the circumstances prevailing on the Kenya coast in the late nineteenth century, they should have done otherwise. Diversity and a common fate was the basis of their strength, along with guns and powder.

Whether of necessity or choice, the greatest achievement of the Children of Ham was cooperating to build and protect villages that provided refuge to others. Rabai, Fuladoyo, Witu, and Gosha prospered not only because they were defended, but because they were open. In the time they lasted as maroon settlements, each admitted all friendly comers, fugitive slave, freed slave, and otherwise. Gosha proved partly an exception; they returned runaways to their Somali allies and admitted runaways from their enemies. Otherwise, no potential resident was turned away, no resident driven out. They incorporated outsiders, accommodated differences in their crude political organizations, traded and allied with neighbors, and communicated over wide areas. Though aliens of the coast, living in exile,

---

[6] For Jones's first two wives, see ch. 5. His third, whom he married in 1883, was Roman Catholic, much to the horror of CMS missionaries. Rabai Conference minutes, 24 Sep. 1883, G3A5/O1(1883), CMS. Jones found each of his wives in India, where they had been freed and educated by missionaries. Regarding the esteem associated with Galla female slaves, who originated from northeast Africa and were sold in the Red Sea and Indian Ocean ports. Christie, *Cholera Epidemics*, 137-8,

they aspired to join something larger than themselves. Their attempts in this respect, even while challenging authority, reflected their desire to merge with established coastal Kenya cultures. Shedding their identities as former slaves, however, was not the prerogative of the Children of Ham, who failed to gain acceptance as equals within the communities that had once enslaved them.

Freed slaves and fugitive slaves influenced the course of major developments on the Kenya coast. Ex-slave communities in particular exercised power along the coastline, at least until Britain abolished the legal status of slavery. By sustaining and enlarging their settlements, freed slaves and *watoro* weakened the slave plantation economy, challenged the local authority of Busaidi and British officials, reshuffled local social, political, and religious alignments, and created new, though hardly revolutionary, coastal societies. Some communities of ex-slave descendants, such as the WaMisheni at Rabai and the Gosha on the Juba river, still survive.[7] Generally speaking the economic and political forces accompanying colonial rule destroyed ex-slave settlements and undermined ex-slave communities. During the cataclysmic 1890s, punctuated by war and climatic disasters, thousands of ex-slaves and slaves were scattered or killed. Ex-slave communities also tended to atomize as individual members became mobile economically. The Children of Ham responded more readily than other Africans to long-term wage employment. They also became more dependent on it, because most were landless and kinless. Pace Cooper, ex-slaves generally lacked the family ties and capital resources that enabled African peasants, such as the Miji Kenda and the *mahaji* squatters, to participate in the cash economy as cashcroppers. Ex-slaves were far more visible in the colonial bureaucratic apparatus established during the early stages of capitalist development. Missionary societies, imperial companies, and colonial administrations depended heavily on ex-slave (and slave) porters in connecting and sustaining their far-flung activities until the advent of railways and motorized road transport, and employed hundreds of ex-slaves to fill positions as interpreters, clerks, policemen, registrars, telegraphers, teachers, servants, and headmen.

The extent of their activities and the relationship of ex-slaves to major historical developments has not yet been fully explored. This study of the Kenya coast emerged because the previous works of Mbotela, Temu, Bennett, Zein, Harris, Ranger, Strayer, Strobel, Mirza, and Romero, though dealing at least in part with ex-slaves, were restricted either to one place (usually Mombasa or Frere Town), one group, or isolated episodes.[8] Books promising broad treatment have

---

[7] A few WaMisheni were living in Rabai in the early 1980s. Herlehy and Morton, "The WaMisheni of Rabai," 254-81. The Gosha, still awaiting a full study, rose in population from 8,259 in 1921 to 14,000 in 1945. Auden report, 22 May 1921, CP 2, KNA; "Somali Handbook," I, 127, FJL. They were visited as recently as 1959. A.H.J. Prins, "The Somali Bantu," *Bulletin of the International Committee on Urgent Anthropological and Ethnological Research*, 3(1960), 28-31.

[8] Mbotela, *Uhuru wa Utumwa*; A.J. Temu, "The Role of the Bombay Africans on the Mombasa Coast, 1874-1904," *Hadith 3* (Nairobi: East African Publishing House, 1971), 6-15; idem, *British Protestant Missions* (London: Longmans, 1972); Bennett, "The Church Missionary Society at Mombasa," 159-94; Zein, *Sacred Meadows;*

delivered less. Cooper purports to cover Zanzibar as well as the Kenya Coast, but he drew most of his evidence with regard to the latter from Mombasa and Malindi, and selectively at that.[9] Only broadly-focused research may do justice to ex-slaves, who of necessity were on the move and alert to broader movements still. By no means is the examination of freed slaves and fugitive slaves on the Kenya coast, or East Africa, near completion; systematic archival and field research on East Africa's largest maroon community, the Gosha, has yet to be undertaken, and other maroon and freed slave settlements can be added to the list: e.g., on the Tana river, in the Pangani hinterland; on Pemba island; and on Zanzibar itself. For all of these areas, as well as for the Mrima coast, detailed studies of the early colonial period are overdue.

More research is also needed on fugitive slaves in other areas of Africa for the period when slavery was practiced. Publications relative to slavery have multiplied in recent years, but more often than not they ignore fugitives and other ex-slaves when discussing slavery and deal with them as part of the post-emancipation period.[10] During slavery, ex-slaves--and especially fugitives--, did not fit into niches acceptable to authority, and the natural preference, then and since, has been to think of them as slaves rather than as individuals clinging to some form of freedom. In words reminiscent of an East Africa Protectorate official, a noted authority commented recently that fugitive slaves in Africa constituted but a "minority" of slaves who had "deserted" their masters. A few ran away, in other words, but they lacked significant reasons for doing so.[11] Rather than acknowledge flight as a phenomenon in its own right, too often the wish has been to will it away.

Ranger, Dance and Society; J.E. Harris, ed. *The Recollections of James Juma Mbotela* (Nairobi: East African Publishing House, 1977) and idem, *Repatriates and Refugees in a Colonial Society: the Case of Kenya* (Washington DC: Howard University Press, 1987); Strayer, *Mission Communities*; Strobel, *Muslim Women in Mombasa*; idem, "Slavery and Reproductive Labor in Mombasa," 111-29; Romero, "'Where Have All the Slaves Gone?'," 497-512; Mirza and Strobel, *Three Swahili Women*.

[9] Cooper, *Plantation Slavery*; idem, *From Slaves to Squatters*.

[10] An example of this tendency is found in the introduction to Miers and Kopytoff, *Slavery in Africa*, and Miers and Roberts, *The End of Slavery*. See also J.L. Watson, *Asian and African Systems of Slavery* (Berkeley: University of California Press, 1980) and Robertson and Klein, *Women and Slavery in Africa*. A notable exception is Lovejoy, *Transformations in Slavery*, in which the importance of fugitive slave activity during the pre-abolition period is recognized. Ironically, Miers and Roberts' *The End of Slavery* itself contains a number of references to flight, marronage, and other forms of resistance to slavery long before abolition (see R. Dumett and M. Johnson, "Britain and the Suppression of Slavery in the Gold Coast Colony, Ashanti, and the Northern Territories," 78, 89-91; A. Isaacman and A. Rosenthal, "Slaves, Soldiers, and Police: Power and Dependency among the Chikunda of Mozambique, ca. 1825-1920," 223-34; Herlehy and Morton, "The WaMisheni of Rabai," 254-67; R. Roberts, "The End of Slavery in the French Soudan, 1905-1914," 284-87; Cassanelli, "The Ending of Slavery in Italian Somalia," 321-3; D. Northrup, "The Ending of Slavery in the Eastern Belgian Congo," 467.

[11] Kopytoff, "The Cultural Context of African Abolition," 485-6

Research on flight, marronage, and other forms of resistance has nevertheless succeeded in staking its claim as important to the study of slavery and the slave trade in Africa. In the 1970s Garfield, Akinola, and Oroge published formative work with reference to Sao Tome, Nigeria, and Zanzibar, respectively, while even Cooper discussed flight and marronage as a form of slave resistance.[12] In the 1980s the extent of resistance gradually unfolded in articles and theses relative to all regions of sub-Saharan Africa. The first monograph on slave resistance, by Ross on the South African cape, also appeared. Important to the growth of resistance studies in general was the stimulus provided by Lovejoy's research in Northern Nigeria and his writing on African slavery.[13] One of the hypotheses to suggest itself from these studies is that wherever slavery was practiced in Africa, slaves were struggling to extricate themselves, while fugitive slaves and freed slaves helped to weaken the institution and hasten its abolition. Their history, though visible still in only outline form, draws into question the

---

[12] R. Garfield, "A History of Sao Tome Island, 1470-1655" (Evanston: Northwestern University Ph.D. Thesis, 1971), 1-145; G.A. Akinola, "Slavery and Slave Revolts in the Sultanate of Zanzibar in the Nineteenth Century," *Journal of the Historical Society of Nigeria* 6, 2 (Dec. 1972), 215-28; E.A. Oroge, "The Fugitive Slave Crisis of 1859: a Factor in the Growth of Anti-British Feelings among the Yoruba," *Odu*, 12 (Jul. 1975), 40-54; and idem, "The Fugitive Slave Question in Anglo-Egba Relations, 1861-1886," *Journal of the Historical Society of Nigeria*, 8, 1(Dec. 1975), 61-80; Cooper, *Plantation Slavery*, esp. 200-210; see also Morton, "Slaves, Fugitives, and Freedmen."

[13] R. Roberts and M.A. Klein, "The Banamba Slave Exodus of 1905 and the Decline of Slavery in the Western Sudan," *JAH*, 21 (1980), 375-94; P.E. Lovejoy, ed., *The Ideology of Slavery in Africa* (Beverly Hills: Sage, 1981), esp. D. Northrup, "The Ideological Context of Slavery in Southeastern Nigeria in the 19th Century"(114-18); B. Agiri "Slavery in Yoruba Society in the 19th Century" (141-43); and P.E. Lovejoy, "Slavery in the Sokoto Caliphate"(230-39); R. Ross, *Cape of Torments: Slavery and Resistance in South Africa* (London: Routledge & Kegan Paul, 1983); Lovejoy, *Transformations in Slavery*, 246-55; Glassman, "The Witu Sultanate"; P. Delius, *The Land Belongs to Us: the Pedi Polity, the Boers and the British in the Nineteenth-century Transvaal* (Berkeley: University of California Press, 1984), 37, 95, 138-9, 142-7, 162; P.E. Lovejoy, ed. *Africans in Bondage: Studies in Slavery and the Slave Trade* (Madison: African Studies Program, University of Wisconsin, 1986), esp. Lovejoy, "Problems of Slave Control in the Sokoto Caliphate" (249-65) and A. Isaacman, "Ex-Slaves, Transfrontiersmen, and the Slave Trade: the Chikunda of the Zambesi Valley, 1850-1900" (278-301); P.E. Lovejoy, "Fugitive Slaves: Resistance to Slavery in the Sokoto Caliphate," in G.Y. Okihiro, ed. *In Resistance: Studies in African, Caribbean, and Afro-American History* (Amherst, University of Massachusetts Press, 1986), 71-95; Cassanelli, "Bantu Former Slave Communities," 216-38; J.C.Miller, *Way of Death: Merchant Capitalism and the Angolan Slave Trade, 1730-1830* (Madison: University of Wisconsin Press, 1988), 38-9, 129-30, 134, 161, 269-74, 384-6; J.C. Armstrong and N.A. Worden, "The Slaves, 1652-1834," in R. Elphick and H. Giliomee, ed., *The Shaping of South African Society, 1652-1840* (Middletown: Wesleyan University Press, 1989), 149-62.

theory that in Africa slaves thought of themselves as dependents best understood through the study of African forms of clientage and kinship.[14]

Needed at this stage are detailed monographs. Each shall be welcome for several reasons. More knowledge about fugitive slaves and freed slaves will extend understanding of African slavery for one, and will contribute to the growing literature in comparative world slavery for another. As well the necessary scouting around the byways, crevices, and retreats inhabited by ex-slaves will chance to uncover important features of life in general that have sofar escaped the notice of historians following well-trodden paths. By their very nature, fugitive slaves and freed slaves involved everyone around them, near and far, and their history will give expression to fundamental forces at work in the time and place of their lives. Reconstructing the ex-slave past nevertheless is tedious work, because few of these beleaguered souls or their descendants craved visibility. Few left anything in writing, and references to them are scattered randomly, buried away, usually surfacing one bit at a time in a document, if not in an archive. The task invites comparison with a series of archaeological digs, each requiring thousands of items to be collected, assembled and reassembled, compared, integrated, and ordered so as to reveal at times no more than a glimpse of the past. Without their history, however, understanding what slavery meant to those who experienced it will remain difficult. Slaves in Africa are largely mute; they have left little direct evidence of their thinking or feelings, whereas the deeds of freed slaves and fugitive slaves, as testified by the Children of Ham, speak with eloquence.

---

[14] For the most recent statement of this position, I. Kopytoff, "The Cultural Context of African Abolition."

Appendix

THE BOMBAY AFRICANS

Apart from three persons, the Bombay Africans arrived in Frere Town between November 1873 and December 1876. George and Priscilla David and Polly Christian Nyondo had worked in Rabai and Mombasa for the East Africa Mission since 1864. William Jones and Ishmael Semler worked with the Davids and Polly Nyondo, but they had returned to India by 1870. Semler journeyed to Mombasa in 1875, and Jones followed the next year. Arrivees were as follows:

Year	Number	Comments
1864	3	George David, Priscilla Christian (later married to David), and Polly Christian (later married to Isaac Nyondo)
1873 (Nov.)	20	Included four of the five Bombay veterans of the Livingstone Search Expedition: Carus Farrar, Mathew Wellington, Benjamin Rutton and Richard Rutton.
1874 (Jan.)	14	
1875 (Feb.)	51	Two groups
1876 (Jan.)	43	Included 13 children
(Dec.)	5	Included 2 children
	136	TOTAL

The following list, consisting of 116 names of first generation Bombay Africans, has been compiled from CMS correspondence files. Some names are missing, and the surnames of six have not been determined. Care has been taken to determine the authenticity of the names listed and to exclude the names of freedslave (*mateka*) women who took Bombay husbands.

(*) denotes an individual who settled first at Rabai. Relationships of persons with like surname are indicated when known.

Ainsworth, James (also known as
  Assura, Aswara)
*Baker, Lucy
*Baker, Samson (husband of Lucy)
Baraka, James [1]
Baraka (wife of James)
*Brown,Manassah[2]
*Candy, Julia
*Baker, Samson (husband of
*Candy, Thomas(husband
  of Julia)
Casar(Caesar), Sophy
Casar (husband of Sophy)
*Christian, Aaron
*Connop, John
*Connop, Ephraim
*Connop, Jane
David, George
David, Priscilla (wife of George)
*Dickson, Jeremiah
*Dickson, Susan (wife of Jeremiah)
Dixon, James[3]
Dowman, Harriet
Dowman, Richard (husband of
  Harriet)
*Faithful, Abraham
*Faithful, Hannah (wife of
  Abraham)
*Farrar, Carus
Farrar, Charles
Farrar, Clement
*Ferry, Joseph
Francis, Mary
Francis (Mary's husband)
*Frank, Ellen
*Frank, Francis (husband of Ellen)
*Gibson, Joseph
*Gibson, Louisa (wife of Joseph)
*Grey, Monica
*Grey, Ruben
Isenberg, Miriam

Isenberg, Samuel (husband of
  Miriam)
Isenberg, William
Japhet, A.
*Jerrom, Bessy
*Jerrom, Frances
*Jerrom, Nicholas
*Jerrom, Niger
*Johnson(Johnstone), Josiah
*Johnstone, Jonah
*Jones, Sally[4]
*Jones, William Henry
Keating, Robert
King, Joshua
Maidment, Henry[5]
Maidment (first wife of Henry)
Malcomb, Deborah
Malcomb, Zebedee (husband of
  Deborah)
Manuel, Mary
Manuel, F. (husband of Mary)
Mark, Emma
Mark, J. (husband of Emma)
*Mason, Patience
*Mason, Thomas
*Matchett, Aaron
Matchett, Abel
*Matchett, Abraham
*Matchett, Adam
*Matchett, Apolos
*Matchett, Caroline
*Matchett, Eliza
*Matchett, Jemina (Amina)
Matchett, Octavia (wife of Abel)
*Matchett, Sadika
Mitchell, Jonah
Mitchell, Rebecca (wife of Jonah)
*Moffat, Prudence
*Morris, Agatha
*Morris, Solomon (husband of
  Agatha)

---

[1] It is possible that James Baraka and James Dixon, whose name appears on an 1881 map of Frere Town, were one in the same person.

[2] Manassah Brown married Selina, the widow of John Scott.

[3] See footnote 1

---

[4] Sally Jones was the second of William Jones's three wives. She died in 1877. Jones met and married Sally, as he did his first and third wives, in India. They were all of Galla origin.

[5] In 1879 after the death of his wife, Maidment married the daughter of James Baraka.

*Nazareth, Joseph
*Nelson, David
*Paul, Andrew
 Rigby, Jesse
 Rigby, S. (husband of Jesse)
 Rigby, Lucy
 Rigby, Philip (husband of Lucy)
 Rodgers (husband of Louisa, a
   mateka)
*Rodgers, Fanny
*Rogers, Samuel (husband of
   Fanny)
 Russell, Enoch
 Russell, Rose (wife of Enoch)
 Rutton, Benjamin
*Rutton, Janet
 Rutton, Maria (wife of Benjamin)
*Rutton, Richard (husband of
   Janet)
*Scott, John
*Scott, Selina (wife of John)[6]
 Semler, Dora
 Semler, Ishmael (husband of
   Dora)[7]
 Simeon, I.
 Smith, Tom
 Smith, Esther (wfie of Tom)
 Wainwright, Jacob
*Wellington, Francis
*Wellington, Hannah
 Wellington, Isabella
 Wellington, Lazurus[8]
 Wellington, Mathew[9]
 Williams, Henry
 Williams, Mary (wfie of Henry)
 Willing, Moses
 Willing, Victoria (wife of Moses)
*Wilson, Martha
*Wilson, Philip

Surnames unknown:

Luke
Bessie
Shadrack
Dolby[10]
Owen
Sarah

---

[6] See footnote 2.

[7] Dora was Semler's second wife. In 1864 Grace Semler accompanied Ishmael to Rabai, where she died in 1866.

[8] Lazurus married Sarah, a *mateka*.

[9] Mathew married Ruth, a *mateka*.

[10] This name, which appears on the Frere Town map of 1881, belongs perhaps to one of the few semi-educated freed slaves who came to Frere Town, not from Bombay, but from one of the British patrol boats on which they worked as interpreters. Dolby is a name preserved in Rabai among the Brenn family, which has *mateka* antecedents.

Abbreviations

Ag	Acting
AgAdmin	Acting Administrator
AJIAI	*Africa: Journal of the International African Institute*
BA	Bombay African
b.	bin (son of)
bw.	bwana
C.	
Cd. }	Command number (parliamentary papers)
Cmmd.	
CMS	Church Missionary Society (in footnotes, CMS Archives, London)
CP	Coast Province Correspondence, Kenya National Archives
DC	District Commissioner
DC/MAL	District Commissioner, Malindi
DC/MSA	District Commissioner, Mombasa
EAP	East Africa Protectorate
EAR	East African Railways, Director General Archives
FJL	Fort Jesus Library, Fort Jesus, Mombasa
FO	Foreign Office Correspondence, Public Record Office, Kew Gardens, London
IBEACO	Imperial British East Africa Company
IJAHS	*International Journal of African Historical Studies*
JAH	*Journal of African History*
JRAI	*Journal of the Royal Anthropological Institute*
KNA	Kenya National Archives, Nairobi
MAL	Malindi district records
MMSA	Methodist Missionary Society Archives, London
MMU	Managing Member, Uganda Railways
MSA	Mombasa district records
MSS. Afr.	Africa Manuscripts
MSS. Brit. Emp.	British Empire Manuscripts
MT$	Maria Theresa dollar
NS	New Series
PC	Provincial commissioner
PRGS	*Proceedings of the Royal Geographical Society*
QR	Quarterly report
RH	Rhodes House Library, Oxford
RIEACO	Royal Italian East Africa Company
teleg.	telegram
UMCA	Universities' Mission to Central Africa
UMFC	United Methodist Free Church

Glossary of Swahili and Miji Kenda Terms

Ajamaa
"Those from another land." Rabai term for ex-slave WaMisheni

akida
junior military officer

askari
policeman, soldier

barani
coastal mainland

buibui
dark colored (usu. black) cloth worn as a cape by a Muslim woman to cover her torso, head, and face

heshima
honor, respectfulness

kanga
cloth wrapper worn by lower class women and slaves

kaya
fortified settlement of the Miji Kenda; meeting place of the senior elders (vaya)

khadi
see qadi

kishenzi
barbaric, defiled, uncivilized

kurya tsoga
lit., "to eat the cut," ritual brotherhood practiced by the Miji Kenda with outsiders

liwali (ma)
city and district governor appointed by the sultan of Zanzibar

madarasa
Islamic schools for young children

mahaji
Muslim converts settled in rural coastal districts

majini
human (as opposed to angelic) spirits, of malevolent and benevolent types

maliwali
see liwali

masuria
see suria

mateka
a captive of war, used with refered to slaves seized by the British naval patrol and placed in the care of missionaries

maulidi
celebrations of the Prophet's birthday, often associated with processional music and dancing

mfu
carcass of a dead animal; corpse of a slave

mjoli
fellow slave

mkufu
see ukufu

mtumwa
slave

mvaya
senior grade of eldership of the Miji Kenda (see kaya)

mwungwana
free-born, civilized person of respectable status

qadi
Sw. khadi (ma), city and district judge appointed by the sultan of Zanzibar

suria (ma)
slave concubine

tamim (ma)
senior elder of either of the Mombasa moieties (Tisa Taifa, Theletha Taifa)

uanga
WaMisheni sorcery associated with cannibalism

ukufu
from the Arabic kafa'a, the principle of marriage to a woman of equal status

ushenzi
barbarism, defilement

utawa	seclusion enforced on waungwana women to prevent their defilement
vijakazi	female slave children
vitwana	male slave children
vivyalia	slaves' children
waanga	practicioners of uanga
wahuru	slaves freed by the British government
waganga	ritual and herbal healers
waja	"newcomers," i.e., slaves, esp. new slaves
wajakazi	adult female slaves
wajinga	"fools," used with reference to raw slaves
wakengi	"restless ones," maroons of the Utenzi forest near Witu
WaMisheni	"people of the mission," ex-slave residents of Rabai
WaShenzi	persons of low inherited status, often used with reference to slaves in general (esp. in Lamu)
watumwa	slaves
watumwa wa nyumba	domestic slaves
watwana	adult male slaves
waungwana	freeborn persons of respectable status
wazalia	slaves' children

Sources

REPOSITORIES

CHURCH MISSIONARY SOCIETY ARCHIVES, LONDON

CA5 Series, letters, reports. (M1-3)Mission Books, Vol. I-III, 1842-1863; (M4) East Africa Mission Despatches, 1875-76; (M5); East Africa Mission, 1877; (M6); East Africa Mission, 1879; (01) Miscellaneous, 1851-1880; (03) H.K. Binns, 1876-1880; (05) W.B. Chancellor, 1873-1874; (06) G. David, 1875-1880; (07) G. Deimler, 1856-1867; (09) J.J. Erhardt, 1851-1855; (10) C.W. Forster, 1875-1876; (11) J.W. Handford, 1876-1880; (12) W. Harris, 1875-1879; (14) W.H. Jones, 1878; (16) J.L. Krapf, 1841-1880; (17) J.W.A. Lamb, 1876-1878; (18) A. Menzies, 1879-1880; (21) C. Pfefferle, 1851; (22) C.A. Praeger, 1877; (23) W.S. Price, 1874-1876; (24) J. Rebmann, 1846-1875; (25) W.F.A.H. Russell, 1876-1878; (26) T.H. Sparshott, 1868-1875; (27) J.R. Streeter, 1877-1880

CA6 Series, letters, reports: (14) J.T. Last, 1877-1880

G3A5 Series, letters. (01) 1881-1884; (02-05) 1885-1888; (06)1889-1890; (07-13) 1891-1897; (14) 1898-1899; (15) 1900-1901; (16) 1902-1903; (17) 1904-1907; (18) 1908-1910; (19) 1911-1914; (L3-4) Feb. 1883-Oct. 1887; (L4-7) Nov. 1887-Nov. 1894; (L7-8) Dec. 1894 onwards; (L9) 1901-190; (L10) Nov. 1906-1913.

CI3 Series, letters. (35) J.G. Deimler, 1855-1879; (48) C.W. Isenberg, 1837-1864; (67) W.S. Price, 1850-1873

EAST AFRICAN (KENYA) RAILWAYS, NAIROBI

Letters to Foreign Office No. 1(20/12/95 - 18/2/97)

FORT JESUS LIBRARY, MOMBASA

J.R.W. Pigott diaries, 1889; W.H. Beech typescript, n.d. ("Swahili life"); Somali handbook, part 1, 1945

KENYA NATIONAL ARCHIVES, NAIROBI

Vault Collection. Rev. H.K. and Mrs. A.K.F. Binns, Diaries, Vols. 1-III, 1878/1883, and photo albums.

Coast Province (CP) Collection. 1/16,Telegraphists(native); 1/37, Quarterly district reports ending 30 Jun. 1911; 1/60 Non-european clerical staff; 1/60A, Non-European clerical staff; 2/73, Rabai political record book; 2/84, Marriages for freed slaves; 3/233, Quarterly district reports ending 30 Jun. 1912, 5/336, Giriama Rising; 5/361, Settlement of freed slaves at Tezo; 6/409, Sacred places (kaya) of natives; 6/442,Malindi administration report; 7/115, Coconut commission; 8/171, Encroachment on crown lands; 9/272, CMS station, Giriama; 9/285, Housing non-European clerical staff Mombasa; 11/71A, Annual reports; 11/101, Alienated land in Rabai district; 13/5, John Price and wife; 15/36, Non-European clerical staff, vol. I; 16/1/2, Native tribes and their customs, 1929/

51; 18/65, Population estimates, vol. I; 20/112, John Price, clerk; 20/128a,Land settlement Malindi; 20/136, Handing Over Reports, Nyika 1915/18; 24/205, R. Brenn, administrative officer; 47/1123, Slavery; 61/133, Report on Gobwen sub-District, 1913; 62/13, Village headmen, 1906/11; 62/46, Compensation, Taka-ungu Liwali, slaves of; 63/48, Rabai station 1909; 63/270A,Provincial handing over reports, 1909, 1911; 64/26, Zanzibar sultan mainland property, 1906/12; 64/26A, Zanzibar sultan mainland property, 1912/13; 64/62, Mazrui land, 1908/12; 64/252A, Christian African converts, 1912/13; 64/261, Inspection re-ports, Malindi district, 1909/12; 65/3, Malindi inward, 1910; 65/4, Miscel-laneous inward, 1894/96; 67/14, Arabic letters translated, 1894/1901; 67/15, Rabai inward, 1896/98; 68/19 Kismayu inward, 1893/94; 68/20, Tanaland in-ward, 1896/1900; 69/20, Lamu inward, 1899; 71/24, Departmental outward, 1901/02; 71/25, Malindi inward, 1901/02; 71/28, Malindi outward, 1901/02; 72/31, Mombasa inward, 1910; 72/32, Mombasa outward, 1909; 72/34, De-partmental inward, 1900; 72/35, Departmental inward, 1903; 73/36, Miscel-laneous inward, 1901; 73/37, Miscellaneous inward, 1902; 73/39, Miscellaneous outward, 1900; 73/40, Departmental 1906; 74/41. Rabai inward, 1901/03, 74/ 43. Malindi inward, 1898/1900; 74/45, Jubaland inward, 1895/98; 75/46, Ma-lindi inward, 1895/98; 76/51, Zanzibar outward, 1899; 77/55, Zanzibar inward, 1893; 77/56, Zanzibar inward; 77/58, Departmental outward, 1908/10; 78/61, Collectors outward, 1906; 78/62, Collectors outward, 1907; 78/65, Kismayu inward, 1899; 79/68. Rabai inward, 1899/1900; 80/74, Rabai inward, 1909; 80/ 79, Miscellaneous inward, 1900/05; 80/83, Special and separate outward.; 81/84, Foreign and miscellaneous inward, 1898; 81/85,Foreign and miscellaneous inward, 1899; 81/87, Miscellaneous inward, 1899; 81/88, Miscellaneous outward, 1899; 82/91. Commissioner inward, 1903; 82/93, Commissioner circular orders; 82/94, Foreign and miscellaneous outward, 1898; 83/98, Foreign and miscellaneous inward, 1899; 83/100, Local inward, 1898; 84/106, Miscel-laneous outward, 1908; 84/108, Public prosecutor outward,1899/1909; 85/111, Sub-commissioner to commissioner outward, 1903; 85/112, Outward corres-pondence, High Commissioner, 1907; 85/114, Departmental, 1895; 85/115, Malindi inward, 1906; 86/118, Malindi outward, 1896/1900; 87/126, Malindi outward, 1906; 87/127, Rabai inward, 1907; 87/132, Governor outward, 1908; 87/133, Rabai outward, 1906; 88/142, Departmental inward, 1910; 89/144, Commissioner outward, 1905' 89/146, Commissioner outward, 1901/02; 89/ 147, Rabai outward, 1901/02; 90/150, Departmental outward; 90/153, Depart-mental and subcommisioner outward, 1899; 90/154, Commissioner inward, 1898; 92/157, Departmental inward, Vol. II, 1899; 92/158, Subcommissioner to ag commissioner inward,1899; 93/162, Departmental inward, Vol. II, 1898; 93/ 163, Departmental inward, Vol. II, 1895/96; 93/164, Departmental inward, Vol. I, 1895/96; 93/165, Departmental inward, 1897; 94/166, Outward, 1906/07; 95/ 175, Commissioner and consul-general outward, 1900; 96/178, Commissioner and consul-general, 1898; 96/179, Foreign and miscellaneous, 1897' 96/181. Malindi outward, 1910; 96/182, Malindi inward/outward, 1909; 97/185, Malindi outward, 1907; 97/187, Rabai outward, 1896/98; 98/190, Railway survey, 1891/95; 98/1, Miscellan-eous, 1899/1950; 98/192, Miscellaneous, 1900/10; 99/196, Malindi inward,

1903; 99/198, Rabai inward, 1910; 99/205, Demi-official, 1899/1907; 103/17, Malindi inward, 1908; 104/22, Miscellaneous inward, 1902/07; 104/34, Malindi outward, 1908; 108/74, Death Sentence for Jonah Nicolas, 1916; 109/89, General correspondence, books I-IV, 1895/1904; 109/89, Proclamations and public notices, 1895; 109/90, General correspondence agreements, 1891; 109/91, 1895/98; 110/91,General correspondence agreements, 1895; ADD MS/2,, Zanzibar, 1894/95; ADD MS/3, Zanzibar inward, 1895/96; ADD MS/5, Commissioner to subcommissioner outward, 1899; ADD MS/6, Subcommissioner outward, 1895/96; ADD MS/7, Departmental outward, 1907; ADD MS/8, Foreign and miscellaneous, 1895/99;CP 2,Jubaland administration, 1909/24; Miscellaneous Correspondence (no cover); Serial no. 3, Mombasa inward, 1895; Serial no. 5, Commissioner to subcommissioner outward, 1899; Serial no. 6, Mombasa outward, 1895/96; Serial no. 8, Foreign and miscellaneous, 1895/96.

District Commissioner, Malindi (DC/MAL); 1/1, Annual reports, 1910/26; 2/1, Political record book, 1913/16; 2/2, Political record book, 1913/16; 2/3, Anthropological and historical, 1913/49; 5/1, Register, 1906/08.

District Commissioner, Mombasa (DC/MSA): 1/1, Annual reports, 1909; 3/1, Political record book, 1914; 3/3, Political record book, n.d.; 3/4, Political record book, 1914/16; 6, Political record book, no. 2; 7/2, Memorandum, 1915; 8, Takaungu subdistrict annual report, 1908/09; 8/1, Miscellaneous, 1908; 8/2, Miscellaneous, n.d.; 8/3, Miscellaneous, 1900; 8/5, Miscellaneous, n.d.; 9, Malindi district annual report, 1908/09.

District Commissioner, Kilifi (KFI); 11, Political record book, vol. I; 12, Political record book, vol. II; 13, Political record book, vol. III.

Kwale District Political record book, vol. I.

Native Tribes and Their Customs, Vol. I, Part 2 (Tribes of the Hinterland).

Rabai Sub-District Political record book.

METHODIST MISSION, RIBE
Baptism register, 1896/1913; Land titles, n.d., 1893/98.

METHODIST MISSIONARY SOCIETY ARCHIVES, LONDON
N/T Series: 46, William During; 105, East African missionaries biographical facts

PUBLIC RECORD OFFICE, LONDON
Foreign Office Correspondence, Africa (FO 2)
57 Imperial British East Africa Company
Foreign Office Correspondence, Slave Trade (FO 84): 1574, Jan./Jun. 1880; 1575, Jul./Dec. 1880; 1599, Jan./Jun. 1881; 1600, Jul./Sep. 1881; 1601, Oct./ Dec. 1881; 1620, Jan./Mar. 1882; 1621; Apr./Jun. 1882; 1622, Jul./Sep. 18821 1623, Oct./Dec. 1882; 1630; Jan./ May 1882; 1631, Jun./Dec. 1882; 1644, Jan./Jul. 1883; 1645, Aug./Dec. 1883; 1677, Jan./May 1884; 1678, Jun./Sep. 1884; 1679, Oct./Dec. 1884; 1724, Jan./Mar. 1885; 1725, Apr./May 1885; 1726, Jun. 1885; 1727,. Jul./Aug. 1885; 1728; 1 Sep./16 Oct. 1885; 1729, 17 Oct./Dec. 1885; 1772, Jan./ Feb. 1886; 1773, Mar./May 1886; 1774, Jun./Aug. 1886; 1775, Sep./Oct. 1886; 1776, Nov./Dec. 1886; 1851, Jan./Feb. 1887;

1852, Mar./Jun. 1887; 1853, Jul./Aug. 1887; 1854, Sep./Dec. 1887; 1906, Jan./Apr. 1888; 1907, May/Jun. 1888; 1908, Jul./Aug. 1888; 1909, 1 Sep./13 Oct. 1888; 1910, 22 Oct./25 Nov. 1888; 1911, Dec. 1888; 2066, Nov./Dec. 1890; 2146, Jan./Feb. 1891; 2147, Mar./Apr. 1891; 2148, May/Jul. 1891; 2149, Aug./Oct. 1891; 2150, Nov./Dec. 1891; 2229, Jan./Feb. 1892; 2230, Mar./Apr. 1892; 2231, May/Jun. 1892.

Foreign Office Confidential Prints, Africa (FO 403): 93, Jan./Jun. 1885;94, Jun./Oct. 1885; 95, Oct./Dec. 1885; 96, Jan./Mar. 1886; 97, Apr./Jun. 1886; 98, Jul./Sep. 1886; 99, Oct./Dec. 1886; 100, Jan./Mar. 1887; 101, Apr./Jun. 1887; 102, Jul./Sep. 1887; 103, Oct./Dec. 1887; 104, Jan./Mar. 1888; 105, Apr./Jun. 1888; 106, Jul./Sep. 1888; 107, Oct./Dec. 1888; 117, Jan./Mar. 1889; 118, Apr./Jun. 1889; 119, Jul/Sep. 1889; 120, Oct./Dec. 1889; 136, Jan/ Mar. 1890; 137, Apr./Jun. 1890; 138, Jul./Sep. 1890; 139, Oct./Dec. 1890; 158, Apr./Jun. 1891; 159, Jul/Sep. 1891; 161, Gazette extract, 6 Jan. 1891; 172, Jul./Sep. 1892; 173, Oct./Dec. 1892; 181, Jan./Mar. 1893; 182, Apr./Jun. 1893; 183, Jul./Sep. 1893; 184, Oct./Dec. 1893; 193, Jan./Mar. 1894; 194, Apr./Jun. 1894; 195, Jul./Sep. 1894; 196, Oct./Dec. 1894; 208, Jan./Mar. 1895; 209, Apr./Jun. 1895; 210, Jul./Sep. 1895; 211, Oct./Dec. 1895; 225, Jan./Mar. 1896; 226, Apr./Jun. 1896; 227, Jul./Sep. 1896; 228, Oct./Dec. 1896; 241, Jan./Mar. 1897; 242, Apr./Jun. 1897; 243, Jul./Sep. 1897; 244, Oct./Dec. 1897; 260, Jan./Mar. 1898; 261, Apr./Jun. 1898; 262, Jul./Sep. 1898; 263, Oct./Dec. 1898; 280, Jan./Mar. 1899; 281, Apr./Jun. 1899; 282, Jul./Sep. 1899; 283, Oct./Dec. 1899; 293, Jan./Mar. 1900; 294, Apr./Jun.1900; 295, Jul./Sep. 1900; 296, Oct./Dec. 1900.

Foreign Office Confidential Prints, Slave Trade (FO 541):13,1Apr.1858/31 Mar. 1859; 14, 1 Apr. 1859/31 Mar. 1860; 15, 1868; 18, 1871; 19, 1872; 20, 1875; 21, 1877; 22, 1878; 25, 1883; 26, 1884; 27, 1887; 28, 1888; 29, Jan./ Jun. 1889; 30, Jul./Oct. 1889; 31, Nov./Dec. 1889; 32A, Memorandum; 32B, Euan-Smith memorandum; 33, Treaties; 35, Jan./Aug. 1890; 36, Sep./Dec. 1890; 41, 1892; 47, 1879; 48, 1880; 49, 1881; 50, 1886.

RHODES HOUSE LIBRARY, OXFORD
British Empire Manuscripts (MSS. Brit. Emp.): s. 18, British and Foreign Anti-Slavery Society Papers, C.H. Allen corres-pondence, c. 48 to c. 71; s. 22, British and Foreign Anti-Slavery Society Papers,East Africa and IBEA, G2, G3, G5, G7.; s. 99, Lugard Papers, East Africa letterbook, 1888/92; s. 290, Ernest Gedge diaries, notebooks, correspondence, 1889/91; s. 294, A.C. Hollis auto-biography, vol. II.
Africa Manuscripts (MSS. Afr.):s. 16, Waller papers; s. 49, R. Thornton diaries, vol. III; s. 528-530, Pringle papers, vols. I-II, 1891/92; s. 1494 Mazrui photograph.

ROYAL GEOGRAPHICAL SOCIETY, LONDON
Library Manuscripts (Lbr. Mss.): Dr. Sir John Kirk, 1881/1910

SCHOOL OF ORIENTAL AND AFRICAN STUDIES, LONDON
    Mackinnon Papers: Euan-Smith 10, 1872/73; 11, 1874/76; 12, 1877/78;
13, 1888/89; 14, 1890; 15, 1890; 16, 1891.   Gerald Waller 243, 1877/78;
244, 1879; 245, 1879; 246, 1879/80; 251, 1877, 1880, 1885.

UNITED SOCIETY FOR THE PROPAGATION OF THE GOSPEL,
    LONDON
    Steere Letters, 1878-1889

ORAL TESTIMONIES. Copies of these interviews with ex-slave descendants
and Miji Kenda are deposited at Bird Memorial Library, Syracuse University.

    Interview Notebook, 4 Nov./2 Dec. 1970   Trans. of E.D. Ngala Tuva,
Nguvu ni marauka, Nairobi: Acme, 1954; RABAI: Befukwe wa Kagumba,
Philip Mabruki, Mburusi wa Kunya, Group interview (Rabai Shikadabu), Silas
Makinda, Tsinga wa Saha, Edward K. Binns, Gideon Ngale, Bendegba wa Be-
dzuare, Johnson Henry, Julia Paul, Ambari Washe, Kongoni; Daba wa Karisa;
Katherine Alfred, Karuku wa Murenje, Kalama wa Mwatsuma, Opoloto, Djuadje
wa Mugindo, John Gideon; Harry Fanjo, Bemwasindo wa Mumba, Sheikh Mwi-
dadi Johari, Mwajita wa Mufuko, Benyaetinga wa Rau, and Dzoro wa Gofya;
MAZERAS: Gulani wa Tsingo and William George Kombo; RIBE: Chimwenga wa Ndoro.

    Interview Notebooks, February/September 1973, vols. I-IV (All interviews
in Rabai unless noted otherwise)
    Volume I: Mbuni divisions, Mbrusi's family, Palm notes, Mbrusi wa
Kunya biographical and general notes, Karuku wa Badala, ngoma for curing
child; Rabai, Ngamani, and Jomvu; Sammy Gandani, Francis Frederick Fukwe,
Gibson Ngome, Befukwe wa Kagumba, Joseph Benyai Tinga.
    Volume II: Joseph Tinga (cont.); Nyungu songs; Makaburini grave
markers, Ribe grave markers, Gibson Ngome, Emmanuel Deimler, Kijala Jayo
(Ruruma), Ernest William, Mkamba wa Benyoka, James Lawrence Deimler,
Young Kalama Tappen, Johnson Henry, Debwani bin Ramadhani, Darwish bin
Mohammed, (Mombasa), Tsochizi wa Tsimba, Johnson Henry, Thomas Rich-
ard Manyenze, Lewa wa Muta, Nathaniel Betsui Gandani, Kasimu wa Ngao,
Betindi wa Mruu, Ernest William, Maggie Kokola Edward, Stanley Saburi,
Besaha wa Dzuyia, Maria Deimler Muzo (Mombasa), Malanga wa Bedena, Fran-
cis Joseph Khamisi (Nairobi), Edward Kinross Binns.
    Volume III: Harry Fanjo, Rabai, Justine Fussel Gore (Jimba), Tumu
wa Lewa (Jimba), Walter Elija Mwang'ombe, James Lawrence Deimler,
Bechumbu, Emmanuel Deimler, Tsochizi wa Tsimba, Rabai, Debwani bin Ramadhani, Maria Deimler Muzo (Mombasa), Jimmy Arthur Vincent, Abel
Stephen Brown Baraka, Timothy Manyenzi's matanga, Betsuma wa Wanje,
Tsuma wa Mumba, Bechitsau, Kalume wa Mcharo, Silas Edward, Stanley Saburi, Ngao of Hodi Boys, Mbrusi wa Kunya, Gibson Samuel, Matebwe wa

Katembe, Rabai, Rawson Gilbert Ngbwede, Abdallah bin Khamisi, Maggie Edward's matanga, Lwambi wa Dena, Stanley Saburi, Mkamba wa Benyoka, Washe wa Chisongo, Mbogo wa Kinda, Ngolo wa Chita, Johnson Henry, Chombo wa Bedena.

Volume IV: Biographical notes on Gideon Amuri, Hannah Andrew, Nancy Andrew, Lizzie Archie, Lucas Baraka, Brown Baraka, Jonathan Baya, Jafeth Benyamvula, Jonathan Bewashe, George Bemwakondo, Alexander Binns, Robin Brenn, James Clarage, Paul Dawa, James R. Deimler, Paul Fanjo, Henry Farazi, F.L. Gore, Glayfair Hamisi, S.J. Harrison, F. Jacobs, P. Jiburani, S. Joha, W. Jones, G. Jeremiah, E. Juma, A. Kaginga, D. Kuvaka, S. Kango, A. Kombe, P. Mabruki,T. Majaliwa, S. Maftaha, P. Mwamba, E. Magapi, H. Matchett, P. Macbride, E. Mabruki, T. Mapenzi, J. Mabruki, L. Mgandi, N. Mgomba, E. Mruu, G.Mtsunga, J. Mtwana, S. Mkenda, P. Mwanjemi, E. Mwang'ombe, J. Mwaringa, H. Mwamagongo, Foster Nasibu, A. Noah, J.E. Pande, A. Paul, O.Ramshaw, J. Rimba, D. Sadala, S. Salim, R. Sarare, M. Saro, K. Scott, S. Suria, S.B. Umari, A. Walle, E. Wilington, A. Mambo; Interviews with Chombo wa Bedena (cont.), Befukwe wa Kagumba, Rabai, Debwani bin Ramadhani, Joseph Binns, James Lawrence Deimler.

Volume V: James Lawrence Deimler(cont.), Nellie Peter Mwamba/Bessie David Maraga, Silina Sylvanos, Mbrusi wa Kunya, Patience Foster, Emmanuel Deimler, Siri's matanga, Hilda Aaron, Bemkoka Morris,Hannah Wewato, Mama Mashaka, Nellie Japhet, Johnson Henry, Silina Mafutaha, Kijala Jayo (Ruruma), Elina David Paul, Rabai, Margeret Simeon Ramshaw, Cheva wa Mkauma, Bedzuyia wa Dawa, personal note, Tuguu wa Baya, Debwani bin Ramadhani, Gideon Ngale, Binns George (Mazeras), Atumia a kaya (Kambi ya Chiefu, Ruruma), Lucas Herbert Mwakampya, Betsama wa Bgwia, notes, Solomon Foster Mwingereza (Chaani, Changanwe), Nellie Japhet, Julius Mwatsama (Magongo, Kamkunji).

PUBLISHED GOVERNMENT DOCUMENTS (GREAT BRITAIN)

ADMIRALTY, Maps:
Africa. East Coast. Kilifi River and Approaches. Sur-veyed by Capt. T.F. Pullen and Officers of the H.M.S. Stork, 1888. London: Admiralty, 1891.
Africa. East Coast. Sketch Survey. Cmmd. C.E. Gissing, R.N., H.M. Vice Consul, Mombasa, 1884. London: Admiralty, 1885.
Africa. East Coast. Zanzibar to Melinda. Surveyed by Commander W.J.L. Wharton, by Commander T.F. Pullen, and A.F. Balfour, 1888-1890. London: Admiratly, 1891.

PARLIAMENT. *Parliamentary Papers* (British Sessional Papers):
C. Series: 209(1870); 420(1871), 340(1871), 383(1871), 657(1872), 820 (1873), 867(1873), 946(1874), 1062(1874), 1064(1874), 1168(1875), 1588 (1876),1521(1876), 1387(1876), 1829(1877), 2139(1878),2422(1879), 2720 (1880), 3052(1881), 3160(1882),3547(1883), 3849(1884), 4523(1885), 4609 (1886), 4776(1886), 4917(1887), 4940(1887), 5111(1877), 5428(1888), 5578

(1888), 5559(1888), 5603(1888), 5315(1888), 5821(1889), 5822(1889), 5901 (1890), 6048(1890), 6049(1890), 6043(1890), 6046(1890), 6211(1890/91), 6254(1890/91), 6373(1891), 6560(1892), 6555(1892), 6817(1892), 6702(1892), 6557(1892), 6955(1893), 7025(1893), 7035(1893), 7707(1895), 8274(1896), 8275(1896), 8394(1897), 8433(1897), 8683(1897), 8858(1898), 9223(1899), 9125(1899), 9502(1899).

Cd. Series: 96(1900), 593(1901), 591(1901), 769(1901), 1389(1902), 1626(1903), 1631(1903), 1534(1903), 2330(1904), 2331(1904), 2684(1906), 2740(1905), 4732(1909).

Cmmd. Series: 1585 (1961).

Precis of Information concerning the British East Africa Protectorate and Zanzibar. London: H.M's Stationery Office, 1901.

NEWSPAPERS, MAGAZINES

Anti-Slavery Reporter. London. 1868-91.
Central Africa . Zanzibar. 1883-1890.
Church Missionary Gleaner. London. 1874-1900.
Church Missionary Intelligencer. London. 1851-1902.
Church Missionary Society Proceedings. London. 1842-1914.
Illustrated London News. London. 1874.
Missionary Echo. London. 1894-1900.
Mombasa Diocesan Magazine. Mombasa. 1903-1908.
Times. London. 1888-1897.
United Methodist Free Churches' Magazine. London. 1863-1885.
Welcome Words, or Juvenile Missionary Magazine of the Methodist Free Churches. London. 1880-1890.

PUBLISHED SOURCES, DISSERTATIONS, AND THESES

Akinola, G.A. "Slavery and Slave Revolts in the Sultanate of Zanzibar in the Nineteenth Century." *Journal of the Historical Society of Nigeria*, 6, 2(Dec. 1972), 215-228.

Allen, J.d.V. "Witu, Swahili History and the Historians. " *State Formation in Eastern Africa.* Edited by A.I. Salim. New York: St. Martin's Press, 1985, 216-49.

Al-Mazrui, Sh. A.b. A. "The History of the Mazru'i Dynasty of Mombasa." Translated by J.R. Ritchie. Typescript, n.d.

Anderson-Morshead, A.E.M. *The History of the Universities' Mission to Central Africa.* London: UMCA, 1909.

Armstrong, J.C. and Worden, N.A. "The Slaves, 1652-1834." *The Shaping of South African Society, 1652-1820.* Edited by R. Elphick and H. Giliomee. Middeltown: Wesleyan University Press, 1989, 109-162.

Barrett, W.E.H. "Notes on the Customs and Beliefs of the Wa-Giriama, etc., British East Africa." *JRAI*, 41(1911), 20-39.

Barton, J.T. Juxon. "Report on the Bajun Islands." *Journal of the East Africa and Uganda Natural History Society* (Mar. 1922), 24-39.

Beech, M.W.H. *Aids to the Study of Ki-Swahili.* London: Kegan Paul, Trench, Trübner, 1918.

Beech, M.W.H. "Slavery on the East Coast of Africa." *Journal of the African Society*, 15, 58(Jan. 1916), 145-9.

Bennett, N.R. "The Church Missionary Society at Mombasa,1873-1894." *Boston University Papers in African History.* Edited by J. Butler. Vol. I. Boston: Boston University Press, 1964.

Berg, F.J. "Mombasa under the Busaidi Sultanate. The City and its Hinterlands in the Nineteenth Century." Madison: University of Wisconsin Ph.D. thesis, 1971.

Berlioux, E.F. *The Slave Trade in Africa in 1872.* London: Edward Marsh, 1872.

Binns, H.K. *A Swahili-English Dictionary.* London: Society for Promoting Christian Knowledge, 1925.

Böcking, G. "Sagen der Wa-Pokomo." *Zeitschrift für Afrikanische und Ozeanische Sprachen*, 2(1896), 33-9.

Boteler, T. *Narrative of a Voyage of Discovery to Africa and Arabia performed in his Majesty's Ships Leven and Baracouta, from 1821 to 1826. under the Command of Capt. F.W. Owen, R.N.* 2 vols. London: Richard Bentley, 1835.

Brantley, C. *The Giriama and Colonial Resistance in Kenya, 1800-1920.* Berkeley: University of California Press, 1981.

Brantley, C. "Gerontocratic Government: Age-Sets in Pre-Colonial Giriama." *AJIAI*, 48, 3(1978), 249-64.

Brenner, R. "Reise in den Galla-Landern, 1867 bis 1868". *Petermann's Mittheilungen* (Gotha), 5(1868), 175-9.

Brenner, R. "Richard Brenner's Forshungen in Ost-Afrika."*Petermann's Mittheilungen* (Gotha), 10(1868), 361-7, 456-65.

Brewin, R. *Memoirs of Mrs. Rebecca Wakefield.* 2nd ed. London: Hamilton, Adams, 1879.

Burton, R.F. *Zanzibar: City, Island and Coast.* 2 vols. London: Tinsley Brothers, 1872.

Cashmore, T.H.R. "Sheikh Mbaruk bin Rashid bin Salim el Mazrui." *Leadership in Eastern Africa: Six Political Biographies.* Edited by N.R. Bennett. Boston: Boston University Press, 1968, 111-37.

Cashmore, T.H.R." Studies in District Administration in the East Africa Protectorate, 1895-1918." Cambridge: University of Cambridge, Jesus College Ph.D. dissertation, 1965.

Cassanelli, L. V. *The Shaping of Somali Society: Reconstructing the History of a Pastoral People, 1600-1900.* Philadelphia: University of Pennsylvania Press, 1982.

Cassanelli, L. V. "Social Construction on the Somali Frontier: Bantu Former Slave Communities in the Nineteenth Century." *The African Frontier: the Reproduction of Traditional African Societies.* Edited by I. Kopytoff. Bloomington: Indiana University Press, 1987, 216-38.

Cerulli, E. *Somali: Scritti vari Editi Ed Inediti.* 2 vols. Rome: Instituto poligrafico, dello stato P.V., 1957.

Chiraghdin, S. "Maisha ya Sheikh Mbaruk bin Rashid Al-Mazrui". *Journal of the East African Swahili Committee,* NS 1, 2(Sep. 1960), 150-79.

Christie, J. *Cholera Epidemics in East Africa.* London: Macmillan, 1876.

Church Missionary Society. *The Slave-Trade of East Africa: Is it to Continue or Be Suppressed?* London: Church Missionary Society, 1868.

Colomb, P.H. *Slave-Catching in the Indian Ocean: a Record of Naval Experiences.* 2nd ed. London: Dawsons of Pall Mall, 1968.

Cooper, F. *From Slaves to Squatters: Plantation Labor and Agriculture in Zanzibar and Coastal Kenya, 1890-1925.* New Haven: Yale University Press, 1980.

Cooper, F. "Islam and Cultural Hegemony: the Ideology of Slaveowners on the East African Coast". *The Ideology of Slavery in Africa.* Edited by P. E. Lovejoy. Beverly Hills: Sage Publications, 1981, 271-307.

Cooper, F. *Plantation Slavery on the East Coast of Africa.* New Haven: Yale University Press, 1977.

Coupland, R. *East Africa and its Invaders, from the Earliest Times to the Death of Seyyid Said in 1856.* Oxford: Clarendon, 1938.

Coupland, R. *The Exploitation of East Africa, 1856-1890. The Slave Trade and the Scramble.* 2nd ed. London: Faber & Faber,1968.

Craufurd, C.H. "Journeys in Gosha and beyond the Deshek Wama (Lake Hardinge)." *Geographical Journal,* 9(1897), 54-8.

Curtin, P.R. (see Romero, P.W.)

Damman, V.E. "Zur Geschichte der Digo."*Zeitschrift für Engeborenen Sprachen,* 34(1944), 53-69.

Darroch, R.G., ed. ""A History of the Pokomo by Mikael Samson (continued)." *Journal of the East Africa and Uganda Natural History Society,* 17, 79/80 (Sep. 1944), 370-94.

Darroch, R.G. ed. "Some Notes on the Early History of the Tribes Living on the Lower Tana, Collected by Mikael Samson and Others." *Journal of the East Africa and Uganda Natural History Society,* 17, 79/80(Sep. 1944), 244-51.

Dawson, E.C. *James Hannington: First Bishop of Eastern Equatorial Africa. A History of His Life and Work, 1847-1885.* 2nd. ed. New York: Negro Universities Press, 1969.

Delius, P. *The Land Belongs to Us: the Pedi Policy, the Boers and the British in the Nineteenth-century Transvaal.* Berkeley: University of California Press, 1984.

de Kiewiet, M.J. "History of the Imperial British East Africa Company, 1876-1895." London: University of London Ph.D. thesis, 1955.

Dumett, R. and Johnson, M. "Britain and the Suppression of Slavery in the Gold Coast Colony, Ashanti, and the Northern Territories," *The End of Slavery*. Edited by S. Miers and R. Roberts. Madison: University ofWisconsin Press, 71-116.

Dundas, F.G. "Exploration of the Rivers Tana and Juba."*The Scottish Geographical Journal*, 9(1893), 113-26.

Dundas, F.G. "Expedition up the Jub River through Somaliland, East Africa." *Geographical Journal*, 9(Mar. 1893), 209-33.

Elliott, F. "Jubaland and its Inhabitants." *Geographical Journal*, 41 (Jun. 1913), 554-61.

Fitzgerald, W.W.A. *Travels in the Coastlands of British East Africa and the Islands of Zanzibar and Pemba*. London: Chapman and Hall, 1898.

Frank, W. *Habari na Desturi za Waribe*. London: Sheldon Press/ Macmillan, 1953.

Fraser, A.Z. *Livingstone and Newstead*. London: John Murray, 1913.

Freeman-Grenville, G.S.P."The Coast, 1498-1840,"in R.Oliver and G.Mathew, ed. *History of East Africa, Vol. I*. Oxford: Clarendon Press, 1963, 129-68.

Garfield, R. "A History of Sao Tome Island, 1470-1655." Evanston: Northwestern University Ph.D. Thesis, 1971.

Glassman, J.P. "Social Rebellion and Swahili Culture: the Response to German Conquest of the Northern Mrima, 1888-1890." Madison: University of Wisconsin Ph.D. Dissertation, 1988.

Glassman, J.P."The Runaway Slave in Coastal Resistance to Zanzibar: the Case of the Witu Sultanate." Madison: University of Wisconsin M.A. Thesis, 1983.

Gray, J. *The British in Mombasa, 1824-1826*. London: Macmillan, 1957.

Greffulhe, H. "Voyage de Lamoo à Zanzibar." *Bulletin de la Société de Géographie et d'Etudes Coloniales de Marseille*, II (1878), 209-17,327-60.

Gregory, R.W. *Foundation of British East Africa*. Reprint. New York: Negro Universities Press, 1969.

Gregory, R.W. *The Great Rift Valley. Being the Narrative of a Journey to Mount Kenya and Lake Baringo*. London: John Murray, 1896.

Guillain, C.*Documents sur l'Histoire, la Géographie et le Commerce de l'Afrique Orientale*. 3 vols. Paris: Arthus Bertrand, 1856.

Gundert, H. *Biography of the Rev. Charles Isenberg, Missionary of the Church Missionary Society to Abyssinia and Western India from 1832 to 1864*. London: Church Missionary Society, 1885.

Hardinge, A.H. *A Diplomatist in the East*. London: Jonathan Cape, 1928.

Harris, C.W. *The Highlands of Aethiopia*. 3 vols. London: Longman, Brown, Green, Longmans, 1844.

Harris, J.E. *The African Presence in Asia: Consequences of the East African Slave Trade*. Evanston: Northwestern University Press,1971.

Harris, J.E. *Repatriates and Refugees in a Colonial Society: the Case of Kenya*. Washington, D.C.: Howard University Press, 1987.

Harris, J.E. Ed. *The Recollections of James Juma Mbotela*. Nairobi: East African Publishing House, 1977.

Haywood, C.W. "The Bajun Islands and Birikau". *Geographical Journal*, 85 (1933), 59-64.

Hemphill, M. deK. "The British Sphere, 1884-94." *History of East Africa, Vol. I.* Edited by R. Oliver and G. Mathew. Oxford: Clarendon, 1963, 391-432.

Herlehy, T.J." An Economic History of the Kenya Coast: the Mijikenda Coconut Palm Economy, 1800-1980." Boston: Boston University Ph.D. dissertation, 1985.

Herlehy, T.J. "Ties that Bind: Palm Wine and Blood-Brotherhood at the Kenya Coast during the 19th Century." *IJAHS*, 17, 2(1984), 285-308.

Herlehy, T.J. and Morton, R.F. "A Coastal Ex-Slave Community in the Regional and Colonial Economy of Kenya: the WaMisheni of Rabai, 1880-1963." *The End of Slavery in Africa.* Edited by S. Miers and R. Roberts. Madison: University of Wisconsin Press, 1988, 254-81.

Hertslet, E. *The Map of Africa by Treaty.* 3 vols. 3rd ed. London: His Majesty's Stationery Office, 1909.

Hinawy, M.A. *Al Akida and Fort Jesus, Mombasa.* 2nd ed. Nairobi: East African Literature Bureau, 1970.

Hogendorn, J. and Lovejoy, P. "The Development and Execution of Frederick Lugard's Policies toward Slavery in Northern Nigeria." *Slavery and Abolition*, 10, 1(1989), 1-43.

Hopkins, A.J. *Trail Blazers and Road Makers. A Brief History of the East Africa Mission of the United Methodist Church.* London:Henry Hooks, 1928.

Hutchinson, E. *The Slave Trade of East Africa.* London: Sampson Low, Marston, Low & Searle, 1874.

Isaacman. A. and Rosenthal, A. "Slaves, Soldiers, and Police: Power and Dependency among the Chikunda of Mozambique, ca. 1825-1920." *The End of Slavery.* Edited by S. Miers and R. Roberts. Madison: University of Wisconsin Press, 220-53.

Jackson, F. *Early Days in East Africa.* 2nd ed. London: Dawsons of Pall Mall, 1969.

Johnson, F., ed. *A Standard English-Swahili Dictionary.* Oxford: Oxford University Press.

Johnston, H.H. *The Kilima-Njaro Expedition.* London: Kegan, Paul, Trench, 1886.

Johnstone, H.B. "Notes on the Customs of the Tribes Occupying Mombasa Sub-District, British East Africa," *JRAI*, 32(1902), 263-72.

Kirk, J. "Visit to the Coast of Somali-land." *PRGS*, 17, 5 (1872/73), 340-42.

Koffsky, P.L. "History of Takaungu, East Africa, 1830-1896." Madison: University of Wisconsin Ph.D. Thesis, 1977.

Kopytoff, I. "The Cultural Context of African Abolition." *The End of Slavery in Africa.* Edited by S. Miers and R. Roberts. Madison: University of Wisconsin Press, 1988, 485-503.

Krapf, J.L. *A Dictionary of the Suahili Language.* 2nd ed. Ridgewood, N.J.: Gregg Press, 1964.

Lewis, I.M. *Peoples of the Horn of Africa:Somali, Afar and Saho.* Ethnographic Survey of Africa: North Eastern Africa, part 1. London: International African Institute, 1955.

Lloyd, C. *The Navy and the Slave Trade. The Suppression of the African Slave Trade in the Nineteenth Century.* London: Frank Cass, 1968.

Lovejoy, P.E., ed. *Africans in Bondage: Studies in Slavery and the Slave Trade.* Madison: African Studies Program, University of Wisconsin, 1988.

Lovejoy, P.E. "Fugitive Slaves:Resistance to Slavery in the Sokoto Caliphate." *In Resistance: Studies in African, Caribbean, and Afro-American History.* Edited by G.Y. Okihiro. Amherst: University of Massachusetts Press, 1986, 71-95.

Lovejoy, P.E., ed. *The Ideology of Slavery in Africa.* Beverly Hills: Sage Publications, 1981.

Lovejoy, P.E. *Transformations in Slavery: a History of Slavery in Africa.* Cambridge: Cambridge University Press, 1983.

Lugard, F.D. *Diaries.* Edited by M. Perham. 4 vols. Evanston: Northwestern University Press, 1959-63.

Lugard, F.D. *The Rise of Our East African Empire: Early Efforts in Nyassaland and Uganda.* 2 vols. Edinburgh: William Blackwood and sons, 1893.

Lyne, R.N. *An Apostle of Empire. Being the Life of Sir Lloyd William Mathews, K.C.M.G.* London: George Allen & Unwin, 1936.

Lyne, R.N. *Zanzibar in Contemporary Times.* Hurst & Blackett, 1905.

Macdonald, J.R.L. *Soldiering and Surveying in British East Africa, 1891-1894.* London: Edward Arnold, 1897.

Mackenzie, D. "A Report on Slavery and the Slave Trade in Zanzibar, Pemba and the Mainland of the British Protectorate of East Africa." *Anti-Slavery Reporter*, 4th series, 15(1895), 69-96.

McDermott, P.L. *British East Africa or IBEA. A History of the Formation and Work of the Imperial British East Africa Company.* London: Chapman & Hall, 1893.

Martin, B.G. *Muslim Brotherhoods in Nineteenth Century Africa.* Cambridge: Cambridge University Press, 1976.

Martin, E.B. *The History of Malindi: a Geographical Analysis of an East African Coastal Town from the Portuguese Period to the Present.* Nairobi: East African Literature Bureau, 1973.

Martin, E.B. "The Geography of Presenti-Day Smuggling in the Western Indian Ocean: the Case of the Dhow". *The Great Circle: Journal of the Australian Association for Maritime History.* 1, 2(Oct. 1979), 18-35.

Mazrui, M.K. *Historia ya Utumwa katika Uislamu na Dini Nyingine.* Nairobi: n.p., 1970.

Mbotela, J. *Uhuru wa Watumwa.* 2nd ed. Nairobi: East African Literature Bureau, 1967.

Miers, S. and Kopytoff, I., ed. *Slavery in Africa: Historical and Anthropological Perspectives.* Madison: University of Wisconsin Press,1977.

Miers, S. and Roberts, R., ed. *The End of Slavery in Africa.* Madison: University of Wisconsin Press, 1988.

Miller, J.C. *Way of Death: Merchant Capitalism and the Angolan Slave Trade.* Madison: University of Wisconsin Press, 1988.

Mirza, S. and Strobel, M., ed.*Three Swahili Women: Life Histories from Mombasa, Kenya.* Bloomington: Indiana University Press, 1989.

Morton, R.F. "A Reappraisal of the History of *wata* Hunters of the Kenya Coast in the Pre-Colonial Era." *Kenya Historical Review*, (1978/79).

Morton, R. F. "The Shungwaya Myth of Miji Kenda Origins: a Problem of Late Nineteenth Century Kenya Coastal History". *IJAHS*, 5, 3(1972), 397-423.

Morton, R.F. "New Evidence Regarding the Shungwaya Myth of Miji Kenda Origins," *IJAHS*, 10, 4(1977), 628-43.

Morton, R.F. "Slaves, Fugitives, and Freedmen on the Kenya Coast,1873-1907." Syracuse: Syracuse University Ph.D. dissertation, 1976.

Moyse-Bartlett, H. *The King's African Rifles: a Study in the Military History of East and Central Africa, 1890-1915.* Aldershott: Gale and Polden, 1956.

Mungeam, G.H. *British Rule in Kenya, 1895-1912: the Establishment of Administration in the East Africa Protectorate.* Oxford:Clarendon Press, 1966.

New, C. *Life, Wanderings, and Labours in Eastern Africa.* 3rd. ed. London: Frank Cass, 1971.

Newman, H.S. *Banani: the Transition of Slavery to Freedom in Zanzibar and Pemba.* 2nd ed. New York: Negro Universities Press, 1969.

Newman, H.S. "East Africa Protectorate." *British East Africa.* Edited by J. Scott Keltie. London: Kegan Paul, Trench, Trübner, 1901, 279-92.

Nichols, C.S. *The Swahili Coast. Politics, Diplomacy and Trade on the East African Littoral, 1798-1856.* London: George Allen & Unwin, 1971.

Ngala, R.G. *Nchi na Desturi za Wagiriama.* Nairobi: Eagle Press, 1949.

Northrup, D. "The Ideological Context of Slavery in Southeastern Nigeria in the 19th Century." *The Ideology of Slavery in Africa.* Edited by P.E. Lovejoy. Berverly Hills: Sage, 1981.

Okihiro, G.Y. ed. *In Resistance: Studies in African, Caribbean, and Afro-American History.* Amherst: University of Massachusetts Press, 1986.

Oliver, R. *The Missionary Factor in East Africa.* 2nd ed. London: Longmans, Green, 1965.

Oliver, R. *Sir Harry Johnstone and the Scramble for Africa.* London: Faber, 1957.

Oliver, R. and Mathew, G. Ed. *History of East Africa, Volume I.* Oxford: Clarendon, 1963.

Oroge, E.A. "The Fugitive Slave Crisis of 1859: a Factor in the Growth of Anti-British Feelings Among the Yoruba." *Odu*, 12(Jul. 1975), 40-54.

Oroge, E.A. "The Fugitive Slave Question in Anglo-Egba Relations, 1861- 1886." *Journal of the Historical Society of Nigeria*, 8, 1 (Dec. 1975), 61-80.

Owen, W. F.W. *Narrative of Voyages to Explore the Shores of Africa, Arabia, and Madagascar.* 2 vols. 2nd ed. London: Gregg International Publishers, 1968.

Parkin, D.J. "Medicines and Men of Influence." *Man*, 3, 3(Sep. 1968), 424-39.

Paulitschke, D. *Ethnographie Nordost-Afrikas.* Berlin: Geographische Verlagshandlung Dietrich Reimer, 1893.

Perham, M. *Lugard: The Years of Authority, 1898-1945.* Hamden: Archon, 1968.

Perham, M. *Lugard: The Years of Adventure, 1858-1898.* Hamden: Archon, 1968.

Peters, C. *New Light on Dark Africa: Being the Narrative of the German Emin Pasha Relief Expedition.* Trans. by H. W. Dulcken. London: Ward, Lock, 1891.

Pouwels, R.L. *Horn and Crescent: Cultural Change and Traditional Islam on the East African Coast, 800-1900.* Cambridge: Cambridge University Press, 1987.

Price, W.S. *My Third Campaign in East Africa: a Story of Missionary Life in Troublous Times.* London: William Hunt, 1890.

Prins, A.H.J. "The Somali Bantu." *Bulletin of the International Committee on Urgent Anthropological and Ethnological Research,* 3(1960), 28-31.

Prins, A.H.J. *The Swahili-Speaking Peoples of Zanzibar and the East African Coast (Arabs, Shirazi and Swahili).* Ethnographic Survey of Africa. East Central Africa, part 12. London: International African Institute, 1967.

Rampley, W.J. *Mathew Wellington. Sole Surviving Link with Dr.Livingstone.* London: Society for Promoting Christian Knowledge, n.d.[ca. 1930].

Ramshaw, R.C. "Stories about East Africa." *Welcome Words,* 16(1882), 158-9.

Ranger, T.O. *Dance and Society in Eastern Africa, 1890-1935.* London: Heinemann, 1975.

Roberts, R. "The End of Slavery in the French Soudan, 1905-1914." *The End of Slavery.* Edited by S. Miers and R. Roberts. Madison: University of Wisconsin Press,282-307.

Roberts, R. and Klein, M.A. "The Banamba Slave Exodus of 1905 and the Decline of Slavery in the Western Sudan." *JAH,* 21(1980), 375-394.

Robertson, C. C. and Kelin, M.A. ed. *Women and Slavery in Africa.* Madison: University of Wisconsin Press, 1983.

Rodd, J.R. *Social and Diplomatic Memories, 1884-1893.* 2 vols. London: Edward Arnold, 1922.

Romero, P.W. "'Where Have All the Slaves Gone?' Emancipation and Post-Emancipation in Lamu, Kenya." *JAH,* 27 (1986), 497-512.

Romero Curtin, P.W. "Laboratory for the Oral History of Slavery: the Island of Lamu on the Kenya Coast." *American Historical Review,* 88, 4(Oct. 1983), 858-82.

Romero Curtin, P.W. "The Sacred Meadows: a Case Study of 'Anthropologyland' vs. 'Historyland'." *History in Africa,* 9 (1982), 337-46.

Ross, R. *Cape of Torments: Slavery and Resistance in South Africa.* London: Routledge & Kegan Paul, 1983.

Salim, A.I. "Sir Ali bin Salim." *Kenya Historical Biographies.* Edited by K. King and A. Salim. Nairobi: East African Publishing House, 1971.

Salim, A.I. *The Swahili-speaking Peoples of Kenya's Coast, 1895-1965.* Nairobi: East African Publishing House, 1973.

Shaw, A.D.*To Chagga and Back: an Account of a Journey to Moshi, the Capital of Chagga, Eastern Equatorial Africa.* London: Church Missionary House, 1887.

Sheriff, A. *Slaves, Spices and Ivory in Zanzibar: Integration of an East African Commercial Empire into the World Economy, 1770-1873.* London: James Currey, 1987.

Sorrenson, M.P.K. *Origins of European Settlement in Kenya*. Nairobi: Oxford University Press, 1968.

Spear, T.T. *The Kaya Complex: a History of the Mijikenda Peoples of the Kenya Coast to 1900*. Nairobi: Kenya Literature Bureau, 1978.

Stigand, C.H.*The Land of Zinj. Being an Account of British East Africa, its Ancient History and Present Inhabitants*. Reprint. London: Frank Cass, 1966.

Stock. E. *The History of the Church Missionary Society: its Environment, its Men and its Work*. 4 vols. London:Church Missionary Society, 1899-1916.

Strayer, R.W. *The Making of Mission Communities in East Africa: Anglicans and Africans in Colonial Kenya, 1875-1935*. London: Heinemann, 1978.

Strobel, M. *Muslim Women in Mombasa, 1890-1975*. New Haven: Yale University Press, 1979.

Strobel, M. "Slavery and Reproductive Labor in Mombasa." *Women and Slavery in Africa*. Edited by C.C. Robertson and M.A. Klein. Madison: University of Wisconsin Press, 1983, 111-29.

Sulivan, G.L. *Dhow-chasing in Zanzibar Waters and on the Eastern Coast of Africa*. London: Sampson Low, Marston, Low & Searle, 1873.

Taylor, W.E. *African Aphorisms, or Saws from Swahili-Land*. 2nd ed. London: Sheldon Press, 1924.

Taylor, W.E.*Giryama Vocabulary and Collections*. London: Society for Promoting Christian Knowledge, 1891.

Temu, A.J. *British Protestant Missions*. London: Longmans, 1972.

Temu, A.J. "The Role of the Bombay Africans(Liberated Africans) on the Mombasa coast, 1874-1901." *Hadith 3*. Edited by B.A. Ogot. Nairobi: East African Publishing House, 1971, 53-81.

Thomas, H.B. "The Death of Dr. Livingstone: Carus Farrar's Narrative."*Uganda Journal*, 14, 2(Sep. 1950), 115-28.

Thomson, J. *Through Masai Land: a Journey of Exploration among the Snowclad Volcanic Mountains and Strange Tribes of Eastern Equatorial Africa*. London: Sampson Low, Marston, Searle & Rivington, 1887.

Tucker, A.R. *Eighteen Years in Uganda and East Africa*. 2nd ed. London, 1911.

Trimingham, J.S. *Islam in East Africa*. Oxford: Clarendon, 1964.

Turton, E.R. "Kirk and the Egyptian Invasion of East Africa in 1875: a Reassessment". *JAH*, 11, 3(1970), 355-70.

Turton, E.R. "The Impact of Mohammad Abdille Hassan in the East Africa Protectorate". *JAH*, 10, 4(1969), 641-57.

Wakefield, E.S. *Koona Koocha, or Dawn upon the Dark Continent*. London: A. Crombie, 1892.

Wakefield, E.W. *Thomas Wakefield: Missionary and Geographical Pioneer in East Equatorial Africa*. London: Religious Tract Society, 1904.

Wakefield, T. "Rev. Thomas Wakefield's Fourth Journey to the Southern Galla Country in 1877." *PRGS*, 4(1882), 368-72.

Wakefield, T. "Routes of Native Caravans from the Coast to the Interior of Eastern Africa." *Journal of the Royal Geographical Society*, 40(1870), 303-38.

Waller, H. *Heligoland for Zanzibar, or One Island Full of Free Men for Two Full of Slaves*. London: Edward Standford, 1893.

Watson, J.L., ed. *Asian and African Systems of Slavery.* Berkeley: University of California Press, 1980.

Werner, A. "A Swahili History of Pate." *Journal of the African Society.* 14, 54 (1915), 148-61, 278-96, 392-413.

Willoughby, J.C. *East Africa and its Big Game: the Narrative of a Sporting Trip from Zanzibar to the Borders of the Masai..* London:Longmans,Green, 1889.

Wray, J.A. *Kenya: our Newest Colony: Reminiscences.* London: Marshall Brothers, n.d.

Yates, W. *Dado: or, Stories of Native Life in East Africa.* London: A. Crombie, 1886.

Ylvisaker, M. *Lamu in the Nineteenth Century: Land, Trade, and Politics.* Boston: Boston University African Studies Center, 1979.

Zein, A.H. M. El- *The Sacred Meadows: a Structural Analysis of Religious Symbolism in an East African Town.* Evanston: Northwestern University Press, 1974.

Index

240

Slavery/slave trade treaties/decrees:
  1845, 16, 66
  1862, 16
  1873, 28, 35, 38, 44, 52, 66,
    166
  1876, 28, 38, 40, 44, 66-7, 166,
    203
  1889, 139, 142n116, 166-8;
  1890, 33n49, 130, 140-3, 167
    n100
  1892, 143
  1907 (abolition), 170-1, 175,
    203
slaves: Digo, 44-5; Duruma, 44-5;
  Galla, 20, 53n6, 205n6; Giriama,
  120; Kamba, 44-5, 141, 166;
  Makua, 61; Miji Kenda, 40, 48, 141;
  Nyassa, 69; Oromo, 25; Pokomo,
  141; population, 1, 20-1 & n5, 161,
  170-1, 180; Rabai, 47; Ribe, 47;
  Sanye, 141; Teita, 141; Yao, 26;
  Zigua, 23, 53n6
slave trade: Bajuni, 38n72; Benadir
  coast, 17, 20, 25; Busaidi, 47;
  coastal Muslims, 11, 44, 48, 66, 68,
  174; Digo, 11, 41; East Africa, 1;
  Gasi Mazrui , 40, 44; Giriama, 11,
  155; Gosha, 25-6, 29; Jomvu, 166;
  Kamba, 48, 157, 174; Lamu, 24,
  35f; Miji Kenda, 1, 11-2, 40, 48,
  157; Mombasa, 66; northern
  Kenya coast, 29, 34, 35, 37, 48;
  pawning, 175n30, 187, 204;
  Pemba, 40, 44, 175; Somali, 1, 20
  & ns4/5, 28-9, 35, 38n72; southern
  Kenya coast, 40, 43-4, 66, 174-5;
  Takaungu Mazrui , 40-1, 48, 50, 66,
  96, 120, 175n30; Witu, 35f; Zanzibar, 175; 1884 famine trade, 38 &
  n72, 40, 48;
small pox, 25n23, 180n48
Smith, Arthur (CMS), 117 & n89
Smith, C.S. (consul-general Zanzibar
  1890-4), 140-143
Smith, Thomas (BA), 59, 63n48, 68-9,
  73
Sokoke, 149, 150 & n19, 151-2, 155,
  181
Sokoke forest, 148n8, 149
Somali people, 19-29, 135-6; expansion of, 15, 16, 23, 14 & n23, 29,

32; Bimal, 26, 28 & n35, 187, 189;
  Darod, 25n23; Geledi, 20n4, 26,
  28; Herti, 21, 24-5, 28; Ogaden
  (Muhammad Zubeir), 21, 24 & n23,
  25 & n28, 26, 29, 187-9; Sheikal,
  28 & n35; Tunni, 24 & n23, 25n25;
  28 & n35, 187

Songolla Mafula, 26, 135-7
sorcery, witchcraft, 198, 201n152
Sparshott, Thomas Henry (CMS), 57 &
  n21, 58, 60, 101
Spear, Thomas T., 8
Starani, 38n72
Steere, Edward (UMCA bishop), 100 &
  n10
Strayer, Robert W., 206
Streeter, John Radford (CMS), 68-76,
  82-7, 102-3, 106
Strobel, Margaret, 206
Sub b. Hamid (liwali of Lamu), 1860-
  84, 1890), 17, 31, 32n48, 35, 38,
  140-1
Suleiman b. Abdullah ("Kimenya"), 80
  n6, 132, 138-9, 139n105, 147
sultans of Zanzibar see Ali b. Said, Bargash b. Said, Khalifa b. Said, Majid
  b. Said, and Seyyid Said
Swahili, 1, 4, 12

Takaungu, 1-3, 12=3, 43, 79, 93-7,
  145f, 172, 180-1 see also Mazrui
  (Zaheri)
Tana river, 133, 206
Tanga, 11, 47
Taru, 124
Taylor, Isaac, 104n27
Taylor, William E (CMS), 48, 74, 104
  & n28, 106-7, 162
Temu, Arnold, 206
Ten-mile strip, 177
Tezo, 150n19, 157-8, 171n13, 180-1
Todd, J. Ross (IBEACO), 136
Tofiki b. Mwidhani, 191-2
Tosiri, Enoch, 82
Tozer, William George (UMCA
  bishop), 100n10
trade, 41; cloth, 95; cotton, 20, 29;
  firearms and powder, 29, 37 & n65,
  41, 50, 135, 189; grain, 16, 20, 43,
  91-5, 135; ivory, 33, 78, 81, 95-6,